Insights in
Decision Making

Hillel J. Einhorn. Photograph by Peter Kiar, Chicago.

Insights in Decision Making

A Tribute to Hillel J. Einhorn

EDITED BY
Robin M. Hogarth

The University of Chicago Press

Chicago and London

The University of Chicago Press, Chicago 60637
The University of Chicago Press, Ltd., London

© 1990 by the University of Chicago
All rights reserved. Published 1990
Printed in the United States of America
99 98 97 96 95 94 93 92 91 90   5 4 3 2 1

Library of Congress Cataloging-in-Publication Data

Insights in decision making : a tribute to Hillel J. Einhorn / edited by Robin M. Hogarth.
   p.   cm.
   Edited versions of papers and comments presented at a conference held June 12–14, 1988, at the University of Chicago.
   Includes bibliographical references.
   ISBN 0-226-34855-5 (alk. paper). — ISBN 0-226-34856-3 (pbk. : alk. paper)
   1. Economics—Psychological aspects—Congresses.   2. Choice (Psychology)—Congresses.   3. Rational expectations (Economic theory)—Congresses.   4. Einhorn, Hillel J., 1941–1987.
I. Einhorn, Hillel J., 1941–1987.   II. Hogarth, Robin M.
HB74.P8I56   1990
330′.01′9—dc20   89-35311
                                                                                              CIP

∞   The paper used in this publication meets the minimum requirements of the American National Standard for Information Sciences—Permanence of Paper for Printed Library Materials, ANSI Z39.48-1984.

ROBIN M. HOGARTH is the Wallace W. Booth Professor of Behavioral Science at the University of Chicago Graduate School of Business and is the director of the Center for Decision Research. He is coeditor of *Rational Choice* and author of *Judgement and Choice*.

Contents

Preface ... ix

Hillel J. Einhorn (1941–1987) ... xiii
    Robin M. Hogarth and Joshua Klayman

PART ONE

Introductory Comments ... 1

1. Compatibility Effects in Judgment and Choice ... 5
    Paul Slovic, Dale Griffin, and Amos Tversky
2. The Costs and Benefits of Vague Information ... 28
    Thomas S. Wallsten
3. Unfinished Tasks: A Research Agenda for Behavioral Decision Theory ... 44
    Ward Edwards

Discussions ... 66
    Howard Kunreuther
    Kenneth R. MacCrimmon

PART TWO

Introductory Comments ... 89

4. When Lives Are in Your Hands: Dilemmas of the Societal Decision Maker ... 91
    Sarah Lichtenstein, Robin Gregory, Paul Slovic, and Willem A. Wagenaar
5. Decomposition and the Control of Error in Decision-Analytic Models ... 107
    Don N. Kleinmuntz

PART THREE

Introductory Comments — 127

6. The Adaptive Decision Maker: Effort and Accuracy in Choice — 129
   John W. Payne, James R. Bettman, and Eric J. Johnson
7. Anticipated Deadline Penalties: Effects on Goal Levels and Task Performance — 154
   Haim Mano

Discussion — 173
   Lola L. Lopes

PART FOUR

Introductory Comments — 177

8. The Potential Nonfalsity of the False Consensus Effect — 179
   Robyn M. Dawes
9. Back to Base Rates — 200
   Maya Bar-Hillel

Discussion — 217
   David Schum

PART FIVE

Introductory Comments — 225

10. Functionalism and Illusionism: Can Integration Be Usefully Achieved? — 227
    Kenneth R. Hammond
11. Strategies in Real-Time, Dynamic Decision Making — 262
    Berndt Brehmer

Discussion — 280
   Michael E. Doherty

PART SIX

Introductory Comments — 293

12. Predicting Utility — 295
    Daniel Kahneman and Jackie Snell
13. Behavioral Game Theory — 311
    Colin F. Camerer

Discussion	337
Baruch Fischhoff	
The Scientific Publications of Hillel J. Einhorn	343
Author Index	347
Subject Index	353

Preface

At the end of 1986, many people knew that Hillel Einhorn was ill; however, his death in January 1987 at the age of 45 was a considerable shock. Hilly had been seriously ill in the past, but he had survived. How could someone whose very being and personality embodied life, enthusiasm, and excitement die in the middle of a flourishing professional career?

This book is a testimony to Hillel Einhorn, both the man and the scholar. It represents one way in which his friends and colleagues have tried to cope with the reality of his death and to remember and honor him. The contributions to this volume represent the edited versions of papers and comments presented at a conference held at the University of Chicago in June 1988 entitled *Insights in Decision Making: Theory and Applications. A Tribute to the Late Hillel J. Einhorn*. Each chapter in this book was specifically written for this conference, and it is significant that every scholar who was asked to contribute to Hilly's memory in this way did so.

The main title of the conference—and of this book (*Insights in Decision Making*)—was chosen to epitomize the nature of Hilly's professional contributions, a stream of *insightful* analyses of issues in decision making. The subtitle—*Theory and Applications*—emphasizes the fact that Hilly's work was concerned with developing and using psychological theory in understanding processes of decision making as well as the importance of practical applications. Hilly was a strong believer in the interplay between theory and practice.

The conference took place from Sunday, 12 June, through Tuesday, 14 June 1988, and was attended by approximately 200 persons, who, for the most part, were active researchers or students in the area of behavioral decision making. The conference itself was preceded by a reception at the McCormick Center Hotel on the evening of Sunday, 12 June, and the papers were presented in the Glen A. Lloyd Auditorium at the University of Chicago Law School. On the evening of Monday, 13 June, most people attending the conference went for an evening dinner cruise on Lake Michigan on the *Spirit of Chicago*. This was a lively event, particularly well appreciated because of unusually hot weather, and provided an occasion for much good fellowship.

Since almost all Hilly's professional contributions dealt with topics in behavioral decision making, it is appropriate to reflect briefly on progress in this field over his professional career, from the late 1960s to the present. Behavioral decision making in the late 1960s could be characterized by heavy reliance on normative frameworks borrowed largely from economics and statistics. In addition, there was a concurrent belief that, through statistical decision theory, it would be possible to help people make better decisions. Experience of the intervening years has modified these views. First, much empirical evidence has shown that models borrowed from economics and statistics do not provide good accounts of individual decision behavior. Thus, current work seeks to link observed behavior to underlying psychological mechanisms and processes. Second, attempts to apply statistical decision theory have revealed both surprising difficulties and opportunities. As a consequence, prescriptive work has become more focused and less encompassing in its goals. Third, the major accomplishments of the field could probably best be characterized by the discovery of several insights into the complex nature of decision making. Moreover, these insights have attracted attention and illuminated issues in both theoretical and applied research in many different areas, for example, accounting, economics, marketing, medicine, public policy, risk analysis, and so on.

The chapters in this book represent a good sample of the wide range of topics now addressed by researchers in behavioral decision making. Some chapters illuminate issues that have already been the subject of much attention such as inconsistency in the expression of preferences and beliefs (Slovic, Griffin, and Tversky), imprecision in assessments of uncertainty (Wallsten), or difficulties in statistical reasoning (Dawes; Bar-Hillel). There are discussions of both conceptual and technical issues in decision analysis that bridge the gap between theory and the practice of helping people make better decisions (Edwards; Lichtenstein et al.; Kleinmuntz); and there are chapters that look closely at the process of how people make well-structured decisions in laboratory situations that are in the best tradition of experimental psychology (Payne, Bettman, and Johnson; Mano). There are also chapters that break new ground by suggesting topics that have received little attention to date. This is the case of Brehmer, who presents a paradigm for studying decision making within dynamic systems; of Camerer, who, inspired by the success of behavioral decision theory, suggests creating a field of "behavioral game theory," thereby providing a mechanism for studying choice behavior at the levels of both individuals and groups; and of the novel investigation by Kahneman and Snell of issues concerning the prediction of one's own preferences. Finally, the chapter by Hammond is a conceptual contribution that suggests ways of integrating two different research traditions.

In addition to this diversity of topics within decision making, the contributors to the conference use and advocate quite different modes of investigation. Nor, as will also be apparent, are they uniform in their appreciation of the contributions made by different approaches to studying decision making. Hilly would have enjoyed this diversity since, cognizant of the complexities of decision making, he believed in the necessity of various approaches. Each approach, however, should be judged by the highest standards.

The organization of the book follows that of the conference itself, with one exception. Following this preface, I have included the obituary that Joshua Klayman and I wrote for the *American Psychologist* (43 [1988]: 656). In fact, this obituary was also included in the printed program of the conference and, as such, was part of the event. It is reproduced here by permission of the American Psychological Association. At the end of the book, the reader will also find a list of Hilly's professional publications.

In preparing their papers for the conference, contributors were not asked to address specific topics in decision making. Instead, they were left free to choose their own topics within the general guidelines of the goals of the conference. The philosophy behind this strategy was that, if one asks some of the best researchers to produce papers, one will obtain a good set of papers that, in an important sense, captures the state of the field at a particular moment in time. However, one will not necessarily obtain a collection of papers that fits together within some logically coherent framework. This has proved to be the case here and renders difficult the task of defining clear categories in which to classify the various chapters. To resolve this problem in the organization of the book, I have simply classified the chapters in the same order in which the papers were presented at the conference, thereby leading to six groupings of chapters corresponding to the six sessions at the conference. This has two advantages. The chapters within each part of the book typically (but not always) deal with similar themes; second, this arrangement allows one to place the discussants' comments directly after the chapters to which they refer. Despite this classification, I have avoided the temptation of providing names or titles for each part since I thought these would be too contrived.

It is my hope that this book will be read not only by those already familiar with the literature in behavioral decision making but also by students and scholars from other areas of inquiry. To facilitate this goal, introductory notes have been provided for each of the six parts in order to situate the context of the chapters and the issues addressed. Readers who are unfamiliar with the field might well be advised to read these notes before deciding on the order in which to read the various chapters. Those already familiar with the literature should also find these notes useful as a guide to the contents.

To hold a conference of the magnitude of this event requires much help and support. First, I would like to thank both the Irving B. Harris Foundation and the National Opinion Research Center for their generous financial support. Much of the editing of the conference volume was also (implicitly) supported by my contract for research on decision making provided by the Office of Naval Research. Second, my colleagues in the Center for Decision Research at the University of Chicago provided me with the much needed moral support and advice necessary to undertake the organization of the conference and also chaired different sessions at the conference itself. For the record, these people were Paul Schoemaker, Joshua Klayman, William Goldstein, Steve Hoch, and George Loewenstein. Third, the conference was the recipient of excellent administrative support from both the staff and the deans of the Graduate School of Business. For the former, I particularly thank Dottie White and Charlesetta Wren; for the latter, I thank Jack Gould and Harry Davis. Finally, I am pleased that the University of Chicago Press agreed to publish the proceedings in this volume. Given the occasion, it is the most appropriate publisher.

Hillel J. Einhorn (1941–1987)

On 8 January 1987, Hillel Einhorn died of Hodgkin's disease at the age of 45. This was his second bout with a disease that had almost claimed his life in 1969, the year in which he started his professional career. Between his two battles with cancer, Hilly contributed greatly to the development of the field of behavioral decision theory.

Hilly was born in Brooklyn, New York, on 12 June 1941. He attended Brooklyn College, where he earned a B.A. majoring in philosophy and an M.A. in experimental psychology. A talented musician, he helped support himself through college playing clarinet and saxophone. In 1966, he married Susan Michaels and enrolled in the Ph.D. program at Wayne State University. Although he started his doctoral studies with the explicit goal of becoming an industrial psychologist, this goal was soon supplanted by the desire to follow an academic career. He received his Ph.D. in 1969 under the supervision of Alan Bass with a major in industrial psychology and a minor in statistics.

Apart from visiting appointments at Carnegie-Mellon University (1971–72) and the Hebrew University of Jerusalem (1977–78 and 1982), Hilly spent his entire professional career at the University of Chicago. He joined the Graduate School of Business as an assistant professor of behavioral science in 1969, was promoted to associate professor in 1973, and to professor in 1976. He also held appointments in the university's Department of Behavioral Sciences. One of his major accomplishments at the Graduate School of Business was to restructure the behavioral science curriculum by providing a specific focus on behavioral decision theory. This new direction led to the founding of the Center for Decision Research in 1977, with Hilly as its first director. The subsequent success of the center was, in no small part, due to his drive and enthusiasm, and its example has been important in establishing the place of behavioral decision making within business schools. In 1986, Hilly was appointed the first Wallace W. Booth Professor in the Graduate School of Business, a considerable honor for a psychologist working in an environment dominated by economists.

Hilly was dedicated to his work and drew great pleasure from each publication. He made major contributions to several topics in decision making, including models of choice strategies, analyses of the effects of imperfect feedback, and the study of judgment in such diverse areas as medical diagnosis, group decision making, risky choice, and causal reasoning. He believed strongly in the importance of a rigorous analytic approach that specifies the assumptions and limitations of one's models. Working at a time when the nature and definition of rational and irrational behavior were often hotly disputed, Hilly defined a reasoned perspective from which the advantages and disadvantages of opposing arguments could be analyzed, although, as he stated himself, such reasoned positions do not typically attract adherents in continuing debates. Hilly also contributed to the development of methods for improving decision making. Aware of human cognitive limitations, he sought to develop procedures that, although not "optimal," were both robust and easy to use.

Three themes could be said to underlie Hilly's work. First, he sought to integrate psychological principles into models of decision making and to bring decision research into the mainstream of psychology. In particular, he saw the important behavioral implications of the conflicts and limitations inherent in human cognition. Second, guided by a strong aesthetic sense, Hilly had a deep appreciation for the latent simplicity, beauty, and efficacy of many natural processes even when observable behaviors seem complex or chaotic. He experienced enormous satisfaction when simple models could be shown to account for complex and apparently contradictory behavior. Third, although he greatly admired rigorous experimental work, he was acutely aware that there can be critical differences between decision making under laboratory conditions and decision making in the real world. He was especially concerned with potential sources of misrepresentation when well-structured and highly simplified environments are used to model processes normally applied to complex and information-rich situations.

Hilly contributed to the academic community in many ways. He was a conscientious reviewer, an active member of the Judgment and Decision Making Society, a stimulating colleague, and an invaluable adviser and supporter for younger researchers. He held high standards for these activities and was critical of others who did not live up to them.

Hilly also had remarkable stage presence and was much in demand as a speaker. Like most great performers, he made it look easy; few realized the extent to which he prepared his talks and how carefully he considered his potential audiences. As a teacher, Hilly captivated students, whether in doctoral seminars or in sessions for M.B.A. students. Finally, Hilly's friends and colleagues will always remember his wonderful sense of humor and the contagious excitement and enthusiasm that pervaded his personal and professional life. For those who knew him well, the loss is hard to bear.

Robin M. Hogarth
Joshua Klayman

Part One

INTRODUCTORY COMMENTS

The three chapters in this first part speak, in quite different ways, to issues concerning how to help people make better decisions by using or modifying models adapted from statistical decision theory. At a general level, the first two chapters (Slovic, Griffin, and Tversky and Wallsten) deal with the fundamental problem of how to elicit information from people that can be used as inputs in decision making. More specifically, Slovic, Griffin, and Tversky discuss how normatively irrelevant factors can affect stated judgments or preferences, and Wallsten treats the issue of whether people are able or willing to express feelings of uncertainty as precise probabilities and the effects this may have on decision making. Both chapters rely heavily on the results of experimental evidence. Edwards's chapter, the third in this part, is broader in scope. He sets forth an agenda of important problems that he thinks should be addressed by decision researchers. In particular, he expresses misgivings concerning the value of the kind of experimental evidence presented by Slovic, Griffin, and Tversky and Wallsten.

The generic problem considered by Slovic, Griffin, and Tversky is one that has attracted much attention over the last two decades. It is the phenomenon that people's judgments and choices are sensitive to the manner in which they are elicited. In other words, ask the same question by different means, and obtain different answers. Moreover, such differences are often robust and systematic and cannot be explained by random error on the part of respondents. From a practical viewpoint, these results raise considerable problems for those who wish to use subjective judgments concerning beliefs and preferences in decision-making models because these models assume that the manner of eliciting information from decision makers should not affect the information obtained. They also suggest the disturbing possibility that unaided, intuitive decisions may be subject to important distortions due to normatively irrelevant factors. However, Slovic, Griffin, and Tversky go beyond simply noting this kind of phenomenon or documenting further evidence of its existence. Instead, they attack the psychologically more interesting issue of why this phenomenon occurs in certain circumstances and propose a specific psychological mechanism of "compatibility" to account for some of these effects. As such, their chapter is an important contribution to understanding problems of systematic variations in people's expressions of preferences or beliefs that are not related to new informational inputs. In his discussion of the chapters in this part, MacCrimmon reviews the history of this topic from a decision-theoretic viewpoint and sketches some alternative accounts of the phenomena discussed by Slovic, Griffin, and Tversky.

From a strictly decision-theoretic viewpoint, Wallsten's chapter is heretical. Noting that there are many circumstances in which people are unwilling, and perhaps even unable, to express their degree of uncertainty about unknown (or future) events in the form of precise probability distributions, he reviews his own experimental program that has investigated the effects of expressing probability estimates in verbal as opposed to numerical form. (For example, describing an event as "likely" to occur as opposed to assessing a specific probability such as .6). An important contribution of his chapter is the description of experiments that have examined whether people's decisions are better or worse when based on verbal as opposed to numerical probability estimates. For the conventional wisdom of most decision analysts, his results are surprising: the differences are minimal. However, Wallsten would be the first to emphasize that these results are based on a limited set of experiments and that it is unclear how they would generalize to other circumstances. Like Slovic, Griffin, and Tversky, Wallsten is interested in psychological processes and also discusses his work on how people assign specific probability phrases to different levels of subjective uncertainty.

As noted above, Edwards both implicitly and explicitly criticizes work of the type reported by Slovic, Griffin, and Tversky and Wallsten. He feels that too much has been made of certain types of experimental results on decision making and that we really know little about the effectiveness of decision making in different types of decision tasks. For example, he is skeptical of the implications of the kinds of results presented by Slovic, Griffin, and Tversky and argues that practitioners (of decision analysis) routinely use procedures to guard themselves against inconsistent judgments. In contrast to the other chapters in this part, which have a heavy psychological orientation, Edwards's main concern is with improving the practice of decision analysis. This leads him to focus on issues such as problem structuring and the invention of hypotheses and options that are currently more in the realm of the "art" as opposed to the "science" of decision making. He also advocates links with other disciplines that could bring synergies to behavioral decision making. At a theoretical level, Edwards discusses one way in which apparently paradoxical decision behavior can be reconciled.

The two discussions of these chapters present additional, and complementary, evidence. Kunreuther relates the issues in all three chapters to real-world decision-making contexts (i.e., outside the experimental laboratory). In contrast, MacCrimmon concentrates on the experimental paradigms and paradoxes that have fueled much of the research in behavioral decision making.

1

Compatibility Effects in Judgment and Choice

PAUL SLOVIC, DALE GRIFFIN,

AMOS TVERSKY

We investigate the hypothesis that the weight of a stimulus attribute is enhanced by its compatibility with the response mode. The first section demonstrates compatibility effects in predictions of market value (study 1) and course grades (study 2). In each case, the weight of a stimulus attribute is greater when it matches the response scale than when it does not. The second section applies the compatibility principle to the study of choice and investigates the hypothesis that preference reversals are caused by the fact that payoffs are weighted more heavily in pricing than in choice, as implied by compatibility. This account is supported in experiments on risky choice (studies 3 and 5) and on time preferences (study 4). Theoretical and practical implications of the compatibility hypothesis are discussed in the last section.

One of the main ideas that has emerged from behavioral decision research in the last two decades is a constructive conception of judgment and choice. According to this view, preferences and beliefs are actually constructed—not merely revealed—in the elicitation process. This conception is entailed by findings that normatively equivalent methods of elicitation often give rise to systematically different responses (see, e.g., Slovic, Fischhoff, and Lichtenstein 1982; Tversky, Sattath, and Slovic 1988). To account for these data within a constructive framework, we seek explanatory principles that relate the characteristics of the task to the attributes of the objects under study. One such notion is the compatibility hypothesis, which states that the weight of a stimulus attribute is enhanced by its compatibility with the response.

The rationale for this hypothesis is twofold. First, noncompatibility between the input and the output requires additional mental operations, which often increase effort and error and may reduce impact. Second, a response

Support for this research was provided by the Air Force Office of Scientific Research grant 88-0007 to Decision Research and grant 89-0064 to Stanford University. Additional support was provided by National Science Foundation grant SES 8712145 to Decision Research. This chapter has benefited from the comments of Robyn Dawes, Gregory Fischer, Robin Hogarth, Eric Johnson, and Daniel Kahneman.

mode may prime or focus attention on the compatible features of the stimulus. Common features, for example, are weighted more heavily in judgments of similarity than in judgments of dissimilarity, whereas distinctive features are weighted more heavily in judgments of dissimilarity (Tversky 1977). Consequently, entities with many common features and many distinctive features (e.g., East Germany and West Germany) are judged as both more similar to each other and as more different from each other than entities with relatively fewer common features and fewer distinctive features (e.g., Sri Lanka and Nepal).

The significance of the compatibility between input and output has long been recognized by students of human performance. Engineering psychologists have discovered that responses to visual displays of information, such as an instrument panel, will be faster and more accurate if the response structure is compatible with the arrangement of the stimuli (Fitts and Seeger 1953; Wickens 1984). For example, the response to a pair of lights will be faster and more accurate if the left light is assigned to the left key and the right light to the right key. Similarly, a square array of four burners on a stove is easier to control with a matching square array of knobs than with a linear array. The concept of compatibility has been extended beyond spatial organization. The reaction time to a stimulus light is faster with a pointing response than with a vocal response, but the vocal response is faster than pointing if the stimulus is presented in an auditory mode (Brainard et al. 1962).

The present chapter investigates the role of compatibility in judgment and choice. As in the study of perceptual-motor performance, we do not have an independent procedure for assessing the compatibility between stimulus elements and response modes. This hinders the development of a general theory, but it does not render the concept meaningless or circular, provided that compatibility can be experimentally manipulated. For example, it seems reasonable to assume that a turn signal in which a left movement indicates a left turn and a right movement indicates a right turn is more compatible than the opposite design. By comparing people's performance with the two turn signals, it is possible to test whether the more compatible design yields better performance. Similarly, it seems reasonable to assume that the monetary payoffs of a bet are more compatible with pricing than with choice because both the payoffs and the prices are expressed in dollars. By comparing choice and pricing, therefore, we can test the hypothesis that the payoffs of a bet loom larger in pricing than in choice.

The research described in this chapter employs the notion of compatibility as a guiding principle that is translated into specific experimental hypotheses. In the first section, we demonstrate compatibility effects in studies of prediction. The next section applies the compatibility hypothesis to the analysis of preference reversals in both risky and riskless choice. Theoretical and practical implications of the findings are addressed in the final section.

PREDICTION

In all the following studies, subjects were either undergraduate students at Stanford University participating for course credit or students at the University of Oregon who responded to an ad in the student newspaper and were paid for their participation.

Study 1: Prediction of Market Value

In our first study, 77 Stanford students were presented with a list of 12 well-known U.S. companies taken from the 1987 *Business Week* Top 100. For each company, students were given two items of information: 1986 *market value* (the total value of the outstanding shares in billions of dollars) and 1987 *profit standing* (rank of the company in terms of its 1987 earnings among the Top 100; see table 1.1). Half the subjects were asked to predict 1987 market value (in billions of dollars). They were informed that, among the Top 100, the highest market value in 1987 was $68.2 billion and that the lowest was $5.1 billion, so their predictions should fall within that range. The remaining subjects were asked to predict each company's rank (from 1 to 100) in market value for 1987. Thus, both groups of subjects received identical information and predicted the same criterion, using a different response scale. Although the two response scales differ in units (dollar vs. rank) and direction (low rank means high market value), the two dependent variables should yield the same ordering of the 12 companies. To encourage careful consideration, a $75 prize was offered for the person whose predictions most nearly matched the actual values. The mean predicted values for each group are presented in table 1.1 along with the actual values.

The compatibility hypothesis states that a predictor will be weighted more heavily when it matches the response scale than when it does not. That is, 1986 market value in dollars (D) should be weighted more heavily by the subjects who predict in dollars (d) than by those who predict in rank (r). By the same token, 1987 profit rank (R) should be weighted more heavily by the subjects who predict in rank than by those who predict in dollars. To investigate this hypothesis, we correlated the criteria with the predictors, estimated the relative weights of the two predictors, and devised a statistical test based on reversals of order.

The product-moment correlations of d with D and R were .93 and .77, respectively, whereas the correlations of r with D and R were .74 and .94. Thus, the correlation between the matched variables was higher than that between the nonmatched variables. It is instructive to examine the compatibility effect in terms of the relative weights of the two predictors in a multiple-regression equation. These values can be computed directly or derived from the correlations between the predictors and the criterion together with the correlation between the predictors. (To make the regression weights positive, the ranking order was reversed.) The multiple regressions for both dollars and

TABLE 1.1
Financial Information for the Twelve Companies Used to Test the Compatibility Hypothesis with the Respective Mean Predictions
(Actual Outcome Values in Parentheses)

	Predictors		Criteria	
	D	R	d	r
	(1986 Market Value, $ Billion)	(1987 Profit Rank, 1 to 100)	(1987 Market Value, $ Billion)	(1987 Market Rank, 1 to 100)
Company				
1 Chevron	18.0	26	21.3	30
			(16.2)	(15)
2 H. J. Heinz	6.2	75	7.3	70
			(5.6)	(84)
3 Coca-Cola	18.1	31	21.6	31
			(14.8)	(17)
4 Westinghouse	9.3	36	12.9	44
			(7.4)	(51)
5 Dow Chemical	15.5	16	20.5	26
			(16.9)	(13)
6 Xerox	7.1	54	9.5	53
			(5.7)	(82)
7 Chrysler	8.2	12	15.5	32
			(5.5)	(90)
8 Kraft	8.4	74	9.0	64
			(7.3)	(53)
9 Hewlett-Packard	14.7	39	17.4	42
			(15.5)	(16)
10 Procter & Gamble	15.6	63	16.3	47
			(13.9)	(25)
11 Kodak	16.9	20	20.9	27
			(13.7)	(26)
12 Johnson & Johnson	15.5	35	18.2	36
			(14.7)	(18)

ranks fit the average data very well with multiple correlations of .99. Let d_i and r_i denote the mean observed predictions of 1987 dollar value and rank, respectively, for a company whose 1986 dollar value is D_i and whose 1987 profit rank is R_i. The multiple-regression equations, then, take the form

$$d_i = \alpha_d D_i + \beta_d R_i,$$
$$r_i = \alpha_r D_i + \beta_r R_i$$

when the independent variables are expressed in standardized units. Thus, α_d and α_r are the regression weights for the 1986 market value (D_i) estimated from the predicted dollars and ranks, respectively. Similarly, β_d and β_r are the corresponding weights for the second predictor, 1987 profit rank. The relative weights for the first predictor in each of the two response modes are

$$A_d = \alpha_d/(\alpha_d + \beta_d),$$
$$A_r = \alpha_r/(\alpha_r + \beta_r).$$

These values measure the relative contribution of D_i in the prediction of dollars and rank, respectively. If the weighting of the dimensions is independent of the response scale, A_d and A_r are expected to be equal, except for minor perturbations due to a nonlinear relation between d and r. As we shall argue next, the compatibility hypothesis implies $A_d > A_r$. Note that A_d is the relative weight of the 1986 market value in dollars, estimated from the prediction of dollars, whereas A_r is the relative weight of the same variable estimated from the prediction of rank. The first index reflects the impact of D_i in a compatible condition (i.e., when the predictions are made in dollars), whereas A_r reflects the impact of D_i in the less compatible condition (i.e., when the predictions are made in ranks). If the compatibility between the predictor and the criterion enhances the weight of that variable, then A_d should exceed A_r.

The values estimated from the regression equations were $A_d = .64$ and $A_r = .32$, in accord with the compatibility hypothesis. Thus, D_i was weighted more than R_i in the prediction of dollars, whereas R_i was weighted more than D_i in the prediction of rank. Moreover, each predictor was weighted about twice as much in the compatible condition as it was in the noncompatible condition. When interpreting the relative weights, here and in later studies, we should keep in mind that they are based on aggregate data, that the predictors (D and R) are correlated, and that the relation between the two criteria (d and r) should be monotone but not necessarily linear. Although these factors do not account for the discrepancy between A_d and A_r, it is desirable to obtain a purely ordinal test of the compatibility hypothesis within the data of each subject that is not open to these objections. The following analysis of order reversals provides a basis for such a test.

The change in the relative weights induced by the response mode could produce reversals in the order of the predictions. In the present study, there were 21 pairs of companies (i, j) in which $D_i > D_j$ and $R_j > R_i$. If D is weighted more heavily than R in the subject's prediction of dollars and R is weighted more heavily than D in the subject's prediction of rank, we would expect $d_i > d_j$ and $r_j > r_i$. The data confirmed this hypothesis. Subjects who predicted dollars favored the company with the higher D 72 percent of the time, whereas subjects who predicted rank favored the company with the higher D only 39 percent of the time. (Ties were excluded from this analysis.) This difference is highly significant ($p < .001$). Note that the subjects did not directly compare the companies; the ordering was inferred from their predictions.

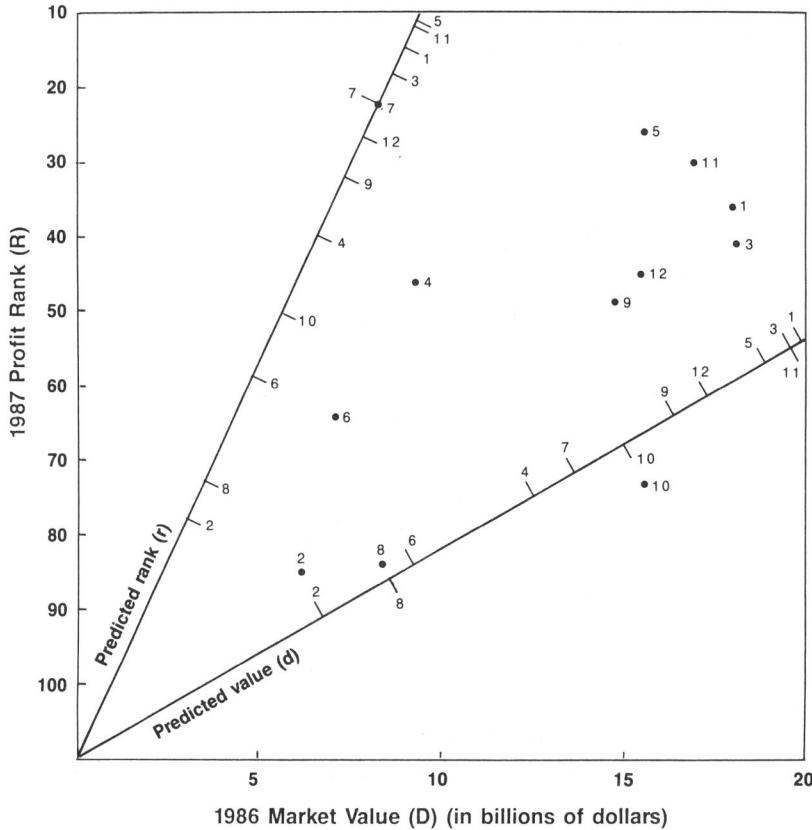

Figure 1.1. A graphic summary of study 1. The dots represent the 12 companies. The slopes of the d and r lines correspond to the weight ratios, α_d/β_d and α_r/β_r, of D to R in the two prediction tasks.

Figure 1.1 provides a graphic summary of the stimuli and the data. Each of the 12 companies is represented as a point in the $D \times R$ plane. Each regression equation defines a set of parallel equal-value lines. The points on any given line are the values of the two predictors that give rise to the same predicted value of the criterion. For the prediction of dollars, for instance, each equal-value line is the set of points for which $\alpha_d D_i + \beta_d R_i$ is a constant. The two prediction lines (d and r) are perpendicular to the equal-value lines for the two criteria. Hence, the predicted order of the companies is given by the order of their projections, denoted by notches. The slopes of the prediction lines are the weight ratios, α_d/β_d and α_r/β_r, of D to R, estimated from d and r, respectively. It is evident from the figure that, in accord with the compatibility hypothesis, the two criteria induced different orders of the 12 companies. For example, the predicted market value of Chevron (no. 1) is higher than that of Dow Chemical (no. 5), but the latter is assigned a higher rank than the former.

Study 2: Prediction of Academic Performance

Our second test of the compatibility hypothesis involves the prediction of a student's grade in a course. Two hundred fifty-eight subjects from the University of Oregon predicted the performance of 10 target students in a history course on the basis of the students' performance in two other courses: English literature and philosophy. For each of the 10 targets, the subjects were given a letter grade (from A+ to D) in one course and a class rank (from 1 to 100) in the other course. Half the subjects predicted the students' grade in history, whereas the other half predicted the students' class rank in history. Each of the four combinations of performance measures (grade/rank) and courses (literature/philosophy) was presented to a different group of subjects. The description of the 10 hypothetical students is presented in table 1.2 along with the mean predictions of grade and rank, rounded to the nearest unit.

The compatibility hypothesis implies that a given predictor (e.g., grade in philosophy) will be given more weight when the criterion is expressed on the same scale (e.g., grade in history) than when it is expressed on a different scale (e.g., rank in history). The relative weight of grades to ranks, then, will be higher in the group that predicts grades than in the group that predicts ranks.

As in the previous study, we first correlated the criteria with the predictors. The (zero-order) correlations of g with G and R were .83 and .82, respectively, whereas the correlations of r with G and R were .70 and .91, in accord with the compatibility hypothesis. We next regressed the mean predictions of grades and ranks (displayed in table 1.2) onto the two predictors. The letter grades were coded D = 1, C− = 2, . . . A+ = 10. (To make the regression

TABLE 1.2
ACADEMIC PERFORMANCE OF THE 10 HYPOTHETICAL STUDENTS USED TO TEST THE COMPATIBILITY HYPOTHESIS, WITH THE RESPECTIVE MEAN PREDICTIONS

	Predictors		Criteria	
Student	G (Grade in Class 1, A+ to D)	R (Rank in Class 2, 1 to 100)	g (Predicted Grade)	r (Predicted Rank)
1	B+	66	C+	48
2	D	93	D	87
3	A	45	B	33
4	C+	34	B−	40
5	A+	6	A	11
6	C−	54	C	54
7	B	59	B−	49
8	A−	72	B−	48
9	C	28	B−	35
10	B−	41	B−	38

weights positive, the ranking order was reversed.) The multiple regressions for both grades and ranks fit the average data very well with multiple correlations of .99. Let g_i and r_i denote the mean observed predictions of grade and rank, respectively, for a student with a grade G_i in one course and a rank R_i in the other course. There was no significant interaction between the scale (rank/grade) and the course (literature/philosophy); therefore, the data for the two courses were pooled. The multiple-regression equations, then, take the form

$$g_i = \alpha_g G_i + \beta_g R_i,$$
$$r_i = \alpha_r G_i + \beta_r R_i,$$

when the independent variables are expressed in standardized units. Thus, α_g and α_r are the regression weights for the grades (G_i) estimated from the predicted grades and ranks, respectively. Similarly, β_g and β_r are the corresponding weights for the second predictor, class rank. The relative weights for the first predictor in each of the two response modes are

$$A_g = \alpha_g/(\alpha_g + \beta_g),$$
$$A_r = \alpha_r/(\alpha_r + \beta_r).$$

These values measure the relative contribution of G_i in the prediction of grade and rank, respectively. Because the grades and ranks are monotonically related, A_g and A_r should be approximately equal if the weighting of the dimensions is independent of the response scale. However, if the match between the predictor and the criterion enhances the weight of the more compatible predictor, then A_g should exceed A_r.

The values estimated from the regression equations were $A_g = .51$ and $A_r = .40$, in accord with the compatibility hypothesis. Thus, grade in philosophy was weighted more heavily in the prediction of grade in history than in the prediction of rank in history. Similarly, rank in philosophy was weighted more heavily in the prediction of rank in history than in the prediction of grade in history.

To obtain an ordinal test of the compatibility hypothesis within the data of each subject, we analyzed the reversals of order induced by the change in weights. There were 21 pairs of students (i, j) in which $G_i > G_j$ and $R_j > R_i$. If G is weighted more heavily than R in the prediction of grades and R is weighted more heavily than G in the prediction of rank, we would expect $g_i > g_j$ and $r_j > r_i$. Indeed, subjects who predicted grades favored the student with the higher G 58 percent of the time, whereas subjects who predicted rank favored the student with the higher G only 42 percent of the time. (Ties were excluded from this analysis.) This difference is statistically significant ($p < .001$). Recall that subjects did not compare students directly; the ordering was inferred from their predictions. Figure 1.2 provides a graphic representation of these data.

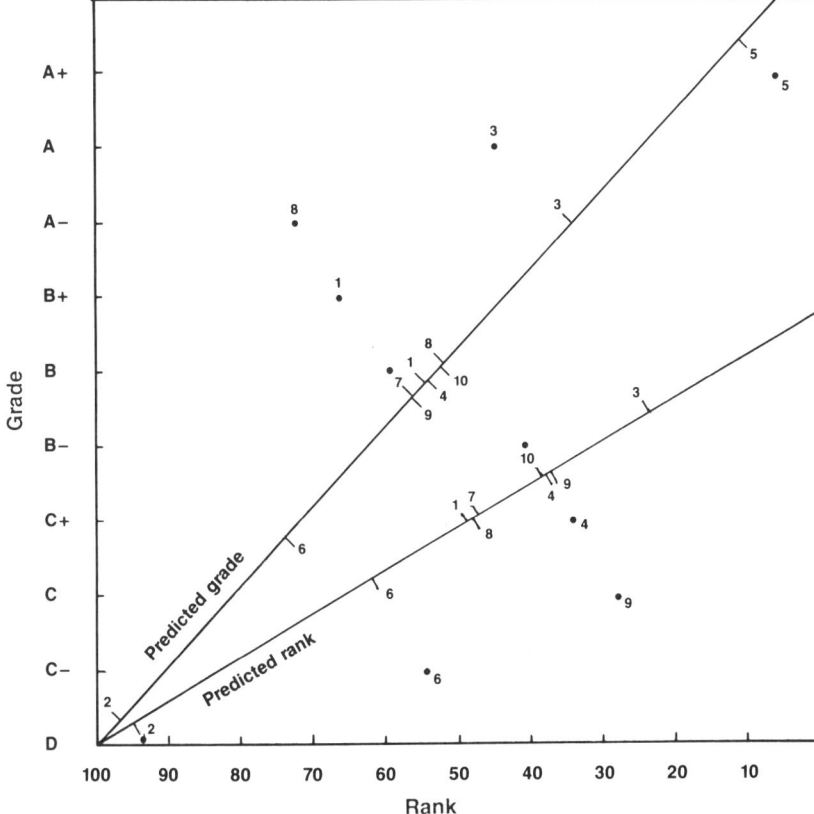

Figure 1.2. A graphic summary of study 2. The dots represent the 10 students. The slopes of the grade and rank lines correspond to the weight ratios, α_g/β_g and α_r/β_r, of grades to ranks in the two prediction tasks.

The compatibility effects observed in the previous two studies may be mediated by a process of anchoring and adjustment. Subjects may use the score on the compatible variable (the attribute that matches the criterion) as an anchor and then adjust this number upward or downward according to the value of the noncompatible variable. Because adjustments of an anchor are generally insufficient (Slovic and Lichtenstein 1971; Tversky and Kahneman 1974), the compatible attribute would be overweighted. An anchoring and adjustment process, therefore, provides a natural mechanism for generating compatibility effects. To test whether compatibility effects occur in the absence of anchoring, we replaced the prediction task described above with a choice task in which the subject is no longer required to make a numerical prediction that would invoke anchoring. The following study, then, investigates the compatibility hypothesis in a context in which anchoring and adjustment are unlikely to play a significant role.

Seventy-eight Stanford undergraduates were presented with 20 pairs of students taken from the list given in table 1.2. In each pair, one student had a higher grade and the other a higher rank. Half the subjects were asked to predict, for each pair, which student would achieve a higher grade in history, whereas the remaining subjects were asked to predict, for each pair, which student would achieve a higher rank in history. Because both groups were asked to predict only which of two students would do better in history, not to make a numerical prediction, their tasks were virtually identical.

Nevertheless, the student with the higher grade was selected 56 percent of the time by the grade group and only 49 percent of the time by the rank group ($p < .05$), indicating that the compatibility effect is present even in a choice task that does not require a quantitative response and is, therefore, unlikely to involve an adjustment of a numerical anchor. The strategy of anchoring and adjustment, however, probably contributes to the compatibility effect observed in numerical predictions.

PREFERENCE

The previous section investigated compatibility effects in prediction and judgment. The present section is concerned with the role of compatibility in decision making in general and preference reversals in particular. A reversal of preference is a pattern of choices in which normatively equivalent elicitation procedures give rise to inconsistent preferences. A well-known example of preference reversal (PR) was discovered by Lichtenstein and Slovic (1971; see also Slovic and Lichtenstein 1968). This phenomenon involves pairs of bets with comparable expected values: an H bet that offers a high probability of winning a relatively small amount of money (e.g., a 35/36 chance to win $4) and an L bet that offers a low probability of winning a moderate amount of money (e.g., an 11/36 chance to win $16). When offered a choice between such bets, most people choose the H bet over the L bet, but, when asked to state the lowest selling price of each bet, the majority state a higher price for the L bet than for the H bet. In general, about half the subjects state prices that are inconsistent with their choices, thereby exhibiting a PR. This pattern of preferences, which violates the standard theory of rational choice, has been observed in numerous experiments, including a study conducted on the floor of a Las Vegas casino (Lichtenstein and Slovic 1973), and it persists even in the presence of monetary incentives designed to promote consistent responses (see, e.g., Grether and Plott 1979; Slovic and Lichtenstein 1983).

Let C_H and C_L denote, respectively, the cash equivalent (or minimum selling price) of the H bet and the L bet, and let ">" and "$\approx$" denote strict preference and indifference, respectively. In this notation, PR is expressed as $H > L$ and $C_L > C_H$. Note that ">" refers to preference between options, whereas ">" refers to the ordering of cash amounts. (Naturally, $X > Y$ implies $X > Y$; i.e., more money is preferred to less.)

It can be shown that PR violates either transitivity or procedure invariance, and possibly both (Tversky, Slovic, and Kahneman, in press). Procedure invariance states that choice and pricing yield the same ordering of options; that is, a bet B is preferred to a cash amount X if and only if the cash equivalent of B, C_B, exceeds X. In particular, $C_B = X$ whenever the decision maker is indifferent between playing the bet B and receiving the cash amount X. If procedure invariance holds, PR reduces to an intrasitivity of the form

$$C_H \approx H > L \approx C_L > C_H.$$

On the other hand, $>$ may be transitive, in which case PR violates procedure invariance. This violation can be produced by either overpricing of L (i.e., $C_L > L$) or underpricing of H (i.e., $H > C_H$).

It follows from this analysis that PR may be caused either by the intransitivity of $>$ or by a failure of procedure invariance that gives rise to a choice-pricing discrepancy. To investigate these possibilities, Tversky, Slovic and Kahneman (in press) extended the traditional design by including, in addition to the bets H and L, a cash amount X that is compared to both. By focusing on all cases in which $C_L > X > C_H$, it is possible to diagnose all PR patterns according to whether they imply an intransitive choice, an overpricing of L, an underpricing of H, or both overpricing of L and underpricing of H. Tversky, Slovic, and Kahneman (in press) applied this analysis to an extensive study of preference reversals, using 18 triples (H, L, X) that covered a wide range of probabilities and payoffs. The diagnostic analysis of the observed response patterns showed that the most important determinant of PR was the overpricing of L. Intransitive choice and the underpricing of H played a relatively minor role, each accounting for less than 10 percent of the total number of reversals.

The compatibility hypothesis offers a simple explanation for the overpricing of L bets. Because the selling price of a bet is expressed in dollars, we expect that the payoffs, which are expressed in the same units, will be weighted more heavily in pricing than in choice. To test this hypothesis, Tversky, Slovic, and Kahneman (in press) have employed a contingent-weighting model in which the relative weight of an attribute varies with the method of elicitation. This analysis differs from the regression analysis discussed in the previous section in two important respects. First, the two attributes of a simple gamble, probability and payoff, combine multiplicatively rather than additively. Consequently, the multiple-regression analysis was applied to the logarithms of the probabilities and the payoffs. Second, the analysis uses only the ordering of the bets by price and by choice. Specifically, assume that a bet $B = (P, X)$ is chosen over $B' = (P', X')$ if and only if

$$\log P + \alpha \log X > \log P' + \alpha \log X'.$$

Similarly, assume that B is priced higher than B' if and only if

$$\log P + \beta \log X > \log P' + \beta \log X'.$$

These relations are equivalent to the assumption that the ordering of bets according to both choice and pricing follows a multiplicative probability-value model with a power function for gains and exponents α and β for choice and pricing, respectively. If the payoff of a bet looms larger in pricing than in choice, as implied by compatibility, β should exceed α.

To test this prediction, Tversky, Slovic, and Kahneman (in press) applied the model outlined above to the data and estimated α and β separately for each subject. Note that a choice between an H bet (P_H, X_H) and an L bet (P_L, X_L) implies an inequality involving α. According to the model, H is chosen over L if and only if

$$\log P_H + \alpha \log X_H > \log P_L + \alpha \log X_L,$$

or, equivalently, whenever

$$R = \log(P_H/P_L)/\log(X_L/X_H) > \alpha.$$

Any comparison of H_i and $L_i (i = 1, \ldots, 18)$ gives rise to an inequality of the form $R_i > \alpha$ or $R_i < \alpha$. For each subject, a value of α was selected so as to minimize the average squared deviations between the model and the data. Specifically, for any subject and any pair of bets (H_i, L_i), define $x_i = 1$ if $H_i > L_i$ and $x_i = 0$ if $L_i > H_i$. A value of α was selected for each subject by minimizing the quadratic loss function

$$F(\alpha) = \sum_{i=1}^{18} f(\alpha, x_i),$$

where

$$f(\alpha, x_i) = \begin{cases} x_i(\alpha - R_i)^2 & \text{if } R_i < \alpha, \\ (1 - x_i)(\alpha - R_i)^2 & \text{if } R_i > \alpha. \end{cases}$$

Exactly the same procedure was used to estimate β, except that the H_i, L_i pairs were ordered by their cash equivalents, excluding ties. In accord with the compatiblity hypthesis, β exceeded α for 87 percent of the subjects ($N = 179$), and the difference between them was significantly positive ($P < .001$). To evaluate the adequacy of the model, the logarithms of the prices were regressed against log P and log X separately for each subject. The median value of the multiple correlation was .95, indicating that the model provided a reasonable fit for individual data.

It should be noted that the contingent-weighting model (with $\beta > \alpha$) implies overpricing of both H and L bets. It can be shown that the predicted effect, however, is substantial for L bets and negligible for H bets. More specifically, let Y_c and Y_p, respectively, be the cash amounts that are equivalent to the bet (P, X) in choice and in pricing. It follows from the model that the discrepancy between choice and pricing, measured by $\log(Y_p/Y_c)$, is proportional to $\log P$. It vanishes when P approaches one, and it is large when P is small. For example, the overpricing effect implied by the model is 20 times larger when the probability of winning (P) is .1 than when it is .9. In general, P is above .9 for H bets and below .5 for L bets. The contingent-weighting model, therefore, explains the major cause of PR, namely, the overpricing of L bets. Additional hypotheses are required to explain second-order effects, such as the occasional intransitivities and the slight underpricing of H bets. In the remainder of this section, we test other implications of the compatibility hypothesis in both risky and riskless choice.

Study 3: Monetary versus Nonmonetary Outcomes

If preference reversals are due primarily to the compatibility of prices and payoffs, their frequency should be substantially reduced when the outcomes of the bets are not expressed in monetary terms. To test this prediction, we constructed six pairs of H and L bets, three with monetary outcomes (as in the usual PR studies) and three with nonmonetary outcomes. Two hundred forty-eight students from the University of Oregon participated in this study. Half the subjects first chose between all six pairs of bets and later assigned a cash equivalent to each bet. The other half of the subjects performed these tasks in the opposite order. There was no significant order effect; therefore, the data for the two groups were combined. Table 1.3 presents the entire set of 12 bets and the percentage of subjects who preferred the H bet over the L bet $(H > L)$, the percentage of subjects who assigned a higher cash equivalent to H than to L $(C_H > C_L)$, and the percentage of preference reversals.

The data show that the percentage of choices of H over L was roughly the same in the monetary and the nonmonetary bets (63 vs. 66 percent) but that the percentage of cases in which C_H exceeds C_L was substantially smaller in the monetary than in the nonmonetary bets (33 vs. 54 percent). Consequently, the overall incidence of predicted PR decreased significantly, from 41 to 24 percent ($p < .01$). Naturally, the pricing response is more compatible with monetary payoffs than with nonmonetary payoffs. Hence the observed reduction in PR with nonmonetary outcomes underscores the role of compatibility in the evaluation of options. Because even the nonmonetary payoffs can be evaluated in monetary terms, albeit with some difficulty, we do not expect the complete elimination of preference reversals in this case.

Study 4: Time Preferences

The compatibility hypothesis entails that preference reversals should not be restricted to risky prospects and that they should also be found in riskless choice. The present study investigates this hypothesis using delayed payoffs

TABLE 1.3
The Monetary and Nonmonetary Bets Used to Test the Compatibility Hypothesis, with the Respective Percentage of Preferences

	$H > L$	$C_H > C_L$	PR
Monetary bets:			
1. H: .94 to win $3	57	26	42
L: .50 to win $6.50			
2. H: .86 to win $7.50	69	21	51
L: .39 to win $17			
3. H: .81 to win $16	63	51	29
L: .19 to win $56			
Mean	63	33	41
Nonmonetary bets			
4. H: .89 to win a 1-week pass good at all movie theatres in town			
L: .33 to win a 1-month pass good at all movie theatres in town			
	65	46	30
5. H: .92 to win an all-expense-paid weekend at an Oregon coastal resort			
	72	56	25
L: .08 to win a 1-week all-expense-paid trip to Hawaii			
6. H: .92 to win a 1-week pass good at all movie theatres in town			
	62	60	16
L: .31 to win dinner for two at a very good restaurant			
Mean	66	54	24

TABLE 1.4
The Options Used in Study 5 and the Respective Percentage of Preferences

S	L	$S > L$	$C_S > C_L$	PR
(1600, 1½)	(2500, 5)	57	12	49
(1600, 1½)	(3550, 10)	72	19	56
(2500, 5)	(3550, 10)	83	29	57
(1525, ½)	(1900, 2½)	83	40	46
Mean		74	25	52

Note. The pair (X, T) denotes the option of receiving X, T years from now.

that differ in size, and length of delay (see Tversky, Slovic, and Kahneman, in press). Consider a delayed payoff of the form (X, T) that offers a payment of X dollars T years from now. Table 1.4 presents four pairs of options that consist of a long-term prospect L (e.g., $2,500, 5 years from now) and a short-term prospect S (e.g., $1,600, 1½ years from now).

One hundred sixty-nine students from the University of Oregon participated in a study of choice between delayed payoffs. Half the subjects first chose between S and L in each pair and later priced all eight options by stating "the smallest immediate cash payment for which you would be willing to exchange the delayed payment." The other subjects performed the choice and pricing tasks in the opposite order. There were no systematic differences between the groups, so their data were combined.

Table 1.4 presents the four pairs of options employed in this study. The table also includes, for each pair, the percentage of subjects who chose S over L ($S > L$), the percentage of subjects who priced S above L ($C_S > C_L$), and the percentage of PR patterns ($S > L$ and $C_L > C_S$). Because both the given payoffs and the stated prices are expressed in dollars, the compatibility hypothesis implies that the payoffs will be weighted more heavily in pricing than in choice. As a consequence, the preference for the short-term option (S) over the long-term option (L) should be greater in choice than in pricing. Table 1.4 confirms this prediction. Overall, S was chosen over L 74 percent of the time, but S was priced higher than L only 25 percent of the time, yielding 52 percent preference reversals, as compared with 3 percent reversals in the opposite direction. The application of the diagnostic analysis described earlier revealed that, as in the case of choice between simple bets, the major determinant of PR was overpricing of the long-term option, as suggested by compatibility (Tversky, Slovic, and Kahneman, in press).

In the pricing task, each option is evaluated singly whereas choice involves a direct comparison between options. The standard demonstrations of PR, therefore, are consistent with the alternative hypothesis that payoffs are weighted more heavily in a singular than in a comparative evaluation. To test this hypothesis against compatibility, we replicated the study presented above with a new group of 184 students from the University of Oregon, with one change. Instead of pricing the options, the subjects were asked to rate the attractiveness of each option on a scale from 0 (not at all attractive) to 20 (extremely attractive). If PR is controlled, in part at least, by the nature of the task (singular vs. comparative), we should expect L to be more popular in rating than in choice. On the other hand, if PR is produced by scale compatibility, there is no obvious reason why rating should differ from choice. Indeed, no discrepancy between choice and rating was observed. Overall, S was chosen over L 75 percent of the time (as in the original study), and the rating of S exceeded the rating of L in 76 percent of the cases. Only 11 percent of the patterns exhibited PR between choice and rating as compared to 52 percent between choice and pricing.

Study 3 showed that the use of nonmonetary prizes greatly reduced the amount of PR, whereas study 4 demonstrated substantial PR in the absence of risk. Evidently, preference reversals are controlled primarily by the compatibility between the price and the payoffs, regardless of the presence or absence of risk.

Study 5: Matching versus Pricing

In addition to pricing and choice, options can be evaluated through a matching procedure in which a decision maker is required to fill in a missing value so as to equate a pair of options. Considerations of compatibility suggest that the attribute on which the match is made will be overweighted relative to another attribute. This hypothesis is tested in the following study, using 12 pairs of H and L bets (displayed in table 1.5). In each pair, one value—either a probability or a payoff—was missing, and the subjects were asked to set the missing value so that they would be indifferent between the two bets. Consider, for example, the bets H (33/36, $50) and L (18/36, $125). If we replace the 18/36 probability in L by a question mark, the subject is asked in effect, What chance to win $125 is equally attractive as a 33/36 chance to win $50? The value set by the subject implies a preference between the original bets. If the value exceeds ½, we infer that the subject prefers H to L, and, if the value is less than ½, we reach the opposite conclusion. Using all four components as missing values, we can infer the preferences from matching either the probability or the payoff of each bet. If the compatibility hypothesis applies to matching, then the attribute on which the match is made will be overweighted relative to the other attribute. As a consequence, the inferred percentage of preferences for H over L should be higher for probability matches than for payoff matches.

Two hundred subjects from the University of Oregon participated in this study. Each subject saw 12 pairs, each consisting of a high-probability bet (H) and a low-probability bet (L). Six of these pairs consisted of bets with relatively small payoffs; the other six pairs consisted of bets with large payoffs, constructed by multiplying the payoffs in the first six pairs by a factor of 25 (see table 1.5). Each pair of bets was evaluated in four ways: direct choice, pricing of each bet individually, matching by providing a missing payoff, and matching by providing a missing probability. Every subject performed both choice and pricing tasks and matched either probabilities or payoffs (no subject matched both probabilities and payoffs). The order in which these tasks were performed was counterbalanced.

The dependent variable of interest is the percentage of responses favoring the H bet over the L bet. These values are presented in table 1.5 for all four tasks. Note that these percentages are directly observed in the choice task and inferred from the stated prices and the probability and payoff matches in the other tasks. Under procedure invariance, all these values should coincide. The overall means showed that the tendency to favor the H bet over the L bet was highest in choice (76 percent) and in probability matching (73 percent) and substantially smaller in payoff matching (47 percent) and in pricing (37 percent). These results demonstrate two types of preference reversals: choice versus pricing and probability matching versus payoff matching.

Choice versus pricing.—The comparison of the results of choice and pric-

TABLE 1.5
Percentage of Responses Favoring the H Bet over the L Bet
for Four Different Elicitation Procedures

	Choice	Probability Matching	Payoff Matching	Pricing
Small bets ($[H]$, $[L]$):				
(35/36, $4), (11/36, $16)	80	79	54	29
(29/36, $2), (7/36, $9)	75	62	44	26
(34/36, $3), (18/36, $6.50)	73	76	70	39
(32/36, $4), (4/36, $40)	69	70	26	42
(34/36, $2.50), (14/36, $8.50)	71	80	43	22
(33/36, $2), (18/36, $5)	56	66	69	18
Mean	71	72	50	29
Large bets ($[H]$, $[L]$):				
(35/36, $100), (11/36, $400)	88	76	69	65
(29/36, $50), (7/36, $225)	83	64	31	55
(34/36, $75), (18/36, $160)	77	79	65	55
(32/36, $100), (4/36, $1,000)	84	68	28	61
(34/36, $65), (14/36, $210)	78	80	36	57
(33/36, $50), (18/36, $125)	68	75	58	46
Mean	80	74	48	56
Overall mean	76	73	49	37

ing in table 1.5 reveals the familiar PR pattern. Subjects preferred the H bet but assigned a higher cash equivalent to the L bet. As was demonstrated earlier, this effect is due primarily to the overpricing of L bets implied by compatibility.

Probability matching versus payoff matching.—The major new result of this study concerns the discrepancy between probability matching and payoff matching. By compatibility, the dimension on which the match is made should be overweighted relative to the other dimension. Probability matching, therefore, should favor the H bet, whereas payoff matching should favor the L bet. Indeed, the tendency to favor the H bet over the L bet was much more pronounced in probability matching than in payoff matching.

Table 1.5 contains two other comparisons of interest: pricing versus payoff matching and choice versus matching. Although the pricing of a bet can be viewed as a special case of payoff matching in which the matched bet has $P = 1$, it appears that the monetary dimension looms even larger in pricing than in payoff matching. This conclusion, however, may not be generally valid since it holds for the small but not for the large bets.

Finally, the least expected feature of table 1.5 concerns the relation between choice and matching. If, relative to choice, probability matching biases the responses in favor of the H bets and payoff matching biases the responses in favor of the L bets, then the choice data should lie between the two matching conditions. The finding that the tendency to favor the H bet is about the

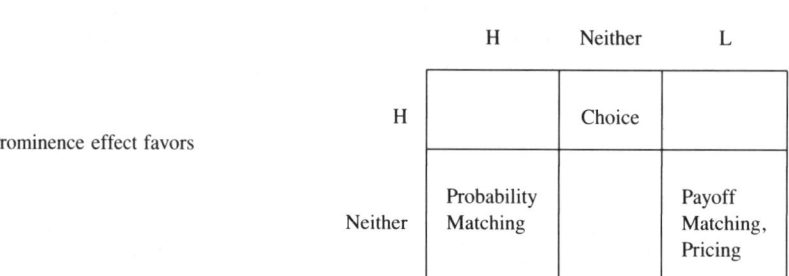

Figure 1.3. Compatibility and prominence effects for four elicitation procedures.

same in direct choice and in probability matching suggests that an additional effect beyond scale compatibility is involved.

The missing factor, we propose, is the prominence effect demonstrated by Tversky, Sattath, and Slovic (1988). In an extensive study of preference, these investigators showed that the more important attribute of an option is weighted more heavily in choice than in matching. In other words, the choice ordering is more lexicographic than that induced by matching. We originally interpreted PR in terms of compatibility rather than prominence (Tversky, Sattath, and Slovic, 1988) because we saw no a priori reason to hypothesize that probability is more important than money. The results of study 5, however, forced us to reconsider the hypothesis that probability is more prominent than money, which is further supported by the finding that the rating of bets is dominated by probability (see Goldstein and Einhorn 1987; Slovic and Lichtenstein 1968; Tversky, Sattath, and Slovic, 1988). It appears to us now that the data of table 1.5 represent the combination of two effects: a compatibility effect that is responsible for the difference between probability matching and payoff matching (including pricing) and a prominence effect that contributes to the relative attractiveness of H bets in choice. This account is illustrated in figure 1.3, which characterizes each of the four elicitation procedures in terms of their compatibility and prominence effects.

Let us examine first the columns of figure 1.3, which represent the effects of the compatibility factor. Recall that the probability matching procedure enhances the significance of P and thereby favors the H bet. Analogously, the compatibility of the payoff matching and pricing procedures with the monetary outcomes enhances the significance of the payoffs and thereby favors the L bet. The choice procedure, however, is neutral with respect to the compatibility factor; hence, it would be expected to lie between the two matching procedures—if compatibility alone were involved. Now consider the rows of figure 1.3. In terms of the prominence factor, the more important dimension (i.e., probability) is expected to loom larger in choice than in either matching procedure. Thus, the tendency to choose the H bet should be greater in choice than in matching if prominence alone were involved. Table 1.5 suggests that both compatibility and prominence are present in the data. The finding that choice and probability matching yield similar results suggests that the two effects have roughly the same impact. It follows from this analysis that compatibility and prominence contribute jointly to the discrepancy between choice and pricing, which may help explain both the size and the robustness of the standard PR. It is noteworthy that each of these effects has been established independently. The demonstrations of compatibility reported in the first part of this paper do not involve prominence, and the prominence effects demonstrated by Tversky, Sattath, and Slovic (1988) do not depend on scale compatibility.

DISCUSSION

Although the notion of compatibility has long been suggested as a possible cause of elicitation effects (see, e.g., Lichtenstein and Slovic 1971; Slovic and MacPhillamy 1974), this hypothesis has not heretofore been tested directly. The present investigations tested several implications of the compatibility hypothesis in studies of prediction and preference. In each of these studies, enhancing the compatibility between a stimulus attribute and the response mode led to increased weighting of that attribute. These findings indicate that compatibility plays an important role in judgment and choice. At the same time, it is evident that this concept requires further theoretical analysis and empirical investigation. Implications of the present work and directions for future studies are discussed below.

The testing and application of the compatibility principle require auxiliary hypotheses about the characteristics of a stimulus attribute that make it more or less compatible with a given response mode. Many features of stimulus attributes and response scales could enhance their compatibility. These include the use of the same units (e.g., grades, ranks), the direction of relations (e.g., whether the correlations between input and output variables are positive or negative), and the numerical correspondence (e.g., similarity) between the values of input and output variables. Although we do not have a general procedure for assessing compatibility, there are many situations in which the compatibility ordering could be assumed with a fair degree of confidence. For example, it seems evident that the prediction of market value in dollars is more compatible with a predictor expressed in dollars than with a predictor expressed in ranks. The same situation exists in the domain of perceptual-motor performance. There is no general theory for assessing the compatibility between an information display and a control panel, yet it is evident that some input-output configurations are much more compatible than others and therefore yield better performance.

Further evidence for compatibility effects in risky choice has been reported by Schkade and Johnson (1989). Using a computer-controlled experiment in which the subject can see only one component of each bet at a time, the investigators were able to measure the amount of time spent by each subject looking at probabilities and at payoffs. Their results showed that the percentage of time spent on payoffs was significantly greater in pricing than in choice. Furthermore, this pattern was particularly pronounced when the subjects produced preference reversals, and it vanished when the subjects produced consistent responses. The conclusion that subjects attend to the payoffs more in pricing than in choice supports the hypothesis that subjects focus their attention on the stimulus components that are most compatible with the response mode. This finding is also consistent with the hypothesis that, in choice between bets, probability is perceived as more important than payoff.

In a second experiment, Schkade and Johnson (1989) compared the pricing of bets to their rating on a 100-point scale. The participants in this study expressed the ratings and the prices using an adjustable pointer. The authors observed that both the initial and the final settings of the pointer were higher for the L bet than for the H bet in pricing and higher for the H bet than for the L bet in rating. The authors attribute the reversal of preference observed in this task to an insufficient adjustment (Slovic and Lichtenstein 1971; Tversky and Kahneman 1974) of the self-generated anchors. The production of these anchors, however, appears to be governed by compatibility. Note that the response scale in the pricing task ranges from zero to the positive payoff, whereas the range of the rating scale (from 0 to 100) matches the probability scale. By compatibility, the payoff is expected to loom larger in pricing than in rating, and the probability is expected to loom larger in rating than in pricing. The notion that the bounded rating scale is more compatible with probability than with money, supported by the process data of Schkade and Johnson, may explain the finding (Goldstein and Einhorn 1987) that the preference for the H bet over the L bet is stronger in rating than in choice, despite the procedural similarity between rating and pricing. An alternative explanation of this result that attributes PR to the mapping of subjective value onto the response scale rather than to the compatibility between stimulus components and response modes was proposed by Goldstein and Einhorn (1987). Their model can accommodate reversals of preference, but it does not predict the variety of compatibility effects described here.

Recent results reported by Delquié and de Neufville (1988) are also consistent with the compatibility hypothesis. These authors employed a double-matching procedure, devised by Hershey and Schoemaker (1985), in which subjects first determine the missing value (e.g., the probability of winning) of an option that would make it equivalent to a second option. Later, the subjects are presented with the option they constructed, and they now have to determine the missing value (e.g., the payoff) of the second option that would make the two options equally attractive. If procedure invariance holds, the latter match should coincide with the given value of the second option. Using both risky and riskless options, Delquié and de Neufville found systematic violations of procedure invariance, which imply that the matched attribute is weighted more heavily than the other attribute—as predicted by compatibility. These findings confirm, in a double-matching design, the conclusion of experiment 5 of the present chapter and of Tversky, Sattath, and Slovic (1988), which were based on a choice-matching design.

The compatibility notion discussed in this paper concerns the correspondence between the scales in which the inputs and the outputs are expressed. In a previous paper (Tversky, Sattath, and Slovic 1988), we have explored a more abstract notion of compatibility that was later called "strategy compatibility" by Fischer and Hawkins (1988). To introduce this concept, we distinguished between qualitative and quantitative choice strategies. Qualitative strategies (e.g., dominance and minimax) are based on purely ordinal criteria, whereas quantitative strategies (e.g., multiattribute utility theory) are based on trade-offs or weighting of the dimensions. We proposed that the qualitative strategy of selecting the option that is superior on the more important dimension is more likely to be employed in the qualitative method of choice, whereas a quantitative strategy based on the trade-offs between the dimensions is more likely to be used in the quantitative method of matching. In this sense, the prominence effect may be attributed to the compatibility between the nature of the task and the nature of the strategy it invokes. (For further discussion of strategy compatibility and its relation to scale compatibility, see Fischer and Hawkins 1988.)

Although compatibility, like anchoring, has a powerful effect on prediction and preference, people are generally unaware of this phenemenon. Such bias seems to operate at a very elementary level of information processing, and it is doubtful whether it can be eliminated by careful instructions or by monetary payoffs. Indeed, the use of incentives to promote careful responses has had little influence on the prevalence of preference reversals (Slovic and Lichtenstein 1983).

The effects of compatibility described in this chapter represent a major source of violations of procedure invariance, namely, the requirement that normatively equivalent elicitation procedures should yield the same ordering of options or events. The failure of procedure invariance complicates the task of the practitioner and the theorist alike. From a practical perspective, the present findings underscore the lability of judgments and choices and make the elicitation task quite problematic. If the decision makers's response depends critically on the method of elicitation, which method should be used, and how can it be justified? At the very least, we need to use multiple procedures (e.g., choice, pricing, rating) and compare their results. If they are consistent, we may have some basis for trusting the judgment; if they are not, further analysis is required.

The assumption of procedure invariance plays an essential role in theories of rational choice. Behavioral research has also demonstrated consistent violations of description invariance by showing that different descriptions of the same decision problem can give rise to systematically different choices. Thus, alternative framings of the same options (e.g., in terms of gains vs. losses or in terms of survival rates vs. mortality rates) produce predictable reversals of preference (Tversky and Kahneman 1986). These failures of description invariance, induced by framing effects, and the failures of procedure invariance, induced by elicitation effects, represent deep and sweeping violations of classical rationality.

Attempts to describe and explain these failures of invariance require choice models of much greater complexity. To account for violations of description invariance, it seems necessary to introduce a framing process, including the determination of a reference point, that takes place prior to the evaluation of prospects (Kahneman and Tversky 1979). To account for violations of procedure invariance, it seems necessary to introduce multiple preference orders (obtained from choice, matching, or pricing) and a contingent-weighting model (Tversky, Sattath, and Slovic 1988) in which the trade-off among attributes is contingent on the method of elicitation. These developments highlight the discrepancy between the normative and the descriptive approaches to decision making. Because invariance—unlike independence or even transitivity—is normatively unassailable and descriptively incorrect, it may not be possible to construct a theory of choice that is both normatively acceptable and descriptively adequate.

REFERENCES

Brainard, R. W., T. S. Irby, P. M. Fitts, and E. Alluisi. 1962. Some variables influencing the rate of gain of information. *Journal of Experimental Psychology* 63:105–10.

Delquié, P., and R. de Neufville. 1988. Response-modes and inconsistencies in preference assessments. Massachusetts Institute of Technology. Typescript.

Fischer, G. W., and S. A. Hawkins. 1988. Preference reversals in multiattribute decision making: Scale compatibility, strategy compatibility, and the prominence effect. Carnegie-Mellon University. Typescript.

Fitts, P. M., and C. M. Seeger. 1953. S-R compatibility: Spatial characteristics of stimulus and response codes. *Journal of Experimental Psychology* 46:199–210.

Goldstein, W. M., and H. J. Einhorn. 1987. Expression theory and the preference reversal phenomena. *Psychological Review* 94:236–54.

Grether, D. M., and C. R. Plott. 1979. Economic theory of choice and the preference reversal phenomenon. *American Economic Review* 69:623–38.

Hershey, J., and P. Schoemaker. 1985. Probability versus certainty equivalence methods in utility measurement: Are they equivalent? *Management Science* 31:1213–31.

Kahneman, D., and A. Tversky. 1979. Prospect theory: An analysis of decision under risk. *Econometrica* 47:263–91.

Lichtenstein, S., and P. Slovic. 1971. Reversals of preference between bids and choices in gambling decisions. *Journal of Experimental Psychology* 89:46–55.

———. 1973. Response-induced reversals of preference in gambling: An extended replication in Las Vegas. *Journal of Experimental Psychology* 101:16–20.

Schkade, D. A., and E. J. Johnson. 1989. Cognitive processes in preference reversals. *Organizational Behavior and Human Performance* 44:203–31.

Slovic, P., B. Fischhoff, and S. Lichtenstein. 1982. Response mode, framing, and information-processing effects in risk assessment. In *New directions for methodology of social and behavioral science: Question framing and response consistency,* ed. R. Hogarth, no. 11, pp. 21–36. San Francisco: Jossey-Bass.

Slovic, P., and S. Lichtenstein. 1968. Relative importance of probabilities and payoffs in risk-taking. *Journal of Experimental Psychology Monograph* 78, no. 3, pt. 2:1–18.

———. 1971. Comparison of Bayesian and regression approaches to the study of information processing in judgment. *Organizational Behavior and Human Performance* 6:649–744.

———. 1983. Preference reversals: A broader perspective. *American Economic Review* 73:596–605.

Slovic, P., and D. MacPhillamy. 1974. Dimensional commensurability and cue utilization in comparative judgment. *Organizational Behavior and Human Performance* 11:172–94.

Tversky, A. 1977. Features of similarity. *Psychological Review* 84:327–52.

Tversky, A., and D. Kahneman. 1974. Judgment under uncertainty: Heuristics and biases. *Science* 185:1124–31.

———. 1986. Rational choice and the framing of decisions. *Journal of Business* 59, no. 4, pt. 2:251–78.

Tversky, A., S. Sattath, and P. Slovic. 1988. Contingent weighting in judgment and choice. *Psychological Review* 95, no. 3:371–84.

Tversky, A., P. Slovic, and D. Kahneman. In press. The causes of preference reversal. *American Economic Review.*

Wickens, C. D. 1984. *Engineering psychology and human performance.* Columbus, Ohio: Merrill.

2

The Costs and Benefits of Vague Information

THOMAS S. WALLSTEN

After distinguishing vagueness from ambiguity, it is argued that events, uncertainty, and the representation of uncertainty can each be either precise or vague. The appropriate form for communicating event uncertainty to a decision maker depends on the nature of the events and of the information base. Precise uncertainties are represented properly by point probabilities or second-order probability distributions, whereas vague uncertainties may be represented in various numerical fashions or linguistically. Although many decision theorists and analysts recommend that all probabilistic judgments be in the form of point-probability estimates, many risk analysts, policymakers, and substantive experts prefer that forecasts be only as precise as warranted by the available information. This chapter supports the latter position by suggesting possible benefits associated with it and suggesting that the costs may be less than commonly feared. Perhaps the most important potential cost of communicating uncertainty linguistically is that of misunderstanding between forecaster and decision maker. However, five experiments show almost equivalent earnings for decisions based on linguistic and numerical information. A theory of decision making given linguistic information, which has been tested on separate data, provides at least a partial rationale for understanding these counterintuitive results.

THERE APPEARS TO BE a fundamental disagreement between decision theorists and analysts, on the one hand, and risk analysts, on the other. The former group suggests that, for purposes of analysis and communication, uncertainty, regardless of its source or nature, should be represented numerically in a man-

---

I was fortunate to spend the fall 1985 semester at the Center for Decision Research at the University of Chicago. During that time, Hilly Einhorn and I engaged in many stimulating discussions and planned collaborative work on choices between linguistic and numerical gambles. While that work never came to pass, those discussions and plans lead ultimately to the theory and supporting experiments reported by Wallsten, Budescu, and Erev (1988) and Wallsten and Erev (in preparation) and summarized in this chapter. I will value always my warm friendship and many interactions with Hilly. Preparation of this chapter was supported by National Science Foundation grant BNS-8608692. I thank David V. Budescu, Robin Hogarth, Lyle V. Jones, Martha Neal, and Rami Zwick for very useful comments on a prior draft of this chapter.

ner consistent with probability theory. However, the latter group suggests that uncertainty should be represented in terms of probability theory only when such a representation is supported by the data base. In other cases, the imprecision of the uncertainty should be explicitly incorporated into the analysis and into any communication to the decision maker.

This chapter attempts to provide an explicit justification for the latter position. It does so by first discussing sources and representations of uncertainty. Subsequent sections of the chapter contrast the views of the two camps as well as the costs and benefits of the two approaches. It is suggested on empirical grounds that the costs of maintaining imprecision may be less than generally feared and therefore may not outweigh the clear benefits. The penultimate section offers a theory that accounts at least in part for this somewhat startling conclusion, and the final section suggests future research necessary to test its limits.

SOURCES AND REPRESENTATIONS OF UNCERTAINTY

Because the concepts of precision and vagueness are so important in what follows, it is useful to begin by defining them and distinguishing the latter from that of ambiguity. A statement or word is *precise* if it is capable of being understood in exactly one way. According to Black (1937), it is *ambiguous* if it can be understood in two or more different, but precise, ways and *vague* if it is not clearly defined or cannot be understood in at least one precise way. This distinction seems worth maintaining. In particular, it might be argued that, when clear communication is a goal, ambiguity can and should be avoided but that, on occasion, vagueness is unavoidable. Dummett (1975), for example, suggested that vague expressions are required to describe values along continua for which equivalence is necessarily intransitive or, in other words, along continua on which events or objects cannot be totally ordered. For example, if we are certain that A is a better teacher than C but cannot judge whether B is better or worse than either A or C, these judgments might be represented by saying that A is good, C mediocre, and B relatively good.

Relying on the concepts of precision and vagueness, but avoiding that of ambiguity, in discussing forms of uncertainty it is useful to employ a $2 \times 2 \times 2$, event type $\times$ uncertainty type $\times$ representation type, taxonomy (shown in table 2.1 and similar to that suggested by Zwick and Wallsten (1989). First, the uncertain events themselves can be precise or vague. Thus, for example, severe health effects, large drops in the stock market, or small rain showers are all vague events, whereas an oral temperature exceeding 101 degrees Fahrenheit, a 1-day decline in the Dow Jones Stock Index of at least 40 points, and a 1-day rainfall between 1 and 2 millimeters are all precise events. Vaguely defined events play important roles in everyday life but occasionally are also useful in situations requiring serious analysis. For example, it might be easier to assess the chances of good weather for a certain military operation than to

TABLE 2.1
Event Type × Uncertainty Type × Evaluation Type Taxonomy

Event Type	Precise[a]		Vague[a]	
	Precise[b]	Vague[b]	Precise[b]	Vague[b]
Precise	1	2	3	4
Vague	5	6	7	8

[a] Uncertainty type.
[b] Representation type.

specify exactly the combinations of temperature, humidity, and wind conditions that would allow the operation to proceed.

Similarly, uncertainty can be precise or vague. To make this distinction, we can build on Dummett's (1975) analysis by saying that uncertainties are vague when the events within a sufficiently rich set cannot be totally ordered with respect to relative likelihood; otherwise, they are precise. Clearly, vague events can have only vague uncertainties, but the uncertainty of a precise event may itself be vague or precise, depending on its source. Vesely and Rasmuson (1984) distinguished physical uncertainty, generally due to stochastic variability or to measurement and sampling error, from uncertainty due to lack of knowledge. Similarly, Whitfield and Wallsten (1989) distinguished uncertainty associated with data from uncertainty associated with the absence of data. Stochastic uncertainty, or uncertainty associated with data, is precise, whereas uncertainty due to lack of knowledge, to absence of data, or to reliance on indirect data is generally vague.

Finally, the representation of uncertainty can be either vague or precise. The representation is precise whenever it is in terms of probability theory, including the use of second-order probability distributions; otherwise, it is vague, such as, for example, when probability intervals or linguistic probabilities are used.

Frequently, the type of uncertainty and its representation are discussed simultaneously. For example, in a recent review, Budescu and Wallsten (1987) defined "a precise uncertainty as one that can be justifiably expressed in terms of either a point probability estimate or a second order distribution over probability values; all other uncertainties are vague" (65). In a similar vein, Easterling (1983) has suggested that the degree of vagueness in an uncertainty depends on how much is known about the probability-generating mechanism. Thus, according to Budescu and Wallsten's (1987) definition, an uncertain probability that itself can be represented as a second-order probability distribution is no less precise than is a probability that can be expressed as a point value. Accordingly, in the Ellsberg (1961) paradigm, the chances of drawing, for example, a red ball out of an urn of an unknown mix of 100 red and black balls are vague (but not ambiguous) because nothing is known about how the urn composition is determined. If, on the other hand, one is told (and believes) that, for example, all possible combinations of the 100 red and black balls are equally likely, then the uncertainty of drawing a red ball would no longer be vague but would be exactly described by a uniform second-order distribution with a well-defined expected value of .5. Note that, according to this terminology, the literature on "ambiguous probabilities" begun by Ellsberg (1961) is really about "vague uncertainties."

This distinction between precise and vague uncertainties is inconsistent with the treatment by such authors as Becker and Brownson (1964), Howard (1988), and others who explicitly suggest that what I call vague uncertainty be represented by a second-order probability distribution. To do so, however, fails to capture the realistic difference between situations in which a second-order probability distribution is truly justified and those in which it is not.

Whereas precise uncertainties should always be represented in terms of probability theory, the vague uncertainty associated with extrapolating beyond available data may be calculated and expressed in probabilistic form if the extrapolation is based on a precise, well-accepted model. However, "the less firm is the basis for extrapolation, the greater is the uncertainty, and virtually always the uncertainty is of a judgmental nature. It is, further, a matter of judgment as to whether the uncertainty is expressible by means of a single probability distribution, or is better expressed in some other fashion" (Budescu and Wallsten 1987, 66).

The points outlined above can all be summarized by referring to the eight cells of table 2.1. Cell 2, in which precise uncertainty about precise events is represented vaguely, might occur in casual conversation, but not otherwise. Cells 1 and 3, which together capture both types of uncertainty about precise events, represent the traditional probabilistic approach of decision theory and analysis. Risk analysts, however, would suggest that cell 4 is appropriate in the presence of a weak or indirect information base. Cells 5 and 6 can never arise because uncertainty about vague events can never be precise. Similarly, cell 7 should never occur because, according to this view, it is incorrect to apply probability theory to vaguely defined events. Thus, when events are vague, analysis and communication should occur only in cell 8.

The fact that not all uncertainties can be measured by unique probability distributions was noted as early as 1921 by both Knight ([1921] 1971) and Keynes ([1921] 1962). Knight distinguished unmeasurable uncertainty from measurable risk, where the latter includes situations for which probability distributions are available on the basis of a priori calculations or past experience. Keynes argued for three types of uncertainty. In one case, the information base is so weak that an individual cannot determine which of two events is more probable or whether in fact they are equally probable. In a second case, the information base allows a rank ordering of events according to probability but does not support the assignment of numerical values. Finally, "in a very special type of case . . . meaning can be given to a numerical comparison of magnitude" (Keynes [1921] 1962, 34). Keynes also suggested that it would occasionally be possible to put bounds on numerical probabilities for events, in which case, he said, the probability is known only vaguely.

CONTRASTING VIEWS ON REPRESENTING UNCERTAINTY

The distinction between risk and uncertainty and among differing levels of measurability of uncertainty was ignored for a good many years and indeed even considered irrelevant to economic approaches to decision theory (Stigler 1971). However, recent years have seen an increase in both theoretical and empirical interests in vague uncertainties. Much of this work has been reviewed by Budescu and Wallsten (1987) and will not be discussed here. Reference should be made, however, at least to Levi's (1980) epistemological theory, according to which, subject to certain constraints, one should maintain credence, or belief, in all probability distributions that are consistent with one's body of knowledge. In a similar vein, Gärdenfors and Sahlin (1982, 1983) have developed a theory in which possible probability distributions are rank ordered according to a measure they call epistemic reliability, indicating the degree to which a particular distribution is consistent with the evidence.

Nevertheless, virtually all decision theories share the idea that degrees of uncertainty regarding events can be represented uniquely and numerically by a probability measure. Savage ([1954] 1972), for example, discussed the concept of "personal probability" at length, considering various objections to it. To the argument that people are differentially confident of their personal probabilities and that this differential confidence might be represented by second-order probabilities Savage replied that this approach immediately leads to an endless hierarchy of higher-order probability distributions. Moreover, he argued, such distributions are unnecessary in that rational choices would be governed only by the expected values of the distributions. Consequently, nothing is to be gained by their introduction. From de Finetti's ([1937] 1964) perspective, precision in estimating subjective probabilities from choices among gambles is only a matter of measurement error. According to de Finetti,

> the scheme of bets gives in principle a method of direct experimental measure of the degree of doubt relative to a given event. If the practical application sometimes runs up against an indeterminateness of this subjective degree of doubt which is to be measured, that is only a consequence of that limited degree of idealization without which it would always be impossible to obtain precision and to develop any theory at all. The indeterminateness is doubtless stronger here than in the physical sciences because of the fact that the magnitude measured is subjective, but the difference is not essential. [150–51]

Although subjectively expected utility theory in the von Neumann and Morgenstern (1947), Savage ([1954] 1972), and de Finetti ([1937] 1964) sense is coming under increasing empirical attack (see, e.g., the review by Machina 1987), alternative models, such as prospect theory (Kahneman and Tversky 1979), persist in representing an individual's subjective uncertainty by real numbers.

Correspondingly, many decision analysts recommend that all uncertainties be expressed to the decision maker in terms of probability distributions. They argue that probability intervals, probability ranges, or linguistic probabilities such as *pretty good chance* are unacceptable. Behn and Vaupel (1982) summarize a vast array of experimental and anecdotal evidence regarding the communication difficulties that may arise when forecasts are made linguistically rather than numerically. According to them, "for a decision maker, ambiguous probability statements are useless. They simply do not provide the information necessary to analyze a decision. . . . to be helpful, . . . forecasts must be specific, numerical statements about the probability that an event will or will not occur" (78–79). Von Winterfeldt and Edwards (1986) also advocate the use of precise probabilities rather than vague words, suggesting and countering various reasons why most people have the opposite communication preferences.

Despite the history of decision theory and the recommendation of thoughtful analysts, there persists a feeling among many policymakers and substantive experts that in many situations it is a mistake to try to represent vague uncertainties precisely. Indeed, a major controversy in the field of risk analysis, as opposed to the field of decision analysis, is the question of how uncertainties are most usefully represented to the decision maker or policymaker. At one extreme is the recommendation not to use numbers at all unless they arise directly from the data. For example, in his presidential address at a meeting of the American Cancer Society, Weinhouse (1982) said that the cancer researcher "should not allow himself to be pressured . . . into putting numbers on risk estimations . . . on the basis of dubious data and uncertain mathematical models. It is very important . . . to remember that in certain instances the most honest and accurate answer is, 'We don't know'" (3472). Somewhat less dogmatically, a committee of the National Research Council wrote that, "while quantitative risk assessment facilitates comparison, such comparison may be illusory or misleading if the use of precise numbers is unjustified" (National Research Council 1981, 15).

The more common recommendation in the risk assessment literature is to obtain numerical estimates but to provide indications of how soft those estimates are or to what degree they depend on theoretical extrapolation rather than on data alone. For example, another National Research Council committee stated, "The degree of uncertainty may be masked to some extent when, in the final form of an assessment, risk is presented as a number with an associated measure of statistical significance. If they are to be most instructive to decision-makers, assessments should provide some insight into qualitative characteristics of the data and interpretations that may impute more or less certainty to the final results" (National Research Council 1983, 165).

When he was administrator of the Environmental Protection Agency, Ruckleshaus said, "If I am going to propose controls that may have serious economic and social effects, I need to have some idea how much confidence should be placed in the estimates of risk that prompted those controls" (1984, 158). He went on, "We must insist on risk calculations being expressed as distributions of estimates and not as magic numbers that can be manipulated without regard to what they really mean. We must try to display more realistic estimates of risk to show a range of probabilities" (161). Finally, in summarizing the current state of risk analysis, Lave suggested that "risk analysis should not attempt to overstate or understate threats, but rather to give the best estimate and the range of uncertainty. Decision-makers can choose the proper amount of conservatism in setting the standard" (Lave 1987, 294).

COSTS AND BENEFITS

Are these recommendations all irrational? I claim that they are not, that they can be justified on both practical and psychological grounds, and that there are benefits to communicating the degree of precision inherent in a probability estimate. But, as the decision analysts suggest, there are costs as well. The costs, however, can be minimized by understanding how people communicate, interpret, and use vague information. The remainder of this chapter enumerates what I perceive to be the benefits and costs of communicating vague uncertainties when the information base does not support more precise statements. It is further suggested that, given our current and as yet very incomplete understanding of how vague information is used, the costs may not be as great as has been feared.

It is noteworthy in this regard that preferences for types of probabilistic forecasts are sensitive to the nature of the information and the outcomes and to the direction of communication (Wallsten et al., in preparation). Generally, numerical expressions are preferred only when the data base warrants them and the situation is important. Otherwise, verbal expressions are preferred because they seem more natural, easy to use, and consistent with the underlying uncertainty. Interestingly, when people are asked unconditionally in which mode they prefer to give forecasts, "verbal" is the usual answer, while "numerical" is the usual unconditional response when asked in which mode they prefer to receive forecasts. It is still an open question why factors predisposing to verbal communication are more salient when giving forecasts but those favoring numerical communication are more salient when receiving them.

I suggest that there are at least two, and possibly three, benefits to using vague probabilities when the information base will not support precise probabilities. The first benefit is that the decision maker retains full control over the decision situation (Feagans and Biller 1981). In other words, if many probability distributions are consistent with the evidence, then the selection of any one by the expert is arbitrary, and so is any subsequent expected value calculation. As suggested by Lave (1987), the expert might indicate the range of possible probabilities, allowing the policymaker to decide how conservative to be in light of this information and of the constituency he or she is serving. Decision analysts do something like this to the degree that they try various probability distributions in their calculations and report the results of the sensitivity analyses.

The fact that in many cases more than one probability distribution is consistent with the available information brings up the second benefit of avoiding misleading precision. In many situations, such as those involving public health, the environment, or applications of technology, the decisions that are being aided by the risk assessment must take into account other considerations in addition to expected value. Slovic and his colleagues (as summarized by Slovic 1987) have demonstrated that perceived risk depends only in part on expected number of fatalities or expected number of adverse events. Two other factors that loom large in individuals' perceptions are degree of dread (depending, e.g., on how controllable, catastrophic, risky to future generations, involuntary, or inequitable the hazard is perceived to be) and the degree to which the risk is unknown (e.g., unobservable, unknown to those exposed, delayed or new and relatively unknown to science). Further, the greater the dread or the less that is known about the hazard, the greater is the desire for strict regulation to reduce the risk. One can infer from these results that people are willing to pay more to reduce risks when the risk estimates are based on sparse or indirect evidence than when they are based on solid relative frequency data. This conclusion is consistent with the range of values attributed to a human life as inferred from an expected value analysis of regulations applied to reduce risks in a variety of contexts (Graham 1982). Further, it is hardly surprising given the general laboratory findings with the Ellsberg (1961) and related paradigms.

To summarize the points made thus far, people generally, and decision makers or policymakers in specific situations, feel best served when representations of uncertainty are as precise as possible, but no more precise than warranted. In a recent literature review, Budescu and Wallsten (1987) recommended that forecasters should "estimate the uncertainty of future events as accurately and precisely as possible, but not . . . give the illusion of more precision than justified by the interpretation of the data" (67). The logical reason for the recommendation is that, when information is sparse, indirect, or inferential, numerous probability distributions are consistent with it. The decision maker loses degrees of control if he or she cannot act according to that distribution that is consistent with the evidence and that satisfies the full range of decision objectives. The psychological reason for Budescu and Wallsten's recommendation is that individuals fear to a greater degree hazards about which little is known. Consequently, the decision maker has to be aware of the strnegth of the information base and behave accordingly.

In addition to the two benefits already suggested of allowing forecasts to be as vague as necessary, there is a third potential benefit. Zimmer (1983) has suggested that people can handle verbal information more optimally than numerical information because they are more skilled at the rules of language than at the rules of arithmetic or probability, and he has presented some data supporting this idea. Our own studies to date (Erev and Cohen, in press; Budescu and Wallsten, in press; Budescu, Weinberg, and Wallsten 1988; Rapoport et al., in press) favor neither this nor the opposite proposition, so that issue is still an open one. However, Zimmer (1984, 1986) suggests further that the mode in which one is required to report one's degree of uncertainty influences the kind of information used to form the judgment. The requirement of precise numerical estimates causes one to rely primarily on information that can be expressed quantitatively, whereas allowing one to respond verbally, or less precisely, encourages the use of qualitative information as well. For example, Zimmer (1986) had subjects forecast the future exchange rate between the U.S. dollar and the Deutsch mark, expressing uncertainty in their judgments either numerically or verbally. On the basis of think-aloud protocols, Zimmer determined that the numerical responders relied on numerical information, such as past exchange rates and patterns of inflation, whereas the verbal responders used this information as well as qualitative information, such as the political climates in the two countries.

There are also costs to expressing uncertainty vaguely. One potential cost, suggested by von Winderfeldt and Edwards (1986), is that the use of vague uncertainties encourages sloppy thinking and lack of responsibility. Specifically, some people avoid numbers because "they invite the collection of data, which is always a nuisance" (von Winterfeldt and Edwards 1986, 100). Of course, one can think sloppily regardless of the mode of forecasting.

What I consider to be a more serious potential cost is that vague communications can be easily reinterpreted, for example, to suggest that the forecasts were right on target after the forecasted situations had been observed. Honesty and vigilance are required to avoid such problems, which I will not discuss further.

But assuming even the best of intentions, there is the very real danger, or cost, of misunderstanding. Behn and Vaupel (1982) provide many examples suggesting this problem. It is here that I believe that the costs may not be as serious as many believe and can be minimized by research on how people understand and use vague uncertainty. I now turn to a discussion of this research.

RESEARCH ON UNDERSTANDING AND USING VAGUE UNCERTAINTIES

Three broadly defined paradigms can be identified for the study of how people understand vaguely defined uncertainties. In one paradigm, the vagueness is represented numerically, either by means of probability ranges or intervals or by leading subjects to believe that point-probability estimates are unreliable (for reasons beyond simply small sample sizes, such as, e.g., by being inferred from unreliable reports). This paradigm is the earliest one to have entered the literature and has received the most study.

The second paradigm for investigating vague information processing is the one that my colleagues and I have been exploring, in which vague uncertainties are represented linguistically. Earlier studies by others looked at phrase-to-number conversions, whereas our more recent work has sought to represent the full vague meaning of a phrase to an individual and to relate that meaning to actual choices or decisions.

The third paradigm probably represents the most common source of vagueness, but, to my knowledge, it is the least studied. This is the case in which the vagueness arises from the nature of the evidence rather than from a summary communication about what the evidence implies. Specifically, the uncertainty is vague when there is no direct connection between the available information and the events in question. The first two paradigms logically follow this one in that they represent a means by which a forecaster, having formed his or her vague judgment, communicates it to a decision maker, and provide a framework for studying how decision makers understand and use such estimates. But the issue of how vague judgments are formed initially on the basis of the raw, indirect data is still open.

Similar conclusions emerge from the first two paradigms, primarily from the work of Einhorn and Hogarth (1985) and their colleagues as well as from our work. Individual differences in understanding vague uncertainties are reliable and substantial. Context effects are real and tend to be in the same directions over individuals. Further, and importantly, a person's decisions are predictable from his or her unique understanding of the vague uncertainty. A surprising result emerging from our research suggests that the costs of vague communications may not be as great as some fear. That is, despite the factors mentioned above, there appears to be little economic difference in the quality of an individual's decisions given vague or precise information.

The classic paper in the first paradigm is, of course, by Ellsberg (1961), who demonstrated that most people prefer a binary gamble based on drawing a ball from an urn of known composition to one based on drawing a ball from an urn of unknown composition. This so-called ambiguity avoidance (which I call vagueness avoidance) has been subsequently replicated by Becker and Brownson (1964), MacCrimmon (1968), and others. In an interesting study, Yates and Zukowski (1976) demonstrated that the subjective vagueness could not be described in terms of the range or variance of a second-order probability distribution. In a related study, Easterling (1983) looked at the Ellsberg phenomenon while imposing various constraints on the unknown probability and found no systematic vagueness avoidance. He hypothesized that this may have been because the constraints rendered the unknown probabilities tractable and they were therefore not considered vague by the subjects.

More recently, Einhorn and Hogarth (1985) have employed a different numerical paradigm to explore vague information processing. In various contexts, their subjects were presented with probabilities known to be unreliable and were then asked either to provide their best estimate of the probability, to choose between gambles, or, in subsequent experiments (Hogarth and Kunreuther, 1989), to bid for selling or buying insurance. All these studies were guided by a model that assumes that one anchors one's probability estimate on the value initially given and then adjusts it upward or downward depending on the perceived degree of vagueness and on one's attitude toward vagueness. These two factors are represented by two parameters estimated uniquely for individual subjects. Individual differences in response to vagueness, and therefore in the parameter values, are great. One result of this line of work is the demonstration that vagueness is not uniformly avoided. In fact, the model predicts well the circumstances under which it is preferred rather than avoided, namely, very low probabilities of gains and large probabilities of losses.

The second paradigm for studying vague information is the one that we have been exploring, in which vague uncertainties are represented linguistically. In a number of experiments (Rapoport, Wallsten, and Cox 1987; Wallsten et al. 1986), we have demonstrated that the vague meanings of probability phrases to individuals can be represented by means of membership functions over the [0, 1] probability interval. Individual differences in meaning are consistent and substantial. Further, the meanings of probability phrases are systematically affected by aspects of the context, including the perceived base rates of the events in question (Wallsten, Fillenbaum, and Cox 1986), the desirability of the events (Cohen 1986), and the direction of communication (Fillenbaum et al. 1987).

Despite these individual and contextual differences, it appears that individuals' choices and bids in gambling contexts are well predicted from their understanding of the phrases and also that people do not operate substantially more poorly (or substantially better either) when the information on which they decide is verbal rather than numerical. It is these results that provide hope that, when communication in vague terms is necessary, the costs due to misunderstanding may not be large.

Specifically, in five experiments to date, we have been unable to establish any real economic advantage to using numerical rather than linguistic probabilistic forecasts. In the first study (Budescu, Weinberg, and Wallsten 1988), subjects initially provided numerical probability estimates and linguistic descriptions regarding the chances of various visible spinners landing on white rather than red. A procedure was used to determine triples for individual subjects that contained an approximately equivalent linguistic phrase, numerical probability, and spinner display. Subsequently, the subjects bid for gambles in which the uncertain event of landing on white was described in one of the three "equivalent" ways. Although in this study subjects did make significantly more money when using the numerical descriptors than they did when using the linguistic descriptors, the amount was very small (1.2 percent for gains and 4.7 percent for losses).

Expecting that the results may have been artifactually due in part to the initial establishment of the triples, we ran three additional studies (two are described by Budescu and Wallsten, in press; the third is nothing more than a complete replication). These experiments used dyads, in which one person was a forecaster and the other a decision maker. The forecaster observed the spinner and then communicated to the decision maker either numerically or linguistically the chances of its landing on white. The decision maker used this information to bid for a gamble involving a possible gain or a possible loss of $1 or $5. In all three experiments, the form of the forecasts (i.e., linguistic or numerical) had no effect on the amount of money made by the dyads.

Erev and Cohen (in press) explored the same issue (among others) in a more real-world context. They had basketball announcers and sports writers estimate both linguistically and numerically the chances of future basketball events occurring (e.g., whether a particular player on one team will get more rebounds than a certain player on the other team during a specific game). Undergraduates used these estimates to make decisions about gambles based on the forecasted events. It should be noted that the actual players and teams were encoded for the undergraduates (e.g., player A will get more rebounds than B in game X), forcing the students to rely on the experts' forecasts alone. The true player and game identities were revealed after the decisions were made so that the games could be watched and the winnings collected. Amounts earned were substantially above chance expectations, but there were no significant differences due to mode of forecasting. A suggestive result was that significantly more money was earned using the forecaster's preferred mode of communication (verbal for three forecasters and numerical for one) rather than his nonpreferred one. But this result needs to be replicated.

The possibility that people may use vague linguistic information as efficiently as numerical information is so counterintuitive that it should not be accepted without considerably more research. At the very least, there must be limits on the range of situations to which such a conclusion applies. However, on the basis of other research, we have developed a theory, and supported it with independent data, that renders these results understandable.

A THEORETICAL RATIONALE AND SOME EVIDENCE

The simplest version of the theory assumes that, when required to act on the basis of a linguistic uncertainty, the individual selects one probability from a set of probability values that are sufficiently well described by the phrase. In terms of the membership function representation of the phrase, a probability is selected whose degree of membership exceeds a specific threshold. The selection is random, but governed by a weighting function that depends on the membership values above the threshold. This notion is analogous to the concept underlying various random-choice models, that choice probabilities depend on response strengths (Luce 1977). The theory is described and modeled mathematically by Wallsten, Budescu, and Erev (1988).

Support for the model comes from a series of studies (Wallsten and Erev, in preparation; also summarized by Wallsten, Budescu, and Erev 1988) in which subjects chose between two binary gambles, $(a, p, 0)$ and $(a, q, 0)$, where a could be won with probability p in the first gamble and with probability q in the other one, otherwise zero. In one gamble, the uncertainty, p, was described linguistically (e.g., the spinner is *likely* to land on white), whereas, in the other, q was easily estimated from a visible spinner. Trials varied in terms of the linguistic expressions, spinner probabilities, and nonzero outcomes employed, but each combination was presented on numerous occasions so that choice probabilities could be estimated. In addition, individual membership functions were empirically determined for each of the phrases. A single parameter, the threshold, was estimated for each subject and used in conjunction with the subject's membership functions to predict his or her choice probabilities.

Nonzero outcomes, a, were manipulated, resulting in choices between gambles for gains or losses of various amounts. Thresholds were insensitive to relatively minor variations in sizes of outcomes but were affected by outcome sign. Specifically, in one experiment, thresholds for one group of subjects were lower when the gambles entailed a possibility of losing $2.50 than they were when they entailed a possibility of winning $2.50. Similarly, it was lower in subjects for whom every trial involved a possible $5.00 loss than it was in those for whom every trial involved a possible $5.00 gain. This result is consistent with Einhorn and Hogarth's (1985) finding that attitude toward vagueness depends in large part on whether the outcomes are gains or losses.

Predictions of choice probabilities were generally excellent, accounting for from about 60 to 97 percent of the variance in individual subjects' data, with a mean of 83 percent. Nevertheless, there were small, but systematic, deviations between the observed and the predicted values. Predictions were virtually perfect for the relatively more precise phrases (which tended also to be the lower ones, such as *doubtful*). However, they were generally too close to .5 (by an average of .03) for the relatively more vague phrases (i.e., for those phrases whose membership functions were relatively broad).

The deviations from predictions based on the simple model described above can be handled by modifying the original theory to assume that, before applying the threshold, the decision maker combines the information conveyed by the phrase with a prior opinion depending on the context. Two points in this development are important for the present discussion.

The first point is that, because context generally operates the same way on all people, to the degree that individuals see the context similarly and share objectives the context will affect their interpretations of the phrases similarly. Indeed, it might be argued that, when an expert and a decision maker have different prior judgments, it is legitimate for the decision maker to incorporate his or hers with the expert's forecast. For example, the decision maker's judgment may be influenced by additional information or by the political or other context within which he or she is operating. In other words, two people, in this case the decision maker and the forecaster, may receive the same vague information in what for them are very different contexts because of different motivations or goals (such as buyers and sellers of insurance; Hogarth and Kunreuther 1989) and legitimately interpret the information in different ways.

The second point, at least equally as important as the first, is that the effect of the threshold is to cause individuals to behave in accordance with the probabilities they believe to be most consistent with the communication. Thus, the full range of vagueness is not considered when making a decision. Perhaps communication does not suffer dramatically because individual differences are smaller in terms of these "most consistent" probabilities than in terms of the full ranges.

CONCLUSION

The theory just outlined provides at least a partial explanation for the observed equally efficient use of linguistic and numerical information, although clearly more research is needed along these lines. For example, it would not be surprising to find that, for some types of information, in some contexts, or for certain kinds of problems, one form of communication leads to more optimal decisions than does the other. Similarly, some individuals may operate more efficiently in one or the other mode.

But, overall, it is beginning to appear on both theoretical and empirical grounds that, when decision makers and forecasters share the same objectives, miscommunication entailed by vague expressions is not as severe as many believe. Because context operates similarly on most people, and because the full range of vagueness is not utilized in making a decision, there may not be an economic penalty to communicating vaguely when the information base warrants it. This possibility, along with the benefits enumerated earlier, suggests that vague probabilistic forecasts may indeed be preferable to precise ones when that is all the information allows.

REFERENCES

Becker, S. W., and F. O. Brownson. 1964. What price ambiguity? or the role of ambiguity in decision-making. *Journal of Political Economy* 72:62–73.

Behn, R. D., and J. W. Vaupel. 1982. *Quick analysis for busy decision makers.* New York: Basic.

Black, M. 1937. Vagueness. *Philosophy of Science* 4:427–55.

Budescu, D. V., and T. S. Wallsten. 1987. Subjective estimation of vague and precise uncertainties. In *Judgmental forecasting,* ed. G. Wright and P. Ayton, 63–82. Chichester: Wiley.

———. In press. Dyadic decisions with numerical and verbal probabilities. *Organizational Behavior and Human Decision Processes.*

Budescu, D. V., S. Weinberg, and T. S. Wallsten. 1988. Decisions based on numerically and verbally expressed uncertainties. *Journal of Experimental Psychology: Human Perception and Performance* 14:281–94.

Cohen, B. L. 1986. The effect of outcome desirability on comparisons of linguistic and numerical probabilities. M.A. thesis, University of North Carolina, Chapel Hill.

de Finetti, B. [1937] 1964. La prévision: Ses lois logiques, ses sources subjectives. *Annales de l'Institut Henri Poincaré* 7:1–68. (English translation in *Studies in subjective probability,* ed. H. E. Kyburg, Jr., and H. E. Smokler. New York: Wiley.)

Dummett, M. 1975. Wang's paradox. *Synthese* 30:301–24.

Easterling, D. V. 1983. Decision making under uncertain risk: Encoding ambiguous probability information. M.A. thesis, University of North Carolina, Chapel Hill.

Einhorn, E. J., and R. M. Hogarth. Ambiguity and uncertainty in probabilistic inference. *Psychological Review* 92:433–61.

Ellsberg, D. 1961. Risk, ambiguity, and the Savage axioms. *Quarterly Journal of Economics* 75:643–69.

Erev, I., and B. L. Cohen. In press. Verbal versus numerical probabilities: Efficiency, biases, and the preference paradox. *Organizational Behavior and Human Decision Processes.*

Feagans, T. B., and W. F. Biller. 1981. Risk assessment: Describing the protection provided by ambient air quality standards. *Environmental Professional* 3:235–47.

Fillenbaum, S., T. S. Wallsten, B. Cohen, and J. A. Cox. 1987. *Some effects of available vocabulary and communication task on the understanding and use of nonnumerical probability expressions.* Report no. 177. Chapel Hill: University of North Carolina, L. L. Thurstone Psychometric Laboratory.

Gärdenfors, P., and N.-E. Sahlin. 1982. Unreliable probabilities, risk taking, and decision making. *Synthese* 53:361–86.

———. 1983. Decision making with unreliable probabilities. *British Journal of Mathematical and Statistical Psychology* 36:240–51.

Graham, J. D. 1982. Some explanations for disparities in lifesaving investments. *Policy Studies Review* 1:692–704.

Hogarth, R., and H. Kunreuther. 1989. Risk, ambiguity, and insurance. *Journal of Risk and Uncertainty* 2:5–35.

Howard, R. A. 1988. Uncertainty about probability: A decision analysis perspective. *Risk Analysis* 8:91–98.

Kahneman, D., and A. Tversky. 1979. Prospect theory: An analysis of decision under risk. *Econometrica* 47:263–91.

Keynes, J. M. [1921] 1962. *A treatise on probability.* London: Macmillan. Reprint, with an introduction by N. R. Hansen. New York: Harper & Row.

Knight, F. H. [1921] 1971. *Risk, uncertainty, and profit.* Reprint, with an introduction by George Stigler. Chicago: University of Chicago Press.

Lave, L. B. 1987. Health and safety risk analyses: Information for better decisions. *Science* 236:291–95.

Levi, I. 1980. *The enterprise of knowledge.* Cambridge, Mass.: MIT Press.

Luce, R. D. 1977. The choice axiom after twenty years. *Journal of Mathematical Psychology* 15:215–33.

MacCrimmon, K. R. 1968. Descriptive and normative implications of the decision-theory postulates. In *Risk and uncertainty,* ed. K. Borch and J. Mossin, 3–32. New York: Macmillan.

Machina, M. J. 1987. Choices under uncertainty: Problems solved and unsolved. *Economic Perspectives* 1:121–54.

National Research Council. Committee on the Institutional Means for Assessment of

Risks to Public Health. 1983. *Risk assessment in the federal government: Managing the process.* Washington, D.C.: National Academy Press.

———. Governing Board Committee on the Assessment of Risk. 1981. *The handling of risk assessments in NRC reports.* Washington, D.C.: U.S. National Research Council.

Rapoport, A., T. S. Wallsten, and J. A. Cox. 1987. Direct and indirect scaling of membership functions of probability phrases. *Mathematical Modelling* 9:397–417.

Rapoport, A., T. S. Wallsten, I. Erev, and B. L. Cohen. In press. Revision of opinion with verbally and numerically expressed uncertainties. *Acta Psychologica.*

Ruckleshaus, W. D. 1984. Risk in a free society. *Risk Analysis* 4:157–62.

Savage, L. J. [1954] 1972. *The foundations of statistics.* New York: Wiley. Rev. ed. New York: Dover.

Slovic, P. 1987. Perception of risk. *Science* 236:280–85.

Stigler, G. 1971. Introduction. In *Risk, uncertainty, and profit,* by F. H. Knight. Chicago: University of Chicago Press.

Vesely, W. E., and D. M. Rasmuson. 1984. Uncertainties in nuclear probabilistic risk analysis. *Risk Analysis* 4:313–22.

von Neumann, J., and O. Morgenstern. 1947. *Theory of games and economic behavior.* New York: Wiley.

von Winterfeldt, D., and W. Edwards. 1986. *Decision analysis and behavioral research.* Cambridge: Cambridge University Press.

Wallsten, T. S., D. V. Budescu, and I. Erev. 1988. Understanding and using linguistic uncertainties. *Acta Psychologica* 68:39–52.

Wallsten, T. S., D. V. Budescu, A. Rapoport, R. Zwick, and B. Forsyth. 1986. Measuring the vague meanings of probability terms. *Journal of Experimental Psychology* 115:348–65.

Wallsten, T. S., and I. Erev. In preparation. Choosing between linguistic and precise gambles: A test of a theory of choice given vague information. Department of Psychology, University of North Carolina, Chapel Hill.

Wallsten, T. S., S. Fillenbaum, and J. A. Cox. 1986. Base rate effects on the interpretation of probability and frequency expressions. *Journal of Memory and Language* 25:571–87.

Wallsten, T. S., R. Zwick, S. Kemp, and D. V. Budescu. In preparation. Factors affecting preferences for verbal or numerical communication of uncertainty. Department of Psychology, University of North Carolina, Chapel Hill.

Weinhouse, S. 1982. Prometheus and Pandora—cancer research on our diamond anniversary: Presidential address. *Cancer Research* 42:3471–74.

Whitfield, R. G., and T. S. Wallsten. 1989. A risk assessment for selected lead-induced health effects: An example of a general methodology. *Risk Analysis* 9:197–207.

Yates, J. F., and L. G. Zukowski. 1976. Characterization of ambiguity in decision making. *Behavioral Science* 21:19–25.

Zimmer, A. C. 1983. Verbal vs. numerical processing of subjective probabilities. In *Decision making under uncertainty,* ed. R. W. Scholz, 159–82. Amsterdam: North-Holland.

———. 1984. A model for the interpretation of verbal predictions. *International Journal of Man-Machine Studies* 20:121–34.

———. 1986. What uncertainty judgments can tell about the underlying subjective probabilities. In *Uncertainty in artificial intelligence,* ed. L. H. Kanal and J. F. Lemmer. Amsterdam: Elsevier.

Zwick, R., and T. S. Wallsten. 1989. Combining stochastic uncertainty and linguistic inexactness: Theory and experimental evaluation of four fuzzy probability models. *International Journal of Man-Machine Studies* 30:69–111.

3

Unfinished Tasks: A Research Agenda for Behavioral Decision Theory

WARD EDWARDS

This chapter attempts to define an empirical research agenda for behavioral decision theory that is oriented toward making decision-analytic tools and procedures better than they now are.

The first item on the agenda is exploration of the ecological validity of the conclusions of behavioral decision research. Available research does not answer the question of whether conclusions reached from experiments done in one decision ecology generalize easily to others. Arguments about use of tools in many but not all nonlaboratory decision contexts invite skepticism of such generalizations. A taxonomy of decision ecologies is needed in order to study the question.

Decision analysts routinely feed inconsistencies in intellectually equivalent quantities elicited by different methods back to respondents in order to obtain improved judgments. Behavioral decision theorists view the same inconsistencies as a basis for questioning decision analysis. Research on the process of feedback and reelicitation is needed.

Issues in structuring of decision problems include option and hypothesis invention and resets. A reset is a failure to take gains or losses from one decision into account in making another decision. Resets are ways of reducing the cost of thinking. Whether to reset in order to simplify a set of decision problems can and should be a deliberate choice.

The chapter ends with a discussion of issues in probability and utility elicitation and with some speculation about emerging relations between decision analysis and such technologies as multiple-criterion decision making, management information systems and decision support systems (MIS-DSS), and artificial intelligence.

HILLY EINHORN BROUGHT his amazing energy, creativity, and intelligence to bear on one of two central tasks of behavioral decision theory: to exploit our knowledge of how decisions should be made in order to understand better how decisions are made.

I am grateful to Thomas Eppel, Robin Hogarth, Amos Tversky, and Detlof von Winterfeldt for important but not always heeded criticisms of an earlier version of this chapter.

The other central task of behavioral decision theory is to use what we know or can learn about how decisions are made to enlarge the tool kit and sharpen the tools of technologists interested in aiding decision makers to make decisions as they should be made. Those technologists come in various brands. Without any intent to exclude, I shall call them all decision analysts.

I believe behavioral decision theory has much to offer decision analysis. I also believe that much of what it has already offered is ignored. Why? In part because busy decision analysts pay less attention to relevant literature than they should. In part because they often find messages in that literature saying that the technologies they use every day will not work at all or will give inappropriate results. Such messages are understandably unappealing, whether correct or not. Though the tools and purposes of decision analysis are prescriptive, not descriptive, decision analysts must elicit numbers from clients. Some, though not all, of the elicitation methods used by decision analysts require that the notion of maximization of expected utility (SEU) be descriptive of human behavior, at least for choices entering the elicitation. Messages from behavioral scientists denying the descriptive validity of SEU even in elicitation tasks are therefore of concern to thoughtful decision analysts. Another message from behavioral scientists to decision analysts (illustrated later in this chapter) is that the inconsistencies among intellectually equivalent numbers obtained by different elicitation methods call decision-analytic methods into question. Decision analysts routinely expect these inconsistencies and exploit them to improve judgments; they see no reason why that fact should lead anyone to question decision-analytic technology.

Often, the evidence on which the messages are based is gathered from people and under conditions quite different from the ones decision analysts normally encounter in their technical work. Moreover, though the procedures labeled inappropriate bear some resemblance to procedures used by decision analysts, they are by no means the same. This is enough to enable decision analysts to reject behavioral decision theory as irrelevant to their lives, and they often (and, to my mind, wrongly) do.

Decision analysts have indeed been slow to accept conclusions about elicitation techniques that can easily be justified on the basis of behavioral studies. They have devoted remarkably little attention to validation either of elicitations or of the decisions to which the analyses lead. Behavioral decision theorists, though they often advocate ecological validity, have not tuned in carefully to what decision analysts know about the ecosystems within which they work. Behavioral decision theorists have not paid much attention to the routine decision-analytic practice of using multiple elicitations of the same quantity and asking respondents to reconcile inconsistencies.

This chapter attempts to define an empirical research agenda for behavioral decision theory that is oriented toward validating decision-analytic procedures and results and toward making decision-analytic tools better than they now are. This obviously is not the only appropriate research agenda for behavioral decision theory. But it would be useful, and the issues it aspires to address are important to understanding as well as improving behavior. First, I discuss some ideas for research on validation of decision-analytic procedures and results. Next, I examine some issues in decision-analytic elicitation, both of problem structures and of probabilities and utilities. The chapter concludes with a few comments on interactions between decision technology and other currently vigorous intellectual technologies.

VALIDATION

Ecological Validity

The idea that I here call ecological validity resembles Brunswik's (1956) goal of representative design. Indeed, Brunswik used the same name for a slightly different idea. The goal of ecological validity that I am advocating seems straightforward and convincing: generalizations from experiments to nonexperimental contexts are most persuasive if the conditions of the experiment resemble the conditions of the nonexperimental context. Many of the conditions needed to make experimentation convenient, or even feasible, have led decision analysts (and others) to question the ecological validity of the resulting experimental data. Bases for such questions have included student subjects, trivial or nonexistent stakes, hypothetical decisions, and boring response modes (e.g., checking options in a booklet).

Is ecological validity needed? The question is in part empirical and can be addressed by means of experiments. The most abundant data concern expertise. A number of studies have looked at experts (e.g., physicians) making hypothetical decisions in booklet tasks concerned with medical-sounding topics, such as lives lost as the result of a hypothetical treatment versus lives saved, and have found results little different from those produced by student subjects. An example appears in Tversky and Kahneman (1986).

Shanteau (e.g., 1988) distinguishes among amateurs, novices, and experts and asserts that most experiments on experts have studied novices rather than true experts because obtaining access and time from the latter is hard. He reviews studies suggesting that true experts, working on the tasks about which they are in fact expert, do quite well, for reasons of substance and also for reasons of style.

Large, real stakes and decision-making procedures less boring than checking off answers in a booklet have been sought and sometimes obtained in behavioral decision research. Lichtenstein and Slovic (1973; see also 1971) and Fryback, Goodman, and Edwards (1973) studied choices among real bets (though not in a standard casino game) in a Las Vegas casino, using its gamblers as subjects. In all studies, patterns of decisions hard to reconcile with the SEU model of rational decision making were found.

The study that most affected my views about ecological validity of procedures was conducted by Slovic, Lichtenstein, and Edwards (1965) and showed that choices among imaginary bets by student subjects using booklets in a classroom setting produced orderly, simple strategies whereas the same choices, made individually in a context in which the chosen bet was played and the money paid, produced far less orderly behavior reflecting much more interest and effort. No help in analyzing the task was offered to subjects in either condition.

A taxonomy of characteristics of decision makers, situations requiring decisions, and procedures for making decisions would facilitate making sense of data concerning the ecological validity of experiments on decision making. Some of the dimensions of that taxonomy are suggested by the preceding discussion: experience and training of the decision maker in the kind of decision being studied, realism of the decision context, availability of tools and advisers, and size of stakes. But which cells of such a taxonomy should behavioral decision theorists study? For behavioral decision theory either to focus exclusively on expert subjects with sophisticated tools making major decisions for high stakes or to ignore that cell would be absurd. A distinguished behavioral decision theorist recently wrote me that "important personal, political, medical and economic decisions and judgments in the real world are made in an informal, intuitive fashion without the use of tools, and there is a big question in the minds of many whether we have relevant tools." If the tools to which he refers are the tools of decision analysis, I certainly agree that most important real-world decisions are made without them, though I consider them to be highly relevant. Tools that are not decision analytic are far more common. Many business and government decisions are based in part on sophisticated financial analyses of their implications. Such analyses are tools. Many important decisions are made by an individual or group decision maker after substantial and sometimes intensive staff input; I consider such staffs to be in a sense tools. (I call these *staffed* decisions.) Important decisions are often made by committees. In some cases, committees are supported by staffs. But many important decisions are made without significant help by decision makers working alone.

It does not seem reasonable to me to expect that the same processes and outputs will be found in personal decisions made casually, perhaps with trivial stakes, in highly sophisticated decisions made after intensive financial analysis and staff study, or in decisions made by committees. Nor do I expect either of those cells of an ecological taxonomy to be identical with what decision analysts encounter in their professional lives. Does a body of ecologically valid experimental data on human decisions exist? For unaided personal decisions for fairly small stakes, it clearly does. For major decisions of any kind, obtaining such data is more difficult since major stakes, knowledge that the decision is "for real," and long experience in making similar decisions are hard to import into laboratory settings. Naturalistic observation of such decisions is clearly feasible and seems like a better approach. The same is true of staffed or committee decisions, though one could easily enough study staffed decisions in a business-game or war-game setting.

Will decision outputs be in some important way different in these different decision ecologies? I do not know but consider it likely. People routinely remark that they use different procedures to make personal decisions than they do to make professional ones, and anecdotal evidence suggests that the statement is true. If financial analysis, staffing, committee consideration, and the like have no effect on the content of decisions, it is hard to explain the ubiquity of such expensive and inconvenient procedures; explanations in terms of legitimating decisions or distributing responsibility seem inadequate to me.

If decisions in different ecologies are different in content and are made differently, how do we achieve ecological validity in studying them? The best we can do is to study a few interesting and important cells of an ecological taxonomy. Some examples include personal decisions, major staffed decisions, committee decisions, and decisions made with decision-analytic help, and there are surely others. I expect the task analysis provided by decision theory to be helpful in studying all of them, but I do not expect conclusions obtained by studying any one to generalize automatically to the others.

Convergent Elicitations

Decision-analytic elicitations deal with the normal inconsistencies by asking respondents to think harder and thus to reconcile conflicting estimates. This procedure is considered to enhance validity by encouraging hard thought. Does it? "The world analysts live in is different from that portrayed in many experiments. Like experimental psychologists, analysts encounter inconsistencies and violations of SEU, and many also see the power of stimuli and response modes in forming judgments. But what experimenters usually consider as the final product of their research is only the beginning for analysts. Observing incoherence, analysts attempt to find reasons for it and seek to resolve it" (von Winterfeldt and Edwards 1986, 384). Virtually every discussion in von Winterfeldt and Edwards (1986) of any elicitation recommends multiple elicitations of the same quantities by different procedures, followed by a discussion of inconsistencies, followed by revision of the elicited quantities by the respondent. Decision analysts routinely expect to obtain and exploit inconsistent judgments. In contrast, many behavioral decision theorists seem to believe that inconsistencies among elicited quantities as a function of the framing of the problem, the method of elicitation, or both do or should present major difficulties to decision analysts:

> The lability of preferences implied by the demonstrations of framing and elicitation effects raises difficult questions concerning the assessment of preferences and values. In the classical analysis, the relation of preference is inferred from observed responses (e.g., choice, matching) and is assumed to reflect the decision maker's underlying utility or

value. But if different elicitation procedures produce different orderings of options, how can preferences and values be defined? And in what sense do they exist? . . . [If preferences] do not satisfy the elementary requirements of invariance, it is unclear how to define a relation of preference that can serve as a basis for the measurement of value. In the absence of well-defined preferences, the foundations of choice theory and decision analysis are called into question. [Tversky, Sattath, and Slovic 1988, 383–84]

The dependence of elicited preferences (and other judgments) on framing and other aspects of elicitation procedure is undeniable. Do decision analysts kid themselves when they nevertheless use elicitations to obtain inputs to analyses? The answer obviously depends on how one feels about the process of seeking inconsistent judgments and then using them to induce the respondent to think harder. Few studies have looked at the issue. John (1984) confronted subjects with obvious ordinal discrepancies between the results of a multiattribute utility model and their intuitive ranking of the options. He gave the subjects the options of rejecting the multiattribute model, adding to it, redefining some attributes, changing weights, changing single-attribute utilities, or changing holistic rankings. All subjects wanted to be consistent; none rejected the multiattribute model or redefined attributes. The most common response was to change weights, followed by changing ratings and/or holistic judgments. Keeney, von Winterfeldt, and Eppel (1988) took this topic into the field, studying reconciliation of multiattribute utility evaluations of future German energy scenarios using ordinary German citizens as respondents in a 2-day workshop setting. Their findings were essentially the same as John's.

Eppel and von Winterfeldt (1988) followed up on a previous study by von Winterfeldt, Eppel, and Ford (1988) concerned with reconciliation of various estimates of the market share for compact disc players in 1990. The most interesting finding of the Eppel and von Winterfeldt study is that active reconciliation is more effective, in the sense of reducing respondents' uncertainty, than just averaging of numerical estimates. Active reconciliation is, of course, the routine decision-analytic procedure.

Decision analysts who ask respondents to reconcile inconsistent judgments obviously think that the more careful judgments that result are also better in some sense. Many behavioral decision theorists feel that judgments are constructed on the fly and depend in an essential way on elicitation method. Some decision analysts agree, but still prefer to base decisions on more careful judgments.

This major validation issue has received less research attention than it deserves. Decision analysts feel, I think correctly, that the elicitation methods they use are being questioned on the basis of research on similar but fundamentally different methods that lead to poorer judgments. The issue is contentious, and more data, especially on what happens in convergent elicitations, would help a great deal.

Expertise

We consider many professional inferrers and decision makers to be expert—but we have remarkably little idea what this means. Most would agree that expertise is not the same as intelligence and that special knowledge, while necessary, is not sufficient. Research on expertise often uses surrogate measures like rank or experience to identify experts. No one defends such measures on grounds other than expediency, and no one has proposed better ones. The range of depth of expertise is wide (Shanteau 1988), and the trade-off between wanting to study truly expert experts and not wanting to work with a sample as small as two or three is obvious.

In a review of expertise in auditing, Bedard (1987) concluded that consensus among experts, often proposed as a defining or at least desirable property of expertise, is as often absent as present. He reaches the same conclusion about stability of judgments over time. Experts do not have a better understanding of their thinking processes than nonexperts do of theirs. Experts often do no better than nonexperts in contexts in which good performance can be identified. The major positive finding in the studies that Bedard reviewed is that experts seem to search for information more systematically and efficiently than nonexperts. They also have more domain knowledge. My own cursory review of the literature on expertise in accounting is as discouraging as Bedard's.

A particularly interesting review of the literature on expertise by Shanteau (1986) reaches pessimistic conclusions similar to Bedard's about comparing judgments made by experts with those made by novices. But Shanteau pays special attention to what might be called stylistic differences. Experts have highly developed perceptual and attentional abilities. They can simplify complex problems. They can recognize exceptional cases. They have a strong sense of responsibility to their task. They are self-confident and tolerant of stress. They can adapt to new conditions. They can do easily what novices must work at. The fact that we persist in believing that experts differ from nonexperts and that such differences are important obviously defines a problem needing research.

Validation of Decision-Analytic Outputs

Decision analysis, as practiced, is a clinical field. It has about the same claim to having been validated as do such other clinical fields as medicine and astrology. Do decision makers who consult decision analysts make wiser decisions than they would have made otherwise? I do not know. The decision-analytic substitute for validity is the usual one: user acceptance. Customers keep coming back, so analysts must be doing something right. Can decision analysis be validated? If so, how?

Decision analysis is a collection of ideas, tools, and techniques that is no more subject to general validation than, say, surgery is. Only piecemeal validation of specific tools and techniques makes sense. I have no ideas at all about validation of problem-structuring techniques. A full discussion of validation of probability assessments can be found in von Winterfeldt and Edwards (1986, 121–31). Validation of utility assessments is harder (see von Winterfeldt and Edwards 1986, 366–67). Many decision analysts would argue that only the input to decision analysis needs validation; combination and decision rules derive from formal models of rationality and so are inherently valid. That old-time religion is good enough for me. Not all clients and decision researchers agree, however. For a review of dissenting opinions, see Fishburn (1988).

If the advantages of decision analysis over intuitive decision making were as great as some of us believe, validation should occur in the marketplace. Companies using decision-analytic procedures should drive competitors out of business. While that test has never been applied (so far as I know), it suggests some interesting experiments. What would happen if decision-analytic techniques were made available to some but not all of the participants in almost any experimental market? Most of us would expect that users of decision analysis would have a competitive edge. The same should be true of skilled users of effective decision aids.

ISSUES IN PROBLEM STRUCTURING

Every decision-analytic procedure starts with elicitations. Elicitation procedures for probabilities and utilities have been extensively studied; for a review of the literature and an attempt to extract from it conclusions about how to proceed, see the relevant chapters of von Winterfeldt and Edwards (1986). Before probabilities or utilities can be elicited, a problem structure must be identified. Some unresolved questions about problem-structure elicitation are discussed below.

My first lecture in any course on decision making, after some banalities about the ubiquity of decisions and the triviality of most of them, starts with a payoff matrix showing acts of the decision maker, states of nature, and numerically defined payoffs associated with each. This choice of a starting place skips over at least three of the most demanding and important unsolved problems in decision theory itself. Where did the acts come from? How did the decision maker identify this particular partitioning of states of nature as most relevant to the problem at hand? What do the numbers presented as payoffs mean? (The third question does not refer to utility; I will explain it later.)

Option Invention

Decision analysts who work in applied settings have long recognized that option invention lies at the heart of their task. A decision maker whose problem is so well formulated that he or she can write down a payoff matrix may not need decision-analytic help. Those who hire me as a consultant often say something like, "I have a month to work on a problem. The physical circumstances are . . . [the decision maker describes them in detail]. We want to meet the following objectives [e.g., bring the project in on time and within budget in the face of unanticipated obstacles] but realize that these objectives are inconsistent. Moreover, we may well encounter more unanticipated problems later but have no idea what they are. What should we do?"

A first response to this daunting challenge is to notice what elements of the problem definition seem most explicit. Almost never are they acts or states; typically, they are objectives. I believe that the discovery that elements of a list of objectives are inconsistent with one another is the most common reason that a decision maker seeks help. A second reason, often linked to the first, is that deadlines are coming and going, not enough is being done, and the decision maker needs to cover his or her assessments.

If this picture is typical, acts must grow out of values, as Pitz, Sachs, and Heerboth (1980), Keeney (1986), and von Winterfeldt and Edwards (1986) have all pointed out. A version of the same line of thought appears in the artificial intelligence literature (see Pearl 1977; Pearl, Leal and Saleh 1980). At least in my own experience, it would be easy to define acts to serve a single value well; the problem is to find acts that serve all the relevant values. This is obviously hard if the relevant values are numerous, the decision maker is less than fully sure what they are, and the trade-offs among them are unknown or a topic of conflict.

Gettys, Manning, and Casey (1981) found that, at least in the context that they used, subjects do a relatively poor job inventing options. However, questions have been raised about Gettys, Manning and Casey's use of consensus as a measure of option quality. I suggest, as Pitz, Sachs, and Heerboth (1980) and others have before, that, if acts grow out of values, a good approach to option invention would be to start by using a very simple value structure, perhaps including only a single value, and inventing acts to serve that value structure well. Typically, acts invented to serve one value well will serve others miserably. But it may be possible to "tweak" a loosely defined act to improve its performance on other values. This idea suggests development of an option invention aid. After value elicitation, the aid should invite its user to invent options that serve the most important value well. These options can be refined or reordered as the list of values is expanded. Dominance or quasidominance can be used to reduce the option set if it grows too large. Though a specific implementation would be context specific, the idea is general.

Option invention is surely the most important single step in decision analysis. Indeed, the most satisfying decision analyses end early because an option is invented that so clearly dominates all others that no further thought is needed, beyond some careful checking to make sure that the option is as dominant as it appears. Yet neither decision theory nor decision-analytic software has much help to offer; both treat options as something to be supplied by the decision maker, normally with little help.

Hypothesis Invention

Related to but less important than option invention is hypothesis invention. If the outcome of an option is uncertain, the decision maker must specify the events on which it depends, here called hypotheses. Such little research as has been done on hypothesis invention (see Gettys et al. 1979; Gettys, Fisher, and Mehle 1978; Fischhoff, Slovic, and Lichtenstein 1978) shows mainly that unaided generation of multiple hypotheses is difficult; too many possibilities get left out. Almost always, the outcomes of real options are not only uncertain but dependent on long chains of events. Detailed specification of such chains may be useless, if possible at all; the resulting structure is too complex. However, risk analysis, sometimes considered a branch of decision analysis, consists primarily of specifying and working with such long, bushy, complex structures.

The most common solutions to the problem of complexity are two, typically used together. One, common in business but less common in personal and governmental decision making, is use of a planning horizon, an arbitrary period of time after which an outcome is to be evaluated. The other, typical when planning horizons do not make sense and often useful when they do, is the use of scenarios. A scenario is simply a future history associated with a given decision. Since almost all real acts can lead to many different futures, scenarios should be used in sets, each set associated with an option. It is natural and sensible to use a set of scenarios as though it enumerated all possible futures resulting from an option even though, taken literally, such a limited set of futures may be absurd. The goal of scenario selection, an extreme form of hypothesis invention, is to make sure that major possible outcomes are covered; the actual future, though not identical with any scenario considered, can therefore be considered a close relative of one. Attainment of this kind of completeness is a key goal of risk analysis. The major intellectual tool that makes an approximation to it possible is liberal use of independence assumptions, often known to be wrong but needed to get on with the task at hand.

A hypothesis generation aid should look for hypotheses that cause the options with which they are associated to produce wide variations on important dimensions of value. The likelihood function may be helpful. A good hypothesis set should invite the collection of highly discriminative data.

A view of option and hypothesis generation to some extent inconsistent with the one presented here is Wohl's (1981) SHOR (stimulus, hypotheses, options, and response) paradigm. Wohl's context is tactical military command and control. The idea is that options grow out of an appreciation of the tactical situation and, consequently, that hypothesis generation precedes option invention. I do not doubt that in some contexts options grow out of hypotheses rather than the other way around; my treatment is based on limited applied experience.

Resets

The third key issue hidden in every payoff matrix I call management of resets; it is less familiar than option and hypothesis invention. In 1962, I wrote,

> Static decision theory . . . conceives of a decision maker who is confronted by a well-defined set of possible courses of action. Associated with each such course of action and each possible state of the world is a value; collectively these values form a payoff matrix. . . . The decision maker executes one of his courses of action, receives the (appropriate) value or payoff . . . and then the world ends. The decision maker (in principle) never gets to make a second decision in which he might apply whatever he may have learned as a consequence of the first. [Edwards 1962a, 1]

The problem is worse than that; not only is learning from experience with decision making excluded from decision theory, but even changes of the decision maker's state, caused, for example, by winning or losing a bet, are inadequately handled. In 1962, though I made a stab at defining the goal of a dynamic decision theory and listing some relevant tools, I did nothing to develop one. Thereafter, I dropped the topic. Not everyone did, however. In 1981, Hogarth reviewed a large collection of research relevant to the topic. His theme was that many of the intellectual errors reported in static decision tasks are functional if tasks are considered as continuous and if adaptive behavior based on feedback and learning is taken into consideration.

The idea of a utility function defined over total assets has been readily available and widely used to tie sets of decisions together. Total assets change as an outcome of most decisions. I know of no other reason than that for using total assets as the argument of a utility function for money (I do not differentiate between value and utility measurement; for a technical discussion of reasons why, see von Winterfeldt and Edwards 1986). As I argued in 1962 (Edwards 1962b) and Kahneman and Tversky argued in 1979, utility defined over total assets makes little sense. Very few of us can come within $10,000 of specifying what our total assets are. A much more natural way of defining an origin for utility functions is to say that zero utility is where you are now— that is, that utility is defined over prospective gains or losses, which are far easier to identify.

This definition of zero utility implies resets. After a transaction is completed and its consequences have been assimilated, the evaluative mechanism built into the human being is reset; it is as though the transaction had never occurred. (Exceptions can obviously be made for massive gains or losses; the question of what *massive* means is empirical.)

The alternative to resetting is some form of accounting, either explicit or intuitive, to keep track of the effects of gains and losses on total fortune. Resetting is easier since any form of accounting takes effort. I conceive of resetting, not as a process, but as the absence of one, and I consider that absence of an effortful process as often appropriate.

Does the notion of resets add anything to the familiar observation that the status quo is the reference point from which gains or losses are in fact evaluated? It clearly grows out of that observation, but, by treating the alternatives of resetting or accounting (intuitive or explicit) as choice options with costs and benefits, it extends the reference point idea. Since the accounting required to take changes in the status quo into account in sequences of decision can be hard, it seems sensible to make a deliberate choice whether to do so. I believe that many decision makers, aided only by casual accounting procedures readily available in the environment, do exactly that. Most of us count our chips when we gamble, thus preventing a too-facile reset.

The issue of how extensive a sequence of decisions to which decision theory applies should be is familiar in abstract decision theory. As Savage put it, "Making an extreme idealization . . . a person has only one decision to make in his whole life. He must namely, decide how to live, and this he might in principle do once and for all. . . . Any claim to realism made by this book . . . is predicated on the idea that some of the individual decision situations into which actual people tend to subdivide the single grand decision do recapitulate in microcosm the mechanism of the idealized grand decision" (Savage 1954, 83). Savage's treatment of what he calls *small worlds* specifies only very abstractly conditions under which such recapitulation in microcosm might occur. The key idea, in language very different from Savage's, is that decision trees must be truncated and the outcomes at the end of each twig treated as certain if that twig is reached, even though they are not.

Savage does not discuss rules relating one small world to another, except that, if various postulates are satisfied, both must recapitulate the *mechanism* of the idealized grand decision. I suggest that it often makes sense to choose to reset when moving from one small world to another. The argument is similar to that for using budgets to control expenditures (discussed below). You might feel, as I do, that your success or lack of it at the poker table last night should have little to do with today's decisions about financial transactions. In that case, you might choose to keep track of your chips but to reset when the game breaks up. Such choices would lead to a context effect in which decisions within one context are linked to one another but not to those made in other contexts. Such context effects seem sensible, if perhaps not formally optimal, to me. They permit exploitation of fairly simple informal accounting mechanisms to avoid paradoxes within a single decision context while maintaining consistent patterns of behavior from one encounter with a decision context to the next, all at low cost for accounting. Obviously, you would want contexts to interact in extreme cases; loss of half your net worth in Las Vegas

TABLE 3.1
KAHNEMAN AND TVERSKY'S VERSION OF THE ALLAIS PARADOX

A. Problem 1

Choose between

A (18)	B[a] (82)
2,500 with probability .33 2,400 with probability .66 0 with probability .01	2,400 with certainty

B. Problem 2

Choose between

A[a] (83)	B (17)
2,500 with probability .33 0 with probability .67	2,400 with probability .34 0 with probability .66

Source: Kahneman and Tversky (1979, 265–66).
Note: $N = 72$ in both problems. The numbers in parentheses represent the proportions of respondents picking each choice.
[a] The preferred option in each pair.

should influence other forms of economic behavior. But such examples should be rare.

Table 3.1 is a version of the Allais paradox (Allais 1953; Allais and Hagen 1979) borrowed from Kahneman and Tversky (1979). It is followed by the mathematics purporting to show that no version of expected utility maximization can be consistent with choosing B and C. Among Kahneman and Tversky's 72 subjects, 82% preferred B over A, and 83% preferred C over D. A preference for B in problem 1 and for C in problem 2 violates any form of SEU maximization. The first preference means that

$$u(\$2,400) > .33u(\$2,500) + .66u(\$2,400) + .01u(\$0), \qquad (1)$$

or

$$.34u(\$2,400) > .33u(\$2,500) + .01u(\$0). \qquad (2)$$

The second preference implies the opposite:

$$.33u(\$2,500) + .67u(\$0) > .34u(\$2,400) + .66u(\$0). \qquad (3)$$

This simplifies to

$$.34u(\$2,400) < .33u(\$2,500) + .01u(\$0). \tag{4}$$

Is the Allais paradox paradoxical or not? I assert that a reset is a necessary condition to produce the paradox. Consider the circumstances of these two successive choices. If the choices are not considered real, it is unclear why anyone should be interested in them. How would one implement a real set of such choices? The language presented to the subjects does not say. One possibility is to present A and B, play the chosen one, and then present and play C and D. If that procedure is used, a reset is required to produce the paradox. Otherwise, the status quo changes after the first play, and a different part of the utility function for money applies to the second choice. To see the point, look at the mathematics that follows table 3.1. The assumption is clearly made that the quantities $u(\$2,500)$, $u(\$2,400)$, and $u(\$0)$ are the same in both equations (1) and (2) and equations (3) and (4). If not, unlikely but acceptable utility functions can be invented to fit any of the possible outcomes and subsequent choices. The experimenter might ask for both choices before playing either. A rational approach by the respondent to making both choices before playing either would be to combine the possible outcomes, and, again, the paradox would disappear. A fancier procedure would be to ask for both choices in advance with the understanding that a coin flip will be used to decide which will be implemented. This procedure does produce the paradox by making the reset intellectually appropriate.

Normatively, we know less about resets than we should. The topic does not easily lend itself to normative thought. Descriptively, we know that respondents in experiments are docile and almost always reset when the experimenter wishes them to. This fact produces such reference point phenomena as treating gains differently from a gift followed by losses, even though the physical consequences are identical. Whether real decision makers, dealing with real decision problems about which they are expert, are as willing to reset as that, I cannot say. I doubt it. The major function that resets serve is economy of thought—fine when the stakes are low and thinking difficult but less important as stakes go up.

Resets and Multiple Transaction Streams

von Winterfeldt and Edwards (1986) argue that transactions are segregated into streams that are thought about separately. If so, it would make sense to assume that a reset normally occurs whenever successive transactions belong to different streams. von Winterfeldt and Edwards identified four such streams in their own lives: wallet and credit card, bank account, capital expenditures, and play money. They defend segregation of transactions into streams as sensible. Anyone who uses a budget to organize decisions about transactions would probably agree since that is what a budget does. Anyone who has been frustrated by the difficulty of transferring money from one budget category to another will acknowledge that such procedures can produce suboptimal resource allocations—and, with ingenious manipulation, violations of dominance and other principles of rational choice. Such procedures, like all that involve resets, may be optimal if cost of thinking is taken into account but are suboptimal otherwise.

The major difficulty in doing research on resets is obtaining access to contexts in which they should not occur. Such contexts will typically involve real, and significant, transactions. Since many social mechanisms (e.g., easy access to credit) are designed to facilitate resets, the obvious places to start looking for research opportunities are contexts in which resets are a problem. Collection agencies for debts are a possibility.

The most interesting issues about resets have to do with how a decision maker can function when they do not occur. The nonoccurrence of a reset implies that the outcomes of earlier decisions should influence later ones. This requires at least an informal kind of accounting. Tversky and Kahneman (1981) have written about psychological accounts but seem to treat them as occurring routinely. The position taken here is that, in executing routine transactions, we try to avoid the need for any kind of accounting, psychological or otherwise, by means of resets. This is a sensible way to hold down the cost of thinking. From either point of view, the question of how psychological accounting works is open to research.

Thaler (1985) has treated intuitive accounting in a spirit similar to that proposed here, but with different results. Basing his arguments on thought-experiment and real data and on prospect theory (Kahneman and Tversky 1979), he argues, in effect, that consumers to some degree control how they perform intuitive accounting. A key issue is whether financial consequences of multiple transactions should or should not be aggregated in dollars before a utility transformation is applied. He argues, on the basis of data and of prospect theory's utility function, that aggregation before transformation is undesirable for gains, desirable for losses or for mixed cases in which aggregation produces a net gain, and unclear for mixed cases in which aggregation produces a net loss. He also associates utility with the circumstances as well as the outcome of a transaction. This idea turns out to have implications to some extent similar to those of the von Winterfeldt–Edwards transaction stream idea discussed above. Thaler's explanation of budgeting is worth quoting: "Individuals face self-control problems in regulating eating, drinking, smoking and consumption generally. The whole mental accounting apparatus . . . can be thought of as part of an individual's solution to these problems. . . . The technology of self-control often implies outright prohibitions because allowing a little bit eventually leads to excesses" (Thaler 1985, 208). While Thaler's treatment is inconsistent with the transaction stream idea, these two lines of thought have a strong family resemblance.

The most troublesome partitions among transactions are of yet another kind, about which we know even less. That is the segregation process that enables us to treat the same kinds of outcomes as unrelated to one another if they arise from distinct decision contexts. Perhaps the most obvious example is the value of a statistical life, which varies from well under $50,000 in some highway design contexts to $10,000,000 or more in the context of nuclear waste disposal.

A closely related phenomenon, in my view, is the willingness, indeed the eagerness, that both individuals and organizations display to use budgeting to manage their financial affairs. Money is a measure of value that is physically transferable and fully substitutable among uses. Yet individuals and organizations routinely deny themselves the flexibility of spending money on whatever use seems best by creating limited categories of expenditures, assigning some of the funds available now or to become available to each category, and making it difficult or impossible to transfer money from one category to another. Why do we deliberately go about limiting the usefulness of this great social invention?

In organizational contexts, the answer is often that budgets facilitate control of one decision maker by another and make easy tracking and prediction of the behavior of large, complex organizations possible. These seem to me to be legitimate goals, and the means often, though not always, fit the ends.

In personal contexts, the justification of budgets as tools by means of which one decision maker controls another makes little sense. Even a single-family budget may be complex enough for tracking and prediction to require subdivision. But surely transfer of funds from one budget category to another should require no more than agreement among relevant decision makers that the transfer should occur. Yet this is seldom so.

I argue that formal or informal personal budgets guide and facilitate resets. That is, we allocate to each transaction stream both rough boundaries on sizes of individual transactions and even rougher ones on totals over a suitable period of time (e.g., a month). This process makes individual decisions about transactions easy to make and enhances consistency of behavior from one decision to the next one of similar kind. When I must decide how elaborate a vacation to take this year, I can often manage to avoid even considering whether the living room needs redecoration.

INPUT ISSUES

The human engineering of decision-analytic procedures is in its infancy mainly because, for the most part, decision analysts are not trained in human engineering and like to think of elicitations as exercises of artistry and because, in most applied and many experimental contexts, convenient validating criteria to use in comparing elicitation procedures do not exist. Decision analysts trained in experimental psychology have produced much of the relevant literature. I shall not review it here; as much as was available up to about 1985 is examined in von Winterfeldt and Edwards (1986). Instead, I will pick out a few especially interesting topics about which our information is meager.

Overconfidence

A substantial experimental literature shows that human probability estimates are typically overconfident (for reviews, see Lichtenstein, Fischhoff, and Phillips 1982; von Winterfeldt and Edwards 1986). Unfortunately, the bulk of the calibration studies that lead to that conclusion use almanac (general information) questions and student subjects. Methodological difficulties so severely plague such experiments that few decision analysts take them seriously—or should. Weather forecasts turn out to be very well calibrated indeed (see Murphy and Winkler 1977). Meteorology may be the only field in which enough probability assessments are available to study calibration outside the psychological laboratory. Twenty years of research on overconfidence have left us unclear about how prevalent it is as well as about how to overcome it.

A manifestation of overconfidence is too-tight credible intervals. Alpert and Raiffa (1982, the first published version of a 1969 progress report) probably were the first to call attention to this problem, but every working decision analyst knows that a respondent, asked to estimate a range within which he or she is 98 percent certain that the true value of a parameter will fall, will routinely make that range too small. (There is nothing special about 98 percent; the same kind of result can be achieved with 50 percent credible intervals.) Seaver, von Winterfeldt, and Edwards (1978) showed that matters can be considerably improved by providing the limits of the interval and asking the respondent to provide the probability, rather than the other way around. Yet, with the response modes so far studied, most credible intervals are almost surely too tight.

Alternative ways of assessing credible intervals are not hard to devise. A search for elicitation procedures that avoid overconfident assessments should be useful.

Very Low Probabilities

Risk analysts, like everyone else, synthesize very low probabilities by multiplying higher ones together. But what if the higher ones are very low too, as they often are? Every valve and pipe in a nuclear power plant is designed not to fail, and indeed failure occurs so seldom that frequentistic information about failure rates may be hard to obtain or interpret. Yet those component failure rates are needed to calculate, say, the probability of a core meltdown. We know very little about how to assess such small probabilities judgmentally. Selvidge (1975) has proposed an approach. von Winterfeldt and Edwards (1986) have supplemented it with the thought that a log odds response mode would help. More ideas are badly needed.

Value Tree Elicitation

Value trees are typically elicited in hierarchical form; a literature exists comparing top-down with bottom-up elicitations. Only the twigs (as I prefer to call what the literature calls leaves; many trees do not have leaves, but all have twigs) have utilities directly associated with them. In principle, one could ignore the superstructure completely. In practice, one seldom wants to do so. The superstructure permits elicitation of weights by procedures less tedious than assessing, say, 32 numbers with appropriate spacing that sum to 1. As usual, such simplifications imply an assumption: in this case, that they do not introduce elicitation errors more severe than would their alternatives. The topic is hard to study because of the absence of a criterion for weights. Still, von Winterfeldt and his colleagues are working on it now.

How abstractly should values be defined? Abstract definition keeps the number of attributes manageably small. Highly specific definition makes utilities easy to assess. The trade-off between these benefits is hard to assess and is surely context dependent. But I know essentially nothing about the rules that should govern that trade-off.

Value-Probability Interactions

Kadane and Winkler (1988) pointed out very recently that probability assessments, even those based on appropriate use of strictly proper scoring rules, should not be expected on formal grounds to yield "correct" probabilities if the assessee has a stake in the occurrence of the event other than that implicit in the assessment of its probability and if the assessee is not risk neutral. The argument applies only to elicitation methods, such as those that use reference gambles or proper scoring rules, that require the assessee to make judgments involving payoffs and then derive the probability being assessed from mathematics based on the assumption of SEU maximization. Moreover the argument applies only if utility is defined as a function either of total wealth or at least of all changes in financial status dependent on the event the probability of which is being assessed. That is, the argument applies only if no resets isolate the main consequences of the event from the consequences involved in its assessment. Kadane and Winkler point out that the issue is important to decision analysis since experts almost always have stakes in the topics about which they are expert. Such elicitation methods are not the only ones available. But it would be useful to study the kind of interaction between assessment and life situation that Kadane and Winkler postulate.

The preceding sample of issues concerned with the human engineering of inputs to decision analysis is far from complete. I do not as yet have enough intuition about human engineering of decision-analytic outputs to do much speculating about them. A few ideas on the topic are latent in von Winterfeldt and Edwards (1986, chap. 11). An obviously crucial point, especially for the design of decision support systems, is that no procedure is likely to be helpful unless the decision maker considers it so (see Holt and Tolcott 1987).

INTERACTIONS WITH OTHER FIELDS

Interactions with Multicriterion Decision Making

Two main differences seem to exist between decision analysis and multiple-criterion decision-making techniques. One is that decision analysis routinely accepts inherently subjective quantities to maximize whereas those interested in multiple-criterion decision making typically do not. The other, less clear cut, is that those interested in multiple-criterion decision making often are unwilling to aggregate across dimensions and therefore define their problem as maximization of one dimension while holding others at acceptable levels—a class of optimization problem for which various mathematical programming tools are appropriate.

Rosenthal (1985) has recently reviewed some of the multiple-criterion decision-making literature from the point of view of how it can profit by using the decision-analytic concept of utility. It is amazing that these highly similar lines of thought have developed so little interaction with each other. Pursuit of such interactions seems likely to be fruitful.

Interactions with MIS-DSS

The designers of management information systems (MIS) and decision support systems (DSS) have for the most part been well aware of decision-analysis concepts and literature. Some decision support systems are explicitly based on decision analysis; some are not. All pursue the crucial objective of eliminating the middle man, the analyst—or, perhaps better put, of providing an automated analyst. In the opinion of most decision analysts, none have yet succeeded. This topic seems destined to merge with the next.

Interactions with Artificial Intelligence

So long as those working on artificial intelligence wanted to mimic human behavior, there was no reason for them to interact with the normative field of decision analysis. Even after researchers interested in expert systems decided that a system capable of being useful in solving a real problem in a real world was worth attending to, the typical tool was the production rule, a statement of the form, If A, B, and C are true, do D. Such rules can be useful but present problems whenever one cannot be quite sure whether A, B, and C are true. Various ad hoc solutions to the problem of quantifying uncertainty were used; some still are. But more and more researchers are coming to recognize that ordinary probabilities, used in other branches of science to deal with quantification of uncertainty for over 300 years, are probably the best tools available for that purpose in artificial intelligence as well. Thus, the possibility of fruitful collaboration between artificial intelligence and decision analysis has just started to open up within the last 5 years or so.

This collaboration seems to me to hold extraordinary promise. I see no reason why rules cannot take probabilistic form. I see no reason why explicit assessments of probabilities and utilities (as well as deterministic rules, where they are relevant) should not be the required inputs to artificially intelligent systems. I do see reasons why explicit assessments of problem structure would be harder to elicit and use without a human analyst to help. I therefore think that the collaboration is most likely to be fruitful in fields like medicine in which the same decision problem is likely to arise enough times to justify the cost of building an artificially intelligent system to deal with it. Major strategic decisions, which are typically one of a kind, will continue to depend on the clinical skills of analysts, though decision support systems with artificial intelligence components will surely help.

The field that researchers on artificial intelligence call knowledge engineering is exactly what decision analysts call elicitation. Versions of it that tend to look for rules can surely be combined with the decision-analytic versions that tend to look for the judgments of utility and probability on which the rules depend.

Introducing utility considerations into artificial intelligence research will add a dimension of concern with values that it does not at present have. Present treatment of objective functions within that research tradition strikes me as primitive.

From the decision-analytic point of view, the great advantage of such a collaboration is that repetitive problems need be dealt with in detail only once. The solution, once embodied in a program, can quite possibly be used without an analyst's help. It is not even that difficult to imagine using an unaided computer program to elicit the needed judgments from the decision maker—which no existing decision support system, in my opinion, can do at all well. I look forward to an exciting next few years as this collaboration, at present nascent, wobbly, and tentative, gains strength and power.

REFERENCES

Allais, M. 1953. Le comportement de l'homme rationnel devant le risque: Critique des postulats et axiomes de l'école américaine. *Econometrica* 21:503–46.

Allais, M., and J. Hagen, eds. 1979. *Expected utility hypotheses and the Allais paradox*. Dordrecht: Reidel.

Alpert, M., and H. Raiffa. 1982. A progress report on the training of probability assessors. In *Judgment under uncertainty: Heuristics and biases,* ed. D. Kahneman, P. Slovic, and A. Tversky, 294–305. Cambridge: Cambridge University Press.

Bedard, J. 1987. Expertise in auditing: Myth or reality. Paper presented at University of Southern California/Deloitte, Haskins, and Sells Audit Judgment Symposium, February.

Brunswik, E. 1956. *Perception and the representative design of psychological experiments*. 2d ed. Berkeley: University of California Press.

Edwards, W. 1962a. Dynamic decision theory and probabilistic information processing. *Human Factors* 4:59–73.

———. 1962b. Subjective probabilities inferred from decisions. *Psychological Review* 69:109–35.
Eppel, T., and D. von Winterfeldt. 1988. Resolving inconsistent forecasts: An experimental study. University of Southern California, Los Angeles. Institute of Safety and Systems Management, Research Center. Typescript.
Fischhoff, B., P. Slovic, and S. Lichtenstein. 1978. Fault trees: Sensitivity of estimated failure probabilities to problem representation. *Journal of Experimental Psychology: Human Perception and Performance* 4:330–34.
Fishburn, P. C. 1988. *Nonlinear preference and utility theory*. Baltimore: Johns Hopkins University Press.
Fryback, D. G., B. C. Goodman, and W. Edwards. 1973. Choices among bets by Las Vegas gamblers: Absolute and contextual effects. *Journal of Experimental Psychology* 98:271–78.
Gettys, C., S. Fisher, and T. Mehle. 1978. *Hypothesis generation and plausibility assessments*. Technical Report no. 15-10-78. Norman: University of Oklahoma, Decision Processes Laboratory.
Gettys, C., C. Manning, and J. Casey. 1981. *An evaluation of human act generation performance*. Technical Report no. 15-8-81. Norman: University of Oklahoma, Decision Processes Laboratory.
Gettys, C., T. Mehle, S. Baca, S. Fisher, and C. Manning. 1979. *A memory retrieval aid for hypothesis generation*. Technical Report no. 27-7-79. Norman: University of Oklahoma, Decision Processes Laboratory.
Hogarth, R. M. 1981. Beyond discrete biases: Functional and dysfunctional aspects of judgmental heuristics. *Psychological Bulletin* 90:197–217.
Holt, V. E., and M. A. Tolcott. 1987. *Impact and potential of decision research on decision aiding*. Reston, Va.: Decision Science Consortium.
John, R. 1984. Value tree analysis of social conflicts about risky technologies. Ph.D. diss., University of Southern California.
Kadane, J. B., and R. L. Winkler. 1988. Separating probability elicitation from utilities. *Journal of the American Statistical Association* 83:357–63.
Kahneman, D., and A. Tversky. 1979. Prospect theory: An analysis of decision under risk. *Econometrica* 47:263–91.
Keeney, R. 1986. *Creating alternatives using value-focused thinking*. Decision Analysis Series, Technical Report. Los Angeles: University of Southern California, Institute of Safety and Systems Management, Systems Science Department.
Keeney, R., D. von Winterfeldt, and T. Eppel. 1988. The public value forum: Eliciting public values in complex policy decisions. Los Angeles: University of Southern California, Institute of Safety and Systems Management, Research Center.
Lichtenstein, S., B. Fischhoff, and L. Phillips. 1982. Calibration of probabilities: The state of the art to 1980. In *Judgment under uncertainty: Heuristics and biases*, ed. D. Kahneman, P. Slovic, and A. Tversky, 306–34. Cambridge: Cambridge University Press.
Lichtenstein, S., and P. Slovic. 1971. Reversals of preferences between bids and choices in gambling decisions. *Journal of Experimental Psychology* 89:46–55.
———. 1973. Response induced reversals of preferences in gambling: An extended replication in Las Vegas. *Journal of Experimental Psychology* 101:16–20.
Murphy, A., and R. Winkler. 1977. Can weather forecasters formulate reliable forecasts of precipitation and temperature? *National Weather Digest* 2:2–9.
Pearl, J. 1977. A framework for processing value judgments. *IEEE Transactions on Systems, Man, and Cybernetics* SMC-7:349–54.
Pearl, J., A. Leal, and J. Saleh. 1980. GODDESS: A goal directed decision structuring system. Report no. UCLA-ENG-8034. Los Angeles: University of California.

Pitz, G., N. Sachs, and J. Heerboth. 1980. Procedures for eliciting choices in the analysis of individual decisions. *Organizational Behavior and Human Performance* 26:398–408.

Rosenthal, R. 1985. Principles of multiobjective optimization. *Decision Sciences* 16:133–52.

Savage, L. 1954. *The foundations of statistics.* New York: Wiley.

Seaver, D., D. von Winterfeldt, and W. Edwards. 1978. Eliciting subjective probability distributions on continuous variables. *Organizational Behavior and Human Performance* 21:379–91.

Selvidge, J. 1975. *Experimental comparison of different methods for assessing the extremes of probability distributions by the fractile method.* Technical Report. Boulder: University of Colorado, Graduate School of Business Administration.

Shanteau, J. 1986. Psychological characteristics of expert decision makers. Paper presented at the University of Southern California Symposium on Audit Judgment and Expert Systems, Los Angeles, February.

———. 1988. Psychological characteristics and strategies of expert decision makers. In *Advances in decision research,* ed. B. Rohrmann, L. R. Beach, C. Vlek, and S. R. Watson. Amsterdam: North-Holland.

Slovic, P., S. Lichtenstein, and W. Edwards. 1965. Boredom induced changes in preferences among bets. *American Journal of Psychology* 78:208–17.

Thaler, R. 1985. Mental accounting and consumer choice. *Marketing Science* 4:199–214.

Tversky, A., and D. Kahneman. 1981. The framing of decisions and the psychology of choice. *Science* 211:453–58.

———. 1986. Rational choice and the framing of decisions. *Journal of Business* 59:S251–S278.

Tversky, A., S. Sattath, and P. Slovic. 1988. Contingent weighting in judgment and choice. *Psychological Review* 95:371–84.

von Winterfeldt, D., and W. Edwards. 1986. *Decision analysis and behavioral research.* New York: Cambridge University Press.

von Winterfeldt, D., T. Eppel, and C. Ford. 1988. An experimental investigation of plural analysis: Estimating the market share of compact disc players in 1990. *Behavioral Science* 33:187–95.

Wohl, J. G. 1981. Force management decision requirements for Air Force tactical command and control. *IEEE Transactions on Systems, Man, and Cybernetics* 11:618–39.

Discussion

HOWARD KUNREUTHER

Hillel Einhorn would have enjoyed these three chapters for at least three reasons. First and foremost, they are all of high-quality and reflect considerable thought by their authors. Second, they all address topics in which he had undertaken research. Together with William Goldstein, Einhorn wrote on the topic of preference reversals, which forms an important part of the chapter by Slovic, Griffin, and Tversky. With Robin Hogarth, he developed a descriptive model of how individuals deal with ambiguity of probabilities, the subject of Wallsten's chapter. Finally, Einhorn was most interested in contrasting normative theories of judgment and choice with descriptive models of individual behavior in the hopes of improving the decision-making process, a theme pursued by Edwards in his chapter.

A third reason why Einhorn would have enjoyed playing a discussant's role here is because he loved a good intellectual fight. All three chapters are provocative and raise a number of important and controversial questions regarding individual decision making under uncertainty and ambiguity. Einhorn had his own inimitable style when it came to discussing and critiquing papers. He made his points clearly and without any malice so that, even if you did not like what he had to say about certain concepts, you always knew that you could have a lively discussion with him about it afterward. He set an excellent example for all of us to emulate. There is no doubt that Hilly would have thoroughly enjoyed the nature of the dialogue and discourse at the conference of which this volume represents the published proceedings.

The easiest way for me to discuss these three excellent chapters is by focusing on two stages of decision making under uncertainty: estimating the probabilities and outcomes associated with different states of nature and specifying a choice between competing alternatives. Although the principal findings presented in these chapters are based on controlled laboratory experiments, they have considerable relevance for current problems facing both the private and the public sectors, as I will attempt to demonstrate.

ESTIMATING PROBABILITIES AND OUTCOMES

Wallsten's chapter directly addresses the issue of how one deals with probabilities when they are either precise or vague. He makes a point, as does

Howard (1988), that decision analysis requires that all uncertainties regarding events be expressed as some type of unique probability measure. Suppose experts disagree on their estimates of some low-probability event such as a nuclear power plant accident. Then one can combine them in some manner (e.g., weight each expert's probability estimate and utilize the resulting mean value). Alternatively, one can undertake sensitivity analyses to determine how important differences in experts' estimates of the probability value affect the choice of alternatives.

There is considerable empirical evidence that suggests that, for many real-world situations, ambiguity regarding probabilities does make a difference in people's willingness to pay to avoid a risk. A number of controlled laboratory experiments, stimulated by the Ellsberg paradox, have borne this out. When confronted with situations in which there was ambiguity associated with probabilities, even sophisticated subjects such as professional actuaries indicated a strong aversion to ambiguity regarding low-probability events (Hogarth and Kunreuther 1988). This group recognized that, from an expected-utility theory point of view, ambiguity should not matter. In their role of making premium recommendations to underwriters it biased their estimates upward, particularly if the potential loss was rather large.

Wallsten is advocating that, for many situations in which there are vague uncertainties, such as in risk assessments (e.g., chance of cancer), it may be more appropriate to provide a verbal rather than a quantitative estimate of the risk. There is no doubt that people feel much more comfortable with this type of information, a fact revealed by an interesting study on managerial perspectives on risk by March and Shapira (1987). For example, one vice president of finance told these authors, "No one is interested in getting quantified measures." Another senior vice president stated, "You don't quantify the risk. You have to be able to feel it" (1408). MacCrimmon and Wehrung (1986), in their study of risk-taking behavior by managers, heard similar comments when they asked executives to rank nine investment alternatives.

Given the discomfort that many people feel with probabilities, what do you do to improve behavior? In situations in which there are vague uncertainties of the type that Wallsten is talking about, a quantitative estimate may be inappropriate. However, this does not necessarily mean that one should utilize verbal statements to express ambiguity and uncertainty. In my opinion, the use of verbal statements is a useful aid only if the decision maker feels that he or she can operate more successfully with this type of information than when presented with a range of numerical examples.

The experimental evidence presented in Wallsten's chapter is somewhat inconclusive on this point. Wallsten's observation that subjects prefer to present forecasts verbally and receive numerical data would be consistent with the findings of an experiment reported in Budescu and Wallsten (1988) in which subjects made significantly less money with verbal than with numerical judgments. Given that individuals prefer receiving quantitative information, it may be appropriate to state that experts are unsure about the actual probabilities and that the range of estimates varies between two specified extremes: P min and P max. This may be more desirable than providing verbal statements such as *highly unlikely* and *almost impossible,* which will be interpreted by each individual in his or her own way.

For low-probability events, we have a special set of problems simply because there is not enough information to estimate the chances of certain events occurring. For example, with respect to nuclear power plants there may not be enough data to determine the chances of an accident. With respect to carcinogenic chemicals, there is often a long latency period between exposure to the toxic chemical and the onset of disease. In addition, there may be a number of other factors that could cause a particular problem. Weinberg (1972) has classified these types of events as "transcientific," indicating that there is no scientific basis for estimating the statistical chances of certain types of accidents occurring even though, epistemologically speaking, these questions are fact. In these situations, it is not at all clear what one should do if one utilized a verbal statement such as *practically impossible.* This may have little meaning to an individual who is greatly concerned with the consequences of a particular event, should it occur.

From a prescriptive viewpoint, there is a clear need for education so that people can understand what is meant by uncertainty with respect to particular risks and the impossibility of achieving zero risks without an extraordinarily high cost (e.g., banning certain products or activities and forgoing the benefits that would be forthcoming from them). In addition, some type of science court may be helpful in indicating basic differences between experts and the assumptions that have been made by different experts in dealing with uncertainty.

Turning to the evaluation of consequences, there are features of many decision problems that lead individuals to introduce attributes that are important to them but that do not naturally fit into a standard decision analysis or expected-utility model. Consider the Allais paradox, which Edwards discusses in his chapter. A principal reason why individuals violate the independence axiom of utility theory is that they view the very small probability (e.g., .01) of getting zero in one of the comparisons between two options as different from the same small increase (of, e.g., .01 from .89 to .90) in another comparison. Behavioral attributes such as regret can be introduced into the problem to explain this behavior; this has been done by Bell (1982) and Loomes and Sugden (1982). Framing the problem as a supergame with four different options (as Edwards does in his chapter) may eliminate the paradox and feelings of potential regret. But this does not mean that the Allais paradox is not real and troublesome. It has assumed importance because it suggests that the evaluation of alternatives is considerably more complicated behaviorally than had originally been assumed.

The work on risk perception by Slovic and his colleagues (Slovic 1987) emphasizes the importance of other attributes in influencing individuals' decisions under uncertainty. When the outcomes from specific events (e.g., a nuclear power plant accident, leakage from a hazardous waste storage facility) are ambiguous, feelings such as fear and dread are important factors to consider in determining what actions to follow. These descriptive findings suggest that prescriptive models of choice need to recognize the multiattribute nature of many problems in which the consequences are ambiguous.

CHOICES BETWEEN ALTERNATIVES

In most decision analysis problems presented in textbooks or published articles, the set of alternatives is well specified, and it is up to the individual to make a choice between them. An important point that Edwards makes in his chapter is that decision analysis can play a critical role in option generation and hypothesis invention. This enables the decision maker to gain better insight into the alternatives actually facing him or her and to develop a meaningful set of hypotheses and techniques for evaluating them.

Once alternatives have been generated, there are two rather general descriptive features of the choice process that should be considered in developing prescriptive models of choice. First, the response mode, framing of choices, and context influence choices between alternatives in ways that are not predicted by normative models of choice. Slovic, Griffin, and Tversky illustrate these phenomena very clearly through a series of controlled experiments that support the compatibility hypothesis whereby the weight of a particular attribute is augmented by its compatibility with the response.

Second, simple rules are often utilized by individuals for reasons of bounded rationality. Furthermore, in many situations they may work almost as well as more complicated rules. The very interesting simulation studies by Payne, Bettman, and Johnson (in this volume) substantiate this point using production systems. The use of threshold models as described in Wallsten's chapter also suggests that individuals utilize simplified rules to ease the cognitive burden of their choice process.

In my opinion, these descriptive findings have important implications for developing prescriptive tools for individual decision makers and for public policy. The first point suggests that how one presents information can determine what course of action is taken; hence, one needs to be very careful in pointing this out to the decision maker. The second point indicates that simple rules may be reasonable to use but that one needs to know in what situations they are most appropriate. I illustrate below the implications of these two features for public policy-making in three areas.

Investing in Public Programs

Consider the following example inspired by Slovic, Griffin, and Tversky's chapter. Table D1 presents three alternative programs for saving lives. The

TABLE D1
Investing in Public Programs

Program	Probability	Lives Saved	Cost ($million)
A: AIDS education	.99	1,000	100
B: AIDS research	.01	100,000	100
C: Highway safety	1	?	100

first two relate to AIDS: program A is an educational program that is almost certain to save 1,000 lives, and program B is a research program that has a low probability of saving 100,000 lives. Both programs cost $100 million. The certainty of saving 1,000 lives in program A suggests that it will be preferred to program B in much the same way that H bets are preferred to L bets in the experiments reported by Slovic, Griffin, and Tversky even though "lives saved" is a nonmonetary outcome.

Should a policymaker be interested in finding ways of justifying program B, then he or she could consider introducing another life-saving program such as program C on highway safety. If it is asked how many lives would have to be saved in program C for a person to be indifferent between programs A and C, the response is likely to be approximately 1,000. However, if the same question is asked in relation to program B, then an individual is likely to respond with a number considerably larger than 1,000. According to the experimental evidence reported by Slovic, Griffin, and Tversky, the attribute on which the match is made is likely to be overweighted owing to compatibility. Hence, using this elicitation approach, program B would be preferred to program A.

Siting Noxious Facilities

There is considerable empirical evidence suggesting that, unless a proposed facility is considered sufficiently safe, communities will be opposed to having it nearby even if offered substantial amounts of compensation (Peele 1987; Kunreuther, Desvousges, and Slovic 1988). In other words, safety is of such importance that it dominates any other consideration. Compensation is therefore viewed by individuals as a bribe in exchange for losing lives rather than as a payment for assuming a small additional risk.

This descriptive finding suggests that people utilize simple rules such as some type of threshold model in dealing with these risks. Attributes such as fear and dread play a very important role in people's attitudes toward noxious facilities that present a risk. Even if the experts present verbal or quantitative information that the chances of an accident are extraordinarily low, residents in the area often do not believe them or focus their attention on the unknown consequences to themselves and future generations. Hence, they are unwilling to make the trade-offs that are implied by any type of compensation program.

For example, Michael Dukakis, as governor of Massachusetts, used a threshold approach in delaying the Seabrook 1 nuclear power plant from operating. The New Hampshire plant, two miles from the Massachusetts border, has not developed evacuation plans that "will protect the lives of the people of Massachusetts living within the ten mile evacuation zone," noted Dukakis. The governor's statement that "the likelihood [of a major accident at Seabrook] is irrelevant" suggests that he was using an outcome threshold (Wessel 1986).

The use of simple rules to justify decisions makes them appealing to individuals who have this role to play. A prescriptive challenge in the spirit of Edwards's chapter is to make available decision-aiding tools such as interactive computer programs that highlight the benefits and costs of alternative actions and therefore encourage trade-offs. To the extent that such approaches are utilized, one may be able to overcome the myth that we can achieve zero risk.

Purchasing Protection after Disaster

There is considerable empirical evidence that suggests that people use relatively simple rules in determining what type of protective activities to invest in regarding low-probability, high-consequence events. People tend to buckle up after they learn of an accident to someone else or have been involved in one themselves. We buy battery cables only after the car does not start. There is interest in buying earthquake insurance following a disaster even though individuals know that the probability of another earthquake occurring is lower than the probability of the first occurring. After the Bhopal disaster in India, chemical companies undertook extensive studies of the operation of their plants and their treatment of chemicals that had the potential to cause catastrophic accidents.

This behavior is consistent with Slovic, Griffin, and Tversky's compatibility hypothesis. Individuals and institutions are likely to overweight the loss dimension following a disaster or accident and hence decide that they should take protective action to avoid such events in the future. Unfortunately, in many cases this may be too late since considerable damage, both economic and physical, will have already occurred.

Prescriptively, there are certain steps that can be taken that shift the weight to certain attributes that are likely to induce an individual to take protective action before a disaster occurs. Consider the seat belt problem, in which individuals appear to place considerable weight on the small chance of an accident per trip by assuming that "it cannot happen to me." One approach for modifying the weights on the different dimensions of the problem is to present probabilistic information using a longer time horizon. Slovic, Fischhoff, and Lichtenstein (1978) experimented with presenting probabilities of an accident in terms of a lifetime of driving rather than individual trips and induced greater interest in seat belts in a controlled laboratory setting. Yet this type of information program would be difficult and costly to implement in a real-world context.

An alternative would be to develop a set of economic incentives for inducing seat belt usage that focused on the costs of not protecting oneself. Fines for not wearing a seat belt are the most well-known example of this approach. Now the problem is framed in terms of the chances of getting caught without a seat belt rather than in terms of the probability of an accident. In addition, law-abiding citizens may decide to buckle up simply because they are required to do so rather than because of their concern with being stopped.

An insurance policy that explicitly states that an injured victim will receive no reimbursement for medical expenses if he or she were not wearing a seat belt at the time of an accident may also increase voluntary usage of belts. Suppose such an incentive induces a group of motorists to buckle up. This suggests that the prospect of not collecting on one's insurance causes individuals to reevaluate the implications of their earlier decision rule that "it cannot happen to me." These individuals are likely to shift some of the weight assigned to the accident probability to the attributes associated with consequences. We are only beginning to understand how individuals weight different attributes associated with a problem and how their concern or worry about the consequences of events translates itself into actions.

CONCLUDING COMMENTS

To conclude my comments, I would like to return to one of Hilly Einhorn's provocative papers on the role that experience plays in the decision-making process (Einhorn 1980). He pointed out that, in an environment in which the majority of the population uses bad decision rules, individuals who use better rules may perform quite well. In other words, one does not have to use optimal rules to survive. He summarized his conclusions by quoting from Erasmus to the effect that "in the land of the blind the one eyed man is king." These three chapters provide a number of interesting directions for overcoming our blind spots in dealing with choice under uncertainty and, in the process, may produce a few more one- and even two-eyed decision makers.

REFERENCES

Bell, D. 1982. Regret in decision making under uncertainty. *Operations Research* 30:961–81.

Budescu, D. S. W., and T. Wallsten. 1988. Decisions based on numerically and verbally expressed uncertainties. *Journal of Experimental Psychology: Human Perception and Performance* 14:281–94.

Einhorn, H. J. 1980. Learning from experience and suboptimal rules in decision making. In *Cognitive processes in choice and decision behavior,* ed. T. S. Wallsten, 1–20. Hillsdale, N.J.: Erlbaum.

Hogarth, R. M., and H. Kunreuther. 1988. Pricing insurance and warranties: Ambiguity and correlated risks. Working paper no. 88-11-01. University of Pennsylvania, Wharton School, Center for Risk and Decision Processes.

Howard, R. 1988. Uncertainty about probability: A decision analysis perspective. *Risk Analysis* 8, no. 1:91–98.

Kunreuther, H., W. Desvousges, and P. Slovic. 1988. Nevada's predicament: Risk perceptions and attitudes toward a high level nuclear waste repository in Nevada. *Environment* 30, no. 8:16–33.

Loomes, G., and R. Sugden. 1982. Regret theory: An alternative theory of rational choice under uncertainty. *Economic Journal* 92:805–24.

MacCrimmon, K. R., and D. A. Wehrung. 1986. *Taking risks: The management of uncertainty.* New York: Free Press.

March, J. G., and Z. Shapira. 1987. Managerial perspectives on risk and risk taking. *Management Science* 33, no. 11:1404–8.

Peele, E. 1987. Innovation process and inventive solutions: A case study of local public acceptance of a proposed nuclear waste packaging and storage facility. In *Symposium on Land Use Management.* New York: Praeger.

Slovic, P. 1987. Perception of risk. *Science* 236:280–85.

Slovic, P., B. Fischhoff, and S. Lichtenstein. 1978. Accident probabilities in seat belt usage: A psychological perspective. *Accident Analysis and Prevention* 10:281–85.

Weinberg, A. 1972. Science and trans-science. *Minerva* 10:209–22.

Wessel, D. 1986. Seabrook unit faces licensing hurdle as Dukakis rejects evacuation plans. *Wall Street Journal,* 22 September, p. 10.

Discussion

KENNETH R. MACCRIMMON

EXPECTED-UTILITY THEORY AS BENCHMARK AND LINK

Expected-utility theory, as developed by Ramsey ([1926] 1931), von Neumann and Morgenstern (1947), and Savage (1954), has proved to be the focal point of many studies of decision making in the latter part of the twentieth century. Contrary to some early opinions, expected-utility theory is not tautological. Its precise formulation, particularly its axiomatic foundations, made clear that actual behavior could conflict with the behavior required by the theory.[1]

Even though behavior in accordance with the theory requires a high order of rationality, the everyday behavior we observe around us can usefully be assessed in terms of deviations from the theory. Many fruitful empirical studies have utilized decision problems in which a person's reflective choices violate expected-utility theory. Such paradoxes have highlighted a series of robust biases and effects in actual decision behavior as well as pointing the way to productive directions for revising the theory.

This widespread reliance on expected-utility theory serves as an important benchmark and an integrating link between otherwise diverse studies. The three chapters in this part are a good illustration of the point; except for a common reliance on expected-utility theory, they would seem quite disconnected. Each chapter, however, utilizes a different one of the three major paradoxes of expected-utility theory. I therefore focus on the use and interrelation of the paradoxes in commenting on the chapters.

Major Themes of the Three Chapters

The chapters by Slovic, Griffin, and Tversky, Wallsten, and Edwards all deal with inadequacies of our current theories of decision making (expected utility and its successors) when confronted with the realities of actual decision making. Let us look first at their main arguments, taking them in order from a more focused attack to a broader one.

Slovic, Griffin, and Tversky.—Many empirical studies have found that people's choices are inconsistent with their valuations of uncertain alternatives. This phenomenon, called preference reversal, is perhaps the most

---

1. I will use the term *expected-utility theory* to refer to all theories in which the representation is a linear expectation of utilities, regardless of the source of the probabilities.

fundamental challenge to our standard theories of preference. How can we understand and explain what is happening? Tversky and his associates propose an explanation based on a compatibility effect. The research described by Slovic, Griffin, and Tversky shows that the numeraire that people are asked to use to value an alternative leads to an undue emphasis on that characteristic of the alternative. So, when people are asked to value an alternative in terms of money, they overemphasize the money aspects; when they are asked to value an alternative in terms of probability, they overemphasize the probability. These compatibility effects are inconsistent not only with expected utility theory but also with various recent revisions of the theory, including Kahneman and Tversky's (1979) prospect theory. Moreover, the authors also show how the compatibility effect applies to preferences among multiple-attribute alternatives in an environment of certainty as well as to beliefs in the form of predictions based on multidimensional stimuli.

Wallsten.—Our standard theories of choice under uncertainty do not necessarily conform to the way people perceive and process information in the real world. Although people are often trained to use numerical probabilities when the underlying events are relatively precise, it is felt to be misleading to use numerical probabilities when the events are vaguely defined or the information is tenuous. Can our theories be adapted to account for using qualitative rather than quantitative beliefs? Wallsten focuses on this issue by considering situations in which the uncertainty cannot easily be translated into probabilities. He presents empirical results showing that the use of linguistic descriptions such as *quite likely* or *improbable* can result in outcomes that are not significantly different from those obtained using numerical probabilities.

Edwards.—Expected-utility theory and its modifications are too narrowly focused on choice. Even casual observation of real decision making reveals that much of the difficulty in making decisions stems from formulating the problem and developing options. How should we study these broader phenomena? Edwards suggests some directions, such as a more explicit use of goals to generate alternatives, developing a better understanding of the decision context, and so forth. He argues that, to be a more complete and more helpful model of decision making, the standard theories need to be extended.

Thus, all three chapters push at the boundaries of current theories, showing their inadequacies in dealing with a person's actual choice behavior. It is important to observe that the problems identified in all three chapters point not only to inadequacies in expected-utility theory but also to inadequacies in prospect theory, weighted-utility theory, and most other generalizations of expected-utility theory.

THE DUAL PAIR PARADIGM AND DECISION PARADOXES

The Dual Pair Paradigm

In considering these three chapters, and indeed in setting a context for any study in the expected-utility tradition, it may be helpful to explore the standard paradigm. By considering the standard paradigm explicitly, we can begin to see connections among various studies that are not obvious on the surface.

The traditional objects of study in behavioral decision theory are binary lotteries. A binary lottery offers one payoff with a particular probability (i.e., if a particular event occurs) and a second payoff with the complementary probability (i.e., if the event does not occur). For example, you receive $100 if a coin falls heads up and have to pay $50 if the coin falls tails up. In the simplest case, the second payoff is zero (i.e., status quo).

The usual approach to using binary lotteries in behavioral decision studies is what I will call the dual pair paradigm. The subject is asked to choose which of two alternatives, call them A and B, she prefers. Then, some other pair, call them A' and B', is generated in such a way that A' is directly associated with A and B' is directly associated with B. The subject's preference between A' and B' is compared with her preference between A and B. A' and B' have been generated in such a way that theory requires that a preference of A over B entails a preference of A' over B'.

There are two common ways for the modified alternatives, A' and B', to be generated: by the experimenter as a systematic modification of the original lotteries (type 1) or by the subject as a result of her valuation of the original lotteries (type 2). Both ways of modifying the original lotteries lead to productive empirical settings, as will be explored below.

Reset Requirements

Before exploring the implications of the dual pair paradigm, consider an important condition that Edwards develops in his chapter. The dual pair paradigm requires that the subject make a reset. She is first asked to consider a choice between A and B and then is told to forget she made such a choice and now consider A' and B'. As I understand Edwards, he claims that such resets are difficult or impossible to do and that the subject is therefore actually making a portfolio decision. That is, Edwards would say that, rather than considering the dual pairs, a person is deciding between the four alternatives A and A', A and B', B and A', and B and B'.

Undoubtedly, it could be the case that a person would think in such portfolio terms even if she were given instructions not to do so, as is standard in such experiments. If Edwards is right in contending that resets do not occur and that choices offered in experiments are automatically converted into portfolio decisions, then doubt is cast on many experimental results.

My belief, based on observing choices in both experiments and real-world decisions, is that people can reset. For example, in management decision making, it is quite common for managers to give subordinates conditional decision rules of the form, "When I'm not around, if the choice of A versus B occurs, choose A, but, if the choice of A' versus B' occurs, choose A'." It would be quite inappropriate for the subordinate to form these choices into a portfolio version. Furthermore, people seem to understand such conditional decision rules and to use them correctly.

Major Paradoxes of Decision

Over the past 40 years, various decision problems, in the dual pair form, have been developed and studied in experiments. Three such problems have achieved prominence over all others: the Allais (1953) paradox, the Ellsberg (1961) paradox, and the Slovic-Lichtenstein paradox (Lichtenstein and Slovic 1971; Slovic and Lichtenstein 1968).[2] With any group of subjects, one can be sure that the presentation of any of these three problems will yield results that contradict expected-utility theory. Hence, they have earned the label *paradox*.

Empirical study of such paradoxes has given us a better understanding of decision behavior and has pointed the way toward useful revision of our theories. Each of the three chapters is focused on one of the three paradoxes, so I explore connections among the paradoxes using the dual pair form.

THE ALLAIS PARADOX AND EDWARDS'S CHAPTER

The Allais Paradox

The oldest paradoxes in expected-utility theory were developed by Allais in the early 1950s. Edwards uses an Allais paradox to present his argument about resets. It is not always recognized that there are various forms of the Allais paradox. Edwards uses the common-consequence form. However, for ease of showing the dual pair paradigm, consider the more transparent common-ratio form. An example may be given as follows:

A: Receive $10,000 with probability 1.00;
B: Receive $20,000 with probability .80.

When offered a choice, most people select A, preferring the sure $10,000 to the 20 percent chance of getting nothing with B. Now construct new alternatives in which A' is based on a 5 percent chance of A (and a 95 percent chance of $0) and B' is based on a 5 percent chance of B (and a 95 percent chance of $0); hence:

A': Receive $10,000 with probability .05;
B': Receive $20,000 with probability .04.

The same person who preferred A to B is now likely to prefer B' to A', arguing that the .01 difference between the probabilities is too small to matter. Expected-utility theory, however, requires that the choice of A over B entails the choice of A' over B'. The choices of A and B' violate the independence (also called substitutability) axiom. The term *common ratio* refers to the probability ratio 5:4, which applies to both pairs. For more details, see MacCrimmon and Larsson (1979), in which both the common-consequence and the common-ratio problems were studied and in which these names were given.

---

2. Heretofore, what I am calling the Slovic-Lichtenstein paradox has been called preference reversal. I discuss reasons for the name change below.

Edwards's Chapter and the Allais Paradox

Edwards objects to the Allais paradox in the dual pair form because it involves resets. He proceeds to reformulate the problem as a portfolio choice. Unfortunately, this change turns an interesting decision problem into an uninteresting one.

In considering the interrelations among decision problems, note that there are two basic errors: segmentation error (type 1), or treating interrelated problems as separate, and aggregation error (type 2), or treating separate problems as interrelated. Since most problems have some connection to other problems, it is necessary to separate them in order to be able to comprehend and solve them. In the process of segmenting problems, some important connections are ignored. Edwards rightly points out the mistakes of type 1, such as using separate budget categories, for example, not considering that the money spent on a vacation could be spent on new furniture.

However, in expressing a concern for errors of type 1, Edwards proceeds to commit the type 2 error—forming separate problems into a portfolio choice. His discussion of a portfolio version of the Allais paradox is correct if the problem is presented as a portfolio choice (which it is not) or if the subject cannot reset (but, as we have seen, subjects can and do reset). While he is quite right to be concerned about whether resets "take" in experiments, the reformulation changes the nature of the Allais problem and downplays the importance of resets in practice.

In any case, the portfolio version of this problem as given by Edwards is uninteresting. On the other hand, the (dual pair) version as stated by Allais has been studied by many researchers and has led to the intriguing general modifications of expected-utility theory, including those by Chew and MacCrimmon (1979), Machina (1982), and Kahneman and Tversky (1979).

So, while I believe that Edwards is mistaken in converting the Allais paradox into the uninteresting portfolio form, I do think he has usefully directed our attention to portfolio problems. This focus is useful in at least two senses. First, we should use better means to obtain resets when we want them in our experiments, and we should monitor subjects' behavior to assure that assumed resets are occurring. Second, we should focus more attention on real portfolio problems since they do occur frequently in real-world decisions but have been relatively neglected in experiments in behavioral decision theory. The interest in portfolio research does not mean, though, that we should convert conditional decision problems into portfolio problems.

THE ELLSBERG PARADOX AND WALLSTEN'S CHAPTER

The Ellsberg Paradox

Ellsberg devised another decision problem of the dual pair form in which both pairs involve experimenter-derived choices. The Ellsberg paradox is addressed to the common distinction made between risk and uncertainty. One form of the Ellsberg paradox (called the event-complement form) nicely illustrates the dual pair format. Consider the following decision problem:

A: $100 if a black card is drawn from a deck with 50 black cards and 50 red cards;
B: $100 if a black card is drawn from a deck with x black cards and $100 - x$ red cards.

Most people would prefer the bet based on the known deck composition (i.e., A) rather than the bet based on the deck in which the card composition is not known (i.e., B). Let us modify A and B simply by changing the color:

A': $100 if a red card is drawn from a deck with 50 black cards and 50 red cards;
B': $100 if a red card is drawn from a deck with x black cards and $100 - x$ red cards.

Here too most people would prefer the bet based on the known deck composition. Unfortunately, the choice of A over B and A' over B' contradicts expected-utility theory.[3] Specifically, it is inconsistent with Savage's (1954) sure-thing principle. Alternatively, if one tries to infer probabilities, one finds that the beliefs for the unknown deck are subadditive and hence not probabilities.

Wallsten's Chapter and the Ellsberg Paradox

The choices that people make for the Ellsberg problem suggest that they make a distinction between precise and vague events. They prefer the bets on the deck with the known composition because they can assign probability .5 to either a red or a black card in deck A (with the 50 black cards and 50 red cards). However, for the B deck, one must resort to second-order probabilities or alternative representations. Second-order probabilities would seem appropriate if we were told the mechanism by which the B deck was generated. However, barring this information, we might have to resort to linguistic descriptions.

Wallsten refers to the Ellsberg paradox several times, and his research is an extension of earlier work dealing with the paradox, although the experiments he describes do not make direct use of the paradox itself. Instead, he picks up on the theme that there are vague events for which it is not appropriate to use numerical probabilities and, he pursues the possibilities of using linguistic statements of beliefs.[4] His emphasis on the terminology *vagueness avoidance* instead of the more usual *ambiguity avoidance* is a useful clarification.

---

3. Note that, in this case, owing to the complementary nature of the probabilities, we must adjust the dual pair paradigm. A choosen over B requires that B' be choosen over A'.
4. Because it seems desirable to preserve the term *probability* for those beliefs satisfying the standard probability axioms, I refer to linguistic *beliefs* rather than linguistic probabilities.

While Wallsten does not deal with the Ellsberg paradox directly, much of his discussion is closely related. The specific source for Wallsten's consideration of vague beliefs is not the Ellsberg paradox but rather the concern of some users of risk analysis who find that the assignment of numerical probabilities to inherently vague events creates a spurious precision. To talk about the probability of cancer being caused by regular eating of peanut butter sandwiches when the linkage is based on a few studies of rats may be very misleading.

Wallsten's table 2.1 indicates eight cases ranging from well-grounded numerical probabilities to imprecise linguistic descriptions. While I find the table useful, I would find it helpful to consider the state of information as well as the precision of the event itself directly. Moreover, it would seem desirable to separate the underlying situation (the event and the information about it) from the belief representation (numerical, ordinal, linguistic, etc.). Hence, I prefer the following categories: event precise, much relevant information available (type 1; e.g., measured rain greater than .1 inches at the weather station at O'Hare airport from 12:00:01 A.M. until 11:59:59 P.M. tomorrow); event precise, very little information available (type 2; e.g., measured rain greater than .1 inches at 123°19′ west longitude and 48°52′ north latitude from 12:00:01 A.M. until 11:59:59 P.M. tomorrow); event vague, much relevant information available (type 3; e.g., the weather was nice at Greenwich Observatory in mid-June several years ago); event vague, very little information available (type 4; e.g., the weather was nice in Seguret in mid-June 1788). For each of these categories, then, one would consider the reasonableness of the varying precision of belief representations: linguistic versus numerical, absolute versus relative (i.e., ordinal), and point versus interval.

Type 1 situations would seem to be ripe for the assignment of numerical probabilities. Type 2 situations are ones in which one might be tempted to resort to linguistic beliefs if more relevant information cannot be collected. However, the first step would seem to be an attempt to collect enough information on which to base numerical probabilities. In type 3 situations, one should try to make the definition of the event more precise and then assign numerical probabilities since the information would support precisely stated beliefs. Type 4 situations require both better specification and more information. The propensity to resort to linguistic belief statements is far stronger in such situations than in the others.

Wallsten and his associates have shown that people can seem to make reasonable decisions with just linguistic descriptions of beliefs after they have been suitably calibrated. This will be encouraging to those users of probability estimates who have felt uncomfortable with numerical probabilities for events that are ill specified or not well grounded in data. On the other hand, Wallsten's subjects who received numerical probability information did at least as well and, as recipients, indicated a preference for receiving numerical probabilities. While Wallsten emphasizes the support the results give for using linguistic probabilities, it seems, correspondingly, that they give at least equal support for sticking with numerical probabilities.

Coming back to the Ellsberg paradox, one wonders how it would be stated in the linguistic terms preferred by Wallsten. Presumably, the bets on deck A could be stated as having a probability of .50, but would the deck B bets be stated as being *equally likely, unknown,* or what? The process by which perceptions of uncertain situations of different types get converted into linguistic statements becomes very important.

The normative implications of Wallsten's research lead us to consider two possibilities: provide the best numerical probabilities, but, if they are very shaky, note it; use the level of precision (numerical, ordinal, linguistic) that most closely mirrors the vagueness in the data. Given that our standard theories are based on numerical probabilities, there would seem to be an impetus toward the first alternative. One wonders why it is not better to provide numerical probabilities but with an indication of the evidence on which they are based? When the event cannot be specified more precisely or better information cannot be obtained, then these cautions should be noted.

The descriptive implications of this research are not as clear cut. Wallsten makes reference to how people might process information linguistically, but the results by themselves do not offer a new predictive theory. Other researchers have focused on building models to capture the actual choice behavior when dealing with vague events, a notable example being Einhorn and Hogarth (1985).

THE SLOVIC-LICHTENSTEIN PARADOX AND SLOVIC, GRIFFIN, AND TVERSKY'S CHAPTER

The Slovic-Lichtenstein Paradox

A third major paradox of expected-utility theory is an example of the type 2 form discussed under "The Dual Pair Paradigm" above. That is, although the experimenter presents the original pair A and B, the subject generates the revised pair A' and B', and her preferences are such that expected-utility theory is contradicted. Heretofore, this problem, developed in the late 1960s by Paul Slovic and Sarah Lichtenstein, has been called preference reversal, but I call it the Slovic-Lichtenstein paradox for two reasons. First, study of the problem has been as widespread as the other two major paradoxes and the developers deserve having their name associated with it. Second, and more important, the term *preference reversal* can be used to describe any of the three paradoxes as well as choices in other problems in which the preference in the second pair is inconsistent with the preference in the first. Hence, the term *preference reversal* should be reserved for more general use rather than for the specific problem first studied by Slovic and Lichtenstein.

The Slovic-Lichtenstein paradox can be illustrated by offering the subject the following choice:

A: Receive $1,000 with probability .99;
B: Receive $10,000 with probability .09.

After making a choice, the subject is asked to provide a certainty equivalence (i.e., price) for A (call this value A') and a certainty equivalence for B (call this value B'). In standard terminology, A is called the P bet and B the $ bet.

Expected-utility theory, and almost all other theories of decision, requires that, if A is chosen over B, then A' should be larger than B'. Yet, in the example given above, many people will choose A over B, yet will give a certainty equivalence for B considerably more than $1,000. Coupled with the fact that their certainty equivalence for A will be less than $1,000, such preferences contradict our theories (expected-utility theory as well as weighted-utility theory, prospect theory, etc.).

Slovic, Griffin, and Tversky's Chapter

A series of results involving the Slovic-Lichtenstein paradox and its extensions is reflected in the Slovic, Griffin, and Tversky chapter. The first part of their chapter deals with prediction and the last half with preference. The preference part covers both decisions under uncertainty and decisions under certainty. The common element is that a two-dimensional stimulus is presented and the response (either prediction or preference) is asked for in terms of one of the two dimensions.

The chapter focuses on a particular explanation, called the compatibility effect, for preference reversals wherein the response dimension will lead to an overweighting of that dimension of the alternatives. Thus, asking for a price for the two alternatives in the Slovic-Lichtenstein paradox leads to payoffs being weighted more than probabilities and (because of the low bound of the P bet) to the $ bet being more overpriced than the P bet.[5]

The compatibility effect is analogous to what MacCrimmon and Smith (1986) called the numeraire hypothesis.[6] In that paper, it was shown that the choosers of the $ bet reversed when probability equivalences were obtained. An efficient design was used in that study in that all the data involving choices, certainty equivalences, and probability equivalences could be checked for some type of preference reversal. Overall, there were eight possible patterns of choices with only two patterns consistent with expected utility. Two patterns were consistent with the numeraire hypothesis (i.e., the compatibility effect) in that the $ bet had a higher certainty equivalence than the P bet but the P bet had a higher probability equivalence than the $ bet. Two patterns were consistent with what was called the response-mode hypothesis wherein

---

5. Note that, in Slovic, Griffin, and Tversky's chapter, the standard labels have been changed. The P bet is now called H and the $ bet L.
6. My decision to work on this problem was stimulated by Goldstein and Einhorn (1987) and, in particular, by a memorable morning in the hills of Santa Barbara spent talking with Hilly Einhorn about preference reversal and related topics.

the two equivalence orders agreed with each other but not with the choice order. The remaining two patterns had no apparent rationale and can be considered as the random base case. The results showed that consistency with expected utility and inconsistency in the form of the numeraire hypothesis were equally prevalent and twice as common as the response-mode hypothesis, which in turn was twice as common as the base (random) case. Hence, in this study, there was strong support for a numeraire/compatibility effect. For further details, see MacCrimmon and Smith (1986).

In 1987 follow-up study, MacCrimmon and Smith (1989) obtained data that raises doubts about the strength of a compatibility (i.e., numeraire) effect. If a compatibility effect is the primary explanation, then obtaining valuations in terms of payoff equivalences in a reference lottery (what Slovic, Griffin, and Tversky call payoff matching) should result in preference reversals. The results with payoff equivalences should be similar to certainty equivalences since they both entail valuations in money terms. However, our results are clear cut; there were no significant asymmetric reversals whenever payoff equivalences were used. There is a hint of the same result in Slovic, Griffin, and Tversky's chapter when they report that, apparently, the monetary dimension looms even larger in pricing than in payoff matching. If any follow-up studies are conducted in which one is trying to put the numeraire/compatibility effect to a true test, the researchers would be well advised to focus on payoff equivalences and seek to explain why different results are obtained than with certainty equivalences. Perhaps there is a primary or secondary effect that involves a distinction between certainty valuation versus uncertainty valuation (i.e., reference-lottery) methods.

My conclusion is that there does seem to be a strong numeraire (compatibility) effect but that this is only one part of a much more complicated explanation. A more complete explanation must take into account other factors, especially an inherent vagueness in people's preferences. Why should our theories require that a person have a precise equivalence (i.e., price) for an uncertain lottery? Even for very simple lotteries, such as those used in the paradox statements above, most people have a hard time providing a reliable single equivalence. The available data show considerable variability in the equivalence (i.e., pricing) responses of subjects. It is surprising to me that very few studies of preference reversal bother to check the reliability of their data. The major discrepancies that we find lead us to place more weight on a theory of vague preferences than on a compatibility effect (MacCrimmon and Smith 1986, 1989). There is not space to develop the notions here, but it would be interesting to consider their interconnections with Wallsten's development of vague beliefs.

Procedure Invariance and Consistent Transaction Modes

Tversky and his associates, in the chapter in this volume and in Tversky, Sattath, and Slovic (1988), and Tversky, Slovic, and Kahneman (in press), describe how preference reversal entails a violation of either transitivity or procedure invariance. However, procedure invariance is not quite correct as stated in those papers because of mixing transaction modes. The correct statement is, "Procedure invariance states that the choice and the valuation yield the same ordering of options *when considered in the same transaction mode*" (italics added). Hence, contrary to Slovic, Griffin, and Tversky, it is not necessarily true that "a bet B is preferred to a cash amount X if and only if the cash equivalence of B, C_B, exceeds X" when cash equivalent is defined as minimum selling price—as they do. As they state it, a person should be indifferent between receiving B and receiving X when X is equal to C_B, yet C_B was the person's selling price of B *if they already had it to sell* rather than their gift equivalence when they did not have it.

To see the importance of keeping the transaction modes straight, let us consider exactly what Slovic, Griffin, and Tversky's expression $C_H = H >^* L = C_L >^* C_H$ *means in terms of their own definitions:* $C_H = H$: receiving the selling price of H is indifferent to giving up H when one holds H; $H >^* L$: receiving H as a gift is preferable to receiving L as a gift; $L = C_L$: receiving the selling price of L is indifferent to giving up L when one holds L; and $C_L >^* C_H$: receiving the monetary amount C_L as a gift is preferable to receiving the monetary amount C_H as a gift (since preference over money is monotonic with money and by definition $C_L > C_H$). Note, then, that one is comparing apples and oranges in that one is using information about selling modes to make inferences about gift modes.

In fact, if one used their formulation to develop a money-pump argument, as is implied, one would be mixing gift modes, selling modes, and buying modes. For a further discussion of the effect of transaction modes in the Slovic-Lichtenstein paradox as well as data comparing selling prices, buying prices, and gift prices, see MacCrimmon and Smith (1987). An earlier discussion of the incorrect conclusions that can result from a failure to differentiate between transaction modes is given in Toda and MacCrimmon (1972).

SUMMARY

Preference Reversal in the Large: The General Concept

In the dual pair paradigm, if someone chooses A over B, then the theory requires that she choose A' over B'. If she prefers B' to A', we can say that she has committed a preference reversal, that is, her preference as manifested in the second set is reversed from what is required by her preference as manifested in the first set. Heretofore, the term *preference reversal* has been used for the particular type of preferences that I have called a Slovic-Lichtenstein paradox. I wish to reclaim the term *preference reversal* for general use.

Note that, for the Allais paradox and the Ellsberg paradox, there is an inconsistency between the ordering of two pairs of choices. Hence, these paradoxes are preference reversals. In particular, they are preference reversals of the choice versus choice form. In contrast, the Slovic-Lichtenstein paradox is due to an inconsistency between the ordering of one pair of choices and the ordering of their certainty equivalences. Hence, it is a preference reversal of the choice versus equivalence form.

Although all the early studies of preference reversal involved certainty equivalences, MacCrimmon and Smith (1986) showed that reversals also occur when valuations are obtained using uncertainty equivalences (e.g., probability equivalences). In their "matching" study, Slovic, Griffin, and Tversky also find preference reversals using noncertainty equivalences.

The consideration of different types of equivalences suggests a focus on a third possible inconsistency: preference reversals of the equivalence versus equivalence form. In research quite distinct from the traditional preference reversal studies, Hershey and Schoemaker (1982) have investigated differences between certainty equivalences and probability equivalences. These comparisons and others were studied by MacCrimmon and Smith (1989) in a study involving all combinations of choice, certainty equivalences, probability equivalences, and payoff equivalences. Asymmetric preference reversals were found for all combinations except those involving payoff equivalences.

My main argument here is that, by constructing a concept of preference reversal in the large, one can see interconnections between strands of research that have heretofore been treated separately.

In summary, then, it helps to have a basic understanding of the standard paradigm to be sure that we are satisfying the requirements that our empirical studies be relevant to theory and that we see the deeper connections among studies that seem unrelated. Virtually all the studies, whether they involve the classic paradoxes, traditional preference reversals, or valuation differences, utilize the dual pair paradigm.

Beyond Expected-Utility Theory

Even when it is clearly wrong, expected-utility theory has proved surprisingly useful. In the years to come, our theories of decision will move further and further away from expected-utility theory, but it should still serve as a benchmark.

Part of the strength of expected utility theory is due to its axiomatic foundations. Even the majority of studies that pay no attention to the axioms are strengthened by the fact that a set of simple axioms implies the expected-utility representation. It is to be hoped that the axiomatic tradition can be continued while modifying the theory to deal with actual behavior.

Slovic, Griffin, and Tversky have shown that the dimension on which alternatives are valued or predicted can have a pronounced effect. This compatibility or numeraire effect should be reflected in theories purporting to deal with actual preferences. Wallsten has drawn our attention to alternative ways of dealing with vague beliefs. As noted above, my own studies have shown that the counterpart concept, vague preferences, can play a key role in understanding preference reversals. All these factors should be considered in revisions and extensions of expected-utility theory.

However, one must realize the limitations of expected-utility theory. It is unlikely to serve a useful role in the aspects of decision making to which Edwards draws our attention—problem formulation and option generation. New ways of theorizing and studying decision behavior are needed.

One person that could have provided the insights into those new directions will sadly not be with us. Hilly Einhorn made important contributions in all the scientific areas (prediction and preference, judgment and decision, certainty and uncertainty) covered by the chapters under consideration here. In addition to pointing out new directions, the chapters serve to remind us of the breadth and importance of Hilly's contributions.

REFERENCES

Allais, M. 1953. Le comportement de l'homme rationnel devant le risque: Critique des postulats et axioms de l'école américaine. *Econometrica* 21:503–46.
Chew, S. H., and K. R. MacCrimmon. 1979. Alpha-nu choice theory: A generalization of expected utility theory. Faculty of Commerce and Business Administration, University of British Columbia. Typescript.
Einhorn, H. J., and R. M. Hogarth. 1985. Ambiguity and uncertainty in probabilistic inference. *Psychological Review* 92:433–61.
Ellsberg, D. 1961. Risk, ambiguity, and the Savage axioms. *Quarterly Journal of Economics* 75:643–69.
Goldstein, W. M., and H. J. Einhorn. 1987. Expression theory and the preference reversal phenomena. *Psychological Review* 94:236–54.
Hershey, J. C., and P. J. H. Schoemaker. 1982. Sources of bias in assessment procedures for utility functions. *Management Science* 28, no. 8:936–54.
Kahneman, D., and A. Tversky. 1979. Prospect theory: An analysis of decision under risk. *Econometrica* 47:263–91.
Lichtenstein, S., and P. Slovic. 1971. Reversals of preference between bids and choices in gambling decisions. *Journal of Experimental Psychology* 89:46–55.
MacCrimmon, K. R., and S. Larsson. 1979. Utility theory: Axioms versus paradoxes. In *Expected utility and the Allais paradox,* ed. M. Allais and O. Hagen, 333–409. Dordrecht: Reidel.
MacCrimmon, K. R., and M. R. Smith. 1986. Imprecise equivalences: Preference reversals in money and probability. Paper presented at the University of California, Santa Barbara, Conference on Preference Reversals, January.
———. 1987. Transaction reversals: Buying and selling lotteries. Faculty of Commerce and Business Administration, University of British Columbia. Typescript.
———. 1989. Choice and valuation: General reversals in preference. Faculty of Commerce and Business Administration, University of British Columbia. Typescript.
Machina, M. 1982. Expected utility analysis without the independence axiom. *Econometrica* 50:277–323.
Ramsey, F. P. [1926] 1931. Truth and probability. In *The foundations of mathematics and other logical essays,* ed. R. Braithwaite. London: Routledge & Kegan Paul.
Savage, L. J. 1954. *The foundations of statistics.* New York: Wiley.
Slovic, P., and S. Lichtenstein. 1968. The relative importance of probabilities and

payoffs in risk-taking. *Journal of Experimental Psychology Monograph* 78, no. 3, pt. 2:1–18.

Toda, M., and K. R. MacCrimmon. 1972. The efficient determination of true preference equivalences. In *Contributions to experimental economics,* ed. H. Sauermann. Tübingen: Mohr.

Tversky, A., S. Sattath, and P. Slovic. 1988. Contingent weighting in judgment and choice. *Psychological Review* 95:371–84.

Tversky, A., P. Slovic, and D. Kahneman. In press. The causes of preference reversal. *American Economic Review.*

von Neumann, J., and O. Morgenstern. 1947. *Theory of games and economic behavior.* 2d ed. Princeton, N.J.: Princeton University Press.

Part Two

INTRODUCTORY COMMENTS

The two chapters in this part are concerned with two quite different issues in the use of decision analysis, the set of techniques for analyzing decisions that have emerged from statistical decision theory (see also Edwards in this volume). One is a broad set of conceptual questions about the applicability of decision analysis, the other a more technical discussion about the manner in which specific judgments should be elicited and aggregated in applications of decision analysis.

In chapter 4, Lichtenstein et al. discuss decision making at the societal level. In particular, how should a societal decision maker, for example, a public official charged with determining health policies, act when taking decisions on behalf of the public? What happens when his or her rational analysis of a situation implies an action that contradicts the wishes of the public he or she represents? This raises a spectrum of new issues for behavioral decision researchers. For example, the axiomatic foundations of the basic decision theory model apply only to a unique decision maker concerned with his or her own welfare. Thus, from a theoretical viewpoint, how does one generalize to a collection of individuals? Second, from a descriptive viewpoint, the problems treated typically fall more within the domain of scholars in the areas of political science or sociology. Nonetheless, Lichtenstein et al. show that both the decision-analytic framework and findings from descriptive research on individual decision making can illuminate several issues. This does not mean that the authors are able to resolve all the dilemmas posed; on the other hand, it is not clear that these issues have been satisfactorily addressed by other disciplines.

As noted above, Kleinmuntz's chapter is a technical contribution to the literature on decision analysis. Underlying the philosophy of decision analysis is the "divide and conquer" strategy. A complex problem is amenable to analysis if it can be broken up into parts and the parts analyzed separately and then reassembled in order to understand the decision as a whole. Kleinmuntz applies this philosophy to the process of eliciting judgments that are to be used as inputs to decision-analytic models. He shows analytically that if quantities to be assessed (e.g., an estimate of a probability) are decomposed so that the assessor can make a series of part judgments that are subsequently aggregated by a formula, there are many circumstances in which this leads to better—in the sense of more reliable—judgments. To do this, Kleinmuntz exploits an approach developed in psychometrics for decomposing judgments into "true" and "error" components and takes advantage of aggregation to eliminate random error. The insights provided by Kleinmuntz's chapter are in delimiting the conditions under which decomposition of judgments leads to more reliable judgments and in suggesting what levels of decomposition and aggregation might be appropriate.

4

When Lives Are in Your Hands: Dilemmas of the Societal Decision Maker

SARAH LICHTENSTEIN, ROBIN GREGORY,
PAUL SLOVIC, AND WILLEM A. WAGENAAR

A societal decision maker (SDM) is a person who makes risky decisions on behalf of others. Most of the time, such decisions should be based on the wishes and beliefs of the affected people. This chapter explores a few cases in which it could be argued that the SDM, in making the decision, should in good conscience disregard the desires or beliefs of the affected people. Several simplifying assumptions are made: the SDM uses decision analysis in making the decision; the affected people speak with one voice on the matter under dispute; the SDM and the people disagree on an issue vital to the decision problem; the SDM cannot delay the decision or otherwise avoid the disagreement; the SDM is motivated only to make the right decision; and the SDM can effectuate an unpopular decision. In this context, the following dilemmas are discussed. What if the people object to the use of decision analysis? What if the people reject the axioms of decision analysis? What risk attitude should the SDM adopt? What concerns should be included in the analysis? What if people are misinformed? What if individual and societal perspectives differ? Do people really want what they say they want? For some of these questions, we argue that the SDM should make decisions against the wishes of the people; for others, we are not sure how to resolve the dispute.

C ONSIDER THE PERSON whose job it is to make risky decisions on behalf of others; that is, decisions with outcomes affecting other people, perhaps many other people, to a far greater degree than the outcomes affect the decision maker. We call such a person a societal decision maker, or SDM. Our society has many such people, making decisions about energy options, drug-testing standards, genetic research, automobile emissions, and the like. Such problems are challenging social issues because the stakes are high and the value issues complicated.

In seeking assistance for these complex problems, it is natural that SDMs would turn to research in decision making for assistance. As people who earn our living by producing and disseminating research results, we would hardly want things to be otherwise.

There is a rich collection of advice available. Over the past several decades, research on decision making has developed a considerable body of knowledge about how risky decisions are made and how they can be improved (e.g., Kahneman, Slovic, and Tversky 1982; Slovic, Lichtenstein, and Fischhoff 1988). Although studies from many disciplines have made important contributions to the topic, in this chapter we focus on contributions from the psychological study of decision making and risk perception. Research in behavioral decision theory examines how individuals and groups actually do make decisions, in contrast to normative prescriptions about how such decisions ought to be made (Einhorn and Hogarth 1981; Slovic, Fischhoff, and Lichtenstein 1977). Studies of public perceptions of risk examine people's expressed opinions about hazardous activities or technologies and attempt to determine how information about uncertain outcomes should be communicated among decision makers, lay people, and technical experts (Slovic 1987).

We have long argued (Fischhoff et al. 1981), and still believe, that policymakers need to take account of public values and perceptions in societal decisions about risk. Failure to do so entails several dangers.

First, the people may know something that the experts are missing. For example, one finding from risk-perception studies (Slovic, Fischhoff, and Lichtenstein 1979) is that experts tend to assess the risks of a technological option in terms of its expected fatalities and injuries whereas lay people typically use a broader evaluation scheme that includes the voluntariness of exposure to a risk, the degree to which it is understood scientifically, and a number of other psychological factors. It is not hard to argue that such richer, more comprehensive views express important criteria that should be included in the decision process.

Second, the disregard of public opinion may result in a decision that cannot be implemented because of outspoken public opposition. Even if it is possible to force the decision on an unwilling public, the outcomes may be quite different from, and worse than, anticipated. Did politicians in 1917 predict that the adoption of the Prohibition amendment to the U.S. Constitution would lead to a law enforcement crisis and the rise of a wealthy, well-armed, and organized underworld?

Finally, the SDM courts trouble in saying, "I know better than you," and, "I'm doing it for your own good." We resented such claims made by our parents when we were young; as adults, we resent them even more. Our society is structured, by and large, democratically; we would not willingly live under authoritarian rule, even the benevolent regime of a technological elite.

But when SDMs look to the research literature for guidance in representing the public's wishes in their decisions, another danger emerges. Experimental results, naively applied to complex social issues, may result in poor social decisions. In order to know which of the experimental findings are relevant, and when, and under what conditions, SDMs need to ask probing questions of the findings and their interpretation. For example, it is important to know why the public and experts view risks differently. Surely the policy implications are different if the public is misinformed about the facts than if the experts are defining the problem too narrowly.

Thus, our starting point is that incorporating public input will usually lead to better social decisions regarding risk, but we do not believe that this happy outcome is guaranteed. We will try, in this chapter, to suggest when and why SDMs might, in good conscience, go against public opinion in order to make a better social decision.

This is a chapter about "oughts" and "shoulds," about ethical dilemmas. We find ourselves with more opinions than skills as ethicists. We present our views forcefully here in the hope that others, whether agreeing or disagreeing with us, will be moved to contribute to ongoing discussions about the proper role of public input; we believe that these issues contain strong implications for the management of risks in our society. We warmly dedicate this chapter to the memory of Hillel Einhorn, who we believe would have approved of our attempts while arguing with us heartily.

SETTING THE STAGE

Our prototypical decision maker is a regulator who forms one link in a chain of command but whose opinions play a decisive role in the regulatory process. Such people do not stand alone in the world of social dilemmas, forced to approach each decision with only their natural instincts and ethics. Instead, we assume that the SDM will use what has been learned about decision making, as an aid to structuring the decision problem and as a guide to evaluating social needs and the probable consequences of alternative actions.

Although a range of prescriptive approaches is available to the decision maker, we advocate the use of decision analysis. Our reasons are straightforward. First, decision analysis is explicit about its assumptions. It makes clear what is being done and what could be done differently. Second, at its core is subjective expected utility theory, with all its prescriptive power. Third, the multiplicity of objectives and consequences that characterize many decision problems can be incorporated into the decision-analytic framework. Unlike cost-benefit analysis, in which economic attributes so often dominate, decision analysis can fuse "hard, objective" knowledge with "soft, subjective" knowledge and values, thereby encouraging the richest, most responsive characterization of problems.

Our view of the efficacy of decision analysis is perhaps broader than that of authors who see the technique as a tool to help express and organize one's already well-formed beliefs and preferences. In contrast, we suspect that in many situations beliefs and preferences are vague, ill formed, or even nonexistent (Fischhoff, Slovic, and Lichtenstein 1980). In working through a decision analysis, then, a user may be not reporting but actually creating beliefs and preferences. This process produces a better understanding of the problem and may lead to new insights. Ideally, when the decision analysis is finished, the right decision seems obvious. The entire decision analysis then provides an elaborate justification for the decision.

Decision analysis is, we believe, the best method for making complex decisions. But it is not perfect; it cannot be expected to capture every possible aspect of the problem and resolve all issues. Thus, one could complete an analysis and then decide to go against its prescriptions. We do not know the conditions under which this might occur. If it does occur, one at least can feel comforted that the decision analysis has illuminated the issues and provided a fuller understanding of the situation.

We recognize that, particularly in the context of the broadly based social problems with which we are concerned, it is not always true that one single individual has sole decision-making power. But this does not materially affect the nature of the dilemmas we address. We therefore assume such sole authority. If, instead, decisions are made in a group (e.g., by a national parliament or by the three-member U.S. Nuclear Regulatory Commission), the reader can suppose that the others' opinions are evenly split and that one person holds the deciding vote. Of course, elected representatives such as members of the U.S. Congress face a more complicated situation in which current decisions (votes) need to be played off against the desire to ensure future coalitions, protect the good of the political party, and so forth. Nevertheless, a basic characteristic of such decision environments is that individuals are expected to act on behalf of, and for the good of, others.

As a further simplification, we here assume that all members of the affected public agree with one another with regard to the critical aspects of the problem under consideration. This is a useful dodge because it means we can use terms like *the public* as if there were only a single public (and we will say *the experts* as if this group, too, were undivided). However, as anyone with experience in public participation or communication knows, the public rarely speaks with one voice; a key to successful interaction is to identify and understand some of the major distinctions that mark the central actors or stakeholder groups (see Edwards and von Winterfeldt 1987). This is an important topic but one that will not be discussed in this chapter.

Furthermore, we assume that the SDM and the affected group disagree on an issue vital to the decision problem. Thus, for whatever reason, what the affected group says it wants is not the same as what the SDM wants or believes or thinks is right. Moreover, the disagreement is consequential. Showing, via sensitivity analysis, that the disagreement would not materially affect the decision would let our SDM off the hook; we thus exclude this possibility.

Let us continue to press our SDM by taking away other possibilities that might forestall the decision or enable the SDM to avoid squarely facing the problem at hand. We do this not because these possibilities are unrealistic but because they provide convenient excuses to ignore the dilemmas that we want to address. We list four such "outs" that we will not permit.

1. The SDM cannot plead limited resources or limited knowledge and just wait until more or better information comes in. At any rate, there is no reason to believe that more resources or knowledge would necessarily bring about agreement between the SDM and the affected group.

2. The SDM is not motivated by other personal or cultural factors such as, "If I decide that way I'll lose my job," or, "Everyone else in my position has always done it this way." Instead, we assume that the entire motivation for the SDM is to make the right decision.

3. The SDM is able to go against the wishes of the affected public without producing so much objection that the goal of the decision is itself threatened or ruined. Clearly, if this were not true, the SDM should take the objections into account. More interesting, to us, is the question of what SDMs should do when it is possible to implement an unpopular decision.

4. The SDM cannot automatically justify a course of action by simply going along with the desires of the affected group. We consider this a fink out of the lowest order. Without the urgency of a central conflict between the group and the SDM, there is probably no need for the decision maker at all and certainly no need for this chapter.

At this point, we have a competent SDM who is responsible for making an important decision using decision analysis; the SDM faces a major dilemma involving a discrepancy between the unanimous wishes of the affected group and the beliefs of the decision maker (or, as often happens, the advice of the experts). We turn now to consider several such dilemmas.

DILEMMAS OF THE SDM

What If People Object to the Use of Decision Analysis?

People may oppose decision analysis because they believe that formal structuring and the codification of values as numbers can never capture the intuitive essence of a complex problem. We reject this view and urge our SDM to reject it. Although a decision analysis can never be complete, the process of constructing it forces the decision maker to think about the problem in an orderly way, which is a virtue for any difficult decision.

People may also object to decision analysis because it calls for explicit trade-offs between attributes such as lives and money (MacGregor and Slovic 1986). They may object to such trade-offs because they believe that the government has deep pockets ("Spend whatever money it takes to save the lives") or because they find such trade-offs morally repugnant. For this dilemma, we have firm advice for the SDM. Go against the public's wishes. We believe that social decisions are made under real resource constraints, that such constraints tacitly imply trade-offs, and that it is better to make the trade-offs explicit. Decision analysis did not invent these trade-offs; if both the approach and its advocates were to vanish tomorrow, the trade-offs would still remain.

This is quite a strong position. However, we declare an even stronger one.

Because awkward trade-offs (between lives and dollars, pollution and jobs, or the safety of the old and the young) are both so prevalent and so difficult to face, it is the responsibility of the SDM to make them explicit and point them out to the public. Being attentive to public opinion does not require fooling people into thinking that tough decisions need not be made.

What If People Reject the Axioms?

There is plenty of evidence in the research literature showing that utility theory is not a good descriptive theory. Some of its descriptive failures may be traced, directly (e.g., Tversky 1969) or indirectly (e.g., Slovic and Lichtenstein 1983), to violations of one or more axioms. One response to these findings, currently much in vogue, is to invent new versions of utility theory that omit the offending axiom in an effort to make utility theory more descriptively accurate (see Machina 1987). Although we admire much of this work for its creativity, we are not convinced that our SDMs should adopt this new approach.

One reason for sticking with the axioms is that, when they are presented to subjects in transparent form, they are less likely to be violated than when they are not made explicit (Tversky and Kahneman 1986). One view of the experiments showing violations of rationality is that they are designed to study our customary intuitions and decision habits to gain insight into how people think but that the underlying structure of the tasks is sometimes not obvious, even tricky. Tversky's (1969) subjects, for example, vigorously proclaimed that they neither violated nor wanted to violate transitivity, although they did make intransitive choices. It is possible that, if the public were to apply as much careful thought to, say, Allais's paradox as did Savage (1972, 101–3), they, like he, might end in accepting the sure-thing principle despite strong initial intuitions against it.

It might be wrong to be too optimistic, however, about the public's eventual acceptance of the axioms. People may ascribe, instead, to Samuelson's (1950) suggestion that they should "satisfy their preferences and let the axioms satisfy themselves." For example, Lichtenstein interviewed some preference reversal subjects extensively (Lichtenstein and Slovic 1971). One subject, when he came to understand that the pattern of his responses could be used as a money pump against him, readily agreed to change those responses to make them consistent. But he then plaintively noted that he had been instructed, at the outset, to report his true preferences; he still felt that his original responses were faithful to that instruction. And the majority of Slovic and Tversky's (1974) subjects were unconvinced by Savage's analysis of the Allais problem.

One or more axioms of utility theory are violated whenever choices are made on the basis of the avoidance of ambiguity (Ellsberg 1961). Ambiguity and vagueness about probabilities, even when expressed as second-order probabilities, are formally irrelevant in decision analysis but seem to play a large role in personal beliefs. There is also increasing evidence that the avoidance of ambiguity is affecting public policy. For example, insurers are unwilling to cover chemical and waste-processing firms because it is so difficult to specify the distribution of anticipated claims (Kunreuther 1987). Einhorn and Hogarth (1987) have suggested that ambiguity aversion may explain why some technologies are feared more than their first-order probabilities of failure or accident warrant.

Dislike of ambiguity may be a pure preference, like the preference for a "fair" coin over a coin biased in some unknown way. However, it is possible that what appears to be an aversion to ambiguity really represents other concerns. For example, the public may legitimately recognize that the experts have been wrong before—while being highly confident in their wrong beliefs (Henrion and Fischhoff 1986). Thus, the public might quite rightly trust probabilities based on abundant data more than probabilities assessed by experts lacking such evidence. It would be appropriate for the SDM to include such concerns in the analysis, perhaps by finding some attribute, such as dread or worry, that could serve as a proxy variable for ambiguity. Researchers could help SDMs in this arena by learning more about the structure and correlates of ambiguity aversion.

The jury is still out on the public's eventual acceptance of the axioms of decision theory. But we have a more personal reason for suggesting that SDMs stick to the axioms. We find that, even when we are comfortable with our own violations, we want to hold our SDMs to a higher standard of rational thought. Consider, for example, the theory proposed by Loomes and Sugden (1982), in which transitivity is given up to accommodate feelings of regret. In our own lives, we may make decisions in a way that minimizes regret even if so doing violates transitivity; we might even believe that this is a good thing for us to do. But we do not feel an equivalent need to protect our SDMs from regret in the decisions that they make on our behalf. We, not they, must suffer the consequences, so to hell with their tender feelings. As another example, the SDM might be tempted to prefer options with low ambiguity because a decision made on that basis can be more easily justified and defended to the public (Curley, Yates, and Abrams 1986). We urge our SDM to resist this temptation and make the best decision without regard for later difficulties in justifying it.

In summary, we are inclined to believe that the SDM should stick to the axioms, but we acknowledge that our case for doing so is not strong. Perhaps our best defense of the axioms is a pragmatic one. The SDM who accepts the axioms can get on with analyzing the problem at hand, comforted by the central theorem of decision theory, which states that, when the axioms are accepted, utilities can be measured.

What Risk Attitude Should the SDM Adopt?

Consider a decision situation with one or more attributes having clear, explicit numeraires, such as lives or money. There is plenty of evidence that people's utility curves for such attributes are often risk averse in the domain of gains and risk seeking for losses. Sometimes risk attitudes may apparently reverse with a different response-elicitation method (Hershey and Schoemaker 1985) or a different wording (Tversky and Kahneman 1981). But we suspect that risk attitudes cannot be attributed solely to response biases; our preference for a sure outcome of, say, $50 over a 50-50 gamble paying either $200 or $-$100 is likely echoed in the preferences of many.

The SDM might want to choose a utility function that has the following characteristics: bad outcomes are minimized, catastrophic outcomes are avoided, and the risk of harm is spread equitably among the affected people. Keeney (1980) has explicated the form of a utility function that has each of these characteristics.

Keeney started with n individuals, some or all of whom are at risk of death. If the risk of death to any one individual is independent of the risk to any other, the whole situation can be represented by a vector of probabilities $(p_1, p_2, \ldots, p_n)$ showing the probability, p_i, of death for each individual (more complex lotteries are used to show dependent risks).

These characterizations of risky situations can then be translated into a probability distribution of total number of fatalities, x. If all the deaths are equally bad, the central question is to find the appropriate utility function over x, the number of fatalities. Keeney explores three possibilities.

1. A *risk-neutral* utility function is the only function that will minimize expected fatalities.

2. A *risk-prone* utility function is the only function that is consistent with a preference for risk equity. Keeney defines risk equity as a preference for

$$(p_1, \ldots, p_i, \ldots, p_j, \ldots, p_n)$$

over

$$(p_1, \ldots, p_i + e, \ldots, p_j - e, \ldots, p_n)$$

when the difference between p_i and p_j is less than the difference between $p_i + e$ and $p_j - e$. It follows that the most equitable vector of probabilities is the one in which all the p's are equal. That is, a preference for risk equity is a preference for equally spread risk.

3. A *risk-averse* utility function is the only function that is consistent with a preference for catastrophe avoidance, defined as a preference for probability π of x fatalities over a probability π' of x' fatalities for any $x < x'$ such that $\pi x = \pi' x'$.

One can, thus, achieve only one of the apparently laudable but inconsistent goals of fatality minimization, risk equity, and catastrophe avoidance. Which one should the SDM adopt? We advocate an extreme position, that the SDM should always use a risk-neutral utility function for lives—and for money—for the following reasons.

The SDM surely realizes that the currently considered risk is only one of many. From that perspective, the concept of risk equity gets fuzzy. Is it the SDM's goal, under risk equity, to ensure that all citizens of the country have an equal risk of dying when all regulated activities are taken into account? Short of that absurdity, it is unclear how to choose the number of people and the number of different risks over which risk equity should be sought. If risk equity is difficult to define, risk proneness loses its appeal.

As for catastrophe avoidance, we are ethically uncomfortable with the position that it is better to avoid 10 deaths from a single accident than to avoid one death in each of 10 separate accidents, other things being equal. It seems more compelling to us that it is the moral obligation of the SDM to save as many lives as possible; that implies risk neutrality.

Where money is concerned, a broader perspective will reveal that the current decision is just one of a multitude of demands for expenditures. Any risk attitude other than risk neutrality increases the expected costs and will, in the long run, buy us less. Moreover, risk aversion is sometimes motivated by fears of a large loss. But a possible loss that would threaten the budget of any one individual can be more easily absorbed by the larger budget of a federal agency.

A simplified but not entirely unrealistic conception of many safety decisions is that they involve trade-offs between lives and money. For example, a regulatory agency may have a fixed budget with which to research and regulate a wide variety of risks to life. Alternatively, the agency may realize that there is a limit to the number of different safety regulations that can be imposed on a particular risky industry—too many regulations would bankrupt or collapse the industry. Here, too, the wish to maximize the number of lives saved per dollar spent is consistent only with risk neutrality.

A catastrophic accident, say 100 deaths and 1,000 injuries in an area populated by 100,000 persons, would not only engender great suffering and grief but also place severe strains on community resources such as hospitals and morgues. But these real costs should not be captured by using risk-averse utility functions for death and injury. Instead, they should be included directly as additional attributes in the decision analysis. As to the suffering and grief, we acknowledge that they might be greater than they would be were such deaths and injuries spread out over time and place. But the SDM knows that individual losses are constantly occuring in numbers greater than this—without accompanying newspaper headlines and live television coverage. We believe that the SDM should accept the responsibility of preserving life in small chunks as well as big chunks; risk neutrality fosters this goal.

A concept related to risk equity is called benefit/risk equity. This is the idea, explored experimentally by Keller and Sarin (1988), that it is fair for those who receive more of the benefits to accept more of the risks. As far as we know, this idea is not inconsistent with risk neutrality over number of fatalities, as discussed above.

A further distinction is between the risk to known and unknown lives. We do not know how to advise SDMs regarding the relative importance of these kinds of deaths. We would not want to live in a culture in which the SDM decides not to make a rescue attempt to save a (known) miner now trapped in a cave-in because the rescue money would save more (expected but unknown) lives if spent tomorrow on mine safety. Here may be a case (not well delineated, we admit) in which the SDM should depart from the prescriptions of decision analysis. We fear a possible result of slavish obedience to the analysis: a host of coldhearted regulators disregarding feelings and emotions.

Which Concerns Should Be Included in the Analysis?

We believe that all the attributes that are important to the affected people should be included in the analysis (assuming that the decision is sensitive to those attributes). However, we see some exceptions to this rule.

Attributes that are illegal or for which there is a clear societal consensus of moral objection should be excluded. For example, residents of a community may be opposed to a federally funded building project because they fear that racially mixed construction and operations crews would settle in their area. Such prejudice has been rejected by our society at large and thus should not be given formal standing in the evaluation process.

Other concerns, while valid, may fall outside the SDM's mandate. For example, an SDM charged with making decisions about safety regulations for an existing nuclear reactor should not consider whether the country is becoming too reliant on nuclear power. In this case, the proposed attribute lies outside the bounds of the legislation that grants authority to the SDM; it is a broad social issue that should be played out in some other arena (probably Congress).

A special case of an attribute that may have to be disregarded by the SDM is "not in my backyard," the syndrome whereby each community simultaneously acknowledges the need for a risky facility but refuses to serve as its host. One approach in such cases is for the SDM to emphasize the costs of noncooperation while offering rewards for cooperation (Kunreuther and Kleindorfer 1986). If no community comes through with an acceptance, then the SDM may need to override the narrowly focused interests of any single community in order to serve the broader interests of the region as a whole.

What If People Are Misinformed?

People may disagree with the SDM because they are misinformed about some aspect of a decision. The obvious solution, to inform them, is attractive if it works, but sometimes that may not be feasible.

Communicating the facts may be impossible if the facts are highly complex and technical. For example, scientists are beginning to understand the complex chain of events linking exposure to low-frequency electromagnetic fields (e.g., from electric blankets or can openers) and potentially dangerous changes in human cell structures (Morgan et al. 1987). Without extensive training in areas such as chemistry and cell biology, however, people may be incapable of understanding the risks involved. Thus, resentment may result if the scientists end up saying, "Just take our word for it, folks, this is a risk that should be reduced."

In addition, people may not trust the SDM or the agency represented by the SDM. Thus, whatever they are told is viewed as a probable lie and heavily discounted. In such cases, assurances of trustworthiness are likely to fall on deaf ears. We can suggest that such an agency first eliminate any real causes for distrust and then embark on a long-term strategy of reassurance. But that will not help the SDM in the immediate situation. We know of no remedy for this problem.

People are not very good intuitive scientists. Their views of facts and of possibilities may be inappropriately influenced by cognitive biases and heuristics (Kahneman, Slovic, and Tversky 1982), leading them to a mistaken view of the world. Moreover, such effects can be highly resistant to change (Fischhoff 1982).

Of course, experts and the SDM are also subject to the influence of cognitive biases and heuristics. That is one good reason for using a formal decision-aiding technique like decision analysis. It is far more difficult to disregard relevant base-rate information when one is reminded of it by Bayes's theorem. Similarly, SDMs, like other people, may fail to appreciate the burgeoning growth of exponential functions (Wagenaar and Sagaria 1975). But statisticians (or hand-held calculators) can remedy this failing.

In keeping with our insistence, in this chapter, of holding the SDM to the most difficult case, let us suppose that a vivid, dramatic, but minor accident has artificially elevated (via the availability heuristic) the public's assessment of the probability of disaster for liquid natural gas storage facilities. The accident and resulting change in public views comes just as the SDM is about to issue a new safety regulation governing liquid natural gas storage. The public demands stringency. The experts have studied the situation extensively and have assured the SDM that the regulation need not be as severe as the public demands; the SDM believes the experts' analysis. Newspaper coverage and pubic hearings fail to change the public's beliefs. Let us not suppose that the SDM can say, "Well, it's only money," and issue the stronger regulation. Instead, suppose that the stronger regulation, because of its greater cost, will prevent the implementation of an additional forthcoming safety regulation, one that is expected to save many lives.

What should the SDM do? A dyed-in-the-wool decision analyst may argue that the only thing to do is to analyze this larger problem, looking at both regulations and including such attributes as the effects of the anger and mistrust engendered if the SDM goes against public opinion. This seems sensible, if perhaps prohibitively expensive. But is it really ethical to incorporate, into one's decisions, the public's wrongheadedness? We are not sure.

It is not only facts and possibilities that the public may be misinformed about. They may also be misinformed as to what risk-reduction policies can accomplish. Although specific risks can be reduced, at some cost, Keeney (1988) has noted that the possibility of zero risk is an illusion. Strictly speaking, risk cannot be eliminated; it can only be transferred or delayed. The contrary view, that perfect safety is an attainable goal, can be a source of conflict between the SDM and the affected group, one which the SDM may have little ability to change. Again, we are left with an unanswered question. Is it right for SDMs to alter their decisions in order to appear to be pursuing the illusion of perfect safety?

What If Individual and Societal Perspectives Differ?

In many cases, both the societal and the individual perspective are valid; both can be included in the analysis. Okrent (1987), for example, proposed standards for nuclear power that place separate limits on the risk to whole populations and the risk to any one individual. But what about seat belts? The SDM sees that the costs and consequences of auto accidents extend beyond the immediate victims. Moreover, requiring seat-belt usage nationwide would save hundreds of lives annually. Such savings would likely outweigh the inconvenience of wearing seat belts and may even outweigh the loss of personal freedom entailed by a national law. Should the SDM also include in the analysis the fact that, from an individual perspective, the risk of a fatal accident seems too small to warrant protective action?

Do People Really Want What They Say They Want?

The best way to discover the preferences of the affected group is to ask; answers are generally forthcoming to questions about values. But do people really want what they say they want? Should assertions of preference always be taken at face value?

These are difficult questions on ethical as well as technical grounds. Certainly, it is dangerous to say that a decision maker might know better than someone else what that person really wants; we are rightfully suspicious of people disregarding our wishes "for our own good." Nevertheless, we explore below several skeptical cautions.

First, people's willingness to answer the questions we researchers put to them does not always ensure that they are expressing well-understood and deeply held values, particularly when the questions concern a rare and emotionally laden event. Consider, for example, a patient facing the choice of a radical mastectomy. There may be no way for her to understand the multiplicity of pain, psychological distress, and physical impairment that results from such surgery. How bad is it, really, to be permanently unable to lift one's arm above one's shoulder? We who can do that now do not know.

Second, the way a question is worded can affect the answer. Difficulties may arise especially with emotionally laden terms. With such terms, people may be so impelled by symbolic meanings that they are blinded to differences in how others are using the term. For example, *compensation* may mean *bribery* to some people; this connotation leads them to different values than if the same concept were thought of as *fair payment*.

Other examples of the effect of question framing are myriad (Hogarth 1982). The most troubling ones are those for which it cannot be said that further reflection will reveal the true preference. Some of these involve risk aversion (e.g., Tversky and Kahneman 1981; Hershey and Schoemaker 1985); we have argued above that, in these cases, the SDM should take neither frame, using risk neutrality instead. Other examples cannot be so easily resolved. For example, McNeil et al. (1982) showed that formally equivalent but different ways of presenting information about the probability distribution, over time, of death from a particular kind of cancer led both doctors and patients to have different preferences for surgery versus radiation treatment. Yet neither description can be viewed as a more natural or "correct" way to present probabilistic information than the other.

Third, it is sometimes problematic for a researcher to detect, accurately, the variable that the respondents were attending to. A discouraging cautionary tale has been told by Wagenaar, Keren, and Lichtenstein (1988). They replicated an experiment by Hammerton, Jones-Lee, and Abbott (1982) in which respondents were given a cover story involving an infectious disease on an island with 100 residents and a choice between one of the islanders dying for sure versus each islander having a 1 in 100 chance of dying. Hammerton, Jones-Lee, and Abbott reported that a large majority of subjects preferred the one sure death, which they interpreted as evidence of risk aversion. Wagenaar, Keren, and Lichtenstein found significant differences with apparently minor changes of wording. More disturbing, they found enormous differences when the cover story was changed to one concerning children who had been taken hostage by terrorists (while the underlying structure of the choice remained the same). Respondents then overwhelmingly chose the risk-equitable option (in which each child has a 1 in 100 chance of dying while in hostage). It became clear (after running 1,366 subjects and 11 story variations) that, whatever it was that the subjects were reacting to, it was not the conflict between risk aversion and risk equity. In the face of these results, SDMs seeking guidance on people's preferences should be cautious in generalizing from the research literature.

Finally, expressed preferences are cheap, but are people willing to put their money where their mouths are? It does not necessarily follow that, if I say that I prefer coffee over tea, I will order coffee when it costs twice as much as tea. The risk-perception literature has delineated several attributes (e.g., catastrophe avoidance) that people rely on when describing activities or technologies as risky and when judging the need for risk reduction. SDMs could make use of this information by incorporating these attributes into their analyses. But doing so means that attaining a more desired state on one of these attributes will, usually, entail giving up a bit of some other attribute, perhaps money or lives. It is critically important to examine people's willingness to make such trade-offs. Slovic, Lichtenstein, and Fischhoff (1984) explored the importance of catastrophe avoidance relative to lives lost. Their subjects were asked to choose one of two possible safety measures for a factory. One would reduce the incidence of single-fatality accidents, thereby saving about 30 lives a year. The other would reduce the probability of a multiple-fatality accident (or, in another form, the number of lives lost thereby), thus reducing the expected lives lost by 27 per year. A substantial proportion of the subjects chose the former, suggesting that they did not view catastrophe avoidance as more important than saving three lives. This suggestion needs more direct confirmation. SDMs should be hesitant to incorporate the public's strongly felt desires until the public is asked to put their money where their mouths are.

CONCLUSIONS

Our purpose in writing this chapter is to encourage others to join us in thinking about the ethical problems faced by SDMs in making decisions when their views differ from those of the affected public. We feel compassion for the SDM, struggling to do the right thing in difficult circumstances. We want our SDM to be intellectually well armed with an understanding of decision analysis sufficient to ensure that complex social problems can be viewed from a broad, consistent perspective. We also want our SDM to have a backbone, able to go against (while never ignoring) public desires, and a heart, caring for and respecting (but not always acquiescing to) public views.

This is a tall order, we admit. These are tough problems, unavoidably so. We recognize that the world of laboratory experiments, which is at the root of both behavioral decision theory and risk perception, is a far safer and simpler place than the world faced by SDMs. Yet we also believe that the link between experimental and policy settings is strong.

In an important sense, what the SDM knows has got to be enough; the problems do not allow the luxury of indecision. But neither do they permit complacency; as students of decision making, we are able to tell SDMs far less than they would like to know. One implication is that more research is needed, research about the consequences of SDMs' actions as well as about what people want their SDMs to do. Another implication is that decision theorists should be encouraged to seek out real-world decision-making settings, as rich sources of inspiration and as challenging settings to explore the validity of laboratory-based findings. Finally, we need to learn more about the ethical bases for decision making so that SDMs can feel more secure in knowing when to lead, when to follow, and when to punt.

REFERENCES

Curley, S. P., F. Yates, and R. A. Abrams. 1986. Psychological sources of ambiguity avoidance. *Organizational Behavior and Human Decision Processes* 38:230–56.
Edwards, W., and D. von Winterfeldt. 1987. Public values in risk debates. *Risk Analysis* 7:141–58.
Einhorn, H., and R. Hogarth. 1981. Behavioral decision theory: Processes of judgment and choice. *Annual Review of Psychology* 32:53–88.
―――. 1987. Decision making under ambiguity. In *Rational choice: The contrast between economics and psychology*, ed. R. Hogarth and M. Reder, 41–66. Chicago: University of Chicago Press.
Ellsberg, D. 1961. Risk, ambiguity, and the Savage axioms. *Quarterly Journal of Economics* 75:643–69.
Fischhoff, B. 1982. Debiasing. In *Judgment under uncertainty: Heuristics and biases*, ed. D. Kahneman, P. Slovic, and A. Tversky, 422–44. New York: Cambridge University Press.
Fischhoff, B., S. Lichtenstein, P. Slovic, S. Derby, and R. Keeney. 1981. *Acceptable risk*. New York: Cambridge University Press.
Fischhoff, B., P. Slovic, and S. Lichtenstein. 1980. Knowing what you want: Measuring labile values. In *Cognitive processes in choice and decision behavior*, ed. T. Wallsten, 117–41. Hillsdale, N.J.: Erlbaum.
Hammerton, M., M. W. Jones-Lee, and V. Abbott. 1982. Equity and public risk: Some empirical results. *Operations Research* 30:203–7.
Henrion, M., and B. Fischhoff. 1986. Assessing uncertainty in physical constants. *American Journal of Physics* 54:791–98.
Hershey, J. C., and P. J. H. Schoemaker. 1985. Probability versus certainty equivalence methods in utility measurement: Are they equivalent? *Management Science* 31:1213–31.
Hogarth, R., ed. 1982. *New directions for methodology of social and behavioral science: Question framing and response consistency*. San Francisco: Jossey-Bass.
Kahneman, D., P. Slovic, and A. Tversky, eds. 1982. *Judgment under uncertainty: Heuristics and biases*. New York: Cambridge University Press.
Keeney, R. L. 1980. Equity and public risk. *Operations Research* 28:527–34.
―――. 1988. Facts to guide thinking about life-threatening risks. In *Proceedings of the IEEE 1988 International Conference on Systems, Man, and Cybernetics*. Oxford: Pergamon.
Keller, L. R., and R. K. Sarin. 1988. Equity in social risk: Some empirical observations. *Risk Analysis* 8:135–46.
Kunreuther, H. 1987. The failure of EIL coverage: Gridlock in environmental insurance. *Environment* 29, no. 1:18–20, 31–34.
Kunreuther, H., and P. R. Kleindorfer. 1986. A sealed-bid auction mechanism for siting noxious facilities. *American Economic Review* 76:295–99.
Lichtenstein, S., and P. Slovic. 1971. Reversals of preference between bids and choices in gambling decisions. *Journal of Experimental Psychology* 89:46–55.
Loomes, G., and R. Sugden. 1982. Regret theory: An alternative theory of rational choice under uncertainty. *Economic Journal* 92:805–24.
MacGregor, D., and P. Slovic. 1986. Perceived acceptability of risk analysis as a decision-making approach. *Risk Analysis* 6:245–56.
Machina, M. J. 1987. Choice under uncertainty: Problems solved and unsolved. *Economic Perspectives* 1:121–54.
McNeil, B. J., S. G. Pauker, H. C. Sox, Jr., and A. Tversky. 1982. On the elicitation

of preferences for alternative therapies. *New England Journal of Medicine* 306: 1259–62.

Morgan, M. G., H. K. Florig, I. Nair, and G. L. Hester. 1987. Power-frequency fields: The regulatory dilemma. *Issues in Science and Technology* 3:81–91.

Okrent, D. 1987. The safety goals of the U.S. Nuclear Regulatory Commission. *Science* 236:296–300.

Samuelson, P. A. 1950. Probability and the attempts to measure utility. *Economic Review* (Tokyo) 1:167–73.

Savage, L. J. 1972. *The foundations of statistics*. New York: Dover.

Slovic, P. 1987. Perception of risk. *Science* 236:280–85.

Slovic, P., B. Fischhoff, and S. Lichtenstein. 1977. Behavioral decision theory. *Annual Review of Psychology* 28:1–39.

———. 1979. Rating the risks. *Environment* 21, no. 3:14–20, 36–39.

Slovic, P., and S. Lichtenstein. 1983. Preference reversals: A broader perspective. *American Economic Review* 73:596–605.

Slovic, P., S. Lichtenstein, and B. Fischhoff. 1984. Modeling the societal impact of fatal accidents. *Management Science* 30:464–74.

———. 1988. Decision making. In *Handbook of experimental psychology,* vol. 2, *Learning and cognition,* ed. R. C. Atkinson, R. J. Herrnstein, G. Lindzey, and R. D. Luce, 673–738. New York: Wiley.

Slovic, P., and A. Tversky. 1974. Who accepts Savage's axiom? *Behavioral Science* 19:368–73.

Tversky, A. 1969. Intransitivity of preferences, *Psychological Review* 76:105–10.

Tversky A., and D. Kahneman. 1981. The framing of decisions and the psychology of choice. *Science* 211:453–58.

———. 1986. Rational choice and the framing of decisions. *Journal of Business* 59, no. 4, pt. 2:S251–S278.

Wagenaar, W. A., G. Keren, and S. Lichtenstein. 1988. Islanders and hostages: Deep and surface structures of decision problems. *Acta Psychologica* 67:175–89.

Wagnaar, W. A., and S. D. Sagaria. 1975. Misperception of exponential growth. *Perception and Psychophysics* 18:422–26.

5

Decomposition and the Control of Error in Decision-Analytic Models

DON N. KLEINMUNTZ

Decision-analytic models rely on the general principle of problem decomposition: large and complex decision problems are reduced to a set of relatively simple judgments, and these component judgments are then combined using mathematical rules derived from normative theory. This chapter discusses the value of decomposition as a procedure for improving the consistency of decision making. Various definitions of error and consistency are discussed. Linear decomposition models are argued to be particularly useful for the control of random response errors in the component judgments. Implications for decision-analysis research and practice are considered, and decision makers' evaluations of the costs and benefits of decision analysis are discussed.

ONE OF THE DISTINCTIVE CHARACTERISTICS of decision research is the continuing interaction between descriptive and normative theories of judgment and choice. Historically, this involved a one-sided exchange in which the normative theory was taken as a given—intuitive responses were compared to normative standards of optimality or rationality and, often, found to be deficient (Edwards 1961; Einhorn and Hogarth 1981; Kahneman, Slovic, and Tversky 1982; Rapoport and Wallsten 1972; Slovic, Fischhoff, and Lichtenstein 1977). More recently, the exchange of ideas has become a dialogue. For instance, both psychologists and economists have raised important questions about the descriptive validity of rationality assumptions in economic theory (Hogarth and Reder 1987; Simon 1978). Another recent development has been the use of the results of descriptive studies of decision making to guide attempts to reformulate the axiomatic foundations of utility theory (Bell and Farquhar 1986; Fishburn, 1982, 1988; Machina 1987).

One area that blends normative logic with descriptive insight is the set of techniques known as decision analysis. These techniques represent an engineering approach to decision making, drawing on both normative and descrip-

---

I would like to thank James Dyer and H. V. Ravinder for many suggestions and stimulating ideas about the topics covered in this chapter. Robin Hogarth, Benjamin Kleinmuntz, and David Schkade provided helpful comments on earlier drafts. The comments of the participants of the MIT Judgment and Decision Making Research Seminar are also appreciated.

tive theory to prescribe methods intended to improve the effectiveness of decision making (Howard 1988; von Winterfeldt and Edwards 1986; Winkler 1982). Decision analysis relies on the general principle of problem decomposition: a large and complex decision problem is broken down into a representation consisting of alternatives, beliefs, and preferences. Typically, the decomposition process is the result of a cooperative effort by the decision maker and a decision analyst. The analyst guides and assists the decision maker, who must identify and assess the components. An important contribution of the analyst is to help ensure that these component judgments conform to the requirements of the normative theory so that they can then be combined using mathematical rules derived from that theory. An advantage of this approach is the reduction of information-processing demands since the decision maker can focus sequentially on simpler individual components of the problem. Also, the cognitively demanding task of information combination can be performed by the model, typically implemented on a computer. Furthermore, the framework is general enough to incorporate information from diverse sources, including both "hard" data and "soft" subjective assessments.

One of the important contributions of psychological research to decision analysis has been in understanding the methodological problems associated with the assessment of the component judgments. In particular, research has emphasized the potential for serious errors in the assessment of uncertainty (Hogarth 1975; Lichtenstein, Fischhoff, and Phillips 1982; Wallsten and Budescu 1983) and preference (Farquhar 1984; Fischhoff, Slovic, and Lichtenstein 1980; Hershey, Kunreuther, and Schoemaker 1982). The general conclusion is that these judgments are extraordinarily sensitive to features of assessment procedures like response modes and question formats, aspects of the problem context, the decision maker's own preconceptions, and the interaction between the decision maker and the analyst (Fischhoff 1980). For a variety of reasons, no single assessment methodology has emerged or is likely to emerge as error free (Fischhoff 1982). Practical recommendations for coping with error include using more than one assessment procedure in order to check for consistency and performing sensitivity analysis to determine whether a model is robust over a plausible range of assessment errors (von Winterfeldt and Edwards 1986).

Yet another approach is to build error theories that can help predict and explain the cumulative effect of assessment errors (Fischer 1976; Fischhoff 1980). The purpose of this chapter is to contribute to the development of an error theory of this type. Specifically, I will argue that decision-analytic decompositions that use a linear aggregation rule have a built-in error-control mechanism that can help decision makers achieve greater consistency despite the presence of errors in component assessments. Understanding the nature of this error control can both provide useful insights into the theory and practice of decision analysis and help identify some unresolved issues related to the use of decomposition as a decision-aiding approach.

The chapter is organized as follows. First, various definitions of error in judgment are discussed. Second, the ability of linear decompositions to control response errors are considered. Third, a number of practical issues related to the use of decomposition and some areas for further research are identified. Finally, the chapter concludes with an analysis of the conflicting objectives associated with the use of decomposition in decision analysis.

DEFINITIONS OF ERROR IN JUDGMENT

There are numerous ways to define and measure the quality of judgment and choice. Much of the decision-making literature is concerned in one way or another with the issue of consistency or inconsistency of behavior. Hogarth (1982) draws a distinction between two standards of consistency: logical consistency and process consistency. First, it is important to realize that consistency is a relative concept—behavior is consistent or inconsistent when compared to some criterion or standard. One possible standard is consistency with the rules of a normative system (e.g., utility theory, probability theory, deductive logic, and so on). Hogarth uses the term *logical consistency* to convey the notion that this comparison has an all-or-none quality since responses are either consistent with the logical premises of the normative system or not.

A different comparison can be obtained by examining the consistency of behavioral processes across time or situations. Hogarth uses the term *process consistency* to refer to the extent to which an individual applies the same psychological rule or strategy when making judgments. One form of process consistency is the extent to which an individual applies the same underlying process across different problems. Violations of this type of process consistency have been demonstrated by experimental subjects who reveal different preferences depending on how a decision problem is described (Tversky and Kahneman 1981) or the way in which a response is elicited (Tversky, Sattath, and Slovic 1988). Note that Tversky and Kahneman have argued that these "framing" effects are also a violation of logical consistency. Specifically, they identify a normative rule called invariance: "Two characterizations that the decision maker, on reflection, would view as alternative descriptions of the same problem should lead to the same choice—even without the benefit of such reflection" (Tversky and Kahneman 1987, 69). However, violations of process consistency do not necessarily lead to violations of logical consistency, or vice versa. For instance, a decision maker might reflect on two problem descriptions and decide that they are not alternate descriptions of the same problem. The use of different decision processes in those two problems need not have any normative implications.

Another form of process consistency involves the consistency of responses to the same problem on two independent occasions. This form of response variability might be caused by unpredictable fluctuations in attention or shifts in processing strategy. One approach to analyzing the two forms of process consistency is to use a statistical model of the response process in which judgments are assumed to be jointly determined by systematic and random components (Eliashberg and Hauser 1985; Hershey and Schoemaker 1985; Laskey and Fischer 1987; Wallsten and Budescu 1983). The two components may be interpreted in a number of different ways. For instance, one could view the systematic component as the individual's "true" internal opinion and the random component as distortions introduced in the expression of those judgments. An extreme version of this position is to assume that the internal opinions are logically consistent. Under this assumption, it is possible, in principle, to estimate the normatively appropriate true opinion from the observed judgments (Lindley 1986; Lindley, Tversky, and Brown 1979).

Unfortunately, there are persuasive arguments against the existence of logically consistent internal opinions. Judgments of both probabilities and preferences have been shown to suffer from systematic as well as random response errors. Among the most pervasive systematic effects are response-mode biases—the use of different question forms or response scales producing consistent, predictable differences in assessed probabilities (Hogarth 1975; Wallsten and Budescu 1983) and in assessed preferences (Goldstein and Einhorn 1987; Herskey, Kunreuther, and Schoemaker 1982; Hershey and Schoemaker 1985; Slovic and Lichtenstein 1983). Another problem with assuming well-formed internal opinions is that there seem to be many instances in which both uncertainties and preferences are ambiguous (Einhorn and Hogarth 1985; Fischhoff, Slovic, and Lichtenstein 1980; March 1978). Neither beliefs nor preferences are always known in advance; instead, they are often constructed when needed.

The lack of fixed, precise internal judgments does not preclude the statistical approach to analyzing systematic and random components of judgment: the model assumes that, if the same situation were repeated a number of times and an individual were able to respond to the same question independently each time, then the set of responses would constitute a hypothetical statistical distribution. The expected value of this distribution is the systematic component of judgment; the variance of the hypothetical distribution is the random component. The expected value should be viewed not as a true internal opinion but rather as jointly determined by the person, task, and context. This perspective is general enough to allow for constructed beliefs and preferences: systematic variations in opinions due to differences in question formats, response modes, and other features of the task and context can be modeled by shifts in the expected value of the hypothetical distribution. The variance of the distribution represents both unpredictable response errors and, perhaps, inherently stochastic variability (i.e., vagueness) in underlying opinions (Eliashberg and Hauser 1985).[1]

What is the appropriate standard for consistency in decision making? This

---

1. This partition of judgment into systematic and random components is equivalent to the respective psychometric concepts of validity and reliability. For further discussion, see Wallsten and Budescu (1983, 152–54).

is, of course, a loaded question since there is no reason to presuppose that only one standard exists. Because decision analysis is firmly grounded in a particular normative theory, von Neumann–Morgenstern utility theory, logical consistency has usually been granted precedence. However, recent developments in utility theory have created an embarrassment of riches in the form of a variety of proposals for alternative utility theories (Bell and Farquhar 1986; Fishburn 1988; Machina 1987). Many of these developments involve weakening utility theory axioms related to either transitivity of preferences or independence of preferences and probabilities. The issue is no longer whether decisions ought to be consistent with a normative standard but rather which normative standard to be consistent with. Unfortunately, to date no one has proposed a logical basis for choosing a normative standard for choice. Ultimately, this reduces to resolving such questions of judgment as how much we like the outcomes produced by a normative theory, whether we believe the axioms from which the theory was developed, and how much we value maintaining consistency with particular logical principles (Einhorn and Hogarth 1981, 59–61).

To summarize, the distinction between logical and process consistency is crucial. Furthermore, any assessment of decision analysis that rests solely on considerations of logical consistency is problematic. In the next section, I will consider the value of decision analysis with respect to process consistency.

DECOMPOSITION AND PROCESS CONSISTENCY

Consider two different strategies for making a judgment. One is an unaided intuitive holistic procedure, by means of which the individual does the best he or she can given limited information-processing capabilities. The other strategy is a formal decomposition procedure, by means of which a large number of relatively simple intuitive component judgments are made and a mathematical aggregation rule is used. I will first present some examples of decision-analytic decompositions and then examine the effect that decomposition has on process consistency, considering systematic and random sources of error in turn.

Example 1: Probability assessment.—One could intuitively assess the probability of some uncertain future event A or, instead, use a decomposition that explicitly uses information about the relation between that event and a set of background events, denoted $B_1, \ldots, B_n$. Each of the events B_i could be a single event or a scenario composed of the intersection of multiple events. For instance, one could assess different distributions for the future price of oil conditional either on different developments in the political situation in the Persian Gulf or on a set of more complex political and economic scenarios. In addition, it is also necessary to assess the marginal probability of each conditioning event. The major technical requirement is that the background events form a mutually exclusive and exhaustive set of events. This implies that $pr(B_j \cap B_k) = 0$ for $j \neq k$ and $\sum_{i=1}^{n} pr(B_i) = 1$, so the probability of the target event is

$$pr(A) = \sum_{i=1}^{n} pr(A \mid B_i) pr(B_i). \tag{1}$$

Example 2: Multiattribute evaluation.—Many problems involve evaluating choice alternatives using additive multiattribute utility or value functions; that is, an outcome or an alternative X is described by a set of attributes $x_1, \ldots, x_n$. For instance, different job candidates might be described by their various characteristics and qualifications. The component assessments consist of single-attribute utility assessments $u_i(x_i)$ and scaling constants (or attribute weights) k_i that sum to one. The result is the aggregate utility assessment for each alternative:

$$U(X) = \sum_{i=1}^{n} k_i u_i(x_i). \tag{2}$$

Example 3: Expected utility.—Another common example is the evaluation of risky prospects using subjective expected utility. A prospect P consists of a set of uncertain outcomes denoted x_i. Each outcome has a subjectively assessed probability $p_i(x_i)$ of occurring, where $\sum_{i=1}^{n} p_i(x_i) = 1$. If preferences for the outcomes are described by a utility function $u_x(x_i)$, then the value of the prospect is a linear combination of the utilities of each outcome weighted by the probabilities:

$$EU(P) = \sum_{i=1}^{n} p_i(x_i) u_x(x_i). \tag{3}$$

In all three examples shown above, a linear rule is used to aggregate the component judgments. This has the general form

$$a = \sum_{i=1}^{n} b_i c_i, \tag{4}$$

where a denotes the result of aggregating components weights b_i and component evaluations c_i. The weights (b_i) are assumed to sum to one. Both the weights and the components being averaged are obtained using human judgment and are subject to error. In fact, both the holistic judgments and the component assessments can be analyzed in terms of the statistical approach outlined in the previous section: each judgment has an expected value (systematic portion) and a standard deviation (random portion). While these examples are relatively simple, many more complex decision-analytic decompositions can be constructed from these base cases. For instance, decision trees are hierarchical representations of decision problems that can incorporate multiple instantiations of all three types described above. Thus, understanding the effect of linear decompositions on process consistency is an important first step.

Systematic Error and Convergent Validity

One way to address the issue of systematic error is to compare holistic judgments to those obtained through decomposition. Such comparisons are tests of convergent validity: if the systematic portions of two different judgment procedures agree, then it should be possible to observe a high degree of correlation between judgments obtained using each procedure. A number of studies have examined the correlation between multiattribute utility models and intuitive ratings or rankings of a set of alternatives. For a set of 11 studies, the typical range of correlations was between .7 and .9, which supports the notion that the systematic components converge (von Winterfeldt and Edwards 1986, 364–66). Most of these studies focused on one type of multiattribute utility model, riskless additive models. However, there is also evidence indicating a high degree of convergence between riskless and risky utility models as well as between additive and multiplicative decompositions (Barron, von Winterfeldt, and Fischer 1984; Fischer 1977).

The limited evidence accumulated to date indicates a reasonably high degree of convergence between decomposition models and holistic judgments. This raises serious questions about the efficacy of the decomposition approach for controlling systematic biases in judgment. One reason for using decomposition is that holistic judgment is prone to pervasive systematic errors and biases (Kahneman, Slovic, and Tversky 1982). In those situations in which decomposed and holistic judgments do tend to agree, it seems plausible to conclude that decomposition neither increases nor decreases the frequency or severity of systematic response errors—the implication is that decomposition may faithfully reproduce the shortcomings of holistic judgments. Some caution in interpreting these results is needed: high correlations simply indicate that the systematic portions of the two judgments are linearly related. Actually to determine that decomposition and holistic judgments are the same requires examining the intercept and the slope of the regression of one on the other—a comparison that is not typically reported in convergent-validity studies.

Clearly, additional investigations of the influence of decomposition models on systematic biases are needed. An important first step should be the continued development of theoretical accounts of the way in which task characteristics like question formats and response modes lead to systematic errors in component judgments. If analysts can predict the direction and size of systematic errors, then it should be possible to select a portfolio of assessment procedures in such a way that biases cancel each other out. For instance, a known bias in one component could be countered by inducing an opposing bias in another component.

Random Error and Models of Judgment

There have been numerous studies that used statistical methods to develop descriptive models and measure random response errors in holistic judgment (Einhorn, Kleinmuntz, and Kleinmuntz 1979; Hammond et al. 1975; Slovic and Lichtenstein 1971). In a typical study, an individual is presented with a series of multidimensional stimuli, and responses are recorded. A statistical technique (e.g., multiple regression) is used to fit a model of the functional relation between the stimuli and the judgments. The statistical model usually incorporates an explicit random-error term, whose variability can be estimated along with other model parameters. Using either this measure of variability or a closely related goodness-of-fit measure (e.g., the correlation between predicted and actual judgments), it is possible to assess the consistency of the judgment process directly (Hammond, Hursch, and Todd 1964; Hammond and Summers 1972). In other words, the statistical model explicitly measures the relative contribution of the systematic and random components of holistic judgment.

The ability to separate the systematic and random components of judgments has an important practical implication: it is possible to improve the consistency of judgment by replacing the human decision maker with the systematic portion of the judgment process that is captured in the model (Bowman 1963; Dawes 1971; Goldberg 1970). There is considerable evidence that replacing an expert's judgments with a linear model of the expert leads to superior performance, in large part because the model uses the judge's own knowledge more consistently (Camerer 1981; Dawes 1979). On the other hand, this procedure of bootstrapping the expert is "vulnerable to any misconceptions or biases the judge may have. Implicit in the use of bootstrapping is the assumption that these biases will be less detrimental to performance than the inconsistency of unaided human judgment" (Slovic and Lichtenstein 1971, 722). This assumption is plausible in large part because the systematic components of linear models tend to be insensitive to differences in model formulation or parameter estimation (Dawes and Corrigan 1974; von Winterfeldt and Edwards 1986, 420–47).

The success of bootstrapping suggests that formal models, broadly defined, constitute a useful strategy for controlling one specific source of random error, the inconsistencies introduced by the judge's attempts to combine information intuitively. In fact, the psychological literature clearly supports the use of mathematical aggregation rules in place of intuitive information combination processes (Einhorn 1972; Meehl 1954; Sawyer 1966). However, there is an additional source of random error when using decomposition: the components themselves are judgments and are therefore subject to error and inconsistency. The critical issue is how errors in the component judgments propagate through the aggregation process and influence the resulting aggregated judgment.

Error Propagation in Linear Decomposition

A model of error propagation in linear models was recently proposed by Ravinder, Kleinmuntz, and Dyer (1988; hereafter RKD). The RKD model was originally developed to analyze the effect of decomposition on probability assessment (example 1 above). While the RKD model was intended to deal only with probability assessment, the assumptions are general enough to permit the analysis of almost any linear decomposition that can be formulated as a weighted average, like equation 4.

The basic approach of the RKD model is to analyze both holistic and decomposition-based judgments in terms of their systematic and random components. Thus, the holistic judgment, denoted a', is represented by

$$a' = \alpha' + \delta', \tag{5}$$

where α' is the expected value and δ' is the random error, with standard deviation denoted by σ_0. Similarly, for the weights numbered $i = 1, \ldots, n$,

$$b_i = \beta_i + \delta_i, \tag{6}$$

with the standard deviation of each random δ_i denoted by σ_i. Finally, for the components numbered $i = 1, \ldots, n$,

$$c_i = \gamma_i + \varepsilon_i, \tag{7}$$

with the standard deviation of each random ε_i denoted by τ_i. In addition, the random errors may be correlated: the correlation between each δ_i and δ_j is denoted by ϕ_{ij}, and the correlation between each ε_i and ε_j is denoted by ρ_{ij}. However, the model assumes that errors in the two types of components are not related (in other words, δ_i and ε_j are uncorrelated).

The main results of the RKD model are derived from the following expression for the variance of the decomposition estimate a, denoted σ_d^2:

$$\sigma_d^2 = \sum_{i=1}^{n} \sum_{j=1}^{n} (\gamma_i \sigma_i)(\gamma_j \sigma_j)\phi_{ij} + \sum_{i=1}^{n} \sum_{j=1}^{n} (\beta_i \tau_i)(\beta_j \tau_j)\rho_{ij}$$

$$+ \sum_{i=1}^{n} \sum_{j=1}^{n} (\sigma_i \tau_i)(\sigma_j \tau_j)\phi_{ij}\rho_{ij}. \tag{8}$$

Ravinder, Kleinmuntz, and Dyer provide an extensive analysis of this equation as a function of the characteristics of the component judgments. Four major factors help determine the amount of decomposition error. First, as the component judgments become more precise (i.e., less error), the decomposition estimate also becomes more precise. Not surprisingly, the less error there is in the components, the better the decomposition estimate.

Second, the expected values of the weights (β_i) interact with the amount of error in the component c_i evaluations. Large errors in the assessment of a particular c_i component (i.e., large values of τ_i) increase error in the decomposition estimate most when that component is given a lot of weight (i.e., large β_i). Conversely, assessment errors associated with relatively low-weighted components do not influence the decomposition estimate's error very much. One implication is that, when all the component c_i evaluations are assessed with equal amounts of error, an equal-weighting scheme is desirable (e.g., $\beta_i = 1/n$ for all i). However, if a particular component evaluation is known to be assessed unreliably, then decomposition error is improved by shifting weight away from this component toward those components that are estimated with greater precision.

Third, it is possible to analyze decomposition error as a function of the number of components used. Initially, as components are added to the decomposition, error decreases rapidly. However, this improvement occurs only up to a point: eventually, decomposition error begins to increase, although the rate of increase is relatively slow. An intuitive interpretation of the benefits of decomposition can be obtained by viewing the decomposition model (eq. [4]) as a weighted average of the c_i components. Decomposition tends to reduce random error through an application of the law of large numbers: the averaging process causes the component errors to cancel each other out. However, as the number of components increases, the marginal error-reduction value of each additional component decreases. At the same time, recall that the weights being used in the composite are themselves subject to random error so that eventually the added error-reduction benefit of another c_i term is offset by the error in the associated weight.

The fourth and final factor that influences decomposition error is dependency among the errors in the components. In particular, if the c_i components have positively correlated errors, then the error associated with decomposition will be seriously inflated. Positive dependencies among the component errors undermine the value of decomposition because the quantities being averaged are to some extent redundant, reducing the potential benefit to be derived from averaging.[2]

The RKD model can also be used to distinguish conditions under which decomposition successfully controls error from conditions under which holistic judgments are preferable. The critical factor is the precision of the components relative to the precision of holistic judgments. The case for decomposition is easiest to make when the component judgments are more reliable than the ho-

---

2. Technical issues related to the constraint that the weights must add up to one may complicate this analysis. These considerations are beyond the scope of this chapter.

listic judgment, perhaps because the components are relatively simple stimuli (e.g., single dimensions rather than multidimensional objects). If the components have small enough errors, decomposition is virtually guaranteed to decrease random error. However, even if the components are estimated with no greater amount of reliability than the holistic judgment, there is still considerable potential for the averaging process to improve judgment.

While the RKD model provides a theoretical analysis of the value of decomposition for controlling response error, there have been relatively few direct empirical tests of the effectiveness of decomposition approaches. There are two notable exceptions, both investigating estimation of uncertain quantities like "How many people are employed by hospitals in the United States?" or "How many cigarettes are consumed in the United States in a year?" Armstrong, Denniston, and Gordon (1975) demonstrated an increase in accuracy when subjects provided component judgments (e.g., "How many hospitals are there in the United States?" and "What is the average number of employees in a U.S. hospital?"), which were subsequently combined by the experimenters. In a larger and more elaborate study, MacGregor, Lichtenstein, and Slovic (1988) found that decomposition improved performance in terms of both accuracy and consistency across subjects. Also, performance was most effective when subjects received detailed and explicit instructions on what components to estimate and how to combine them.

IMPLEMENTING DECOMPOSITION

What are the implications of the preceding discussion for the use of decomposition as a decision-aiding technique? There are still a number of open issues surrounding decomposition, particularly with respect to the control of systematic biases. However, decomposition does appear to be an extremely effective method for controlling random error. On the other hand, the way in which decomposition is implemented can influence the probability of success. The following four specific implementation issues are relevant in this regard: methods for reducing the amount of error in the components, the implications of selecting different weighting schemes, the problem of dependent errors, and the appropriate level of detail for decomposition.

Methods for Reducing Component Errors

The reliability of the component judgments is determined largely by judgmental ability and the characteristics of the problem. However, the analyst can use certain methods to reduce the component errors. One approach is to use the bootstrapping approach mentioned earlier. For example, in a multiattribute evaluation problem, rather than assessing the weights for each attribute intuitively, a statistical model can be used to estimate the weights. These model-based estimates are likely to be more precise than intuitive assessments (Hammond et al. 1975; Laskey and Fischer 1987).

Another approach might be to use nested decomposition—that is, the components of a decomposition can themselves be estimated through decomposition. For instance, the earlier discussion of subjective expected utility for evaluating risky prospects (example 3) assumed that the component probabilities and utilities would be assessed intuitively. However, each of the component probabilities could be estimated through a decomposition procedure (e.g., example 1), and the utilities could similarly be obtained through a multiattribute decomposition (e.g., example 2). In fact, in some cases it may be possible to extend nesting to multiple levels (e.g., decompose the component probabilities of the component probabilities, and so on). However, there are limits to this approach in practice since the number of judgments required from the decision maker could be quite large.

A less promising approach is to try to obtain multiple independent judgments of the same component and take the average. This approach fails in practice because an individual is not likely to be able to provide repeated independent opinions. Another technique is to use multiple judges: selected component judgments can be delegated to experts who have specialized knowledge about that component. For instance, estimates of probabilities of decision outcomes might be elicited from scientists or engineers, and judgments of values or preferences can be provided by the decision maker (Hammond and Adelman 1976). Although there is little direct evidence on this issue, it seems plausible that experts will be able to provide more reliable judgments in their area of expertise than a novice could (Wallsten and Budescu 1983).

Picking the Best Weighting Scheme

From the perspective of controlling decomposition error, the ideal set of weights is one that maximizes the influence of precisely estimated components and minimizes the influence of unreliable components. However, random assessment errors in the weights themselves are a concern. One method for dealing with this problem is to use a unit weighting scheme, applying a predetermined set of equal weights to the components. The advantage is that random assessment errors associated with the weights are removed. Unfortunately, this advantage is offset by the introduction of a systematic bias since the judgmentally selected weights are unlikely to match the unit weights precisely.

On the other hand, under fairly general conditions, the size of the systematic bias due to simplified weights will be negligible, thus making the trade-off relatively attractive. The condition is either that the number of components be large or that the intercorrelation among components be positive. In choice problems, the latter usually occurs when dominated alternatives are present among the set of choice alternatives (Einhorn 1976; Einhorn and Hogarth 1975; Einhorn and McCoach 1977; von Winterfeldt and Edwards 1986, chap. 11). Some care should be taken in interpreting these conditions: specifically, intercorrelation among components should not be confused with correlated errors as discussed in the RKD model. For instance, Einhorn and Hogarth's analysis of the sensitivity of models to different weighting schemes treats a set of judgment problems as a sample over which different decomposition models are compared. Thus, in their analysis, the correlation of components refers to the correlation of components over the entire set of judgment problems, whereas the RKD model considers only a single judgment problem at a time.

Dealing with Dependent Errors

In fact, one of the most serious threats to decomposition's error-reduction potential is the presence of dependent errors. Any time two judgments are based on shared information, there is a strong possibility of dependent errors. An example would be judgments obtained using an anchoring-and-adjustment strategy (Tversky and Kahneman 1974). Previous research on this strategy has focused on problems with inappropriate choices of an anchor or the tendency to adjust insufficiently from the anchor. But if two different judgments share the same anchor, then any errors in the anchor will be present in both judgments. In fact, in many preference-assessment methods, a sequence of judgments is obtained, creating linkages between successive judgments. For instance, the results of one assessment may be used as an anchor for the next assessment, inducing a positive serial correlation in the response errors (Laskey and Fischer 1987). Furthermore, factors like question presentation formats and response modes can strongly influence the anchoring process (Johnson and Schkade 1989; Schkade and Johnson 1989).

More broadly, dependent errors may result because shared information is used as the basis for different component judgments. A decision maker may consider the same published reports, data bases, or expert advice in making different component judgments. To the extent that there are errors in the common information sources, these errors may carry through to each component judgment. A common version of this problem involves using multiple experts for forecasting: since the experts may have formulated their opinions using shared information, statistically dependent errors reduce the accuracy of aggregate probability assessments and predictions (Clemen and Winkler 1985; Hogarth 1978; Winkler 1981).

Additional research is needed on the distribution of response errors associated with various assessment procedures. Analytic approaches like the RKD model predict the implications of different component-error distributions for the effectiveness of decomposition, but they do not predict what those component errors will look like in practice. Measurement of the variances and covariances of assessment errors in a variety of assessment domains may be informative. Empirical studies could use variations on test-retest reliability designs. A decision maker could assess component judgments on two different occasions, and the correlations between repeated assessments could then be used to estimate the response errors. Another method would be to examine the statistical relation between holistic judgment and the assessed components. This is the approach that Laskey and Fischer (1987) successfully used to identify problems with serial autocorrelation of response errors in multi-attribute utility decompositions.

Choosing the Appropriate Level of Detail

A critical issue in implementing a decomposition is determining how much detail to include in the model. For instance, in multiattribute evaluations, the analyst has considerable leeway in determining how many attributes to include. The RKD model's analysis of random error suggests that the relation between the precision of decomposition and the number of components is single peaked: adding detail to the model helps control error, but only up to a point. Beyond that point, the incremental error associated with a new attribute may outweigh any error-cancellation effect. If a component is known to be assessed unreliably, it will probably not be worth including in the analysis.

On the other hand, there may be systematic error associated with choosing the wrong level of detail: specifically, there are a number of studies suggesting that there are problems with models that incorporate too few components. For instance, in multiattribute-evaluation models, using an incomplete set of factors may, under certain conditions, lead to biased evaluations (Aschenbrenner 1977; Barron 1987; Barron and Kleinmuntz 1986). Another example involves the use of fault trees to estimate the probability of a complex system's failure. When trees are pruned, incorporating specific failure events in a catchall "other problems" category, decision makers systematically underestimate the probability of the missing events. Furthermore, they are unaware that the problem was incompletely represented—what is out of sight is also out of mind (Fischhoff, Slovic, and Lichtenstein 1978). It is important to note that, at present, the RKD model does not address any systematic sources of error. In particular, the analytic framework should be extended to include these issues of "model underspecification"—assessing the sensitivity of decomposition models to missing components.

Valuable information on assessment errors and model underspecification might be derived by analyzing published reports of decision analyses. An example is provided by Politser and Fineberg (1988), who examined the model-underspecification issue through a meta-analysis of published analyses of decision problems in clinical medicine. Their review examined 24 analyses that incorporated a decision tree and expected-utility calculations and found a relation between the complexity of the analysis and the clarity of the results: complexity was measured by the number of terminal branches in the decision tree, whereas clarity was assessed in terms of the expected utility to be gained by performing the analysis (Lindley 1986). The results indicated a strong positive correlation between the complexity of the tree and the clarity of the results: simpler trees had small differences between the value of alternatives, whereas trees with more branches had larger differences in the value of competing alternatives.

Politser and Fineberg use their results to raise important questions about the value of overly simplified analyses. In particular, they point out that many textbook discussions of decision analysis suggest that simple models are adequate since they capture the "essence" of the decision problem. In contrast, their results suggest that the missing components do in fact undermine the value of the results. Since smaller models tend to produce smaller differences in the evaluation of alternatives, conducting only a simplified analysis may underemphasize the differences between alternatives. Of course, common sense would dictate that increased complexity and detail will not always improve an analysis. Larger models require greater expenditures of effort from both the analyst and the decision maker, as they struggle to cope with the added detail and complexity.

Since the benefits of added complexity are likely to diminish on the margin, and since the negative consequences are likely to escalate correspondingly, it seems plausible to argue that there is some optimal intermediate level of complexity that appropriately balances these conflicting goals (Coombs and Avrunin 1977). Of course, the tough question for decision analysts is to determine whether current modeling practices are above or below this level of optimal complexity. While the answer is not immediately apparent, a number of the research strategies discussed above may provide some insight. These include extending analytic frameworks like the RKD model to address issues of model completeness; carrying out experimental investigations of different methods and approaches for decomposition, including explicitly examining the effectiveness of decompositions that vary in level of detail; and analyzing the characteristics of published examples of decision analysis. These three approaches should be viewed as complementary since theoretical analyses, laboratory experiments, and field studies each have compensating strengths and weaknesses.

THE COSTS AND BENEFITS OF DECISION ANALYSIS

Given the points raised above, should decision makers use decision analysis? The relevant question for many decision makers is not whether to use simple or complex models but whether to use a simplified model or rely on unaided intuition (Behn and Vaupel 1982). This perspective emphasizes the fact that it is the decision maker who ultimately must determine the extent to which decomposition and formal analysis should be used. Recent research on the selection of decision strategies has emphasized the cognitive trade-offs between various dimensions of alternative strategies (e.g., the effort required to use a strategy vs. the quality of the resulting decision). Different strategies are selected under different task conditions if the values of these dimensions change (Payne 1982). A generalization of this cost-benefit view is to formulate the strategy-selection process as a metadecision problem, in which one "decides how to choose" (Einhorn and Hogarth 1981, 69). Thus, each decision strategy can be viewed as a multidimensional object, with the dimensions corresponding to the associated costs and benefits.

In this chapter, I have focused on two of these dimensions, the control of random and systematic response errors, respectively, and have touched on two others, logical consistency with normative principles and the effort required to implement decomposition. In particular, decomposition methods require considerable additional effort but appear to promote process consistency under fairly general conditions. There are a number of other costs and benefits that may also influence the use of decision-analytic models. The costs include resistance to the use of quantification and failure to appreciate the limitations of formal models (Howard 1980); reluctance to reveal sensitive information in an analysis (Keeney 1982); and reliance on the uncertain interpersonal and technical skills of the decision analyst (Fischhoff 1980). The benefits include forcing assumptions to be scrutinized and justified (Hogarth 1987, chap. 9); the development of insight and understanding of complex problems through "immersion" in the details of the problem (Howard 1980); and the promotion of consensus formation, conflict resolution, and communication (Edwards 1977; Hammond 1965; Hammond and Adelman 1976; Raiffa 1982).

How do we decide how to choose? The role of intuitive judgment is inescapable since it is the decision maker who must assess how different strategies (e.g., decomposition, intuition) measure up and, ultimately, balance these conflicting objectives. This decision is complicated by the many uncertainties and ambiguities associated with the cost-benefit dimensions. For example, many of the purported benefits of decision analysis are notoriously difficult to evaluate objectively, if they can be evaluated at all (Fischhoff 1980), whereas many of the costs of using decision analysis are readily apparent. Since decision makers are more likely to attend to factors they know more about, the perceived costs of using decision analysis may outweigh the perceived benefits in their minds (Kleinmuntz and Schkade 1989). Furthermore, the lack of accurate and unambiguous feedback about the effectiveness of decision analysis can lead to overconfidence in one's abilities (Einhorn 1980; Einhorn and Hogarth 1978). The unverified claims of analysts and decision makers about the efficacy of decision analysis should be treated with a measure of skepticism.

An increased sensitivity to decision makers' perceptions of the costs and benefits of analysis can be helpful. For instance, recognizing that decision makers are more concerned with conserving cost and cognitive effort than with issues of strict logical consistency has led to the development of simplified modeling techniques (Einhorn and McCoach 1977; Gardiner and Edwards 1975). These linear decomposition approaches are valuable because the component judgments tend to be less complex and are therefore less effortful and, perhaps, more reliable; the underlying linear decomposition promotes process consistency; these models often do a good job approximating more complex models (Dawes and Corrigan 1974); and choosing a linear approximation when the normative model is nonlinear increases the chance that less technically sophisticated decision makers can understand and use the model (Dyer and Larsen 1984).

While I have discussed a number of issues related to the effectiveness and implementation of decision analysis, the fundamental question can be stated quite succinctly. Are decomposition-based decision-analytic models more effective than unaided intuitive judgment? Normative decision theorists have typically framed this question in terms of logical consistency: decision analysis helps decision makers conform to normative principles that they might violate otherwise. This chapter has focused on a different standard, process consistency: decision analysis helps decision makers control judgment errors because of the way that decomposition-based models combine the errors in the component judgments. These perspectives can both be used to frame questions about the effectiveness of decision analysis. Logical consistency defines an ideal that decision-analytic models help us attain. In contrast, process consistency defines unaided intuition as a baseline that decision aids and models help us surpass. Both perspectives provide useful insights into the real benefits of decision analysis.

REFERENCES

Armstrong, J. S., W. B. Denniston, and M. M. Gordon. 1975. The use of a decomposition principle in making judgments. *Organizational Behavior and Human Performance* 14:257–63.

Aschenbrenner, K. M. 1977. Influence of attribute formulation on the evaluation of apartments by multiattribute utility procedures. In *Decision making and change in human affairs*, ed. H. Jungermann and G. de Zeeuw. Dordrecht: Reidel.

Barron, F. H. 1987. Influence of missing attributes on selecting a best multiattributed alternative. *Decision Sciences* 18:194–205.

Barron, F. H., and D. N. Kleinmuntz. 1986. Sensitivity in value loss of linear models to attribute completeness. In *New directions in research on decision making*, ed. B. Brehmer, H. Jungermann, P. Lorens, and G. Sevon. Amsterdam: Elsevier.

Barron, F. H., D. von Winterfeldt, and G. W. Fischer. 1984. Theoretical and empirical relationships between risky and riskless utility functions. *Acta Psychologica* 56:233–44.

Behn, R. D., and J. W. Vaupel. 1982. *Quick analysis for busy decision makers*. New York: Basic.

Bell, D. E., and P. H. Farquhar. 1986. Perspectives on utility theory. *Operations Research* 34:179–83.

Bowman, E. H. 1963. Consistency and optimality in managerial decision making. *Management Science* 9:310–21.

Camerer, C. 1981. General conditions for the success of bootstrapping models. *Organizational Behavior and Human Performance* 27:411–22.

Clemen, R. T., and R. L. Winkler. 1985. Limits for the precision and value of information from dependent sources. *Operations Research* 22:427–42.

Coombs, C. H., and G. S. Avrunin. 1977. Single-peaked functions and the theory of preference. *Psychological Review* 84:216–30.

Dawes, R. M. 1971. A case study of graduate admissions: Application of three principles of human decision making. *American Psychologist* 26:180–88.
———. 1979. The robust beauty of improper linear models in decision making. *American Psychologist* 34:95–106.
Dawes, R. M., and B. Corrigan. 1974. Linear models in decision making. *Psychological Bulletin* 81:95–106.
Dyer, J. S., and J. B. Larsen. 1984. Using multiple objectives to approximate normative models. *Annals of Operations Research* 2:39–58.
Edwards, W. 1961. Behavioral decision theory. *Annual Review of Psychology* 12:473–98.
———. 1977. Use of multiattribute utility measurement for social decision making. In *Conflicting objectives in decisions*, ed. D. E. Bell, R. L. Keeney, and H. Raiffa. New York: Wiley.
Einhorn, H. J. 1972. Expert measurement and mechanical combination. *Organizational Behavior and Human Performance* 7:86–106.
———. 1976. Equal weighting in multi-attribute models: A rationale, an example, plus some extensions. In *Proceedings of the conference on topical research in accounting*, ed. M. Schiff and G. Sorter. New York: New York University Press.
———. 1980. Learning from experience and suboptimal rules in decision making. In *Cognitive processes in choice and decision behavior*, ed. T. S. Wallsten. Hillsdale, N.J.: Erlbaum.
Einhorn, H. J., and R. M. Hogarth. 1975. Unit weighting schemes for decision making. *Organizational Behavior and Human Performance* 13:171–92.
———. 1978. Confidence in judgment: Persistence of the illusion of validity. *Psychological Review* 85:395–416.
———. 1981. Behavioral decision theory: Processes of judgment and choice. *Annual Review of Psychology* 32:53–88.
———. 1985. Ambiguity and uncertainty in probabilistic inference. *Psychological Review* 92:433–61.
Einhorn, H. J., D. N. Kleinmuntz, and B. Kleinmuntz. 1979. Linear regression *and* process-tracing models of judgment. *Psychological Review* 86:465–85.
Einhorn, H. J., and W. McCoach. 1977. A simple multi-attribute procedure for evaluation. *Behavioral Science* 22:270–82.
Eliashberg, J., and J. R. Hauser. 1985. A measurement error approach for modeling consumer risk preferences. *Management Science* 31:1–25.
Farquhar, P. H. 1984. Utility assessment methods. *Management Science* 30:1283–1300.
Fischer, G. W. 1976. Multidimensional utility models for risky and riskless choice. *Organizational Behavior and Human Performance* 17:127–46.
———. 1977. Convergent validation of decomposed multiattribute utility assessment procedures for risky and riskless decisions. *Organizational Behavior and Human Performance* 18:295–315.
Fischhoff, B. 1980. Clinical decision analysis. *Operations Research* 28:28–43.
———. 1982. Debiasing. In *Judgment under uncertainty: Heuristics and biases*, ed. D. Kahneman, P. Slovic, and A. Tversky. New York: Cambridge University Press.
Fischhoff, B., P. Slovic, and S. Lichtenstein. 1978. Fault trees: Sensitivity of estimated failure probabilities to problem representation. *Journal of Experimental Psychology: Human Perception and Performance* 4:330–44.
———. 1980. Knowing what you want: Measuring labile values. In *Cognitive processes in choice and decision behavior*, ed. T. S. Wallsten. Hillsdale, N.J.: Erlbaum.
Fishburn, P. C. 1982. Nontransitive measurable utility. *Journal of Mathematical Psychology* 26:31–67.

———. 1988. *Nonlinear preference and utility theory.* Baltimore: Johns Hopkins University Press.
Gardiner, P. C., and W. Edwards. 1975. Public values: Multiattribute-utility measurement for social decision making. In *Human judgment and decision processes,* ed. M. F. Kaplan and S. Schwartz. New York: Academic.
Goldberg, L. R. 1970. Man vs. model of man: A rationale, plus some evidence, for a method of improving on clinical inferences. *Psychological Bulletin* 73:422–32.
Goldstein, W. M., and H. J. Einhorn. 1987. Expression theory and the preference reversal phenomena. *Psychological Review* 94:236–54.
Hammond, K. R. 1965. New directions in research on conflict resolution. *Journal of Social Issues* 21:44–66.
Hammond, K. R., and L. Adelman. 1976. Science, values, and human judgment. *Science* 194:389–96.
Hammond, K. R., C. J. Hursch, and F. J. Todd. 1964. Analyzing the components of clinical inference. *Psychological Review* 71:438–56.
Hammond, K. R., T. R. Stewart, B. Brehmer, and D. O. Steinmann. 1975. Social judgment theory. In *Human judgment and decision processes,* ed. M. F. Kaplan and S. Schwartz. New York: Academic.
Hammond, K. R., and D. A. Summers. 1972. Cognitive control. *Psychological Review* 79:58–67.
Hershey, J. C., H. C. Kunreuther, and P. J. H. Schoemaker. 1982. Sources of bias in assessment procedures for utility functions. *Management Science* 28:936–54.
Hershey, J. C., and P. J. H. Schoemaker. 1985. Probability versus certainty equivalence methods in utility measurement: Are they equivalent? *Management Science* 31:1213–31.
Hogarth, R. M. 1975. Cognitive processes and the assessment of subjective probability distributions. *Journal of the American Statistical Association* 70:271–89.
———. 1978. A note on aggregating opinions. *Organizational Behavior and Human Performance* 21:40–46.
———. 1982. On the surprise and delight of inconsistent responses. In *Question framing and response consistency,* ed. R. M. Hogarth. San Francisco: Jossey-Bass.
———. 1987. *Judgement and choice: The psychology of decision.* 2d ed. Chichester: Wiley.
Hogarth, R. M., and M. W. Reder, eds. 1987. *Rational choice: The contrast between economics and psychology.* Chicago: University of Chicago Press.
Howard, R. A. 1980. An assessment of decision analysis. *Operations Research* 28:4–27.
———. 1988. Decision analysis: Practice and promise. *Management Science* 34:679–95.
Johnson, E. J., and D. A. Schkade. 1989. Bias in utility assessments: Further evidence and explanations. *Management Science,* 35:406–24.
Kahneman, D., P. Slovic, and A. Tversky, eds. 1982. *Judgment under uncertainty: Heuristics and biases.* New York: Cambridge University Press.
Keeney, R. L. 1982. Decision analysis: An overview. *Operations Research* 30:803–38.
Kleinmuntz, D. N., and D. A. Schkade. 1989. The cognitive implications of information displays in computer-supported decision making. Working paper no. 2010-88. Massachusetts Institute of Technology, Sloan School of Management.
Laskey, K. B., and G. W. Fischer. 1987. Estimating utility functions in the presence of response error. *Management Science* 33:965–80.
Lichtenstein, S., B. Fischhoff, and L. Phillips. 1982. Calibration of probabilities: The state of the art to 1980. In *Judgment under uncertainty: Heuristics and biases,* ed. D. Kahneman, P. Slovic, and A. Tversky. New York: Cambridge University Press.

Lindley, D. V. 1986. The reconciliation of decision analyses. *Operations Research* 34:289–95.

Lindley, D. V., A. Tversky, and R. V. Brown. 1979. On the reconciliation of probability assessments (with discussion). *Journal of the Royal Statistical Society,* ser. A, 142:146–80.

MacGregor, D., S. Lichtenstein, and P. Slovic. 1988. Structuring knowledge retrieval: An analysis of decomposed quantitative judgments. *Organizational Behavior and Human Decision Processes* 42:303–23.

Machina, M. J. 1987. Decision-making in the presence of risk. *Science* 236:537–43.

March, J. G. 1978. Bounded rationality, ambiguity, and the engineering of choice. *Bell Journal of Economics* 9:587–608.

Meehl, P. E. 1954. *Clinical vs. statistical prediction.* Minneapolis: University of Minnesota Press.

Payne, J. W. 1982. Contingent decision behavior. *Psychological Bulletin* 92:382–402.

Politser, P. E., and H. V. Fineberg. 1988. Toward predicting the value of a medical decision analysis. Harvard University, School of Public Health. Typescript.

Raiffa, H. 1982. *The art and science of negotiation.* Cambridge, Mass.: Harvard University Press, Belknap Press.

Rapoport, A., and T. S. Wallsten. 1972. Individual decision behavior. *Annual Review of Psychology* 23:131–75.

Ravinder, H. V., D. N. Kleinmuntz, and J. S. Dyer. 1988. The reliability of subjective probabilities obtained through decomposition. *Management Science* 34:186–99.

Sawyer, J. 1966. Measurement *and* prediction: Clinical *and* statistical. *Psychological Bulletin* 66:178–200.

Schkade, D. A., and E. J. Johnson. 1989. Cognitive processes in preference reversals. *Organizational Behavior and Human Decision Processes* 44:203–31.

Simon, H. A. 1978. Rationality as process and as product of thought. *American Economic Review* 68:1–16.

Slovic, P., B. Fischhoff, and S. Lichtenstein. 1977. Behavioral decision theory. *Annual Review of Psychology* 28:1–39.

Slovic, P., and S. Lichtenstein. 1971. Comparison of Bayesian and regression approaches to the study of information processing in judgment. *Organizational Behavior and Human Performance* 6:649–744.

———. 1983. Preference reversals: A broader perspective. *American Economic Review* 73:596–605.

Tversky, A., and D. Kahneman. 1974. Judgment under uncertainty: Heuristics and biases. *Science* 185:1124–31.

———. 1981. The framing of decisions and the psychology of choice. *Science* 211:281–99.

———. 1987. Rational choice and the framing of decisions. In *Rational choice: The contrast between economics and psychology,* ed. R. M. Hogarth and M. W. Reder. Chicago: University of Chicago Press.

Tversky, A., S. Sattath, and P. Slovic. 1988. Contingent weighting in judgment and choice. *Psychological Review* 95:371–84.

von Winterfeldt, D., and W. Edwards. 1986. *Decision analysis and behavioral research.* New York: Cambridge University Press.

Wallsten, T. S., and D. V. Budescu. 1983. Encoding subjective probabilities: A psychological and psychometric review. *Management Science* 29:151–73.

Winkler, R. L. 1981. Combining probability distributions from dependent information sources. *Management Science* 27:479–88.

———. 1982. Research directions in decision making under uncertainty. *Decision Sciences* 13:517–33.

Part Three

INTRODUCTORY COMMENTS

These chapters are detailed psychological investigations of how people make specific choices in well-structured tasks. As Lopes emphasizes in her discussion both chapters represent a multiple-method approach in that each uses different means of studying a particular phenomenon. This is a welcome development in experimental research in decision making, which for too long has depended on studies conducted within the confines of a single methodology.

The general topic studied by Payne, Bettman, and Johnson is fundamental: given that people are limited in their ability to process information, how do they adapt their decision strategies as a function of the characteristics of the tasks with which they are confronted? Payne, Bettman, and Johnson use an old argument but give it new meaning. The argument is that there are costs associated with thinking or deciding that are represented by the amount of mental effort expended in reaching specific choices. This notion is modeled here by showing that different strategies for choice involve combinations of different mental operations and that, if each mental operation has a cost, then so does each strategy. Payne, Bettman, and Johnson review their work on these issues, which has been conducted with two complementary methodologies. First, they use mathematical simulation techniques to model how different choice strategies perform when confronted with tasks involving differing characteristics on which performance can be measured on two dimensions, efficacy of outcomes and effort. The former is considered relative to the benchmarks of normative models, the latter to the number of mental operations or EIPs (i.e., elementary information processes). Second, they examine the actual performance of human subjects performing the same tasks as simulated strategies. An innovative aspect of these studies is the computer technology, "Mouselab," developed by these authors for monitoring subjects' choices in a manner that permits characterization of their strategies. This work is applauded by Lopes in her discussion; however, she points out that so far it has been applied only to well-structured choice tasks. She looks forward to the day when Payne, Bettman, and Johnson are able to achieve the "impossible," which is to extend these kinds of techniques to messier, ill-structured problems.

Mano's chapter deals with a problem that, to date, has received little attention in the decision making literature—"why and how an individual selects a particular goal level" in a specific task. For example, imagine a production worker whose remuneration depends on the number of units of output satisfactorily completed within a given period of time. How many units of output should the worker aim to achieve, and what governs the selection of this goal? Mano investigates this process using two different frameworks. In one, he assumes an economic cost-benefit approach. In the other, he postulates a more psychological approach involving a mental strategy of anchoring and adjustment. Interestingly, he shows that both theoretical frameworks are complementary and lead to identical predictions. Mano also uses two experimental methodologies or types of data: one is the testing of theoretical predictions by observation of outputs (selection of goals) in an experimental task; the other is protocol analysis, that is, examination of self-reports of what subjects are doing in the process of the experimental task. Both yield similar conclusions. In her comments on Mano's chapter, Lopes raises interesting questions about the nature of the adjustment process assumed in models of anchoring and adjustment, pointing out, inter alia, that much work remains to be done in explicating what psychological processes are involved in adjustment.

6

The Adaptive Decision Maker: Effort and Accuracy in Choice

JOHN W. PAYNE, JAMES R. BETTMAN,
and ERIC J. JOHNSON

Research has shown that the strategies people use to evaluate and choose among a set of multiattribute alternatives are highly sensitive to a variety of task and context variables. This chapter reviews a program of research concerned with better understanding how decision-making behavior is contingent on properties of the decision task. The perspective adopted is that strategy selection is a function of both costs, primarily the effort required to use a decision rule, and benefits, primarily the ability of a strategy to select the best alternative. A series of experiments involving both Monte Carlo simulation and process-tracing techniques is reported that support the effort-accuracy framework. Unresolved issues of learning, bottom-up as well as top-down processing, and the role of incentives in strategy selection are then discussed. Finally, an implication of adaptive decision behavior for improving decisions by designing information displays that make effective processing easier is outlined.

IN HIS DISSERTATION RESEARCH, Hillel Einhorn examined a question that is central to behavioral decision research and of substantial applied interest. How do people evaluate and choose among a set of multiattribute alternatives (Einhorn 1970, 1971)? Einhorn concluded that no single model such as additive utility was likely to be an adequate general representation of evaluative decision making. He proposed that conditions should be specified under which various models apply as representations of human decision making. The work described in this chapter follows Einhorn's suggestion and considers why decision makers, given a particular decision task, select one particular decision strategy instead of others.

Contingent strategy selection reflects the fascinating ability of individuals to adapt to a wide variety of environmental conditions. The issue of strategy selection also reflects a growing concern in cognitive psychology with the regulation of cognition, or metacognition (Brown et al. 1983). The research

---

The research reported in this chapter was supported by a contract from the Perceptual Science Programs, Office of Naval Research. Each author contributed equally to all phases of this project.

program described in this chapter emphasizes the adaptivity of human decision behavior to task demands and the cognitive control question of how one decides how to decide.

DECIDING HOW TO DECIDE

The most frequently advocated approach to explaining strategy selection is to assume that strategies have differing advantages and disadvantages and to hypothesize that an individual selects the strategy that is best for the task (Beach and Mitchell 1978). Several factors, such as the chance of making an error (Thorngate 1980), avoidance of conflict (Hogarth 1987), and justifiability (Tversky 1972), can affect decision makers' perceptions of the appropriateness of a strategy for a particular task and hence can affect strategy selection. However, our research has focused on the role played in strategy choice by the cognitive effort (mental resources) required to execute a strategy in a specific task environment.

The idea that decision making is influenced by considerations of cognitive effort is an old one (e.g., Simon 1955; Marschak 1968). It seems obvious, for example, that different strategies require different amounts of computational effort. Expected-utility maximization, for instance, requires a person to process all relevant problem information and to trade off values and beliefs. The lexicographic choice rule (Tversky 1969), on the other hand, chooses the alternative that is best on the most important attribute, ignoring much of the potentially relevant problem information.

At a more precise level of analysis, however, a comparison among decision strategies in terms of cognitive effort is more difficult. In part, this is because decision strategies proposed in the literature have varied widely in terms of their formal expression. Some have been proposed as formal mathematical models (e.g., elimination by aspects; Tversky 1972) and others as verbal process descriptions (e.g., the majority-of-confirming-dimensions rule; Russo and Dosher 1983). The research described here developed a language that could be used to express a diverse set of decision strategies in terms of a common set of elementary information processes. That language allows strategy selection to be investigated at a detailed information-processing level rather than at a more general level of analysis, such as comparisons of analytic versus nonanalytic (Beach and Mitchell 1978) or analytic versus intuitive strategies (Hammond 1986). One can examine, for instance, how cognitive effort is affected by both the amount of information to be processed and the specific mix of elementary information processes used.

In addition to cognitive effort, we have been concerned with how the use of simplified decision rules affects the accuracy of decisions. For example, a simple equal-weighting strategy can closely approximate the accuracy of an optimal-weighting rule in some task environments (Einhorn and Hogarth 1975).

The rest of this chapter is organized as follows. First, studies that test and elaborate the implications of an effort-accuracy framework for strategy selection are briefly reviewed. The studies include Monte Carlo simulations of how the effort and accuracy of different strategies might vary across task environments, an empirical test of various models of subjects' effort using different decision strategies in different choice environments, and experiments that examine whether the actual decision behaviors exhibited by subjects across different task environments are consistent with the efficient processing patterns identified by the simulation. Some unresolved issues relating to the effort-accuracy framework are then considered, such as the extent to which strategies may be not so much selected as they are constructed throughout the decision process. Such construction may allow individuals to notice and exploit structure in the choice set in ways that reduce effort (Bettman 1979). Finally, some implications of our research for decision aiding are described.

EFFORT, ACCURACY, AND CHOICE ENVIRONMENTS

As typically formulated, decision problems consist of three basic components: the alternatives available to the decision maker; events or contingencies that relate actions to outcomes as well as their associated probabilities; and the values associated with the outcomes. These informational elements, along with a goal statement (such as "choose the preferred alternative"), represent the task environment presented to a decision maker. The decision maker's internal representation of this task environment is the individual's problem space, containing the solution (i.e., the preferred alternative), which must be identified (Newell and Simon 1972). Generally, decision tasks become more difficult with more alternatives, multiple contingencies, and multiple conflicting dimensions of value.

Much research supports Einhorn's suggestion (1970, 1971) that an individual will utilize a number of different information-processing strategies to solve decision tasks (Abelson and Levi 1985). Sometimes the strategies involve an exhaustive use of the available information in a form of compensatory processing. However, often the strategies used are heuristics that simplify search through the problem space either by disregarding some problem information or simplifying the processing done on particular elements of the problem. Examples of the latter are within-attribute comparison as opposed to the combining of information across attributes (Russo and Dosher 1983). Alternative heuristics such as elimination by aspects (EBA), satisficing (SAT), lexicographic choice (LEX), and equal weighting (EQW) represent different simplification strategies for search through the problem space. For example, the EQW rule reduces processing by ignoring any different weights for the decision outcomes while still examining the values for all outcomes. The LEX rule, on the other hand, uses the weights to limit search to one or a few of the most important attributes and simplifies processing by using only comparisons of one outcome value to another. More generally, people seem to react to the discrepancy between information-processing demands and information-processing capacity in decision making by selectively processing a subset of the available information and/or selectively applying to that information operations that are easier to perform.

The use of heuristics that save effort can also lead to serious decision errors (Tversky 1969). However, some cognitive simplifications can both save effort and maintain reasonably high levels of accuracy in a given task environment (Einhorn and Hogarth 1975). This point is crucial; we do not believe that heuristics and biases should be viewed as synonymous. Rather, we argue that the use of heuristics often represents intelligent, if not optimal, decision making. Given this perspective, characterizing the effort required to use various heuristics and the accuracy of those heuristics in various task environments is essential. In the next section, we report Monte Carlo simulation experiments that provide estimates of accuracy and effort for several heuristics in different decision-task environments. Decision makers can potentially use such estimates to both save effort and maintain accuracy by selecting different heuristics for different task environments. In later sections, we examine whether decision makers in fact adapt to different tasks in ways that the simulations suggest are relatively efficient (i.e., that maintain accuracy with savings in effort).

MONTE CARLO SIMULATIONS OF EFFORT AND ACCURACY IN CHOICE

The two main purposes of the simulation studies were to characterize the effort and accuracy of various strategies in different decision environments and to develop insights into how processing might change if efficient effort-accuracy trade-offs were desired in selecting decision strategies. The simulations provide a task analysis of the problem of strategy selection in decision making. Additional details on the simulations can be found in Johnson and Payne (1985) and Payne, Bettman, and Johnson (1988).

Measuring Strategy Effort

Building on the ideas of Newell and Simon (1972), 10 decision strategies were decomposed into elementary information processes (EIPs). The set of strategies included weighted additive (WADD), EBA, EQW, LEX, majority of confirming dimensions (MCD), SAT, lexicographic semiorder (LEXSEMI), two combined strategies, and a random-choice rule. Each decision strategy was viewed as a specific sequence of EIPs, such as reading the values of two alternatives on an attribute, comparing them, and so forth. The set of EIPs used in the simulations included operators to *read* an alternative's value on an attribute into working memory, *compare* two alternatives on an attribute, *add* the values of two attributes in working memory, calculate the size of the *difference* of two alternatives for an attribute, weight one value by another (*product*), *eliminate* an alternative from consideration, *move* to the next element of the task environment, and *choose* the preferred alternative and end the process.

A count of the total number of EIPs used by a strategy to reach a decision in a particular choice environment provides a straightforward measure of the effort associated with the use of that decision strategy in that environment.[1] Several areas of cognitive research use EIP counts to measure processing load (e.g., Card, Moran, and Newell 1983).

To illustrate how EIP counts of effort would be determined, consider the set of EIPs given above and a simple decision problem involving two options (A and B), two events with probabilities (weights), and two payoff values per option (one payoff for each of the two possible outcomes). For an elimination-by-aspects rule, the process might proceed as follows. First, the decision maker finds the most probable outcome (most important attribute; throughout this chapter we use the terms *outcome* and *attribute* interchangeably). This involves reading the two probability values and comparing the two values to determine which is larger (two *reads* and one *compare*). Next, the decision maker might acquire an explicit cutoff value and then compare the payoff values on the most probable outcome for each option against that cutoff value. If the first option (A) failed the cutoff and the second option (B) passed, then a choice of B would be made. This process of comparing options to the cutoff involves three *reads*, two *compares*, one *elimination*, and one *choice*. Thus, the entire decision process consists of five *reads*, three *compares*, one *elimination*, and one *choice*, for a total EIP count of 10.

In contrast, if the WADD rule were used on the same size decision problem (two options, two events, and four payoff values), one might proceed as follows. First, the probability of event 1 and the payoff of option A given event 1 would be acquired (two *reads*). Next, the payoff would be multiplied by the probability (one *product*). The process would be repeated for the next probability and payoff, and the two products would be added, for a total of four *reads*, two *products*, and one *addition*. The same process would be repeated for option B. Finally, the overall values for A and B would be compared (one *compare*) and the option with the largest value chosen (one *choice*). The total EIP count would be 16 (eight *reads*, four *products*, two *additions*, one *compare*, and one *choice*).

A particular set of EIPs, like the one given above, requires a theoretical judgment regarding the appropriate level of decomposition. For instance, the product operator might itself be decomposed into more elementary processes. We hypothesized, however, that a reasonable approximation of the

---

1. Different EIPs may require different levels of effort. For example, comparing two values may be easier than adding or multiplying them. Hence, the operator counts could be weighted by some measure of the effort required for each individual operator, such as the time estimates mentioned below. The results remain essentially the same whether a weighted or an unweighted EIP count is used to measure effort.

cognitive effort associated with a strategy could be obtained from the level of decomposition outlined above. An experimental test of this hypothesis is reported below.

The strategies examined in the simulations differed in several ways, for example, amount of information processed, selectivity in processing, and form of processing. For example, the WADD process involves no selectivity in processing. The values of each alternative on all the relevant attributes and all the relative importances (weights) of the attributes are considered. The WADD strategy also uses alternative-based processing: all information about the multiple attribute values of a single alternative is processed before information about a second alternative is considered. In contrast, EBA selectively attends to a subset of the available information. The processing of information is also attribute based. That is, information about the values of several alternatives on a single attribute is processed before information about a second attribute is processed. When the results of the simulation are presented in table 6.1 below, the form of processing and selectivity are indicated for each rule as an aid in interpreting those results.

Measuring Accuracy

Accuracy of choice could be defined by basic principles of coherence, such as avoiding selection of dominated alternatives or intransitive patterns of preferences. However, more specific criteria for choice accuracy can be developed in certain types of task environments. For instance, the expected-utility (EU) model is generally suggested as a normative decision procedure for risky choice because it can be derived from more basic principles. A special case of the EU model, the maximization of expected value (EV), has been used as a criterion to investigate the accuracy of decision heuristics via computer simulation (Thorngate 1980). A similar model, the WADD rule, is often used as a criterion for decision effectiveness in multiattribute choice (Zakay and Wooler 1984).

In our research, we have emphasized a measure of accuracy that considers the performance of a heuristic relative to the upper and lower baseline strategies of maximization of EV (or the equivalent WADD value) and of random choice. The accuracy measure provides an indication of the relative performance of heuristics:

$$\text{relative accuracy} = \frac{EV_{\text{heuristic-rule choice}} - EV_{\text{random-rule choice}}}{EV_{\text{expected-value choice}} - EV_{\text{random-rule choice}}}.$$

This measure is bounded by a value of 1.0 for the EV rule and an average value of 0 for the random rule. While we have relied primarily on this measure of relative accuracy, we have used other measures with similar results (Johnson and Payne 1985). Note, incidentally, that an EV strategy represents a complete use of the information in the problem statement. A random-choice rule, in contrast, uses none of the information.

Task and Context Environments

Several aspects of choice tasks were investigated in the simulations, including number of alternatives, number of attributes (outcomes), time pressure, dispersion of probabilities within each gamble, and the possibility or absence of dominated alternatives. Task size (i.e., the number of alternatives and the number of attributes) was included in the simulation because variations in choice-problem size have produced some of the clearest examples of contingent decision behavior (Payne 1982). Time pressure was of particular interest since the use of a normative decision strategy like EV maximization may be less attractive or infeasible under time constraints (Simon 1981). Under time pressure, deciding how to choose becomes a selection of the best of the available heuristics, not a choice between using some heuristic or the optimal normative rule. To illustrate the dispersion-of-probabilities variable, a four-outcome gamble with a low degree of dispersion might have probabilities of .30, .20, .22, and .28 for the four outcomes. In contrast, a gamble with a high degree of dispersion might have probabilities of, for example, .68, .12, .05, and .15. This variable was included because Thorngate (1980) had suggested that probability information may be relatively unimportant in making accurate risky choices (see also Beach 1983). Finally, the absence or possibility of dominated alternatives was included because McClelland (1978), among others, has suggested that the use of certain simplification procedures, such as the EQW strategy, is dependent on the presence of dominated alternatives.

Time constraints, number of alternatives, and number of attributes represent task variables, which are variables associated with general characteristics of the decision problem and not dependent on the particular values of the alternatives. Dominance possible or absent and dispersion of probabilities, on the other hand, represent context variables, which are variables associated with the particular values of the alternatives (Payne 1982).

Results

Table 6.1 summarizes the results of our simulations for the two context variables and the two extreme time-pressure conditions (absent and severe). These results support four major conclusions. First, the simulations show that heuristics, in at least some task environments, can approximate the accuracy of normative rules with substantial savings in effort. For example, in an environment characterized by high dispersion in probabilities, dominance possible, and no time constraint, the LEX strategy achieved a 90 percent relative accuracy score, with only about 40 percent of the effort that would be needed to use a normative strategy like EV (i.e., 60 as opposed to 160 EIPs).

Second, no single heuristic did well across all decision environments. For instance, in the no-time-pressure condition, when the dispersion in proba-

TABLE 6.1
SIMULATION RESULTS FOR ACCURACY AND EFFORT OF HEURISTICS

Strategy	Processing Form	Processing Selectivity	Time Pressure Absent						Severe Time Pressure			
			Dominance Possible		Dominance Not Possible				Dominance Possible		Dominance Not Possible	
			Low Dispersion	High Dispersion	Low Dispersion	High Dispersion			Low Dispersion	High Dispersion	Low Dispersion	High Dispersion
WADD	Alternative	No										
RA			1.0	1.0	1.0	1.0			.28	.28	.12	.24
UOC			160	160	160	160			NA	NA	NA	NA
EQW	Alternative	No										
RA			.89	.67	.41	.27			.72	.55	.26	.18
UOC			85	85	85	85			NA	NA	NA	NA
LEX	Attribute	Yes										
RA			.69	.90	.67	.90			.47	.59	.48	.60
UOC			60	60	60	60			NA	NA	NA	NA
LEXSEMI	Attribute	Yes										
RA			.71	.87	.64	.77			.40	.49	.43	.51
UOC			87	78	79	81			NA	NA	NA	NA

	Type	Comp.	WADD	EQW	LEX	LEXSEMI	SAT	MCD	EBA+WADD	EBA+MCD
EBA	Attribute	Yes								
RA			.67	.66	.54	.56	.49	.65	.48	.61
UOC			87	88	82	82	NA	NA	NA	NA
SAT	Alternative	Yes								
RA			.32	.31	.03	.07	.30	.23	.06	.04
UOC			49	49	61	61	NA	NA	NA	NA
MCD	Attribute	No								
RA			.62	.48	.07	.09	.23	.17	−.02	.02
UOC			148	148	141	140	NA	NA	NA	NA
EBA + WADD	Mixed	Yes								
RA			.84	.79	.69	.66	.43	.48	.27	.43
UOC			104	106	102	102	NA	NA	NA	NA
EBA + MCD	Attribute	Yes								
RA			.69	.59	.29	.31	.44	.49	.27	.36
UOC			89	89	86	86	NA	NA	NA	NA

Note. RA = relative accuracy (95 percent confidence interval width = ±.029). UOC = unweighted operations count (95 percent confidence interval width = ±2.75). WADD = weighted-additive strategy. EQW = equal weighing strategy. LEX = lexicographic choice strategy. LEXSEMI = lexicographic semiorder strategy. EBA = elimination-by-aspects strategy. SAT = satisficing strategy. MCD = majority-of-confirming-dimensions strategy. EBA + WADD = combined elimination-by-aspects plus weighted-additive strategy. EBA + MCD = combined elimination-by-aspects plus majority-of-confirming-dimensions strategy. The UOC is marked NA in the severe time-pressure conditions because the operations count was constrained to be approximately 50 for all rules in these conditions.

bilities varied from high to low, the accuracy of the LEX rule dropped from 90 to 69 percent. In contrast, the alternative simplification represented by the EQW strategy produced an increase in accuracy from 67 to 89 percent as dispersion in probabilities went from high to low. The existence of efficient heuristics and the sensitivity of heuristics to changes in task environments are highlighted by figure 6.1, which shows the relative effort and accuracy associated with different strategies in two different environments. One prediction that can be drawn from figure 6.1 concerns the relative effort and accuracy of the EQW and LEX strategies as a function of dispersion in probabilities. Note that, for the EQW strategy in a low-dispersion environment and the LEX strategy under high dispersion, the accuracy obtained is roughly equal. However, less effort is required in the high-dispersion condition. Thus, a decision maker desiring relatively high levels of accuracy could maintain that accuracy across contexts through a shift in strategies, but with a substantial savings in effort in the high-dispersion environment. More generally, figure 6.1 and other results reported in Johnson and Payne (1985) and Payne, Bettman, and Johnson (1988) suggest that, in order to achieve both a reasonably high level of accuracy and low effort, a decision maker would have to use a repertoire of strategies, with strategy selection contingent on situational demands.

A third conclusion was that both the effort and the accuracy of strategies were differently affected by number of alternatives, number of attributes, and

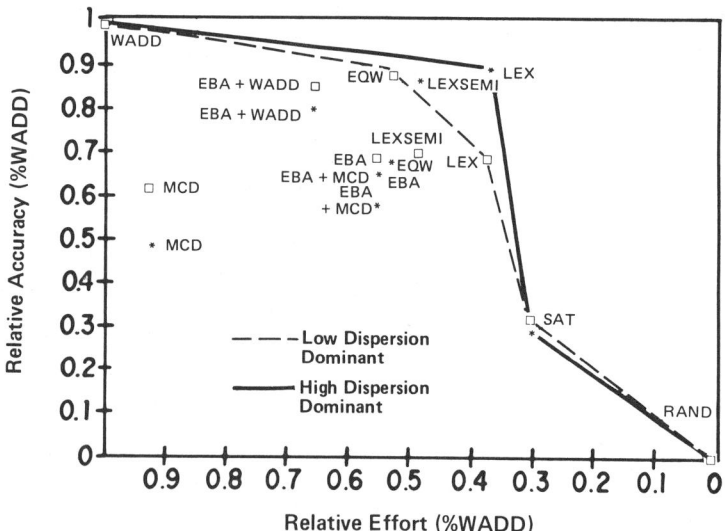

Figure 6.1. Effort-accuracy trade-offs for various decision strategies in the low-dispersion (□) and high-dispersion (*) environments in which dominance is possible. The lines join the most efficient pure strategies for each environment.

the possibility or absence of dominance. For example, the effort required to use heuristics such as EBA increased much more slowly than the effort required to use the WADD rule as the number of alternatives increased. This simulation result is compatible with substantial empirical research showing strategy shifts due to the number of alternatives (Payne 1982). The decision task characterized by dominance absent and low dispersion in probabilities was one in which no heuristic did particularly well in terms of accuracy. The accuracy score of the best simple heuristic, LEX, was only .67, or .22 less than the accuracy score for the best heuristic in the other environments. Since a decision maker would not be able to reduce effort appreciably without suffering a substantial loss in accuracy in this type of task environment, such an environment should be perceived as particularly difficult. In fact, when asked, subjects report that decisions in the dominance absent, low-dispersion choice environments are more difficult. Subjects also take longer to make decisions in this environment than in the other three environments, representing combinations of dominance possible or absent and dispersion.

Fourth, time constraints were shown to have different effects on the various decision strategies. The WADD rule, for example, showed a reduction in accuracy from the baseline value of 1.0 under no time pressure to an average accuracy of only .12 under the most severe time constraint in the dominance absent, low-dispersion environment. Strategies that require many EIPs show degraded performance under time pressure because such procedures must be truncated when time runs out.[2] In contrast, the EBA heuristic was relatively unaffected by time pressure. The average accuracy across environments was only reduced from .69 under no time pressure to .56 with severe time pressure. More generally, under high time pressure, strategies that process at least some information about all alternatives as soon as possible performed best.

The simulation results indicated what a decision maker could do to adapt to various decision environments. The results clearly suggested that a decision maker could maintain a high level of accuracy and minimize effort by using a diverse set of heuristics, changing rules as context and task characteristics change.

Note, however, that the simulation results alone do not identify which particular strategy a decision maker will select in a given decision task. That would depend on the degree to which a decision maker was willing to trade decreases in accuracy for savings in effort. This trade-off might depend on factors such as the decision maker's goal structure, the size of the payoffs, and the need to justify a decision. We will discuss the role of such factors in strategy selection in more detail below, but it is important to recognize that the

---

2. Depending on the definition of the particular strategy, the alternative selected when time ran out was either the best alternative processed up to the point time ran out or an alternative randomly chosen from those alternatives not yet eliminated when time ran out.

simulation indicates general changes in processing that might be expected regardless of any particular trade-off between effort and accuracy, for example, the effect of dispersion on the attractiveness of a LEX versus an EQW strategy.

Thus, the results of the simulation yield interesting predictions about the general patterns of processing that might characterize decision makers desiring to make efficient accuracy-effort trade-offs. However, the simulation work itself would remain only suggestive without further validation. For example, the simulation makes the crucial assumption that EIP counts represent reasonable measures of effort. Both this assumption and the predicted patterns of processing can be examined experimentally with actual decision makers. The next two sections report this empirical work.

COGNITIVE EFFORT IN CHOICE

The research reported in this section examined the assumption that EIP counts provide a measure of cognitive effort. Decision makers made choices using different prescribed strategies for choice sets varying in size. Both decision latencies and self-reports of decision difficulty were obtained as measures of strategy-execution effort. The crucial question was whether models based on EIP counts could predict these two indicators of cognitive effort in choice. In addition, we characterized how the effort required by subjects to use different decision strategies varied as task size (number of alternatives and number of attributes) varied. Given space constraints, the following description of our methods and results is necessarily limited (for more details, see Bettman, Johnson, and Payne, in press).

Overview of Method

Seven subjects were trained to use six different decision strategies: WADD, EQW, LEX, EBA, SAT, and MCD. Each strategy was used by each subject in a separate session to make 20 decisions ranging in problem size from two to six alternatives and from two to four attributes. The decision problems involved selection among job candidates. For each session, subjects were to use the prescribed rule exactly as given to them to make their selections. Subjects used the MOUSELAB computer-based information acquisition system to acquire information and make their decisions (Johnson et al. 1988). Subjects used a mouse as a pointing device to move a cursor around a screen containing the probabilities and outcome values in a matrix format. When the cursor pointed to a cell of the matrix, the information in that cell was displayed, and all other information remained concealed. The computer-based acquisition system monitored the subjects' information sequences and recorded latencies for each acquisition, the overall time for each problem, any errors made by the subject (i.e., departures from the prescribed search pattern or choice), and the choice. In addition, subjects rated the difficulty of each choice and the effort each choice required on two response scales presented at the end of each decision problem. Subjects also provided data in a seventh session for 12 choice problems of various sizes on which the subject was free to use any strategy desired.

Results

As expected, decision problems of increasing complexity (i.e., more alternatives and/or more attributes) took longer and were viewed as more effortful. Of greater interest, the effects of task complexity varied by strategy. Compared to other strategies, the WADD rule showed much more rapid increases in response time and somewhat more rapid increases in self-reports of effort as a function of increased task complexity. Thus, there was evidence of a strategy × task interaction in terms of these two indicators of cognitive effort.

The central question of interest, however, was whether the EIP framework could predict the effort required by each strategy in the various task environments. To answer this question, we used regression analyses to assess the degree to which four alternative models of effort based on EIPs fit the observed response times and self-reports of effort. The simplest model treated each EIP as equally effortful and summed the numbers of each component EIP to get an overall measure of effort (the *equal-weighted EIP* model). The second model allowed the effort required by each individual EIP to vary by using counts for each of the individual EIPs as separate independent variables (the *weighted EIP* model). A third model allowed the effortfulness of the individual EIPs to vary across rules (the *weighted EIP by rule* model). While such a variation is possible, of course, the goal of developing a unifying framework for describing the effort of decision strategies would be much more difficult if the sequence of operations or the rule used affected the effort required for individual EIPs. The fourth model allowed the required effort for each EIP to vary across individuals but not rules (the *weighted EIP by individual* model) on the basis of the expectation that some individuals would find certain EIPs relatively more effortful than other individuals would. A fifth model based simply on the amount of information processsed was also assessed as a baseline model of decision effort (the *information acquisition* model). This last model implies that the specific type of processing done on the information acquired makes little or no difference in determining decision effort.

Overall, the results yielded strong support for the EIP approach to strategy effort. A model of effort based on weighted EIP counts provided good fits for response times ($R^2 = .84$) and self-reports of effort ($R^2 = .59$). In addition, the fit of the weighted EIP model to the data was statistically superior to that of the baseline model of information acquisition and to that of the equal-weighted EIP model. Thus, it appears that a model of cognitive effort in choice requires not only concern for the amount of information processed but also different weighting of the particular processes (EIPs) applied to that information. Interestingly, the estimates of the time taken for each EIP were mostly in line with prior cognitive research. For example, the *read* EIP combines encoding information with the motor activity of moving the mouse. Its estimated latency is 1.19 seconds. This estimate is plausible since it might consist of the movement of the mouse, estimated to be in the range of .2–.8 seconds by Johnson et al. (1988), and an eye fixation, estimated to require a minimum of .2 seconds (Russo 1978). *Additions* and *subtractions* both take less than 1 second, with estimates of .84 and .32, respectively. These values are not significantly different and are consistent with those provided by Dansereau (1969), Groen and Parkman (1972), and others (see Chase 1978, table 3, p. 76). Our estimate for the *product* EIP, 2.23 seconds, is larger than that commonly reported in the literature. The time for *compares* is very short, .08 seconds, and that for *eliminations,* 1.80 seconds, is relatively long. This may reflect the collinearity of *compares* and *eliminations*.

The weights for the various EIPs were essentially the same regardless of the decision strategy used. That is, the fits for the more complex weighted EIP by rule model were essentially the same as the fits for the weighted EIP model. This supports the assumption of independence of EIPs across rules.

The results showed significant individual differences in the effort associated with individual EIPs, suggesting that individuals may choose different decision strategies in part because component EIPs may be relatively more or less effortful across individuals. In fact, Bettman, Johnson, and Payne (in press) show that the processing patterns used by subjects in an unconstrained choice environment were related to the relative costs of certain EIPs, although the limited number of subjects in that study precluded any strong conclusions. Subjects for whom arithmetic operators were relatively more difficult, as indicated by the coefficients for the various EIPs, showed greater selectivity in processing.

To summarize, we found strong support for the EIP approach to conceptualizing and measuring the effort of executing a particular choice strategy in a specific task environment. Next, we examine whether the general patterns of processing predicted by the simulation agree with the processing patterns exhibited by decision makers adapting to variations in dispersion of probabilities and time pressure. Such a match, together with the success of the EIP approach to measuring effort reported above, would provide powerful support for our proposed approach to contingent strategy selection. In the next section, therefore, we consider adaptivity in strategy selection when both effort and accuracy may be valued and when subjects are free to use any information-processing strategy they wish in making a choice.

ADAPTIVE STRATEGY SELECTION

The experiments asked the following two questions. To what extent do people vary their information-processing behavior as a function of context effects, such as the dispersion of probabilities, and task effects, such as time pressure? Are these changes in processing in the directions suggested by the simulation work described earlier? Again, the method and results can only be summarized. Details can be found in Payne, Bettman, and Johnson (1988).

Method

Two experiments were conducted in which subjects were asked to make a series of choices from sets of risky options. Each choice set contained four risky options, with each option offering four possible outcomes (attributes). For any given outcome, the probability was the same for all four options. Thus, there was only one set of probabilities for each set of four alternatives. The payoffs ranged from $.01 to $9.99. Dominated options were possible. At the end of an experiment, subjects actually played one gamble and received the amount of money that they won. The sets varied in terms of two factors: presence or absence of time pressure and high or low dispersion in probabilities. In terms of the simulation, the no-time-pressure conditions correspond to the dominance possible, low- and high-dispersion conditions shown in figure 6.1. The high-time-pressure sets correspond to conditions not shown in figure 6.1, but the general patterns of results for such conditions were briefly discussed in the section describing the simulation results. In the first experiment, the time-pressure condition involved a 15-second time constraint. In the second experiment, half the subjects had a 15-second constraint. The other half had a more moderate 25-second time constraint. Also, in the second experiment, subjects returned for a second experimental session that was similar to the first except that the time constraint was at the level they had not yet experienced; that is, the time pressure for the second session was set at 25 seconds if the subject was in the 15-second condition on the first day, and vice versa. For comparison, the average response time for the no-time-pressure conditions was 44 seconds.

The design was a complete within-subjects procedure, with a total of 40 randomly ordered decision problems in an experimental session, 10 in each of the four dispersion by time pressure conditions. This design was motivated by the desire to provide the strongest possible test of adaptivity in decision making (i.e., the same subject would be expected to switch strategies from one trial to the next). The subjects were not provided any accuracy feedback in these experiments for two reasons. It is the exception, rather than the rule, for probabilistic decision problems to provide immediate and clear outcome feedback (Einhorn 1980). To the extent that adaptivity is exhibited in such situations, it suggests that adaptivity is crucial enough to decision makers that they will guide themselves to it without the need for explicit feedback.

Information acquisitions, response times, and choices were monitored using the MOUSELAB system (Johnson, Payne, et al. 1988). For the time-constrained trials, the MOUSELAB system ensured that subjects could not collect any additional information once the available time had expired. A clock on the display screen was used to indicate the time left as it counted down.

Results

Overall, the results for subjects' actual decision behaviors validated the patterns predicted by the simulation. Subjects showed a substantial degree of adaptivity in decision making, although this adaptivity was not perfect.

More specifically, subjects processed less information, were more selective in processing, and tended to process more by attribute when dispersion in probabilities was high rather than low. Moreover, accuracy was equivalent for the two dispersion conditions. Thus, subjects showed an ability to take advantage of changes in the structure of the available alternatives so as to reduce processing load while maintaining accuracy. Recall that this prediction was drawn from the simulation results.

At the level of individual subject behavior, there was evidence that subjects who were more adaptive in their patterns of processing (i.e., relatively more selective and attribute-based processors in high-dispersion environments) also performed better in terms of relative accuracy scores. What is important, this increase in performance was not accompanied by a significant increase in effort. Hence, more adaptive subjects also appeared to be more efficient decision makers.

Several effects of time pressure were also demonstrated. First, under severe time pressure, people accelerated their processing (i.e., less time was spent per item of information acquired), selectively focused on a subset of the more important information, and changed their pattern of processing in the direction of relatively more attribute-based processing. This general pattern of results is consistent with the simulation, which suggested that an efficient strategy under severe time pressure was one that involved selective and attribute-based processing.

The effects of time pressure were substantially less for those subjects with a 25- as opposed to a 15-second constraint. In the more moderate condition, subjects showed evidence of acceleration in processing and some selectivity in processing but no evidence of a shift in the pattern of processing. These results suggested a possible hierarchy of responses to time pressure. First, people may try to respond to time pressure simply by working faster. If this is insufficient, people may then focus on a subset of the available information. Finally, if that is still insufficient, people may change processing strategies, for example, from alternative-based processing to attribute-based processing.

Although these results suggest high adaptivity, there was evidence to suggest that the adaptivity to time pressure was not perfect on a trial-by-trial basis. When the responses to the no-time-pressure condition were compared for the two groups of subjects in the second experiment, some carryover from behavior generated in response to the time-pressure trials to performance on the no-time-pressure trials was detected. Specifically, subjects who had the more severe 15-second time constraint showed comparatively more attribute-based processing, even in the no-time-pressure trials.

To summarize, the results provided strong evidence of adaptivity in decision making. While not perfectly adaptive, our subjects were able to change processing strategies in ways that the simulation indicated were appropriate. Taken together, the results of the simulation, models of cognitive effort, and experiments in adaptive decision making provide strong and consistent support for the proposed EIP approach to strategy selection. We believe that this approach provides a more systematic approach to characterizing effort and accuracy for decision strategies than any other currently available. It is our belief that further application of this conceptualization to problems of contingent strategy selection would be very fruitful.

Although we are excited by the progress made thus far, there are several incomplete aspects of our framework. The next section examines several of these issues.

SOME UNRESOLVED ISSUES

Implicit in our approach is a top-down view of strategy selection. When deciding how to decide, a decision maker is assumed to evaluate the costs and benefits of the various strategies known to him or her and to select that strategy that is in some sense best for the environment. We now believe that this view is too restrictive. While we still espouse an effort-accuracy viewpoint and the idea of multiple strategy use, we have begun to consider several broader concerns that lead to a more complex view of contingent decision behavior.

Assessing How Well One Is Doing

In order to adapt to task demands, it seems reasonable that individuals must determine, even if roughly, how well they are doing. The notion of adjustment via effort-accuracy trade-offs, in particular, implies the ability to generate ideas about the degree of effort and accuracy characterizing one's decision process. Our data on adaptivity in strategy use suggest that people can learn to change behavior as a function of task and context variables. Yet none of the experiments provided subjects with explicit accuracy or outcome feedback. Thus, how do people learn when and how to change decision strategies?

In the absence of explicit feedback, individuals must somehow generate their own feedback about effort and accuracy. This is not too difficult to imagine for effort. In the course of solving a decision problem, the decision maker has a fairly rich data base available about how effortful or difficult he or she is finding the decision. This process feedback (Anzai and Simon 1979) could provide the basis for a change in strategy. To illustrate, consider a faculty member asked to identify a small number (three) of job candidates to be brought in for an interview. Assume that over 100 applications have been received. Also assume that the faculty member is inexperienced at this task and that he or she wants to do a good job. Initially, we suspect that the faculty member would try to evaluate each application in great depth. However, at some point that person would likely recognize that the process is becoming increasingly effortful and would think about a change in processing strategy. One implication of such readily available process feedback on effort is that considerations of effort will play a prominent role in strategy selection.

Self-generation of accuracy feedback is not as obvious. One possibility is that, along with process feedback, people have some general knowledge of the properties of a reasonable strategy. For example, decision makers might believe that a good strategy involves looking first at the most important information for all alternatives and then looking at other information as desired or as time allows. Some data supporting such general beliefs about good decision strategies are reported in Payne, Bettman, and Johnson (1988). With such knowledge, the individual could not only ascertain the effort required during the course of making a decision but also determine how closely this decision process resembled his or her notion of what a good strategy should entail. In the absence of environmental constraints the match between the strategy used and notions of a good strategy should presumably be close, and the individual's accuracy assessment would be high. However, if there were severe environmental constraints (e.g., great time pressure), the individual may feel that the strategy, either as executed or while executing, did not match his or her notion of a reasonable strategy. For example, important information may not have been examined before time ran out. Klein (1983) reports data supporting this kind of learning about the task during decision making. The individual could then adjust the decision process to be more in line with his or her notion of reasonableness, either on line or the next time such a decision is faced.

Recently, Reder (1987) has considered strategy changes without explicit feedback in a task dealing with question-answering strategies and proposed a "feeling of knowing" process that is related to our ideas. She argues that people may develop strategies that are adaptive to different problem environments by trying to minimize effort while maintaining a feeling of knowing that a reasonable answer is being produced. An interesting issue is how well calibrated such feelings of knowing may be in the area of decision making and how they are affected by decision-task properties.

The possibility that process feedback provides information about both the effort and the accuracy of making a decision raises another question. Under what conditions will explicit feedback about effort and accuracy be used by decision makers? Creyer, Bettman, and Payne (in press) found that explicit feedback on the time used to make a decision (a measure of effort used) had no effect on decision processes. Of greater interest, explicit accuracy feedback also had little effect on decision problems similar to the high dispersion in probabilities (weights) choice problems used in Payne, Bettman, and Johnson (1988) and discussed above. On the other hand, explicit accuracy feedback did change processing and improve performance for those decision problems involving low dispersion in weights (probabilities). One explanation of these results is that explicit accuracy feedback is needed only to supplement process feedback for those situations in which the decision maker is faced with more difficult problems. When asked to rate decision problems according to degree of difficulty, subjects rated low-dispersion problems as more difficult than high-dispersion problems.

Although there is a large literature on feedback, learning, and judgment (Brehmer 1980; Einhorn 1980), issues regarding learning and contingent strategy selection in decision making are just beginning to be explored. However, a better understanding of the role of process feedback and strategy selection seems crucial for building a more complete model of the adaptive use of heuristics in decision making. As discussed in Johnson and Payne (1985), learning mechanisms in decision making also offer a solution to the infinite-regress difficulty associated with the hypothesis that people decide how to choose. Such strategy decisions are not made often, but the relation between task and context variables and the efficiency of a decision strategy is learned over time. Finally, as discussed next, process feedback may also be important in understanding the construction of decision processes (Bettman 1979) as well as their selection.

A Constructive View of Choice and Editing

As noted above, effort-accuracy frameworks for strategy selection often implicitly assume a top-down process. That is, information about the task is used to assess the costs and benefits of various strategies, and the best strategy is then selected and applied to solving the choice problem. There are data supporting such a goal-directed process of strategy selection (Payne 1976). Nonetheless, heuristic problem solvers not only use information extracted from the initial problem definition in deciding how to search but also utilize information from states already explored in the problem space to identify promising paths for search (Langley et al. 1987). That is, as people learn about the problem structure during the course of making a decision, they may change their processing to exploit this structure. This view of strategy selection as an opportunistic process (Hayes-Roth and Hayes-Roth 1979) also suggests that editing processes (Kahneman and Tversky 1979) are a crucial component of adaptivity.

Editing processes have been proposed as an important component of choice (Kahneman and Tversky 1979; Goldstein and Einhorn 1987), with individuals supposedly editing choice problems into simpler forms before choosing. Editing could involve cancellation of outcomes that are identical across alternatives, eliminating dominated alternatives, or combining of equal payoff outcomes, for example. To the extent that editing can simplify choice, it is potentially a major component in understanding the role of cognitive effort and adaptivity to different decision environments.

Whereas Kahneman and Tversky (1979) and Goldstein and Einhorn (1987) argue that editing processes come first, with alternatives edited and then the simplified options evaluated, we argue instead that editing occurs throughout a choice, whenever individuals notice some structure in the choice environment that can be exploited. Hence, editing can be a bottom-up process, driven by the data, as well as a priori or top down. Thus, one might not decide a priori to eliminate dominated alternatives but might eliminate such alternatives only if noticed during the course of processing.

The editing process itself may be adaptive in that the particular editing operations used may be a function of problem states already explored. Different types of processing will leave different traces in working memory, and these traces will be more or less compatible with different editing operations. For example, processing a pair of alternatives using an attribute-based form of processing will facilitate the detection of dominance, whereas an alternative-based form of processing would discourage such detection. Hence, different choice strategies enable different editing operations during the course of processing. Therefore, different choice environment properties will affect editing because they affect strategy selection. This is likely to be particularly true for the effects of information display. Slovic (1972), for example, has argued for a principle of concreteness, which states that individuals tend to use information in the form in which it is displayed. To the extent that this is true, display should exert a strong influence on editing processes by encouraging or discouraging various types of processing.

This opportunistic view of editing implies a more constructive view of choice (Bettman 1979)—that people develop simplifications and strategies as they progress in a decision process rather than invoking them a priori. Which regularities in the task environment (if any) are noted and exploited can profoundly affect the course of the decision process, so the sequence of editing operations can have a major effect on the resultant process and decision (Tversky and Kahneman 1986).

Amazingly, almost nothing is known about editing processes. Such research topics as what features of a decision task are noticed and exploited, how this changes with display format, and studies of the determinants of focus of attention in decision making are badly needed. We agree with Yates, Jagacinski, and Faber (1978) that events affecting attention in the real world are likely to be numerous and powerful and that such events are not just experimental nuisance factors.

Incentives and Strategy Selection

As stated at the beginning of this chapter, the major focus of our research has been on the role of cognitive effort in strategy selection. Questions of strategy accuracy have played an important, but secondary, role in our research. In particular, we have not emphasized the direct role of incentives in strategy selection, although subjects in our studies do receive compensation tied to performance. However, it is clear that an effort-accuracy framework for strategy selection must deal with incentive effects more directly.

The effort-accuracy framework implies that people should utilize strategies that provide greater accuracy at the cost of greater effort when the incentives associated with accuracy are increased. However, as pointed out by several authors (Tversky and Kahneman 1986; Wright and Aboul-Ezz 1988), incentives sometimes enhance performance and at other times have no effect. We have obtained similar mixed results in our own research. Sometimes incentive effects are in the direction predicted by our framework, in that people increase the amount of processing, are less selective in processing, and process more by alternative than by attribute when goals and incentives are structured to emphasize accuracy more than effort (Creyer, Bettman, and Payne, in press). At other times, however, we have found incentive effects either difficult to detect or in directions opposite from those predicted. For example, Simonson (1987) found that the frequency with which the context variable of asymmetric dominance relations (Huber, Payne, and Puto 1982) affects choice is *larger* with an increased need to justify one's decision. To the extent that the need to justify or be accountable for a decision affects the desire to make a good decision (Beach and Mitchell 1978; Tetlock 1985), this finding seems contrary to what one would expect.

One solution to the ambiguity of this research is the common distinction between working harder and working smarter. Tversky and Kahneman (1986), for example, argue that incentives work by focusing attention and prolonging deliberation. That is, incentives cause people to work harder but not necessarily smarter (see also Einhorn and Hogarth 1986). However, if people do not change strategies but just work harder, this may have the paradoxical effect of increasing error in decisions through increased effort applied to executing a flawed strategy (Arkes, Dawes, and Christensen 1986). It is also important to recognize that incentives will not eliminate errors if a normative strategy is impossible to use because of information-processing limitations or environmental factors such as severe time pressure (Simon 1981). Finally, any shift in strategy due to incentives would seem to require awareness of alternative strategies. In some cases, incentives may have limited effect because of a lack of awareness of any better decision strategy than the one currently being used. Thus, one important direction for research on strategy selection is to understand better when and how incentives will affect processing and choice.

To this point, we have reviewed basic questions in the area of behavioral decision research. However, as indicated in the theme of this volume, the work of Hillel Einhorn was concerned with both theory and application. Consequently, we will end this chapter with a discussion of one implication of our program of research for improving decisions.

DESIGNING DECISION DISPLAYS

An exciting application of the effort-accuracy approach is guiding the design of information displays to facilitate better decision making. By designing displays that make more effective processing easier, decision performance should be improved. Like Slovic (1972), we suspect that decision makers are greatly influenced by the form of the information presented and are unlikely to transform information so that it will fit strategies. By making better strategies easier to use, the application of more efficient decision heuristics can be encouraged.

An excellent demonstration of decision aiding through information display changes is provided by Russo (1977). Russo argued that using unit-price information in the supermarket was unduly effortful, requiring that consumers locate the various unit-price tags spread throughout the shelf and remember these values until other brands could be located. He reduced the required effort by combining all unit-price tags into a single list, sorted by unit price. A field study comparing the existing shelf tags and the list showed that the list produced a 2 percent decrease in the average price paid, representing 11 percent of the savings possible by always buying the least expensive brand. More generally, encouraging the use of efficient strategies by making them easier to execute has important implications for providing product information to the public (Bettman, Payne, and Staelin 1986).

Johnson, Payne, and Bettman (1988) show that the design of information displays can have important consequences on the frequency of one of the most dramatic decision errors, the preference reversal (Lichtenstein and Slovic 1971). In the preference reversal paradigm, subjects choose among and give monetary equivalents for two gambles. Preference reversals occur when a subject indicates a choice of one gamble but gives a higher monetary equivalent for the other gamble in the pair. In the typical preference reversal experiment, the probabilities are described as fractions, a consequence of using a roulette wheel to determine outcomes. Johnson, Payne, and Bettman suggested that these fractions ($^{29}/_{36}$, e.g.) discouraged the use of expectation strategies and facilitated the use of heuristic strategies, producing reversals. They manipulated the way identical probabilities were displayed, ranging from simple decimals (.8) to quite complex fractions ($^{284}/_{355}$). The complex fractions produced almost twice as many reversals as the decimals. Further, process-tracing measures, collected with MOUSELAB, were consistent with the notion that the simpler displays encouraged using expectation strategies.

Together, these examples illustrate the principle of passive decision support. In contrast to more active approaches that replace human cognitive processes to aid decisions, better decisions can be encouraged by designing displays that passively encourage more accurate strategies by making them easier to execute. Such reductions in execution effort can be achieved by using formats that make operations such as comparisons easier or by making individual pieces of data easier to process, for example.

CONCLUSION

A major finding of the last 20 years of decision research is that an individual will use many different strategies in making a decision, contingent on task demands (Einhorn and Hogarth 1981; Payne 1982; Abelson and Levi 1985). The use of multiple strategies raises the fundamental issue of how people decide to decide. This chapter reviews a program of research directed at understanding the adaptive use of strategies in decision making. While people clearly sometimes make decisions that violate certain principles of rationality (Tversky 1969), it is also becoming clear that decision makers often adapt in directions representing efficient effort-accuracy trade-offs.

REFERENCES

Abelson, R. P., and A. Levi. 1985. Decision making and decision theory. In *The handbook of social psychology,* vol. 1, ed. G. Lindzey and E. Aronson. New York: Random House.
Anzai, Y., and H. A. Simon. 1979. The theory of learning by doing. *Psychological Review* 86:124–40.
Arkes H. R., R. M. Dawes, and C. Christensen. 1986. Factors influencing the use of a decision rule in a probabilistic task. *Organizational Behavior and Human Decision Processes* 37:93–110.
Beach, L. R. 1983. Muddling through: A response to Yates and Goldstein. *Organizational Behavior and Human Performance* 31:47–53.
Beach, L. R. and T. R. Mitchell. 1978. A contingency model for the selection of decision strategies. *Academy of Management Review* 3:439–49.
Bettman, J. R. 1979. *An information processing theory of consumer choice.* Reading, Mass.: Addison-Wesley.
Bettman, J. R., E. J. Johnson, and J. W. Payne. In press. A componential analysis of cognitive effort in choice. *Organizational Behavior and Human Decision Processes.*
Bettman, J. R., J. W. Payne, and R. Staelin. 1986. Cognitive considerations in designing effective labels for presenting risk information. *Journal of Marketing and Public Policy* 5:1–28.
Brehmer, B. 1980. In a word: Not from experience. *Acta Psychologica* 45:223–41.
Brown, A. L., J. D. Bransford, R. A. Ferrara, and J. C. Campione. 1983. Learning, remembering, and understanding. In *Handbook of child psychology,* ed. P. H. Mussen, vol. 3, *Cognitive development,* ed. J. H. Flavell and E. M. Markman. New York: Wiley.
Card, S. K., T. P. Moran, and A. Newell. 1983. *The psychology of human-computer interaction.* Hillsdale, N.J.: Erlbaum.
Chase, W. G. 1978. Elementary information processes. In *Handbook of learning and cognitive processes,* vol. 5, ed. W. K. Estes. Hillsdale, N.J.: Erlbaum.
Creyer, E. H., J. R. Bettman, and J. W. Payne. In press. The impact of accuracy and effort feedback and goals on adaptive decision behavior. *Journal of Behavioral Decision Making.*
Dansereau, D. F. 1969. An information processing model of mental multiplication. Ph.D. diss., Carnegie-Mellon University.
Einhorn, H. J. 1970. Use of nonlinear, noncompensatory models in decision making. *Psychological Bulletin* 73:221–30.
———. 1971. Use of nonlinear, noncompensatory models as a function of task and amount of information. *Organizational Behavior and Human Performance* 6:1–27.
———. 1980. Learning from experience and suboptimal rules in decision making. In *Cognitive processes in choice and decision behavior,* ed. T. S. Wallsten. Hillsdale, N.J.: Erlbaum.

Einhorn, H. J., and R. M. Hogarth. 1975. Unit weighting schemes for decision making. *Organizational Behavior and Human Performance* 13:171–92.

———. 1981. Behavioral decision theory: Processes of judgment and choice. *Annual Review of Psychology* 32:53–88.

———. 1986. Decision making under ambiguity. *Journal of Business* 59:S225–S250.

Goldstein, W. M., and H. J. Einhorn. 1987. Expression theory and the preference reversal phenomena. *Psychological Review* 94:236–54.

Groen, G. J., and J. M. Parkman. 1972. A chronometric analysis of simple addition. *Psychological Review* 79:329–43.

Hammond, K. R. 1986. A theoretically based review of theory and research in judgment and decision making. Report no. 260. University of Colorado, Institute of Cognitive Science, Center for Research on Judgment and Policy.

Hayes-Roth, B., and F. Hayes-Roth. 1979. A cognitive model of planning. *Cognitive Science* 3:275–310.

Hogarth, R. M. 1987. *Judgement and choice.* 2d ed. New York: Wiley.

Huber, J., J. W. Payne, and C. Puto. 1982. Adding asymmetrically dominated alternatives: Violations of regularity and the similarity hypothesis. *Journal of Consumer Research* 9:90–98.

Johnson, E. J., and J. W. Payne. 1985. Effort and accuracy in choice. *Management Science* 31:395–414.

Johnson, E. J., J. W. Payne, and J. R. Bettman. 1988. Information displays and preference reversals. *Organizational Behavior and Human Decision Processes* 42:1–21.

Johnson, E. J., J. W. Payne, D. A. Schkade, and J. R. Bettman. 1988. Monitoring information processing and decisions: The MOUSELAB system. Duke University, Fuqua School of Business, Center for Decision Studies. Working Paper.

Kahneman, D., and A. Tversky. 1979. Prospect theory: An analysis of decision making under risk. *Econometrica* 47:263–91.

Klein, N. M. 1983. Utility and decision strategies: A second look at the rational decision maker. *Organizational Behavioral and Human Performance* 31:1–25.

Langley, P., H. A. Simon, G. L. Bradshaw, and J. M. Zytkow. 1987. *Scientific discovery.* Cambridge, Mass.: MIT Press.

Lichtenstein, S., and P. Slovic. 1971. Reversals of preference between bids and choices in gambling decisions. *Journal of Experimental Psychology* 89:46–55.

McClelland, G. H. 1978. Equal versus differential weighting for multiattribute decisions. University of Colorado, Boulder. Typescript.

Marschak, J. 1968. Decision making: Economic aspects. In *International encyclopedia of the social sciences,* vol. 4, ed. D. L. Stills. New York: Macmillan.

Newell, A., and H. A. Simon. 1972. *Human problem solving.* Englewood Ciffs, N.J.: Prentice-Hall.

Payne, J. W. 1976. Task complexity and contingent processing in decision making: An information search and protocol analysis. *Organizational Behavior and Human Performance* 16:366–87.

———. 1982. Contingent decision behavior. *Psychological Bulletin* 92:382–402.

Payne, J. W., J. R. Bettman, and E. J. Johnson. 1988. Adaptive strategy selection in decision making. *Journal of Experimental Psychology: Learning, Memory, and Cognition* 14:534–52.

Reder, L. M. 1987. Strategy selection in question answering. *Cognitive Psychology* 19:90–138.

Russo, J. E. 1977. The value of unit price information. *Journal of Marketing Research* 14:193–201.

———. 1978. Eye fixations can save the world: Critical evaluation and comparison between eye fixations and other information processing methodologies. In *Advances in consumer research,* vol. 5, ed. H. K. Hunt. Ann Arbor, Mich.: Association for Consumer Research.

Russo, J. E., and B. A. Dosher. 1983. Strategies for multiattribute binary choice. *Journal of Experimental Psychology: Learning, Memory, and Cognition* 9:676–96.

Simon, H. A. 1955. A behavioral model of rational choice. *Quarterly Journal of Economics* 69:99–118.

———. 1981. *The sciences of the artificial.* 2d ed. Cambridge, Mass.: MIT Press.

Simonson, I. 1987. Justification processes in choice. Ph.D. diss., Duke University.

Slovic, P. 1972. From Shakespeare to Simon: Speculations—and some evidence—about man's ability to process information. *Oregon Research Institute Research Bulletin,* vol. 12, no. 12.

Tetlock, P. E. 1985. Accountability: The neglected social context of judgment and choice. *Research in Organizational Behavior* 7:297–332.

Thorngate, W. 1980. Efficient decision heuristics. *Behavioral Science* 25:219–25.

Tversky, A. 1969. Intransitivity of preferences. *Psychological Review* 76:31–48.

———. 1972. Elimination by aspects: A theory of choice. *Psychological Review* 79:281–99.

Tversky, A., and D. Kahneman. 1986. Rational choice and the framing of decisions. *Journal of Business* 59:S251–S278.

Wright, W. F., and M. E. Aboul-Ezz. 1988. Effects of extrinsic incentives on the quality of frequency assessments. *Organizational Behavior and Human Decision Processes* 41:143–52.

Yates, J. F., C. M. Jagacinski, and M. D. Faber. 1978. Evaluation of partially described multiattribute options. *Organizational Behavior and Human Performance* 21:240–51.

Zakay, D., and S. Wooler. 1984. Time pressure, training and decision effectiveness. *Ergonomics* 27:273–84.

7

Anticipated Deadline Penalties: Effects on Goal Levels and Task Performance

HAIM MANO

This chapter examines the effects of anticipated deadline penalties on self-selected goals and performance. It advances and tests the hypothesis, based on both a cost-benefit input-output model and an anchoring-and-adjustment process, that steeper penalties lead to lower self-selected goal levels. The findings support the hypothesis and also indicate that heavier penalties had a dysfunctional effect on subsequent task performance quality. In an additional experiment, verbal protocols collected while subjects performed the same task provided further evidence supporting the use of anchoring-and-adjustment strategies.

IN THE COURSE OF EVERYDAY LIFE, impending deadlines force us to adjust so that the negative consequences of missing a predetermined schedule can be avoided. Adjustments may take the form of speeding up the pace of work, neglecting or ignoring less important aspects of the activity, lowering performance quality, attempting to reschedule other activities, and so on. By these adaptive responses we may avoid the penalty associated with missing the deadline, such as the fine for an expired parking meter, the embarrassment of being late for a meeting, or the possible financial loss incurred by a late submission of a contract bid. That is, a deadline involves an explicit or implicit penalty incurred for failing to reach some required goal level before a predetermined time. This study examines the effects of anticipated deadline penalties on the goal-setting process that precedes performance in a cognitive task and on subsequent performance in that task.

To date, relatively little theoretical and empirical attention has been devoted to the role of deadlines and time pressure in determining the processes and outcomes of judgment and choice. Past research has focused on three issues: how time pressure affects the way decisions are made, identifying the aspects of the available information that most influence the decision-making process under time pressure, and the effect of deadlines on decision outcomes.

I am grateful to Elisabeth W. Case, Robin M. Hogarth, and Joshua Klayman for helpful comments on earlier drafts of this chapter.

Results of this research have shown, first, that time pressure may alter the decision process by inducing the use of simpler decision strategies (Ben Zur and Breznitz 1980; Christensen-Szalanski 1978, 1980; Mano 1988; Payne, Bettman, and Johnson 1988; Wright 1974; Wright and Weitz 1977) or the acceleration of the rate of cognitive processing, that is, using the same decision strategy but processing information faster (Ben Zur and Breznitz 1980; Mano 1988; Payne, Bettman, and Johnson 1988). Second, people under time pressure overweight negative evidence and become more risk averse (Ben Zur and Breznitz 1980; Hanson, Keating, and Terry 1974; Janis and Mann 1977; Wright 1974; Wright and Weitz 1977). Third, short deadlines are detrimental to the quality of decision outcomes (Goldberger and Breznitz 1982; Janis and Mann 1977; Zakay and Wooler 1984).

An important aspect of decision making under deadlines that has not received attention is the judgment of the amount and quality of work to be accomplished under a deadline. Such judgments—usually formed prior to but sometimes also during task performance—may reflect perceptions of both task difficulty and individual ability as well as the decision maker's aspired objective or goal level. For example, when faced with the task of deciding how many simple additions to complete in 1 minute, we are aware that it is harder to complete 20 than 15; also, we may know how many similar activities we usually perform in 20 seconds. Thus, setting a goal level, that is, allowing the decision maker to lower or raise the anticipated performance level, is of interest because it is a critical element in dealing with and adjusting to deadlines.

The main objective of this study is to examine the process by which goal levels are selected when people make decisions under deadlines involving the threat of a penalty. In particular, the study considers the effect of different deadline penalties on the process of selecting a goal and on subsequent performance in the task involving that goal.

The view taken in this study is that decision makers attempt to make adaptive responses to environmental demands by choosing goal levels deemed most appropriate both for specific decision environments and their own needs (Hogarth 1981; Payne, Bettman, and Johnson 1988, in this volume). This adaptiveness is evidenced by purposive and flexible decision behavior. Purposive decision behavior implies that some ways of deciding are better than others (Einhorn and Hogarth 1981); flexibility, on the other hand, is expressed in the ability to adjust to task requirements by choosing from an array of possible decision strategies. Thus, when deciding on future goal levels, decision makers are viewed as engaging in a dynamic process in which they aim to select goal levels that will maximize net benefits.

This chapter is organized as follows. First, two parallel models for the selection of goal levels under deadlines involving the threat of a penalty are presented: an input-output cost-benefit model and an anchoring-and-adjustment process model. Also, two possible theoretical mechanisms mediating between deadline penalties and subsequent task performance are considered. In the empirical part of the chapter, the first study tests the predictions implied by the two models and examines the effect of deadline penalties on performance. In the second study, the decision process leading to the selection of a goal level is examined in detail, using verbal protocols. Finally, implications of the models and results are discussed.

GOAL SETTING: A DECISION-MAKING APPROACH

Everyday tasks and professional activities often require people to judge the level of performance to be accomplished in a given amount of time. Many of these tasks can be analyzed in terms of units of action, and one is therefore asked to estimate the number of units expected to be completed successfully during a predetermined time period, that is, to set a goal level. Attaining a higher level of performance, that is, successfully completing more units of action, leads to higher payoffs, but missing the deadline or failing to reach the declared goal level may lead to a penalty. Past research indicates that both goal-level selection and task performance are affected by a host of individual and environmental factors such as ability, feedback, or rewards (Locke et al. 1981). This literature, however, has not investigated the judgmental processes performed while a goal level is chosen.

An Input-Output Cost-Benefit Model

Why is a particular goal level selected? One appealing perspective is that the decision maker chooses a goal using a cost-benefit evaluation (Beach and Mitchell 1978; Einhorn and Hogarth 1981; Payne 1982). According to this view, the decision maker evaluates the different goal levels' costs and benefits and selects the goal that maximizes net benefits, given task characteristics.

Consider the case in which a task has to be completed by an individual in a given period of time. Without loss of generality, let the amount of time be 1 unit, and let Q be the expected quality of the completed task determined as follows:

$$Q = f\{\text{work, task difficulty, individual ability}\}; \qquad (1a)$$

that is, Q is assumed to increase with exerted work, decrease with task difficulty, and increase with individual ability. Let w denote exerted work, which is defined as

$$w = (\text{effort/unit time})(\text{amount of time}). \qquad (1b)$$

By working harder (or longer) one can expect to achieve higher levels of quality. However, work is not a free good; higher levels of work are accompanied by escalating levels of disutility. Define this utility by $U(w)$ ($U[w] \leq 0$), and assume that it monotonically decreases in w with $U' < 0$, and $U'' < 0$.

Consider now that the decision maker is facing a task of a required quality-goal level, C (e.g., the threshold of a pass/fail criterion). Let $U(Q \geq C)$ denote the utility if the goal is attained and $P(Q \geq C|w)$ the decision maker's subjective probability of success given the w level of work. It is assumed that $P(Q \geq C|w)$ is monotonically increasing with w (i.e., the more one works, the better the chances of achieving C; cf. Yates and Kulik 1977) and decreasing with goal level (i.e., the higher C, the smaller the probability of success). Also, as work increases, the probability of success reaches an asymptote determined by task difficulty or individual ability.

Now consider that, if the task is not completed by the deadline, some penalty F (= constant) will be imposed on the decision maker. Let $U(F)$ represent the disutility associated with this penalty. The decision maker is thus viewed as facing the situation in which every level of possible effort is accompanied by subjective estimates of the probabilities of success and failure. Hence, the expected utility of work is

$$\mathrm{EU}(w|C) = P(Q \geq C|w)[U(Q \geq C) + U(w)] \\ + [1 - P(Q \geq C|w)][U(Q < C) + U(w) + U(F)], \quad (2)$$

where $U(Q < C)$ represents the disutility of not obtaining the specified goal. By assuming that this disutility is absorbed (or incorporated) in the penalty, that is, setting $U(Q < C) = 0$, equation (2) reduces to

$$\mathrm{EU}(w|C) = U(w) + P(Q \geq C|w)U(Q \geq C) \\ + [1 - P(Q \geq C|w)]U(F). \quad (3)$$

Equation (3) provides a parsimonious representation of the trade-offs faced by the decision maker. Every level of work is accompanied by its certain disutility, $U(w)$, and a "gamble" with $U(Q \geq C)$ as the gain and $U(F)$ as the loss. This poses an approach-avoidance conflict arising from the compromise between the goods and bads of work. By working more, one increases not only the probability of a positive payoff but also the disutility of work. Thus, for a given goal level, the decision maker can be viewed as attempting to maximize $\mathrm{EU}(w)$ over w.

The three terms in equation (3) are now considered to determine the requirements for obtaining a maximum and are illustrated in figure 7.1a. The first term, $U(w)$, represents the certain disutility of work (curve 1). The second term, $P(Q \geq C|w)U(Q \geq C)$, represents the expected possible goods from w (curve 2). As w increases, these goods asymptote to a maximum (determined by the product of $U(Q \geq C)$ and the highest probability for completing the task before the deadline). The third term, $P(Q < C|w)U(F)$, represents the expected disutility associated with the penalty (curve 3); no work guarantees the penalty, but more work decreases the probability of failure;

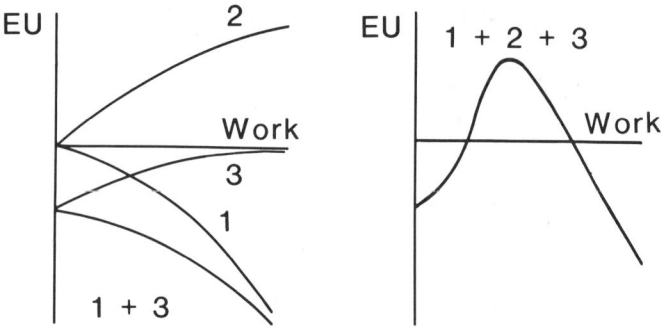

Figure 7.1. Single peakedness in the approach-avoidance conflict. Curve 1 represents disutility of invested work, curve 2 expected utility if goal is achieved, and curve 3 expected negative payoff from penalty if goal is not achieved.

hence, the deadline bads are bounded between $U(F)$ and zero. Thus, the total effect of the bads (curve 1 + 3 in fig. 7.1a) eventually escalates.

The overall utility of the goods and the bads (i.e., curve 1 + 2 + 3) is illustrated in figure 7.1b. Formally, for an optimum level of work to exist, the only necessary condition is that bads escalate faster than goods satiate (Coombs and Avrunin 1977). Under the assumptions made, this condition exists for any C because the goods, $P(Q \geq C|w)U(Q \geq C)$, satiate and the bads, $U(w) + [1 - P(Q \geq C|w)]U(F)$, escalate. Moreover, even if the assumption for work disutility is changed so that work has a convex disutility function, that is, the marginal values of losses decrease with larger magnitudes of work, for single peakedness to exist it is sufficient that the utility function for losses reaches a higher absolute value than the utility function for gains.

Consider now the case in which the decision maker can choose a goal level, c, and assume a monotonic relation between a goal level and its corresponding utility. Note that, if the goal level is lowered, the utility of successful performance decreases, but the probability of success and of avoiding the deadline penalty increases. Thus, the selection of a goal level entails an approach-avoidance conflict; the decision maker attempts to resolve the conflict by selecting the most appropriate combination of goal and resources levels (Coombs and Avrunin 1977), formally addressed by maximizing

$$\text{EU}(w, c) = U(w) + P(Q \geq c|w)U(c) + [1 - P(Q \geq c|w)]U(F). \quad (4)$$

When the effects of a heavier penalty are considered within the posited cost-benefit evaluation, a more severe penalty would cause one to lower the goal level. For, other things being equal, when the severity of the penalty increases, by reducing the aspired goal level the decision maker increases the probability of success and, therefore, decreases the chances of incurring the higher penalty; that is, the decision maker may lose some benefit associated with a higher goal level but will gain by decreasing the chances of getting the heavier penalty.

A Process Model

While the cost-benefit rationale predicts the outcomes of judgment, equally important is the need to understand the process of how such judgments are formed. In this work, it is proposed that the judgmental process of goal setting follows an anchoring-and-adjustment strategy whereby people first anchor on the most important or readily available information and then adjust this for any additional factors (Einhorn and Hogarth 1985; Hogarth 1981; Tversky and Kahneman 1974). Specifically, the present study adopts Einhorn and Hogarth's (1985) anchoring-and-adjustment model of judgments under uncertainty. In this model, the anchor reflects previous information about the topic, and the adjustment is the net result of mental simulations in which people imagine how things might turn out in the future (or how things could have turned out otherwise in the past). In Einhorn and Hogarth's (1985) study, the model was applied to predict subject-assessed likelihoods of uncertain events based on ambiguous information; as hypothesized, subjects first anchored on the probability reflected in the available information and then adjusted for how things might have turned out otherwise because of the nature of the ambiguous information.

Given the uncertainty regarding the outcomes of performance contingent on selecting particular goal levels, it is postulated that judgments of aspired goal levels are subject to this anchoring-and-adjusting strategy. First, people's assessments focus on their past rate of success in the task, which serves as the initial anchor; then, this rate is adjusted for the amount of ambiguity perceived in how things might turn out in the future. For example, when adjusting from the anchor, the decision maker may consider such questions as, How and why might I do better than before? How or why might I do worse? It is also assumed that the resulting balance of the answers to these questions reflects the severity of the penalty contrasted with the benefits of the reward.

Specifically, under this constructive mental simulation, decision makers facing tasks under a deadline with a penalty are viewed as asking themselves, How likely am I to complete the task successfully before the deadline? How much do I really know about my chances to succeed in this particular task? If I fail, how is the penalty going to affect me? The process of answering these questions forms the basis of the simulation of how things may turn out and what their consequences might be. Under these circumstances, steeper deadline penalties and their associated stress are likely to increase attention paid to the possibility of failure and, thus, highlight the negative consequences of failing to achieve goals.

To summarize, the cost-benefit model predicts that stricter penalties decrease goal levels, but it does not specify the process of how these judgments are formed. It is assumed that the judgmental process can be explained by an information-processing model that involves anchoring on past experience and adjusting for what might occur in the future. The two proposed rationales consider the same underlying decision but in different degrees of generality and, thus, complement one another (Einhorn, Kleinmuntz, and Kleinmuntz 1979).

With the above considerations in mind, the major objectives of this study are to examine whether people achieve appropriate cost-benefit trade-offs in lowering self-selected goal levels in response to stricter possible penalties and the influence of past rates of success and deadline penalties on selected goal levels.

The present study will also examine subsequent performance in the task following the declaration of the goal level. Of particular interest is whether selected goal level and penalty-induced stress could affect performance. Two explanatory mechanisms could apply in this case, and both predict lower performance levels for subjects facing the steeper penalty. First, Locke's goal theory (Locke et al. 1981) argues that task performance is regulated by task difficulty, with lower and less challenging goals leading to lower effort and lower levels of performance. Thus, if as postulated by the cost-benefit model, stricter penalties lead to lower selected goal levels, the lower goals may, in turn, lower performance. A second mechanism, stress, also predicts lower levels of performance in the presence of deadline penalties. Specifically, deadline penalties are assumed to induce stress, and greater stress might have detrimental effects on performance (Janis 1982; Janis and Mann 1977; Keinan 1987).

METHOD

Overview

This experiment manipulated the severity of deadline penalties and examined its effects on subject-selected goal levels and subsequent task performance. First, subjects practiced a task for 1 minute and were provided performance feedback on their practice task. Next, after being exposed to one of two possible levels of penalty severity if their declared goal was not met, they declared their goal as to the number of activities they expected to perform successfully during a similar 3-minute task. Analyses focused on self-selected goal levels, performance quality, self-reports of effort, and their interrelations.

Subjects and Design

The subjects were 48 undergraduates enrolled in an elective course at the Washington University School of Business. The design involved a two-level between-subjects factor of deadline-penalty severity.

Procedure and Materials

A modified version of the perceptual speed task (Moran and Mefferd 1959) was used. In the original version, subjects are presented with rows of random digits and are required, in a given amount of time, to circle the first digit in each row and then cross out digits in each row that are identical with that row's first digit. Performance can be measured by speed (number of lines covered and digits marked), accuracy (number of correct digits found), and errors (number of correct digits omitted and digits incorrectly marked).

Subjects responded anonymously using six-page booklets distributed in class. On the first page, subjects were informed that they were endowed with 200 "task points," each worth 1 cent, and that in the main experimental task they would attempt to achieve a given level of performance. If they performed satisfactorily by reaching the goal, they would be awarded additional task points; if, however, the goal was not met, they would lose points. Subjects were also informed that, after the experiment, one out of every five participants would be selected by lottery and paid in cash for each of his or her task points.

Subjects were then introduced to the task. It was explained that they had to carry out as quickly and as precisely as they could a series of searches. Specifically, they would be presented with rows of 32 one-digit numbers, and their task was to circle the first digit in each row and then cross out every remaining digit in that row that was the same as that first digit. The task was further clarified, and then a completed sample of three 32-digit rows was provided. At the bottom of the first page, subjects were prompted to ask the experimenter any clarifying questions and were requested not to turn to the next page until a signal was given by the experimenter.

On the second page, subjects read instructions regarding the practice task. They were informed that during the 1-minute practice task they would have to work as fast and as accurately as they could; after the minute the experimenter would announce how many digits should have been crossed out in each row of the practice task. Based on this feedback, they would have to estimate their speed and accuracy and, later, write down (declare) how many rows of numbers they could cover, without any errors, during the main task, which would last 3 minutes. It was further explained that, if in the main task all the declared rows were covered without error, they would win additional points. However, in case of failure, either because all declared rows were not covered or because of any errors in the declared rows, they would incur a penalty (i.e., lose points). At this stage, no mention was made as to the exact amount of points to be won or lost.

Subjects were prompted to ask any clarifying questions and then waited for the experimenter's signal before turning to work on the practice task. When the signal was given, subjects turned to the third page and started working on the practice task of 30 32-digit rows. Time was monitored by the experimenter. At the end of the minute, subjects stopped crossing out digits, and the experimenter provided the feedback by announcing the correct number of digits that had to be crossed in each line of the practice task. At the foot of the third page, subjects recorded the number of rows covered and the number of errors they had made during that minute. For the subjects' convenience, the rows were arranged in blocks of five.

On the fourth page, subjects were given the details of the task point allocation schedule. For every row declared and covered correctly, they would win 20 points (i.e., a potential of 20 cents per row). Subjects were then exposed to their experimental condition. Half the subjects faced a low-severity penalty (losing 25 of the original 200 points) if their goal were not met. The other half, in the high-severity condition, stood to lose 150 points for the same failure. Subjects then declared the number of rows they expected to cover correctly during the 3-minute main task. Thus, if all the declared rows were successfully covered, subjects expected each line to increase their payoff by 20 points, resulting in a final payoff of $200 + 20X$ (declared number of rows) points; no extra points were added for rows beyond those declared. Failure to achieve their declared goal prior to the time limit, however, would lead to the imposition of the penalty and a final payoff of 200 − penalty points.

The declaration was written at the bottom of the fourth page. Following this, subjects were given the experimenter's signal to turn to the fifth page to start on the main task. This consisted of 40 32-digit rows arranged in blocks of five. Time was monitored by the experimenter, who announced the amount of time left after 2 minutes had elapsed.

At the end of the third minute, subjects stopped crossing out digits and turned to the sixth and final page, where they answered, on 11-point scales, three questions regarding the amount of cognitive effort exerted during task performance. The first question asked them to rate the amount of effort exerted to perform the task that they had just completed, the second how hard they had to push themselves to keep going, and the third how much mental energy was required while working on the task. The answers were verbally anchored at the extremes and the middle (e.g., very little effort, moderate effort, and very high effort). The effort-related variables were elicited in order to assess the potential mediating role of cognitive effort on performance quality.

After the questionnaires were collected, the lottery drawing took place. Lottery winners were referred to an assistant, who, after class, examined their questionnaires and paid them their accumulated task points. All subjects were debriefed in a subsequent class session.

RESULTS

Two of the 48 subjects, one in each condition, did not record their declaration of number of rows to be covered in the main experimental task and were not included in the statistical analyses.

Practice Task

There were no statistically significant differences between the two groups concerning the number of rows covered or errors (omissions) in the practice task. On the average, subjects covered 11.24 rows and had .54 errors.

Selected Aspiration–Goal Level

The number of rows declared reflects the subject's aspirations concerning task performance. It is the number of rows that the subject believes can be covered without committing any errors. Subjects in the low-penalty condition declared, on the average, 30.39 rows, whereas subjects in the high-penalty condition declared 27.22 rows, $t(45) = 1.70$, $p < .05$, one tailed. Therefore, as hypothesized by the cost-benefit rationale, higher penalties decreased aspiration levels.

The process by which these judgments were formed was hypothesized to be as follows. First, the number of rows covered successfully during the practice minute should have served as the anchor on which subjects based their judgment. Before learning the size of the deadline penalty, an initial judgment could be obtained by multiplying this number by three to reflect the triple amount of time available in the main task. Also, this anticipation of future performance could be adjusted for possible improvement, due to learning, or decrement, due to fatigue. (At this point, it is noteworthy that the relatively small number of errors in the practice task—.54 per 11.24 rows—was not related to the declaration, $r = -.10$, NS.) After learning the deadline penalty, however, it was hypothesized that subjects facing the steeper penalty would adopt lower goal levels than subjects facing the more lenient penalty.

Across the two experimental groups, the correlation between number of rows covered in the practice and declared goal level was .45 ($p < .01$). However, when this relation is examined for each of the two groups separately, a different picture emerges. For the low-penalty condition, the coefficient was .79 ($p < .001$); for the high-penalty condition, the corresponding figure was .06 (NS). This significant difference between correlation coefficients ($z = 3.19$, $p < .002$) highlights the differences in the judgmental processes adopted by the two groups and suggests that subjects facing the lower penalty were more heavily anchored on the number of rows covered in the practice task.

For the low-penalty group, the average of the ratio of rows declared to rows in practice was 2.77, whereas for the high-penalty group it was 2.51, $t(44) = 1.47$, $p = .07$, one tailed. The higher value of this ratio as well as the strong relation between rows declared and rows in practice suggests that subjects facing the lower penalty obtained their goal level by, first, tripling the number of rows covered in practice and, then, lowering the product by about 8 percent. The 8 percent decrease can be viewed as an attempt to avoid the penalty or an anticipation that future performance would decrease slightly over time. Thus, for the low-penalty group, judgment was heavily based on the number of rows covered in the practice task, and only minor adjustments were made with the potential penalty in mind.

For the high-penalty group, the hypothesized goal-setting process implies that, after anchoring on the triple of rows in practice, the penalty would produce a stronger adjustment away from the anchor. Indeed, both the lower declaration and the lower ratio of rows declared to rows in practice suggest that there was a stronger adjustment due to the penalty. Moreover, the lack of correlation between declaration and rows in practice indicates that subjects facing the higher penalty did not remain heavily anchored on number of rows in practice. That is, even though the penalty triggered a stronger adjustment, the extent of the adjustment varied significantly across subjects (as evidenced by the low correlation between the anchor and the final outcome).

Overall, the previous analyses suggest that subjects used an anchoring-and-adjustment strategy when forming judgments of future goal levels and that the strategy of selecting a goal level was influenced by performance in the practice task and the penalty level. Furthermore, because of the anticipated penalty level, subjects in the two experimental conditions assigned different weights to the practice and the penalty. Nonetheless, outcome-level data do not always provide direct evidence for process-level behavior. In order to support and investigate further the postulated judgmental process, concurrent verbal protocols were collected from 16 additional subjects; these results will be presented later.

There are other variables, not measured in the present study, that could have influenced the adjustment process, especially for the high-penalty group. For example, it is possible that the steeper penalty highlighted individual differences and affected risk-taking attitudes. This possibility is suggested by the observation that, for the high-penalty condition only, the fewer the number of rows covered in the practice task, the smaller the variability in the number of declared rows. Specifically, when the 23 high-penalty subjects are arranged into three groups (of seven, eight, and eight) and ranked in ascending order according to number of rows covered in the practice task, the standard deviations of the declared goals for each group, respectively, were 2.52, 4.59, and 9.99. That is, higher performance in the practice task led some subjects to higher levels of risk taking in their future performance, but it led others to more conservative assessments. However, this is a tentative explanation, and the issue deserves further attention.

Performance Quality and Task Difficulty

The total number of correct digits marked before the deadline (correct) and the number of digits omitted in the declared and covered lines (errors) both provide indirect measures of performance quality in the main task (digits incorrectly marked were not detected). Analyses were performed on an index of performance: the difference between number of correct and number of errors divided by number of rows declared or covered. Specifically, for subjects who covered less than their declared goal level, the index was calculated only for rows covered, whereas, for subjects who covered more than their declaration, the index was calculated for rows declared. Thus, the index represents the average quality level for each declared and covered row. Performance without errors would result in an index of about 3.2 (there were 32 random digits per row). Using the index, the low-penalty group was found to be more accurate than the group facing the higher penalty (3.18 vs. 3.05, $t[44] = 2.16$, $p < .02$, one tailed).

With regards to the relation between declared goal level and task performance, Locke's goal-setting theory suggests that, when a performance goal is set, performance is likely to be higher if the goal is difficult than if it is easy (Locke et al 1981). Declared goal level and performance were highly correlated ($r = .49$, $p < .01$), lending support to the contention that more difficult goals lead to higher performance quality.

As seen so far, higher penalties led to the selection of lower goal levels and to lower levels of performance quality. Also, goal levels and performance quality were positively correlated. These results could suggest that task performance was influenced by both the penalty-induced stress and the lower goal level. A regression analysis, with goal level and penalty predicting performance quality, revealed a strong effect for goal level and a low-to-moderate effect for penalty, $t(43) = 3.27$, $p < .005$ for goal, $t(43) = 1.51$, $p = .14$ for penalty. However, two observations are noteworthy. First, this regression assumes that performance was mediated by the selected goal level; an alternative conceptualization might be that performance and goal level were both directly influenced by the severity of the deadline penalty. Second, the effect of the penalty-induced stress is evinced by the fact that the heavier penalty led subjects, first, to lower their aspired performance level and, then, despite having less to accomplish, to perform worse.

The question of course remains whether the penalty induced stress or the decrease in goal level led to reduction in performance beyond the decrease attributable to the other factor. The design of the present experiment cannot provide conclusive support for one or the other explanation. However, a combination of both explanations is always plausible.

Perceived Effort

While a heavier deadline penalty may require more effort—so that the penalty can be avoided—at the same time, the decrease in goal level, due to the heavier penalty, may justify a lower effort level (Mano 1988). That is, the amount of exerted effort may be influenced upward by the heavier penalty and downward by the lower self-selected goal level. Therefore, no specific predictions can be made concerning the effect of the deadline penalty on cognitive effort.

Since the intercorrelations of the three cognitive-effort-related questions, answered immediately after the main task, were high (from .41 to .61, all

p's < .01), they were averaged into one scale, defined as overall perceived effort (reliability alpha = .71). The averages for this index were 6.82 in the low-penalty group and 7.09 in the high (NS). Also, there was no relation between perceived effort and the index of performance quality ($r = .01$, NS). There was thus no relation between perceived effort and deadline penalty or performance quality.

VERBAL PROTOCOLS

In order to examine the judgmental process employed while subjects selected the goal level, concurrent verbal protocols were collected from 16 additional subjects, who were run individually and responded to the stimuli used in the main experiment. Eight subjects were assigned to the low-penalty questionnaire and eight to the high-penalty questionnaire. Subjects were instructed to perform the task while thinking aloud; in particular, immediately after subjects decided on the goal level, they were prompted to explain why that particular value was chosen. Responses were tape-recorded and protocols transcribed.

All but one subject's protocols on goal selection started with a mention of the number of rows correctly covered in the practice task and the triple amount available in the main task. It is clear, therefore, that this value served as the subjects' initial anchor for both the low- and high-deadline-penalty groups. This is an important process finding because it supports the hypothesis that, despite the low correlation between practice and expressed goal in the high-penalty condition, the number of rows covered in the practice task did serve as the initial anchor for subjects facing the stricter penalty. Furthermore, it suggests that there was more individual variability in the adjustment process undertaken by subjects facing the higher deadline penalty.

But most subjects' decisions on goal level did not end with "triple the practice." As the typical protocols presented below show, subjects in both conditions became risk averse in forming their aspirations and adjusted downward. Still, as in the main experiment, the decrease of the lower-penalty subjects was less pronounced than that of the high-penalty subjects, from 32.6 to 30.5 for low penalty as opposed to from 36.4 to 28.7 for the high-penalty subjects. (The difference in the decreases between the two groups was significant, $t[14] = 2.14$, $p < .03$.) Also, while the correlation between number of rows covered in the practice task and declared goal level was .96 for the low-penalty group, that coefficient was only .11 for the high-penalty group ($z = 2.9$, $p < .003$). These results highlight the low value placed on the anchor and the high variability in adjustment by subjects in the high-penalty group.

To illustrate, consider the following excerpts from some subjects in the low penalty condition from the protocols collected while they formed their aspiration judgments:

Subject 101.—"Practice was 10 and lasted one minute. I did 10 perfectly in one minute; I assume I could do 30 in three minutes. At the same time, working long, efficiency comes down a bit. 25 I think."

Subject 103.—"I am picking 23 rows because of this—I completed 8 rows in one minute correctly, therefore I am doing 8 times 3, which is 24. Because, when I get to the second minute, I think I will slow down, so I am subtracting one row, only one row because I think I will get better as I do it."

Subject 106.—"31; I did eleven with three errors so I figure if I slow down a little bit, I'll be around 30. But my errors were reduced towards the end. I was getting a little better at it. So I thought I might be able to go a little faster at the end."

Now consider typical protocols from subjects facing the stricter penalty:

Subject 201.—"The task lasts three minutes. And 14 a minute. Umm . . . I worked as fast as I can, out of the gate to begin with. Any penalty, I lose 150 points. I lose money. So, I say 30 rows, so I'll go slower, won't make any errors."

Subject 202.—"I am going to say 30. I pick those based on the fact that I did 12 before in one minute. If I did three minutes I would think that I could do 36, but I am assuming that after a couple of minutes, it will get more tiring, and I'll slow down some. I know I will make more errors as I go on, so I figure I will probably slow down some. So, 30."

Subject 205.—"I covered 14, times three is 42. But I am going to go down and keep up the accuracy. Umm . . . Probably about 35. No. About 33 to make sure I am accurate. I can cover more with speed. But if I want to keep all 150 points, then I better be sure of my accuracy. So I will say 33."

Subject 207.—"Number of rows in three minutes. That has to be more than I just did . . . , so, I'll say 20. Well, I don't want it to be too large. If I had there only one minute and I did 13, I don't want really to make it three times because my errors will probably increase too. So I will choose, say, in-between number. I was thinking of it in terms of that: to make sure that I can limit my number of mistakes and just reduce my risk. . . . That I could actually complete the whole thing. I just wanted to minimize my risk."

Consider too the protocol of a heavy-penalty subject, the only one whose protocol did not start with a mention of the practice task:

Subject 203.—"I think I would choose 25, because I don't want to lose 150 out of the 200 points by not being able to complete 30 and at the process I was going I would complete 30. But I want to make sure that I get all the rows I choose correctly. So, I took about 5 off. I figure that's about what I could cover."

These excerpts highlight several important features of the decision process. First, subjects' judgments of aspirations followed a dynamic pattern that was initiated with the triple of the practice rate and proceeded to incorporate expectations about future efficiency in task performance. These expectations were predominantly risk averse, as evidenced by subjects' lowering the initial triple-rate anchor. Second, risk aversion was more prevalent for the high-penalty subjects, whose thoughts were dominated by the possible loss of task points. Third, and most important, subjects constructed scenarios of how things might develop in the future. As clearly demonstrated by statements like "I think I will slow down," "I might be able to go a little faster," "I'll go slower, won't make any errors," "I am assuming that after a couple of minutes, it will get more tiring, and I'll slow down some," or "My errors will probably increase too," the scenarios dealt with imagining what might take place during actual task execution.

The features outlined above support the postulated process of anchoring and adjusting by imagining. In conjunction with the output data obtained in this and the main experiment, they indicate that the heavier deadline penalty produced different emphases in anticipations and imaginability of future events.

DISCUSSION

The present study raised three issues concerning the effect of threats associated with failed performance in a time-limited task. Does the threat of a steeper penalty reduce self-selected goal levels? How is the judgment of the goal level formed? How is performance quality in the task affected by the threat of the penalty?

Regarding the first question, as hypothesized, a steeper penalty induced a lower aspiration level for a time-limited task. This finding supports the cost-benefit postulate that higher potential losses are compensated by decreases in aspiration levels.

The process by which judgments of aspiration levels were formed followed an anchoring-and-adjustment strategy whereby the decision maker anchored on past performance and then adjusted for the potential threats of the penalty. It is important to note that the effect of the penalty on judgment formation was examined with two different and independent methodologies, questionnaire and concurrent verbal protocols. Thus, even though the results of the questionnaire study by itself provide only weak evidence for the hypothesized judgment-formation process, this is considerably strengthened by the corroborating findings of the verbal protocols.

Of special interest is the allocation of weights to the anchoring-and-adjustment factors in the two experimental conditions. In the process of goal formation, subjects in the low-penalty condition weighed the anchor heavily and made only minor adjustments for the penalty; as a result, the final judgments correlated strongly with the anchor. Subjects under the severe penalty, however, made stronger adjustments away from the anchor, yet, despite their initial anchor on the triple of the number of rows covered in the practice task, they selected goal levels that were not correlated with this figure. This is probably because factors such as stress, responses to ambiguity, and individual differences in risk attitudes were stronger for judgments performed under the threat of the heavier penalty. Overall, these results highlight that, besides considerations of task difficulty and individual ability, a major factor affecting the willingness to select and commit to a goal is the perceived severity of the consequences if the goal level is not achieved.

Adjustments made in the low-penalty condition were proportional to the anchor and appear appropriate for the task at hand. In the high-penalty condition, however, the anchor received little weight and did not influence the final result of the judgmental process. This may be indicative of some dysfunctionality on the part of the decision maker facing the stress induced by the steeper penalty. However, these results stand in contrast to the prevailing notion that adjustments are sometimes dysfunctional because they are typically insufficient (Tversky and Kahneman 1974). In the context of the present study, adjustments could be viewed as weak and functional in the low-penalty condition and as strong and dysfunctional in the high-penalty condition.

The present results also have implications for understanding the role of anticipated penalties and other task characteristics on judgmental processes. The contrast between aspiration levels set under milder and steeper penalties suggests that by increasing stress some imbalance may be induced, which, in turn, may lead to overreactive corrections. Support for the overreactive nature of the adjustment in the high-penalty condition is provided both by the lack of correlation between the number of rows covered in practice and the chosen goal and by the heightened risk aversion found in the verbal protocols. This suggests that, given the sequential and dynamic nature of anchoring-and-adjusting processes, judgment formation is guided by prevalent task characteristics. The different allocation of weights distributed to the anchoring-and-adjusting factors appears to be a function of these factors' relative salience.

A constructive imagination process constituted the core of the anchoring-and-adjustment strategy (Einhorn and Hogarth 1985) and provided the underlying structure for the posited cost-benefit trade-off. In particular, subjects anchored on the concrete available values of past experience and then imagined how performance might be different in the future and the consequences of possible failure. Moreover, under the heavier penalty, people paid more attention to the risks and imagined worse outcomes. These results demonstrate the crucial role of imagination in determining how past experience and possible consequences may affect expectations about future performance.

The importance of imagination in judgment and choice has been highlighted recently by Einhorn and Hogarth (1985) and Kahneman and Tversky (1982). Both studies describe a decision-making process that commences at initial concrete conditions and proceeds to construct possible outcomes of varying likelihood. Kahneman and Tversky provide a constructive version of the availability heuristic: "There appear to be many situations in which questions about events are answered by an operation that resembles the running of a simulation model. . . . we construe the output of a simulation as an assessment of the ease with which the model could produce different outcomes, given its initial conditions and operating parameters" (1982, 201). In Einhorn and Hogarth's (1985) anchoring-and-adjusting model of judgments under uncertainty, events that are closer to the anchor are more easily imaginable and, therefore, have a greater effect on the final judgment. The results of the present study also suggest that the judgmental process of forming a goal level is governed by an initial comparison with the concrete (past experience) followed by imagining the consequences of future action, with greater threats leading to lower goal levels. Taken together, the evidence we have so far on the role of imagination in judgment suggests that what appears closer to the concrete is more imaginable than the remote. This "surprising tidiness of the rules that govern mental simulations" (Kahneman and Tversky 1982, 206) stands in some contrast with the common notion that imagination is driven by the unexpected.

Why did steeper penalties lead to lower levels of performance? It appears that emphasis on the higher threat and possible negative consequences of failure generated by the anticipated penalty was maladaptive and hindered performance. Similar stress-generated dysfunctional behavior patterns have been identified in situations calling for emergency decisions when people believed that there was limited time to deliberate (Janis and Mann 1977). Even though the nature of the phenomena studied here and those reported in the stress literature differ in the severity of their consequences, the dysfunctional effects of stress on performance were similar. These similarities suggest that, from the standpoint of decision research, the processes and outcomes of deciding under stress require further theoretical and empirical attention.

Stress, however, is only one explanation for the lower performance of subjects facing steeper penalties. Lower performance could also have been mediated by the selection of lower goals (Locke et al. 1981). The present experimental design cannot distinguish whether penalty independently affected selection of goal level and task performance or whether task performance was influenced only by selected goal level. Further research is needed to delineate how stress and selected or assigned goal levels jointly interact to affect performance in a cognitive task.

An important implication of the data on dysfunctional task performance involves the nature of the task employed here. Detection of specific signals in a mass of material under conditions of deadline is an activity performed by various professions (e.g., auditing, quality control, etc.). As the results indicate, for these activities the threat of severe penalties might be counterproductive both with respect to the intended goal levels and with respect to the quality of performance during execution. For example, consider the case of an inspector who has to decide what percentage of produced items to inspect during a 1-day inspection. If the consequences of unsuccessful on-time completion are severe, the inspector's intended percentage goal level is likely to decrease. The natural assumption may be that such a decrease in goal level will be appropriate because, while quantity may decrease, quality is likely to increase. However, the present study suggests that the quality of inspection, even for these fewer items, is also likely to decrease. Thus, severe anticipated penalties incur a double cost, lower goals and lower levels of performance.

On the other hand, the artificiality of the particular task employed here should be acknowledged as an important caveat in interpreting the generalizability of the judgment processes and, in particular, the performance results. Nonetheless, this artificial task allowed for a more detailed and controlled inspection of the hypothesized relations.

Finally, using decision-theoretic models offers a promising approach for investigating the goal-setting process. Ultimately, all actions are based on expectations of future consequences. So far, however, the role of individual judgments and choices in determining aspired goal levels has not been a major focus in the goal-setting literature. Nor have aspirations, intentions, and task performance been of much interest to behavioral decision research. As the present study demonstrates, some progress can be made by concentrating on why and how an individual selects a particular goal level.

REFERENCES

Beach, L. R., and T. R. Mitchell. 1978. A contingency model for the selection of decision strategies. *Academy of Management Review* 3:439–49.

Ben Zur, H., and S. J. Breznitz. 1980. The effects of time pressure on risky choice behavior. *Acta Psychologica* 47:89–104.

Christensen-Szalanski, J. J. J. 1978. Problem solving strategies: A selection mechanism, some implications, and some data. *Organizational Behavior and Human Performance* 22:307–23.

———. 1980. A further examination of the selection of problem solving strategies: The effects of deadlines and analytic aptitudes. *Organizational Behavior and Human Performance* 25:107–22.

Coombs, C. H., and G. S. Avrunin. 1977. Single peaked functions and the theory of preference. *Psychological Review* 84:216–30.

Einhorn, H. J., and R. M. Hogarth. 1981. Behavioral decision theory: Processes of judgment and choice. *Annual Review of Psychology* 32:53–88.

———. 1985. Ambiguity and uncertainty in probabilistic inference. *Psychological Review* 92:433–61.

Einhorn, H. J., D. N. Kleinmuntz, and B. Kleinmuntz. 1979. Linear regression *and* process-tracing models of judgment. *Psychological Review* 86:465–85.

Goldberger, L., and S. Breznitz. 1982. *Handbook of stress: Theoretical and clinical aspects.* New York: Free Press.

Hanson, R. D., J. D. Keating, and C. Terry. 1974. The effects of mandatory time limits in the voting booth on liberal-conservative voting patterns. *Journal of Applied Psychology* 4:336–42.

Hogarth, R. M. 1981. Beyond discrete biases: Functional and dysfunctional aspects of judgmental heuristics. *Psychological Bulletin* 90:197–217.

Janis, I. L. 1982. Decisionmaking under stress. In *Handbook of stress,* ed. L. Goldberger and S. Breznitz. New York: Free Press.

Janis, I. L., and L. Mann. 1977. *Decision making: A psychological analysis of conflict, choice, and commitment.* New York: Free Press.

Kahneman, D., and A. Tversky. 1982. The simulation heuristic. In *Judgment under uncertainty: Heuristics and biases,* ed. D. Kahneman, P. Slovic, and A. Tversky, 201–8. New York: Cambridge University Press.

Keinan, G. 1987. Decision making under stress: Scanning of alternatives under controllable and uncontrollable threats. *Journal of Personality and Social Psychology* 52:639–44.

Locke, E. A., K. M. Shaw, L. M. Saari, and G. P. Latham. 1981. Goal setting and task performance: 1969–1980. *Psychological Bulletin* 90:125–52.

Mano, H. 1988. Deadlines and cognitive effort: A cost-benefit approach. Washington University, St. Louis, John M. Olin School of Business. Typescript.

Moran, L. J., and R. B. Mefferd. 1959. Repetitive psychometric measures. *Psychological Reports* 5:269–75.

Payne, J. W. 1982. Contingent decision behavior. *Psychological Bulletin* 92:382–402.

Payne, J. W., J. R. Bettman, and E. J. Johnson. 1988. Adaptive strategy selection in decision making. *Journal of Experimental Psychology: Learning, Memory, and Cognition* 14:534–52.

Tversky, A., and D. Kahneman. 1974. Judgment under uncertainty: Heuristics and biases. *Science* 185:1124–31.

Wright, P. 1974. The harassed decision maker: Time pressure, distraction, and the use of evidence. *Journal of Applied Psychology* 59:55–61.

Wright, P., and B. Weitz. 1977. Time horizon effects on product evaluation strategies. *Journal of Marketing Research* 14:429–43.

Yates, F. J., and R. M. Kulik. 1977. Effort control and judgments. *Organizational Behavior and Human Performance* 20:54–65.

Zakay, D., and S. Wooler. 1984. Time pressure, training and decision effectiveness. *Ergonomics* 27:273–84.

Discussion

LOLA L. LOPES

The chapters by Payne, Bettman, and Johnson and by Mano are fitting contributions to this volume in honor of Hillel Einhorn not only because they are interesting and insightful contributions to the literature on judgment and decision making but also because they exemplify one of the prime virtues of Einhorn's own work, that of methodological and theoretical diversity. Beginning with his dissertation work (Einhorn 1970, 1971) and continuing throughout his later collaborations with others (e.g., Einhorn and Hogarth 1985; Einhorn, Kleinmuntz, and Kleinmuntz 1979; Goldstein and Einhorn 1987), Einhorn juxtaposed ideas and techniques ordinarily kept separate—choice and judgment, process and product, qualitative and quantitative—and in so doing opened up new conceptual territory. In a discipline that is, for the most part, organized around schools of thought that encompass both theoretical and methodological issues, I am more than a little pleased to be asked to give my thoughts on a pair of chapters that cross boundaries and draw strength from multiple perspectives.

Mano has taken important first steps toward understanding how people set goals under external constraints. His theoretical approach has merged cost-benefit notions with a process-oriented focus on anchoring and adjustment, and his experimental approach has made use of both quantitative data and verbal protocols. In general, both data sources support the idea that subjects anchor their goals for future performances on the outcome of past performances and then adjust in order to allow for error.

Mano's study has raised for me two interesting questions that deserve further thought. The first has to do with the psychological processes by means of which people who are using an anchor-and-adjust strategy compute the magnitude of the adjustment. Actually, most of what we know about anchoring and adjustment has to do with how the anchor is set. It seems, though, that this is often a rather uninteresting part of the process, at least in the sense that, once an anchor-and-adjust strategy is assumed, the anchor is obvious given the task.

How the adjustment is made is less obvious. In the case at point, the adjustment might be based on an explicit consideration of the magnitude of the penalty for which one is adjusting. For example, the adjustment might reflect the fact that, at 20 points per declared row accurately completed, a 150-point penalty for shortfalls amounts to a 7.5-row penalty. Although subjects in tasks such as Tversky and Kahneman's (1974) serial multiplication task sometimes base an anchor on computations, no subject in Mano's task appeared to use computations in figuring an adjustment. Instead, Mano's subjects (as do most subjects in anchoring-and-adjustment experiments) appeared to choose their adjustment magnitude by means of some rough-and-ready analogical process. In itself, this is interesting since the subjects were business students who presumably have the ability and the cognitive schemata necessary to use the information analytically.

Whether the analogical processes subjects actually use can be systematically modeled remains unclear. Nevertheless, it seems feasible at the least to attack simple quantitative questions about the process such as whether adjustments are additive (i.e., subtracting a constant number of rows independent of the magnitude of the anchor) or multiplicative (i.e., reducing the anchor by a constant proportion).

The second question raised by Mano's chapter concerns the function of goals in human performance. In Mano's task, as in an early study of my own (Lopes 1976), subjects' goals were assumed to function primarily as estimates of their future performance. Certainly, such estimates are important in rational planning. But goals have other functions as well, one of which is to gain increased control over future outcomes. Several of Mano's protocols suggest that such control strategies played a part in subjects' goal setting in the dangerous, high-penalty condition. For example, subject 201 explained his goal by saying, "The task lasts three minutes. And 14 a minute. Umm . . . I worked as fast as I can, out of the gate to begin with. Any penalty, I lose 150 points. I lose money. So, I say 30 rows, *so I'll go slower, won't make any errors*" (emphasis added). Here, it is clear that the adjustment does not correspond at all to an estimate—even a conservative estimate. Instead, it is a strategic choice aimed at guaranteeing an apparently acceptable outcome.

If Mano's chapter shows the early promise of basing research on multiple theoretical sources and multiple experimental methods, the chapter by Payne, Bettman, and Johnson shows the mature fruits of pursuing such a strategy over a period of years. The experiments that they summarize convey forcefully just how much can be accomplished when a complicated scientific problem is surrounded and attacked mercilessly using multiple methods on multiple fronts. By integrating the insights achieved by three quite different sorts of studies (i.e., computer simulations of effort-accuracy trade-offs for different choice rules, benchmark studies of "pure case" performances in which subjects make choices using prespecified rules, and unconstrained experimental studies of subjects' choice efficiency in a variety of systematically manipulated task environments), they have given us a full-bodied picture of the adapting and adaptive human decision maker.

As an aside, although Newell and Simon (1972) pioneered the technique of analyzing cognitive performances by breaking them into their EIPs, or elementary information processes, Payne, Bettman, and Johnson clearly take the prize for applying the idea in a generative context. Unlike the originators of the technique, who model single-subject, single-trial performances, Payne, Bettman, and Johnson relate their analysis to a general problem area and by so doing are able to generate new, testable predictions, something that does not easily follow from applications of the technique to particular performances.

The general discussion that the authors provide at the end of the chapter is a far better commentary on their work than I can provide here. But there are two themes that they address that I consider to be particularly noteworthy and that I would like to elaborate on a bit. The first theme is that the decision-making process is one of constructing strategies on the fly rather than selecting and executing a decision rule from some preexisting library of rules. In other words, the process is seen to be cybernetic rather than ballistic. The second and related theme concerns the issue of how decision makers monitor the effectiveness of their strategies in achieving personal goals, thus raising the important question of what people consider to constitute a good decision.

In their work so far, Payne, Bettman, and Johnson have used conformity to decisions prescribed by the weighted adding (WADD) or expected-value (EV) rules as working definitions of good or accurate decisions, always, of course, keeping efficiency considerations in mind. This has been a useful first approach to a difficult problem, as evinced by the coherent and interpretable body of research that they have produced to date. But decision makers may have strategic goals other than matching the hypothetical choices made by these rules, and, if that is so, we would do well to extend our sights to understanding what it is that people try to achieve when they choose one way rather than another.

One important possibility is that people's strategies may reflect their personal theories of what decision situations and decision failures are like. For example, subjects describing the reasons for their choices may indicate that they are trying to avoid future regret or perhaps trying to guarantee an acceptable worst-case outcome. Goals such as these suggest that people's conceptions of the choice environment are highly sophisticated and that they have well worked-out notions of what is important to them not only in terms of the material benefits to be achieved by the choice but also in terms of the psychological benefits to be enjoyed both during the process of choosing and during the period of self-assessment that follows the denouement of the final consequences of choice, that is, once all uncertainty about final outcomes and final preferences has been resolved. The techniques pioneered by Payne, Bettman, and Johnson seem ideally suited to further our understanding of the multiple goals that people attempt to satisfy and the degree to which they are capable of choosing so as actually to attain their intended ends.

In what they have achieved so far, Payne, Bettman, and Johnson have already done the difficult, and we thank them for it. Let me close, however, by asking whether they might now attempt what may be impossible. In laboratory tasks such as most of us pursue, the decision situation comes well structured for the subject. For example, the MOUSELAB technology that these authors have created presents subjects with choices displayed in a matrix format, neatly arrayed with alternatives on one axis and attributes on another. In the real world, however, decision problems hardly ever come prestructured. Worse yet, in many cases it is not possible to get a homogeneous structure even with effort since information about the various alternatives is often incomplete or inherently heterogeneous. Classified listings of apartments for rent provide a handy case in point.

When people make choices in messy domains such as these, not only do they have to construct their choice strategy on line, as Payne, Bettman, and Johnson have already pointed out, but they also have to structure the problem on line. In other words, as the choice process proceeds, people's task understanding deepens as they discover what the attributes are on which the alternatives differ. As methodologists, we are all sensitive to this fact, as evinced by the strong feelings of some that within-subjects experiments are poor for understanding intuitive choice processes since mere exposure to a within-subjects variable may sensitize subjects to the variable's potential importance. But as theoreticians and substantive experimentalists we have tended to ignore the important difference between well-structured and ill-structured choice domains.

Payne, Bettman, and Johnson have shown us how a concerted, creative, and multifaceted attack on a problem can yield a coherent picture of a complex cognitive process. The problem of understanding choice in ill-structured domains seems ripe for their picking, though I expect that it will be messy and difficult to contain. I look forward to what these authors will do in the future as they extend their attack to the new issues raised here and in their own final discussion.

REFERENCES

Einhorn, H. J. 1970. The use of nonlinear, noncompensatory models in decision making. *Psychological Bulletin* 73:221–30.

———. 1971. Use of nonlinear, noncompensatory models as a function of task and amount of information. *Organizational Behavior and Human Performance* 6:1–27.

Einhorn, H. J., and R. M. Hogarth. 1985. Ambiguity and uncertainty in probabilistic inference. *Psychological Review* 92:433–61.

Einhorn, H. J., D. N. Kleinmuntz, and B. Kleinmuntz. 1979. Linear regression *and* process-tracing models of judgment. *Psychological Review* 86:465–85.

Goldstein, W. M., and H. J. Einhorn. 1987. Expression theory and the preference reversal phenomena. *Psychological Review* 94:236–54.

Lopes, L. L. 1976. Individual strategies in goal-setting. *Organizational Behavior and Human Performance* 15:268–77.

Newell, A., and H. A. Simon. 1972. *Human problem solving.* Englewood Cliffs, N.J.: Prentice-Hall.

Tversky, A., and D. Kahneman. 1974. Judgment under uncertainty: Heuristics and biases. *Science* 185:1124–31.

Part Four

INTRODUCTORY COMMENTS

An important area of interest in behavioral decision making is the investigation of people's ability to think probabilistically. Do people make inferences about uncertain situations according to the rules of probability theory? For example, does the revision of probabilistic opinions follow the dictates of Bayes's theorem? Do people consider sample size when making inferences from samples to populations? Do people understand the probabilistic implications of conjunctions of events? Since initially attracting attention in the early 1960s, this work can be characterized as having gone through several phases. In sequence, these have been as follows. People are quite good "intuitive statisticians." People are "conservative" in their revision of probabilities compared to Bayes's theorem. People do not reason probabilistically at all; instead, they use heuristic decision strategies that frequently imply biased judgments. It is not that people cannot reason probabilistically so much as that the kinds of experimental tasks they are asked to do, or the probabilistic rules used to evaluate their judgments, are not representative of decision tasks in more naturally occurring environments. Finally, we need to delineate the kinds of probabilistic judgments people can and cannot do. What are the limitations of the probabilistic models with which we judge people's inferential abilities?

In other words, from some rather simple and contrary initial positions, the development of work on this topic has steadily become more sophisticated. Researchers have also become more circumspect in how they evaluate the reasoning abilities of others. These trends are exemplified in the chapters and the discussion included in this part.

Dawes considers a "bias" investigated primarily in social psychology and known as the "false consensus effect." In everyday parlance, this could be described as the bias of believing that our own behavior is more typical of the behavior of others than is in fact the case—in other words, a bias induced by believing that others would do what we would do in the same circumstances. As Dawes points out, there are some 135 articles in the literature documenting this bias; however, as he also demonstrates, a fairly simple application of probability theory shows that the bias is not a "bias." If anything, Dawes argues that it is the authors of those 135 articles rather than their subjects who have made inferential errors. In discussing the "false consensus effect," Dawes emphasizes the fact that intuitive "causal" reasoning often exerts undue influence on our inferences and that many correct inferences can be made by appeal to statistical reasoning. His chapter, however, also illustrates that, whereas statistical reasoning may be simple from a purely mathematical viewpoint, its subtleties often escape us. In his discussion of Dawes's chapter, Schum relates some of the underlying statistical principles to an examination of the evidence from a murder trial in Scotland. Specifically, he considers how the model that Dawes uses to examine false consensus applies to predicting the verdict of a 15-person jury.

In her chapter, Bar-Hillel discusses some of the puzzling effects associated with what is known as the "base-rate" fallacy, the tendency when making predictions about specific cases to ignore characteristics about the underlying population of cases that are relevant to the predictive task. As she indicates, ignoring base rates is a robust although not universal phenomenon. As she also shows, the base-rate phenomenon is not as simple as was previously thought. There are often considerable problems in defining the base rate from a normative viewpoint, and experimental subjects are quite obstinate in the way their responses to experimental base-rate questions do not conform with what one might expect. Bar-Hillel also suggests some graphic methods by which different types of base rates might be made salient.

Finally, in commenting on Bar-Hillel's chapter, Schum both emphasizes the subtle nature of statistical reasoning and questions some of the conclusions about human inference that psychologists reach on the basis of experimental tasks using "contrived, verbally described scenarios."

8

The Potential Nonfalsity of the False Consensus Effect

ROBYN M. DAWES

The purported "false consensus effect" is described as an egotistic bias to believe that others in a group of which one is a member will respond like oneself—for example, in agreeing or refusing to engage in a particular behavior or in endorsing or rejecting a particular attitude or opinion statement. The effect is defined as existing whenever a correlation is discovered within a target item between individuals' endorsement or rejection and their estimates of the proportion of other people who endorse or reject it. The rationale for this definition is that, because there is only one true endorsement rate, systematic deviations from it in the direction of one's own behavior constitute a bias. This chapter presents statistical arguments challenging the entire conception and definition of "false consensus." First, since individuals who agree or disagree have different information available about a single group member's response (their own), they should—according to normative Bayesian principles—make different estimates. They should treat their own responses in the same manner in which they would treat information about how some other single individual in a group responded, and they generally do. A correlational analysis yields the same conclusion, in fact exactly the same estimates as a Bayesian one; individual yes-no responses are correlated with the base rates of yes responses to various items; correlation is symmetric, and therefore, just as base rates yield valid diagnostic information in predicting individual responses (a "deductive" inference), individual responses yield valid diagnostic information in predicting base rates (an "inductive" inference), not just within individuals across items, but within items across individuals as well. A statistically valid definition of a false consensus effect depends on such predictions' being insufficiently regressive. Empirical data in several contexts studied indicate that instead estimates are too regressive (a "false uniqueness" effect). Finally, I speculate that experimenters' failure to realize that their definition of false consensus is itself false may be related to the same types of biases that these experimenters typically study in other people.

Every man is in his own person the whole human race, with not a detail lacking; I am the whole human race without a detail lacking; I have studied the human race with diligence and strong interest all these years in my own person; in myself I find in big or little proportion every quality and every defect that is findable in the mass of the race.
—Mark Twain (quoted in DeVoto 1922)

According to Robert Kennedy, the President tried constantly to put himself in Kruschev's position. Once during the [Cuban missile] crisis, he even described to Ben Bradlee of the *Washington Post* how he thought he would feel if in the Kremlin, but he cautioned Bradlee that his words were off the record. 'It isn't wise politically to understand Kruschev's problem in this way.'

—Neustadt and May 1986

THOMAS SCHELLING WROTE roughly twenty years ago that "you can sit in your armchair and try to predict how people behave by asking yourself how you would behave if you had your wits about you. You get free of charge a lot of vicarious empirical behavior" (Schelling 1966, 150). At about the time that Schelling was writing that passage, Lyndon Johnson proposed to the North Vietnamese that they stop their "aggression in the south" in exchange for our help in building up a Mekong Delta system much like the Tennessee Valley Authority. Those of us who thought the same way as Schelling concluded that, since we would not give up the fight to unify our country, the proposal would be rejected. We were correct. (Of course, we might have been just lucky in our predictions and unlucky in our lives.)

The simple heuristic is that you can inquire about yourself in order to make predictions about others. In the last 10 years, a number of social psychologists have published about 135 articles on this heuristic, which leads to what is termed a *false consensus effect* and is characterized as an *egotistic* bias to think that other people behave the same way we do. The first finding about use of this heuristic was published by Ross, Greene, and House in 1977. Stanford students were asked to engage in a number of activities, one of which was to walk around the Stanford campus with a big sign reading "Repent!" Students either agreed to engage in this activity or refused and then were asked to estimate the proportion of Stanford students who would agree. The students who agreed made an average estimate that 63.5 percent of Stanford students would agree, whereas, among those who refused, the average estimate was 23.3 percent. That result led to a definition of the false consensus effect (as stated in two recent review articles): "False consensus refers to an egocentric bias that occurs when people estimate consensus for their own behavior. Specifically, the false consensus hypothesis holds that people who engage in a given behavior will estimate that behavior to be more common than it is estimated to be by the people who engage in the alternative behavior" (Mullen et al. 1985, 262).

Much the same definition is given by Marks and Miller (1987, 74):

> The paradigm for examining the false consensus bias is a simple one. Individuals are generally asked to indicate their attitude or behavior on a dichotomous measure (*yes* or *no, agree* or *disagree*). They are then asked to estimate the percentage of their peers who would respond one way or the other. (Sometimes the order of these two ratings is counter-

balanced.) Individuals are said to perceive the false consensus when their estimate of consensus for their own position exceeds the estimate for it made by those who endorse the opposite position. Thus, the bias is relative to the perception of those who endorse a position opposite or alternative to one's own view.

Now consider Schelling's assertion; if two different analysts came to different conclusions about what they would do in this situation—having their wits about them or not—they would be demonstrating the false consensus effect if they were willing to generalize from their different conclusions to other people. The effect rests on believing oneself to be diagnostic—not causal because clearly your own behavior does not cause other people's behavior. You see yourself as representative of others. According to the analysis that consensus reasoning is necessarily false, believing oneself to be representative, hence diagnostic, is illegitimate.

This view of false consensus has, however, been modified. The basic argument is that a positive association between one's position and target behavior when actual target behavior is held constant (i.e., within items) indicates that at least some subjects in the experiment have perceived relatively more consensus than they should have "because not everyone can be right" (Ross and Sicoly 1979, 222). Therefore, any between-subjects, within-items association between subjects' own positions and the target position is "defined away" (Hoch 1987). But Hoch has also argued that a within-subjects, between-items relation is legitimate because, in fact, items do vary in their rate of endorsement. Thus, I may estimate a higher endorsement probability for those items that I endorse than for those items that I reject without violating normative prediction principles.

Hoch's distinction puts those of us who think like Schelling in a bit of a bind. Suppose that one of us endorses item or alternative A but rejects alternative B across a set of nonexclusive options and that the other does the reverse. It is legitimate for each of us to postulate a higher probability of endorsement by others for the alternative we endorse than for the alternative we reject. But if, simultaneously, that leads to a higher estimate within each alternative from the person endorsing it than from the person rejecting it, then we have done something illegitimate (and if we have a larger number of alternatives, that result is virtually certain to occur unless one of us makes higher estimates for all alternatives than the other does). Further, how are we to deal with the possibility of reframing each binary alternative as two separate ones, each requiring an endorsement or rejection? For example, we may ask the question "Will you carry this signboard?" (yes/no) as two separate questions—"I am willing to carry this signboard" (yes/no) and "I am not willing to carry this signboard" (yes/no).

This chapter challenges the conception that consensus reasoning is necessarily false and presents theoretical reasons (and some empirical evidence) that people who engage in this supposedly false and egocentric bias tend to be more accurate than those who do not. The basic idea is that the problem with which subjects are presented is not to state (by some burst of omniscience) the true probability of endorsement but to estimate it, that the normative principles of estimation are based on the samples available, and that, if different people do different things, they have different samples of behavior available to them.

Let us return to the Stanford example and suppose that, instead of asking subjects what they are willing to do, the investigators asked for estimates on the basis of information about what some particular other student was willing to do. For example, the question is what percentage of Stanford students will walk around the campus with a big sign that reads "Repent!" and the investigators tell one subject that the previous subject agreed to the request but tell another subject that the previous subject refused. What should these subjects' estimates be? Suppose the subjects are good Bayesians and, believing the situation to be a confusing one, decide to postulate the most extreme prior possible—a uniform one. Each has an observation, although those observations conflict. Consider the subject who is told that the previous subject agreed. What should the mean of that subject's posterior distribution be? It is the integral from zero to one of $p \times p$ divided by .5 (the prior probability of a "success" from a uniform prior), for, if the probability is a certain value p, the prior subject will agree with probability p. Thus, it is $(p^3/3)/.5 = 2p^3/3$ evaluated at zero and one, or 2/3. Thus, if a subject has a uniform prior, is told that someone else agreed to walk around campus with a big sign that says "Repent!" and is a good Bayesian, that subject should estimate that two-thirds of the Stanford students would agree. Conversely, if another subject is told that the previous subject refused, then the mean of that subject's posterior is 1/3 (= $[p^2/2 - p^3/3]/.5$ evaluated at zero and one).

What is the difference if subjects have access to their own willingness or refusal rather than to that of the prior subject? It may be difficult for subjects to think of themselves as randomly selected individuals. From the perspective of the estimation problem, however, the current subject and the prior subject are *exchangeable*. They are both just Stanford students. Therefore, it is quite reasonable for subjects to estimate 67 percent if they themselves agree and 33 percent if they themselves refuse. In fact, there is empirical evidence that people do treat their own response exactly the same way they treat a response from a randomly selected person in their own group in making such estimates. Sherman, Presson, and Chassin (1984) have discovered that equivalence. Where subjects make a choice and then find out the choice of a single other person, own response and the other person's response are weighted equally in estimating the frequency of group response—except for "ego-threatening" alternatives. (Sherman, Presson, and Chassin found that subjects who were told that they had failed in a task at which one other subject had succeeded estimated lower probabilities of success than did those told that they had succeeded but that one other had failed. Interestingly, in other research, Sherman [Sherman, Chassin, et al. 1984] finds one other departure from normatively correct use of consensus—when people are asked about good qualities. I have them, but that does not mean that other people have them.)

Let me go into some mathematics of a concrete example. Suppose you are a Berkeley student asked to estimate endorsement frequency of Berkeley students to 16 items from the California Psychological Inventory (CPI; Gough 1986). (See the appendix.) You know from Berkeley norms that the 16 items have base rates of endorsement ranging in steps of .10 from .15 to .85, where the endorsements of men and women were very, very close, a maximum 4 percent difference. For example, 15 percent of Berkeley students state that several times a week they feel that "something dreadful is about to happen," whereas 85 percent believe that their "right to speak their mind" is very important. Let us suppose hypothetically that I tell you the characteristics of items, which is that there are two of each type ranging from .15 to .85 endorsement frequency, but not which items have which endorsement frequencies. I now ask you to estimate the endorsement frequency of each item on the basis of only your own response and your knowledge of the distribution of base rates. How could you do so optimally? The answer turns out to be rather simple.

One method is based on noting that there is a correlation between items and individual endorsements. When an item, for example, has an 85 percent endorsement rate and endorsements I_i are coded one for yes and zero for no, .85 is paired with 85 percent ones and 15 percent zeros. With a 15 percent endorsement rate, .15 is paired with 15 percent ones and 85 percent zeros. So there is a correlation. What is it?

First, consider the covariance between the I_i endorsements ($I_i = 1$ for agree, 0 for disagree) and the proportion of people who endorse an item. The expectation of the cross-product term can be computed by noting that paired with each item with an endorsement p_i is an expected proportion p_i of ones and $1 - p$ of zeros. Because anything multiplied by zero is zero, the expectation of their product is simply the expectation of p_i^2. But the mean endorsement rate and the mean of the item endorsement rates are equivalent, call it $\bar{p}$. Hence, the covariance is $E(p_i^2) - \bar{p}^2$, or simply the variance of the item endorsements.

The correlation coefficient is equal to the covariance, which is a variance of the p's, divided by the square root of the variance of the p's multiplied by the variance of the endorsements. Thus,

$$r = \text{var}(p)/\sqrt{\text{var}(p)\text{var}(I)} = \sqrt{\text{var}(p)/\text{var}(I)}. \tag{1}$$

In the example,

$$r = \sqrt{.0525/.25} = .4583. \tag{1a}$$

Now suppose you wish to make your predictions to minimize mean square error. By standard regression analysis, if your own response is I_i, your prediction should be

$$p'_i = \frac{\sqrt{\text{var}(p)}}{\sqrt{\text{var}(I)}} \sqrt{\frac{\text{var}(p)}{\text{var}(I)}} (I_i - \bar{p}) + \bar{p}$$

$$= \frac{\text{var}(p)}{\text{var}(I)} (I_i - \bar{p}) + \bar{p}. \qquad (2)$$

In the example,

$$p'_i = \frac{.0525}{.25} (I_i - .5) + .5, \qquad (2a)$$

or .605 when $I_i = 1$ and .395 when $I_i = 0$.

The general principle is intuitively clear. If all the items in a particular set have endorsement rates close to .50, predictability is nil. To the degree to which the variance of the p's approaches the variances of the I_i's, prediction improves. If the variance of the p's equals the variance of the I_i's, prediction is perfect. That would mean that every item had an endorsement rate of 100 percent of zero. If that were the case, own response *would* be perfectly predicted.

Moreover, the prediction is always different for those who say yes than for those who say no. In fact, this difference d is simply the variance of p divided by the variance of I:

$$d = \left[\frac{\text{var}(p)}{\text{var}(I)}(1 - \bar{p}) + \bar{p}\right] - \left[\frac{\text{var}(p)}{\text{var}(I)}(0 - \bar{p}) + \bar{p}\right] = \frac{\text{var}(p)}{\text{var}(I)}. \qquad (3)$$

In the particular example of the CPI items, your prediction should be .605 if you endorse an item and .395 if you reject it. This prediction entails no theory about anybody (no causality—my responding this way does not cause other people to respond this way; other people responding this way do not cause me to respond this way). It results simply because there has to be a correlation between individual responses and base rates.

Exactly the same results are obtained from a Bayesian analysis, as I have proved elsewhere (Dawes 1989). Here, I will just show this equivalence for a person who endorses an item. From equation (2), that person's prediction should be

$$p'_i = \frac{\text{var}(p)}{\text{var}(I)}(1 - \bar{p}) + \bar{p}, \qquad (4)$$

but, since var$(I) = \bar{p}(1 - \bar{p})$, equation (4) reduces to

$$p'_i = \frac{\text{var}(p)}{\bar{p}} + \bar{p} = \frac{\text{var}(p) + \bar{p}^2}{\bar{p}} = \frac{E(p_i^2)}{\bar{p}}. \quad (4a)$$

The Bayesian analysis leads to a mean of the posterior for that person that is equal to

$$p'_i = \int_0^1 pf(p)/\bar{p} = \frac{E(p_i^2)}{\bar{p}}. \quad (4b)$$

An aspect of this argument that upsets people is that it appears to fit with Nisbett and Ross's "unnerving conclusion" that, as a result of irrational judgment, "logically required deductions from group tendencies to individual cases are stubbornly resisted and normatively dubious inductions from individual cases to group tendencies are willingly embraced" (Nisbett and Ross 1980, 150, following a discussion of "manipulated base rates versus the representativeness criterion"). Since our only two predictions are .605 and .395, our inductive correlation is 1.00—possibly an unnerving result. What should be noted, however, is that both deduction and induction are perfectly legitimate processes provided that they are conducted properly. The greater strength of the deduction prediction in the exercise is reflected in the variance of the deductive predictions—.05250 as opposed to .011025 for the inductive predictions (= .105²). (A little tedious algebra demonstrates that the variance of predicted base rates is [var(p_i)]²/var(I_i)], which will always be less than var[p_i] because var[p_i] ≤ var [I_i].)

At this point, I usually hear three immediate objections to the idea of predicting base rates from one's own response. How is the person predicting supposed to know the distributions of the p_i's, the I_i, and, in particular var(p)/var(I)? Base rates for which groups, anyway (any individual is after all a member of many groups)? Own response presents a sample of size $N = 1$, and a sample of size $N = 1$ is too small a sample from which to make an inference.

The answer to the first question is that of course the individual does not know the base rates (or priors), but that does not prevent him or her from having some ideas about their distribution. If, for example, the distribution is a 2-point one concentrated at 1.00 and .00, then one's own response is perfectly diagnostic. But that will clearly be unreasonable in a context in which questions are asked. For example, I analyzed the Stanford signboard study assuming a uniform prior. "But that's an unreasonable assumption," the critic counters, and my response to that is, "Gotcha!" For the critic is responding not to the mere existence of an across-subjects, within-items correlation between response and estimate but to the implicit model on which the actual estimates are based. The definition of the supposedly false concensus effect, however, is based purely on the existence of the correlation. *Any* model with a var(p) > 0 predicts a different estimate based on a yes than on a no response.

Thus, people who believed that there is some variability across items but who do not believe that the variability is so great as to constitute a uniform distribution should give estimates that depart from $\bar{p}$, but by less than .167. (By asking each item in both positive and negative frames, we can assume that a subject assuming consistency on the part of group members will believe $\bar{p}$ to be .50; thus, average estimates greater than .67 for items to which he or she responds yes or less than .33 for no could be interpreted as evidence of a *truly* false consensus effect.) The question of whether a consensus effect is false is equivalent to the question of whether an estimate is *insufficiently regressive*. We know that in other contexts people make predictions that are insufficiently regressive, but later I will review some evidence that in this context we often find the reverse effect.

Sufficiently or insufficiently regressive according to what model? First, according to a "reasonable" model. Subjects surely have some idea of the variability of response in an identified group of which they are a member across a domain of items—for example, regarding food preferences or political beliefs. The implicit model can be checked by assuming that the subject is a good estimator and noting that the difference in estimation for yes and no responses should equal var(p)/var(I). Note not only that such a check assumes statistical optimality on the part of the subjects but also that other factors affecting the estimates are not systematically related to the subjects' own responses—an assumption that is dubious if the sample of items is small.

Second, according to the subject's own implicit model. Here, we do not assume statistical optimality on the part of the subject but rather check to see how well the subject's differences in estimates match that subject's own value of var(p)/var(I) computed across the entire set of items. Again, granting the ceteris paribus assumption that other factors influencing subjects' estimates are not systematically related to their own responses, this analysis is based on the principle that internal coherence ("reliability") is a necessary condition for validity—although not a sufficient one.

Now what about the problem that any individual is a member of many groups? First, the multiple-group-membership phenomenon is true of all base-rate analyses. If 90 percent of the accidents in a particular area involve (for whatever reason) blue taxis, that is the base rate. If only 25 percent involve drivers with more than 5 years' experience, that is the base rate. If you know that the taxi was blue and I know that the driver was experienced, we have different base rates ("priors") to consider in evaluating a witness's testimony. Second, the subject is told which group is the target one and is able to use any available information about that group's var(p) in making the estimate.

A final objection is based on the idea that such consensus judgments are based on "the law of small numbers." The answer is that, in proposing belief in this "law," Tversky and Kahneman (1971) argue that people overestimate the degree to which such samples are diagnostic, not that such samples are totally nondiagnostic. Some have generalized the argument to the point of maintaining that samples of size $N = 1$ should not be used at all. The problem with this assertion is that any sample of size $N > 1$ can be considered to be a sequence of samples of size $N = 1$, each of which must have some diagnostic value if the entire sample is to have any. For example, the probability of drawing five spades off the top of a deck of cards can be determined either on the basis of total configurations or on the basis of sequential sampling. It is equal to the number of sets of five spades divided by the number of sets of five cards in the deck, but it is also equal to the probability that the first card is a spade (1/13) multiplied by the probability that the second one is a spade given that the first one is (12/51), and so on. When we look at making an inference from a larger sample, we can look at it in a step-by-step way. If $N = 1$ has no diagnostic validity whatsoever, my first observation cannot change anything, so I have the same prior idea when I look at the second observation as I did when I looked at the first. I iterate the argument and end up with the conclusion that any sample of any size is irrelevant.

I want to cover two other points before I present some data. First, the subject's own response is often not the only information that the subject should use in estimating base rates. Clearly, information based on interaction with other group members is important; in fact, such information may even lead particular subjects to believe that they are atypical of the group of which they are a member and therefore weight their own responses negatively. But the importance of other information is not unique to the consensus context. Generally, for example, there is a positive correlation between people's height and weight; therefore, if I know only that someone is of above-average height, I predict that that person is of above-average weight. If I know that the person has been on a hunger strike for 30 days, I make a different prediction. And so on. Interestingly, as follows from both the correlational and the Bayesian analyses, the less other information available, the more important consensus should be as a predictor of base rates. It follows that we should expect researchers to proclaim a false consensus effect for precisely those odd and unusual activities concerning which subjects have very little nonconsensus information about others' behavior—for example, walking around the Stanford campus with a signboard demanding "Repent!"

A second point—which will be important later in this chapter—is that the size of the group about which base rates are to be estimated is irrelevant. (Note that there has been nothing in the development referring to group size.) I mention this point because, when I first illustrated my conclusions with an example of two items and three people, the most common objection I encountered was, "That's just because each individual accounts for a third of the group!"

Does estimating on the basis of assumed consensus work empirically? Yes.

Mathematical results are applicable to the real world. In a *within-individual* analysis, Hoch (1987) assessed degree of perceived consensus by correlating subjects' responses with their estimates and their accuracy by correlating estimates with true proportions. The frequencies to be estimated were endorsements of a 21-item consumer questionnaire (e.g., "Our family is too heavily in debt today"). Actual endorsement frequencies for various items in a national survey of 3,000 married consumers ranged from 31 to 87 percent. Business school students were asked to fill out this questionnaire and estimate endorsement frequencies either for the survey respondents or for their peers. In addition, both husband and wife of 80 married couples were asked to indicate their agreement with each item on a seven-point Likert scale and to predict their spouse's agreement—without, of course, discussing the questionnaire. With the exception of the M.B.A.s' predictions of the national survey responses, the correlations between consensus and base rates were positive to the point that 65 percent of the subjects could have improved their predictions had they given their own responses more—not less—weight than a "lens" multiple-regression analysis (Hursch, Hammond, and Hursch 1964; Tucker 1964) indicated that they in fact did. Hoch concluded that, whereas 63 percent of the M.B.A. students predicting national survey responses gave their own responses too much weight in their estimates, such overweighting was found in only 24 percent of the consumers predicting peers and in only 16 percent of the married subjects in the spouse condition. Apparently, the M.B.A. students were not like the respondents to the national survey. Well, M.B.A. students are different; for example, most care about money.

The analysis developed in this chapter differs in three important ways from Hoch's. First, Hoch, noting that actual endorsement rates across items differ, argues that the analysis must be limited to within-subjects predictions; he rejects the possibility that a between-subjects, within-items correlation between responses and estimates could not be valid—"because own position is artificially constrained to be orthogonal to target position" (1987, 223). In contrast, I argue that both analyses are equally valid.

Second, Hoch treats the optimal weights on one's own responses as empirically determined. In contrast, I argue that they are analytically determined, specifically from the variance of the item responses. For example, Hoch argues that the M.B.A. students "perceive" (229) too much consensus when estimating the National Survey responses. In contrast, I fearlessly predict that a statistical analysis would reveal that the M.B.A. students' responses just happen to be negatively correlated with the responses in the national survey. It is not a matter of "perceptions." In the very unusual situation in which people in group 1 are estimating the responses of people in group 2, consensus estimates will work for *analytic* reasons if and only if the base rates in groups 1 and 2 are positively correlated—again, for the very simple reason that base rates are correlated with individual responses. In contrast, the response base rates of the group of M.B.A. students cannot be negatively correlated with themselves. Thus, consensus as a basis for estimation is analytically valid.

Third, while Hoch notes the importance of actual similarity between spouses when they are asked to predict each others' responses, he does not consider the importance of the base rates across all his 160 subjects. If there is base-rate variance, then consensus estimates can be used in making predictions about anyone in the sample—for example, in man 1's predictions of the responses of the wife of man 2. Such consensus-based predictions could be as valid as those of predicting one's own spouse. We just do not know.

Let me now describe a study that I recently completed. It was an extensive class project on the validity of interviewing.[1] (All 10 students in this advanced class on judgmental and empirical strategies for evaluating others' attitudes and behaviors opted for this interview project out of several possible ones.) Students interviewed different groups of 20 Carnegie-Mellon students whom they did not know and who made up pseudonyms to preserve anonymity (and who were paid $10). Some of the students used structured interviews, some unstructured ones. After 40 minutes of talk, the students took notes about the interviews while the subjects responded to the 16 items of the CPI (see the appendix)—those with base rates of endorsement for both Berkeley males and females ranging systematically from .85 to .15. (One student taped her 20 interviews.) When all 200 subjects had been interviewed, each student answered the questions himself or herself and then—with full access to the notes taken—made a probability estimate that each of the 20 subjects interviewed would answer each question affirmatively.[2] The instructions for these judgments were as follows:

> In addition, make a *probability judgment* that your judgment that the interviewee answered "yes" or "no" is correct. This probability can be any number from .50 to 1.00. It can be interpreted as your degree of certainty about the correctness of your answer. For example, if you respond that the probability is .60, it means that you believe that there are about 6 chances out of 10 that your judgment is correct. A response of 1.00 means that you are absolutely certain that your judgment is correct. A response of .50 means that your best guess is as likely to be right as wrong. Don't estimate any probability below .50, because you should always be picking the alternative that you think is more likely to be correct. Write your probability judgment next to the question.
>
> To repeat, this probability is a measure of your degree of certainty

---

1. I would like to thank student interviewers Tom Donovan, Victor Forberger, Lauren Howard, Leesa Keys, Jennifer Kim, Deborah McKillop, Joe Melvin, Jane Tshudy, William Walker, and Teresa Williams—all of whom will become coauthors when this study is expanded.
2. Owing to an unfortunate clerical slip, the response alternatives were changed from *agree/disagree* to *yes/no*.

that your chosen alternative is the correct alternative. It is a number from .50 to 1.00 where .50 means complete uncertainty and 1.00 means complete certainty.

You can make most probability judgments in one of two (equivalent) ways:

(i) decide whether the interviewee said "yes" or "no" and make a judgment between .50 and 1.00 of your probability of being correct; or

(ii) assign a probability p to indicate your judgment of the probability that the person said "yes" and a probability $1 - p$ to indicate your judgment of the probability that the person said "no." (Whichever is higher is your judgment of the more likely response, and the probability assigned to it is your probability that this judgment is correct.) If you use this method you must *still* choose one of the answers as (slightly) more likely—even if both p's assigned are .50; just "flip a mental coin," if you feel totally uncertain.

The student interviewers were not trained in proper scoring rules; therefore, the simplest measure of accuracy is the mean squared difference between probability judgment and response. This MSE is equivalent to the Brier (1950) score.

Table 8.1 presents the MSE based on four criteria: the item base rates, the actual judgments made by the student interviewers, consensus-based estimates, and an overall base-rate prediction of .50. The student interviewers, of course, did not know the true value of var(p)/var(I) and hence that the best consensus predictions were .605 for yes and .395 for no. Instead, the values .67 and .33 were used—as if each interviewer had assumed a uniform distribution of item endorsements. (For the reasons presented in this chapter, .605 and .395 would have been superior; the .67/.37 split represents a worst-case consensus prediction; Hoch [personal communication, 21 March 1988] finds .55 and .45 to work best for his consensus data.) Table 8.1 presents the MSE (= Brier) results for each of the 10 interviewers separately.

The first result is rather striking. All interviewers would have been *more accurate* had they relied exclusively on base rates rather than their impressions formed during the 40-minute interview. Second, the consensus prediction increased accuracy relative to overall base rates for all subjects, except for one tie. Third, the interviewers did gain some information from the interviewees other than what they could have gleaned from their own responses. In the future, I plan a number of additional analyses and conditions: letting the interviewers make their own base-rate estimates, avoiding retrospection by using more interviewers who simply talk to one interviewee, supplying some interviewers with the true item base rates prior to making their estimates, and determining how the interviewers' liking of the interviewee affects use of consensus and base-rate information (either actual or estimated).

I now turn to the question of why people believe in the falsity of the consensus effect—that is, fail to appreciate that, just as individual responses can

TABLE 8.1
RESULTS OF CLASS EXPERIMENT

	I_1	I_2	I_3	I_4	I_5	I_6	I_7	I_8	I_9	I_{10}
Item base rate	.206	.146	.221	.200	.158	.170	.157	.184	.173	.193
Interview	.212	.179	.238	.240	.177	.189	.159	.210	.189	.236
Consensus	.220	.202	.219	.250	.154	.213	.207	.215	.228	.228
Overall base rate	.250	.250	.250	.250	.250	.250	.250	.250	.250	.250

be predicted from base rates (Cronbach 1955; Gage and Cronbach 1955), the inverse prediction can be made as well (mutatis mutandis). There is a body of empirical work concerning the failure to integrate base-rate information into judgments of individual responses; psychologists and others underneath the ambiguous umbrella labeled *behavioral decision making* study this failure on the part of their subjects. Here, in contrast, the failure is that of the investigators themselves (or at least of the authors of the 134 studies and their reviewers).

While we attend to each others' cognitive limitations and irrationalities, the usual contexts in which we do so are informal ones—for example, as journal reviewers or clever conversationalists. There are rare exceptions involving systematic study, as, for example, reported in Tversky and Kahneman's (1971) original paper on "the law of small numbers," but they are rare. I must confess that I have done no systematic study of my colleagues' belief in the falsity of consensus estimates; I have not even kept a careful count of the number of times I have been told I am wrong, crazy, or guilty of a fallacious algebraic demonstration of an artifact. (I can, in contrast, assert that the number of times I have heard the phrase *of course* is zero, although I hope to hear that phrase with ever-increasing frequency in the future.) What follows is speculative. I will present three principles of incoherence that may, singly or in combination, lead to a failure to understand that consensus estimates can be valid.

1. A prediction or estimation strategy that is known a priori to result in errors is a bad (false) one.

Valid consensus estimates can never be "right on." First, they are regressive and—as do all regressive predictions—result in a distribution of predictive values with a variance smaller than the variance of actual values. Thus, all regressive predictions have to be imperfect (standardized MSE $= 1 - r^2$, not 0). Second, since subjects make a higher prediction for those items they endorse than for those they reject, their predictions must be in the wrong direction a certain proportion of the time—unless, of course, all items have endorsement frequencies of zero or one. In the 16 items, for example, a perfectly representative group of students will make directionally incorrect estimates 30 percent of the time (the average of 15, 25, 35, and 75 percent). Worse yet, both the direction and the magnitude of the error can be predicted in advance. Since the consensus judgment means that people who affirm the item or behavior give a higher estimate than those who do not, those who answer yes will have a tendency to misestimate more than those who answer no when a majority answer no, and vice versa. (This difference is always true when $\bar{p} = .50$, as, for example, in supplying probability judgments to each alternative of a dichotomous question.) Those giving a minority response to an item will misestimate more than those giving a majority response.

Let me illustrate this last assertion about magnitude with an example from Sanders and Mullin (1983). Undergraduates answered yes/no questions on diverse topics ranging from expectation of living past 70 to preferring Italian movies to French ones to "anticipating re-election of Jimmy Carter in 1980," and they also estimated the proportion of college students who would answer yes to each. Not surprisingly, given the analysis outlined above, "the majority subjects generated more accurate comparison information than did the minority" (57). Consider, for example, a student who knew the mean and variance of the item-endorsement frequencies—which are .46 and .0520, respectively. Such a subject would estimate a yes response rate of .57 for items answered yes and .37 for those answered no. The actual average frequencies of yes responses for those items yielding a majority of yeses was .69 and for those items generating a majority of nos .28. Thus, for both types of items, those in the majority would underestimate the amount of consensus, but those in the minority would underestimate it more. The figures are appropriately 10 and 30 percent underestimation, respectively. That is exactly what happened; the acutal figures were 8 and 25 percent. Very close. I am not claiming that subjects knew the mean and variance of the item endorsements, but, when we obtain results virtually identical to those that would be obtained from statistically optimizing subjects who did, it is questionable to ascribe these results to "causes," such as "bad feelings" about holding a minority position.[3]

In one of his last papers (Einhorn 1986), Hilly Einhorn pointed out that optimal—or often even satisficing—strategies of estimation and prediction involve minimizing error, not eliminating it. Using such strategies, therefore, implies accepting the inevitability of error. For an apparently trivial example, consider the old probability-matching experiments, in which subjects were asked to predict the outcome of a binary event with unequal outcome probabilities in which there is no contingency between successive outcomes—for example, a blue chip is drawn from a bookbag with a constant probability of

---

3. I am indebted to Steve Hoch for pointing out the general implications of my analysis for Sanders and Mullin (1983).

.70 independent of previous draws, whereas a red chip is drawn with probability .30. Even when subjects are explicitly told that there is no contingency, have extensive experience that this assertion is true, and are paid for accuracy, they fail to adopt the optimal strategy of predicting the more probable outcome on every trial (cf. Tversky and Edwards 1966). To adopt this optimal strategy would be to accept a priori a known rate of error (e.g., 30 percent in the example—which is the same proportion with which a consensus-based prediction would yield an estimate in the wrong direction in both the data presented in this chapter and in the Sanders and Mullin study). The only way a subject could make a correct prediction on every trial is to probability match response-rate variance with base-rate variance and be extraordinarily lucky—just as the only way to avoid any error at all in making a prediction in a regression problem is to match variance of prediction with variance of outcome, that is, to make a totally nonregressive prediction.

When I was 7 years old, I once had a dream that I had a pet grasshopper in a large matchbox who told me the wisest choice to make whenever I was in doubt—only sometimes it was a gnome the size of a grasshopper. The dream was so pleasant that, when I woke before having to get up, I tried—unsuccessfully—to go back to sleep. Well, as adults we must learn to put away childish things. Only we do not. As Ellen Langer hypothesizes and clearly illustrates (Langer 1975, 1977; Langer and Roth 1975), we persist as adults in treating chance as if it were skill, even—perhaps especially—if we are successful at our work (March and Shapira 1987). The goal of finely developed skill is to eliminate error. Consensus-based estimates entail error; therefore, a consensus effect must be false. I suggest that we are suffer—more or less—from the delusion that deep within is the voice of the grasshopper, which we would hear if we could only listen better. Consequently, we reject consensus as an estimation procedure.

2. Macroconsistency in understanding cognitive biases is too broad and vague a goal for which to strive: Better to catalog effects. We, ourselves, need not be coherent.

As Emerson stated, "a foolish consistency is the hobgoblin of little minds." Many people who refer to this quote neglect the word *foolish*. It is not a trivial qualifier.

I became interested in the logic of the false consensus effect slightly over a year ago while organizing a class project on social judgment for an empirical methods course. The point of the project was to demonstrate well-documented social biases through a brief mail survey of Pittsburgh residents and Carnegie-Mellon University (CMU) students. Questions were dichotomous of a roughly liberal-conservative nature (Canela, Gold, and Dawes, in preparation). Subjects were sampled and identified by group membership: Pittsburgh resident,

CMU undergraduate, or—within CMU undergraduates—students at the College of Fine Arts or the College of Engineering. We approached potential subjects, who were sampled in as near a random way as possible, by phone, and—if receiving a verbal willingness to participate for $5—mailed out the questionnaire. In addition to answering the questions yes or no, subjects were asked to estimate the proportion of yes responses in the group with which they were identified and in a contrasting group (e.g., Pittsburgh resident vs. CMU undergraduate). (The sample of randomly selected CMU undergraduates identified as such was separate from the samples of fine arts and engineering students.) The project was meant to demonstrate five principles.

The first principle was the existence of actual differences between groups in the direction generally believed by casual social observers. Pittsburgh residents were expected to be more conservative than CMU students, engineering students than fine arts students. They were. The second was the existence of a social contrast effect that results in an asymmetric distortion of these differences. The discrepancy between the actual and the judged position for the contrasting group on the contrasting side of the liberal-conservative dimension was expected to be positive and greater than the discrepancy of the subject's group on its side. The third was the existence of an outgroup homogeneity effect. The average estimate of the endorsement frequencies was expected to be closer to zero or one for the contrasting group than for the subject's own group. The fourth was the existence of a true consensus effect within individuals across items. Those subjects who had a higher correlation between own response and estimates were expected to be more accurate than those with a lower correlation—at least when making estimates for their own group. The fifth was the existence of a false consensus effect across individuals within items. Those subjects who had more extreme estimates of yes responses consistent with their own yes/no response to a particular item were expected to be less accurate than those with estimates less discrepant from .50 but consistent. The converse prediction was made for subjects whose estimates were inconsistent with their own responses.

I demonstrated with hypothetical data how each of these principles could be evaluated singly, and the students' response was the normal one: scribble, scribble, scribble. But then *I* began to feel uncomfortable. What was I telling the students? I was stating on the one hand that we exaggerate the differences between ourselves and others (principles 2 and 3) but on the other hand that we exaggerate the similarity (principle 5). Moreover, the exact opposite predictions for the within versus between analysis of the consensus effect began to bother me. I was indeed able on the spur of a question to generate hypothetical data that satisfied both expectations simultaneously—a true consensus effect within and a false one between—but the numbers were so bizarre that I was embarrassed, and even back in the uproar of my own office I could not do much better. (Basically, the sets of estimates of different subjects must have minimal overlap.)

After some months of thought, I came to the conclusion that I was uncomfortable because I was telling the students contradictory things. The contradiction was not within predictions but between predictions and hence at a general level. People cannot both have a consistent tendency to exaggerate the difference between themselves and others and also be prey to the false consensus effect. Of course, it is possible to wave one's hand at assimilation and contrast, but when does contrast start, especially when groups can be defined at varying levels of specificity? Besides, assimilation has never been well established when it is assessed by some method other than having subjects make categorical ratings. My resolution of this broad contradiction was to question whether the false consensus effect was clearly false—which led to diddling with some numbers, then some algebra, then some results, and finally this chapter.

It is easier, of course, simply to catalog social biases as a list of "cognitive illusions," as is done in the penultimate chapter of an excellent text. Moreover, not worrying about incoherence in the "big picture" protects oneself from the inherent vagueness of such pictures and charges of fuzzy thinking. But, if we can (correctly) fault our research subjects for little inconsistencies (e.g., contradictory answers to identical hypothetical questions framed in two different ways), should we not fault ourselves for big ones (e.g., stating that people both do and do not exaggerate the discrepancies between themselves and others, that correlation is symmetric but that only deduction is justifiable)? The solution to this incoherence proposed here is that the false consensus is not false—that the major bias in judging others is to exaggerate the differences between "them" and "us," that egotism consists of believing that we are unique, hence not representative of others. I was reinforced in this resolution when a student interviewer in the study I described earlier indicated that she had learned something very important in the project: "They're all alike, and they all think they are so different!" (But she still did not do as well as the base rates in predicting their responses.)

3. Diagnosticity exists only in a context of causality.

Our poor subjects fail to integrate the base-rate information in the famous blue/green cab problem unless they are told that 85 percent of the accidents in the area involve blue cabs *because* . . . (Bar-Hillel 1980). Our misguided clinical colleagues make horrific representative judgments without considering base rates—"this child's doll play is typical of those who have been abused; therefore she was abused"—and seemingly endless didactic efforts to get them to attend to base rate information fail (Meehl and Rosen 1955; Melton 1988). They are interested in what makes *this* particular individual "tick," and class membership does not provide a causal mechanism—just a probability (and some of us have even been told that we "fail to realize" that "statistics do not apply to the individual"). Well, my response made in isolation does not cause others to respond as I do, nor do their responses cause me to act as they do.

Of course, unless response rate is identical across all questions, there has to be a correlation between one response and another; a little algebra indicates that it is just, once again, $\text{var}(p)/\text{var}(I)$. (This result can be appreciated most easily by noting that the correlation between individual responses partialing out base rate is zero; hence, it equals $\sqrt{\text{var}(p)/\text{var}(I)}$ multiplied by itself.) But how do our own colleagues respond to simple hypothetical demonstrations of this correlation? I have heard the assertion many times that there is a correlation because a single subject "contributes" a lot to the base rate in these examples. "If the group got larger, the correlation would disappear." Of course it does not. The correlation remains constant, and that is easy enough to demonstrate by multiplying the number of hypothetical subjects in the demonstration by 1,000. It is only when this causal explanation of the phenomenon is shown to be wrong that the search for an algebraic error is begun.

We too do not appreciate contingency without causality.

A NOTE ABOUT MAGICAL THINKING

Elster (in preparation) proposes that the belief that one can be diagnostic of others involves an implicit acceptance of "magic." I hope that I have persuaded the reader that it does not. Let me give an example of what I propose to be real magical thinking. Suppose that I use my own response to make *different* predictions about various others' responses on the basis of their relationship with me. For example, suppose I am asked to make predictions about how each of three others will play a particular two-person prisoner's dilemma game and that I know nothing about these others except that I have been told that one of them (I do not know which) has been randomly paired to play the game with me. I then make a prediction that the person with whom I have been randomly paired will be more likely to choose as I choose than will the other two people. According to the argument made here, I should—in a total absence of all other information—use my own response to make the same prediction for all members of a particular group of which I am a member, depending on my beliefs about the variance of group members' responses across a relevant set of choices. There is no reason to think that the person with whom I am paired will act any differently from the other two. Messé and Sivacek (1979) have examined this exact situation and found that subjects do in fact assume more similarity for the choice of the person with whom they have been randomly paired than for the other subjects. It is making such a differential consensus prediction that is magic, however, not making a consensus prediction per se.

APPENDIX

QUESTIONNAIRE
Judgmental Survey Strategies–Spring '88

FORM A

Please answer the following questions yes or no. While that may be difficult for a few, please do not leave any blank. Circle *yes* or *no* at the end of each. Thank you.

1. I think I would like the work of a school teacher. *Yes* No = .45.

2. It often seems that my life has no meaning. *Yes* No = .25.

3. I do not always tell the truth. *Yes* No = .75.

4. My table manners are not quite as good at home as when I am out in company. *Yes* No = .65.

5. Several times a week I feel as if something dreadful is about to happen. *Yes* No = .15.

6. People should not have to pay taxes for the schools if they do not have children. *Yes* No = .15.

7. My daily life is full of things that keep me interested. *Yes* No = .75.

8. Sometimes I feel like swearing. *Yes* No = .85.

9. I regard the right to speak my mind as very important. *Yes* No = .85.

10. I used to like it very much when one of my papers was read to the class in school. *Yes* No = .65.

11. I usually don't like to talk much unless I am with people I know very well. *Yes* No = .55.

12. When in a group of people I have trouble thinking of the right things to talk about. *Yes* No = .35.

13. I usually take an active part in the entertainment at parties. *Yes* No = .45.

14. I cannot keep my mind on one thing. *Yes* No = .25.

15. I enjoy hearing lectures on world affairs. *Yes* No = .55.

16. I refuse to play some games because I am not good at them. *Yes* No = .35.

REFERENCES

Bar-Hillel, M. 1980. The base rate fallacy in probability judgments. *Acta Psychologica* 44:211–33.

Brier, G. W. 1950. Verification of forecasts expressed in terms of probability. *Monthly Weather Review* 75:1–3.

Canela, J. A., E. Gold, and R. M. Dawes. In preparation. The Pittsburgh Conservatism Scale (PCS): Construction and validation of a scale to measure conservatism using the Wilson-Patterson approach. Carnegie Mellon University. Typescript.

Cronbach, L. J. 1955. Processes affecting scores on "understanding others" and "assumed similarity." *Psychological Bulletin* 5:177–93.

Dawes, R. M. 1989. Statistical criteria for establishing a truly false consensus effect. *Journal of Experimental Social Psychology.* 25:1–17.

DeVoto, B. 1922. *Mark Twain in Eruption.* New York: Harper & Row.

Einhorn, H. J. 1986. Accepting error to make less error. *Journal of Personality Assessment* 50, no. 3:387–95.

Elster, J. In preparation. Collective action and social norms. University of Chicago. Typescript.

Gage, N. L., and L. J. Cronbach. 1955. Conceptual and methodological problems in interpersonal perception. *Psychological Review* 62:411–22.

Gough, H. G. 1986. *California Psychological Inventory, form 462.* Palo Alto, Calif.: Consulting Psychologists Press.

Hoch, S. J. 1987. Perceived consensus and predictive accuracy: The pros and cons of projection. *Journal of Personality and Social Psychology* 53:221–34.

Hursch, C. J., K. R. Hammond, and J. L. Hursch. 1964. Some methodological considerations in multiple-case probability studies. *Psychological Review* 71:42–60.

Langer, E. J. 1975. The illusion of control. *Journal of Personality and Social Psychology* 32:311–328.

———. 1977. The psychology of chance. *Journal of Theory and Social Behavior* 7:185–207.

Langer, E. J., and J. Roth. 1975. Heads I win, tails is chance: The illusion of control is a function of the sequence of outcomes in a purely chance task. *Journal of Personality and Social Psychology* 32:951–55.

March, J. G., and Z. Shapira. 1987. Managerial perspectives on risk taking. *Management Science* 33:1404–18.

Marks, G., and N. Miller. 1987. Ten years of research on the false-consensus effect: An empirical and theoretical review. *Psychological Review* 102:72–90.

Meehl, P. E., and A. Rosen. 1955. Antecedent probability and the efficacy of psychometric signs, patterns, or cutting scores. *Psychological Bulletin* 52:194–201.

Melton, G. B. 1988. Psychologists' involvement in cases of child maltreatment: Limits of roles and expertise. Working paper (adopted as a policy statement). Washington, D.C.: American Psychological Association, Division 37, Child, Youth and Family Services.

Messé, L. A., and J. M. Sivacek. 1979. Prediction of others' responses in a mixed-motive game: Self-justification or false consensus? *Journal of Personality and Social Psychology* 37:602–7.

Mullen, B., J. L. Atkins, D. S. Champion, C. Edwards, D. Hardy, J. E. Story, and M. Venderklok. 1985. The false consensus effect: A meta-analysis of 115 hypothesis tests. *Journal of Experimental Social Psychology* 21:263–83.

Neustadt, R. E., and E. R. May. 1986. *Thinking in Time.* New York: Free Press.

Nisbett, R., and L. Ross. 1980. *Human inference: Strategies and shortcomings of social judgment.* Englewood Cliffs, N.J.: Prentice-Hall.

Ross, L., and D. Greene, and P. House. 1977. The "false consensus effect": An egocentric bias in social perception and attribution process. *Journal of Experimental Social Psychology* 13:279–301.

Ross, L., and F. Sicoly. 1979. Egocentric biases in availability and attribution. *Journal of Personality and Social Psychology* 37:322–36.

Sanders, G. S., and B. Mullin. 1983. Accuracy in perceptions of consensus: Differential tendencies of people with majority and minority positions. *European Journal of Social Psychology* 13:57–70.

Schelling, T. C. 1966. [Comments.] In *Strategic interaction and conflict*, ed. K. Archibald, 150. Berkeley, Calif.: University of California Press.

Sherman, S. J., L. Chassin, C. C. Presson, and G. Agostenelli. 1984. The role of the evaluation and similarity in the false consensus effect. *Journal of Personality and Social Psychology* 47:1244–62.

Sherman, S. J., C. C. Presson, and L. Chassin. 1984. Mechanisms underlying the false consensus effect: The special role of threats to the self. *Personality and Social Psychology Bulletin* 10:127–38.

Tversky, A., and W. Edwards. 1966. Information versus reward in binary choice. *Journal of Experimental Psychology* 71:680–83.

Tversky, A., and D. Kahneman. 1971. The belief in the "law of small numbers." *Psychological Bulletin* 76:105–10.

Tucker, L. R. 1964. A suggested alternative formulation in the development by Hursch, Hammond, and Hursch and by Hammond, Hursch, and Todd. *Psychological Review* 71:528–30.

9

Back to Base Rates

MAYA BAR-HILLEL

The existing literature on the base-rate fallacy offers a picture of the conditions under which base rates will or will not be used that is as robust and coherent as the phenomenon itself. This picture is briefly summarized with examples. However, the full base-rate story, especially its normative side, has yet to be told. Open questions, for both empirical and formal research, are sketched. For example, when are base rates thought of as properties of ensembles or of entire populations and when are they interpreted as properties of individual population members? How does this property affect their likelihood of being integrated with other information? When is it normatively appropriate to ignore base rates, to give them small weight in forming a prior, or to combine them with additional information by formal means that differ from Bayes's theorem? A graphic representation for causal versus incidental base rates is offered and possible relations between the base-rate fallacy and counterfactuals and between the base-rate fallacy and Simpson's paradox are suggested.

It is fifteen years since Kahneman and Tversky published the first results of what has come to be known as the base-rate fallacy. In a landmark paper (Kahneman and Tversky 1973), they described the now classic Tom W. and engineer/lawyer studies. In these studies, subjects were provided with a brief personality description of a person and a list of different categories to which the person might belong. The task was to assess the category in which the described person was most likely to be a member. Subjects appeared to base these judgments on the extent to which the given description matched the various category stereotypes, all but ignoring the relative sizes—that is, the base rates—of the different categories. To illustrate, one description read as follows: "Jack is a 45 year old man. He is married and has four children. He is generally conservative, careful, and ambitious. He shows no interest in political and social issues and spends most of his free time on his many hobbies which include home carpentry, sailing, and mathematical puzzles" (Kahneman and Tversky 1973, 241). Subjects presented with this nondiagnostic description gave a mean probability judgment of close to 90 percent that Jack was an engineer—regardless of whether they were told that the description was randomly drawn from a file containing 70 descriptions of engineers and 30 of lawyers or one containing 30 descriptions of engineers and 70 of lawyers. However, according to the standard normative account, formalized by Bayes's theorem, the odds in favor of Jack's being one of the engineers rather than one of the lawyers ought to have been over five times larger in the first case than in the second (7/3 : 3/7 = 5.44).

The base-rate fallacy was initially linked to the representativeness heuristic, according to which "the probability of an uncertain event, or a sample, [is evaluated] by the degree to which it is . . . similar in essential properties to its parent population" (Kahneman and Tversky 1972, 431). It soon became apparent, however, that, while the representativeness heuristic may promote the base-rate fallacy, it is neither a necessary nor a sufficient condition for its occurrence (Bar-Hillel 1984). Base rates are sometimes ignored in tasks that do not call for judgments of representativeness, and they are sometimes utilized in tasks that do.

An example of the former is provided by the cab problem (see, e.g., Bar-Hillel 1980):

> Two cab companies operate in some city, the Blue and the Green (according to the color of cab they run). Eighty-five percent of the cabs in the city are Blue, and 15 percent are Green.
> A cab was involved in a hit-and-run accident at night in which a pedestrian was run over. An eyewitness identified the cab as a Green cab. The court tested the witness's ability to distinguish between Blue and Green cabs under nighttime visibility conditions. It found that the witness was able to identify each color correctly about 80 percent of the time but confused it with the other color about 20 percent of the time.

Although the wording of this problem does not typically invoke the representativeness heuristic, subjects who are asked for the probability that the hit-and-run cab was indeed Green, as stated by the witness, overwhelmingly tend to respond with 80 percent—a response that reflects the witness's accuracy but ignores the low base rate of Green cabs in that city.

Ajzen (1977) provided an example of the converse, namely, base rates that *are* used in spite of the presence of the representativeness heuristic. His subjects were given a brief personality description of Gary W., a graduate student. They estimated the probability that Gary had passed some test. Subjects were told that this test is typically passed by either 75 or 25 percent of those taking it. In response to this problem, subjects did exhibit sensitivity to the stated base rate of pass versus fail in the test. This result can be explained by noting that the rate of test failures is a natural measure of a test's difficulty. The difficulty of a test, in turn, can readily be linked causally to the chances that any individual candidate would pass it. The conclusion is that base rates that can be causally linked to the target outcome will not be ignored. They exert an effect even if Gary's chances of passing the test are also evaluated by how representative he is of a good as opposed to a poor student.

That the existence of causal links between base rates and target outcomes is important in determining whether base rates affect judgment was later confirmed in cab-type problems as well (i.e., in problems that do not require representativeness). Altogether, the experimental literature on the base-rate fallacy has, over the years, painted a reasonably consistent picture, and for some time now it has seemed that we have a fairly robust and comprehensive answer to the question, When and why are base rates ignored? In a nutshell, the answer is as follows (more comprehensive accounts can be found in Bar-Hillel 1980, 1983; Tversky and Kahneman 1982).

Base rates are not ignored for procedural reasons (Tversky and Kahneman 1982) such as the nature of the problem format, the experimental design, or the task requirements—although each of these, when systematically manipulated, can sometimes have some effect on base-rate use. For example, systematically varying the base-rate parameter across problems within subjects draws attention to it and elicits responses that vary with the base rate—but not nearly enough or for the right reasons (i.e., enhanced understanding; Fischhoff and Bar-Hillel 1984). Neither are base rates ignored simply for cognitive convenience, such as reducing mental load or because subjects do not know the normatively appropriate way of utilizing them. Rather, base rates are by and large neglected if and when they are considered to be irrelevant to the prediction at hand.

When base rates refer only to category size and category size is seen to be purely arbitrary, they will generally be used only in the absence of other information. However, in many prediction tasks—both in real life and in the Bayesian tasks that dominate laboratory studies of base-rate neglect—base rates provide only a general informational background on which other information, which typically pertains more directly or specifically to the target case, is added. Thus, in tasks within the social judgment paradigm (Bar-Hillel 1983), such as the engineer/lawyer study, we have, in addition to the base rate, the description of the target individual (labeled *individuating information* by Kahneman and Tversky 1973). In tasks within the textbook-problem paradigm (Bar-Hillel 1983), such as the cab problem, we have, in addition to the base rate, an uncertain category indication (e.g., the color testified to by the witness along with the witness's accuracy rates—labeled *indicant information* by Bar-Hillel 1980). Such information, by virtue of pertaining more directly to the target case, tends to render the arbitrary base rates subjectively irrelevant.

Parenthetically, it is important to note that sometimes (though not in the problems discussed hitherto) more specific information really does override more general information. For example, when predicting the life expectancy of a newborn, knowledge of the life expectancy in that newborn's country overrides worldwide life-expectancy figures. (As we shall see later, distinguishing between cases in which specific information overrides base-rate considerations and cases in which it does not is by no means a trivial matter, either psychologically or normatively.)

Even in the presence of individuating or indicant information, base rates may sometimes influence target judgments—either if the additional information is deemed worthless or if the base rates retain their apparent relevance even in the presence of the additional information. The first could happen when the given description is either too neutral or too contradictory with respect to the alternative prediction categories (Ginosar and Trope 1980). The second could happen if the base rates are seen as conveying more than just category size, as when they are interpreted as a causal tendency or propensity (e.g., when the base rate of candidates failing an exam is taken as a measure of the exam's difficulty). Or it could happen if the indicant information is seen as conveying no more than category size and cannot be interpreted causally (e.g., the Intercom problem; Bar-Hillel 1980).

Finally, two quantitative notes are in order. First, even when base rates are used, they are seldom used in quite the correct fashion from a quantitative point of view. Second, when base rates are neglected, they are not usually totally ignored—at least as evinced in group data—since different people may differ in the extent to which they judge base rates as irrelevant and hence in the extent to which they are inclined to ignore them.

While new base-rate studies continue to appear from time to time (see, e.g., Gigerenzer, Hell, and Blank 1988), it has been quite a while since any of them warranted a significant revision of this general picture. This stated, it may come as a surprise that now, several years after my last in a longish series of base-rate fallacy papers (Bar-Hillel 1980, 1983, 1984; Bar-Hillel and Fischhoff 1980; Fischhoff and Bar-Hillel 1984), I am back to base rates. I share that surprise. Yet here I also want to share some new empirical results and thoughts about base rates. The empirical work was done jointly with Baruch Fischhoff, and the thoughts relating to normative aspects of base-rate use owe much to an unpublished manuscript by Kahneman and Tversky.

SOME NEW BASE-RATE RESULTS

Can Base Rates Dominate Indicant Information?

Some time ago, Fischhoff and I attempted to reverse the base-rate fallacy, in the following sense. Believing that we know the conditions under which base rates are dominated by indicant information, we thought that it should be possible to design a textbook-paradigm base-rate problem in which the base rate would be endowed with the characteristics usually associated with the indicant information, and vice versa. In that case, we might observe a situation in which the base rate will dominate, rather than be dominated by, the indicant information.

For this purpose, we needed to make the base rates causal, as is typical of the indicant information, while at the same time making the indicant information as noncausal and as general as the typical base rate. We had some idea how to achieve this from previous attempts to make base rates causal (e.g., Ajzen 1977; Bar-Hillel 1980; Tversky and Kahneman 1980; Locksley and

Stangor 1984) or indicant information less causal (Bar-Hillel 1980). After some tinkering, we came up with the following story.

> A study of suicide patterns was done in some community. The study showed that, although half the teenage population are boys and half are girls, about 80 percent of teenage suicide attempts are made by girls and 20 percent are made by boys.
>
> A teenager identified only as J. was one of the cases of attempted suicide analyzed in depth by the study. Some of the attempted suicides could not be analyzed at such depth because their files were lost in an unfortunate computer breakdown. Seventy-five percent of the boys' files survived the breakdown and 25 percent of the girls' files.
>
> What do you think are the chances that J. is a girl?

In this question, the base rate is the same as the one successfully employed by Tversky and Kahneman (1980), shown there to induce causal thinking. The indicant information, in turn, is modeled after Bar-Hillel's intercom problem (1980). It applies to the entire population, and there is little of a causal nature that comes to mind in explaining why a lower rate of boys' files were lost than of girls' files—arbitrariness is in the nature of accidents. Thus, we hoped that the modal response to this question would be 80 percent (i.e., the base rate for female suicide attempts).

Table 9.1 shows the results. As can be seen, 26% of 68 respondents gave 80 percent as their reply, thereby making reliance on the base rate, to the total exclusion of the indicant information, the modal response. As also noted in table 9.1, in the typical base-rate problem only about 5 percent of responses rely exclusively on the base rate. Similarly, typically about 50 percent of respondents rely exclusively on the indicant information, as compared to 9 percent here. Nonetheless, a plurality of 47 percent of the subjects, including the median respondent, lay in between the points suggested by the base rate alone and the indicant information alone (i.e., between 80 and 25 percent), which we take as evidence of some integration of both kinds of information.

How much of a success in reversing the familiar effect does this result represent? Though it is the best result that we obtained in a series of several attempts, it lies at the lowest boundary of the typical range of the base-rate fallacy—in which more than 30 percent and up to 75 percent of subjects give responses identical to the implications of the indicant information. In that light, the success is very modest.

Recall, however, that the quintessential characteristic that serves to define the indicant information as such, even when it has an actuarial nature much like the base rate, is that it describes a variable that is differentially distributed in the two population categories (here, boys vs. girls). Hence, by definition, removing this characteristic from the indicant information and conferring it on the base rate cannot be done without reversing the very roles of the base rate and the indicant information. But information that some variable has a different distribution in two groups is a strong invitation to causal thinking: one

TABLE 9.1
RESULTS OF SUICIDE BASE-RATE PROBLEM

Result	This Problem (%)	Typical Standard (%)
Base rate (80%)	26	5
Indicant information (25%)	9	50
Integration (between 25% and 80%)	47	40

cannot help wondering why the variable is not distributed similarly in both and trying to relate the answer to the nature of the two groups. Even if the search for a plausible causal link fails (as we hoped would happen in the suicide problem above), the very effort to find one focuses attention on the indicant information, thereby making it hard to ignore. This property gives the indicant information a built-in advantage over base rates, making the two intrinsically asymmetrical in terms of their effect on people's probabilistic reasoning.

In summary, although it is not difficult to elicit integration of base rates with indicant information by providing the proper cover story, we may have reached the limits of base-rate dominance over indicant information that can be achieved by manipulating cover stories. It can be done, but the effect (25 percent of the subjects totally ignoring the indicant information) is much weaker than its inverse—the domination of base rates by indicant information (occasionally by up to 75 percent of the subjects).

Ensembles versus Individual Cases

While in the previous problem we deliberately attempted to induce base-rate use, in the following one we expected to find the more common neglect, so the results we obtained took us quite by surprise.

Johnson and Finke open a 1985 paper by addressing the following questions to the reader: "Are there more first-born children than second-born children in graduate school? Last year, did more hotel fires originate on the first 10 floors or on the second 10 floors? In baseball games, are more runners thrown out by the pitcher at first base, at second base, or at third base?" Clearly, they went on to answer, "there are more first-borns than second-borns and more hotel floors numbered 1 to 10 than floors numbered 11 to 20, and there are also more runners who reach first base than second or third" (63). The truth of this simple base-rate assertion is a logical consequence of the natural ordering of births, floors, and bases rather than an empirical observation. But a prediction based on the base-rate fallacy would expect answers that reflect only subjects' estimates of the tendencies of firstborns versus secondborns to attend graduate school, of the fire proneness of the various hotel floors, or of the probability of being thrown out at each of the three bases.

Johnson and Finke did not actually present subjects with any of these three questions; they just used them didactically. So we ran the following hotel problem ourselves.

> In a certain town, a large hotel fire recently claimed 20 victims. Consequently, the town set up a committee to inquire into fire precautions in the town's public buildings, the preparedness of the fire brigade, etc. The committee examined witnesses, read files, collected statistics, etc. This being a large town with hotels big and small, fancy and simple, central and peripheral, quite a number of hotel fires had been recorded in the course of the years, though most were of a modest nature and had been quickly contained. The Fire Department records details such as supposed cause, time and place the fire broke out, time till it was put out, etc.
>
> According to your estimate, among all hotel fires recorded in this town over the years, were there more that broke out on lower residential floors (i.e., 1–10) or higher ones (i.e., 11–20)? This town has no hotels with more than 20 floors, and few reach even that height. Kitchens are not located on residential floors.

This question bears some resemblance to a children's riddle in which one is asked why more grass is consumed by white sheep than by black sheep. The intended answer is because there are more white sheep. This answer eludes most listeners, who seem to take their task to be to explain why an *individual* white sheep eats more grass than a black one. Imagine our surprise, then, when we discovered that a majority of our respondents (19 out of 29) chose floors 1–10 as their answer and that only five respondents each chose floors 11–20 or a roughly equal number.

At the moment, we can offer no more than a tentative ad hoc explanation of this result. Though this had not been our intention, our question formulation apparently directed subjects to think about the entire ensemble of first 10 floors versus second 10 floors rather than about individual floors. Moreover, it emphasized that the first category (floors 1–10) was far more numerous than the second one (floors 11–20), thus highlighting the base rate. In contrast, the sheep riddle works not because people are unaware that a large population eats more than a smaller one but because they do not think of the population when asked the riddle. To enhance our understanding of the base-rate fallacy, and perhaps to design debiasing devices to counter it, we need to explore further when population differences are more likely to be attributed to differences in their size and when to differences in the properties of their members. More on that in the final section.

ON THE NORMATIVE ROLE OF BASE RATES

When Base Rates Can Be Safely Ignored

The typical problem that has been utilized for studying the base-rate fallacy has been Bayesian in nature. The base rate provides the prior, and the additional information—individuating or otherwise—provides the likelihood ratio. However, not all problems in which base rates and other information co-occur are cast in this mold. An example follows:

> Two cab companies operate in a certain city, the Blue and the Green (according to the color of cab they run). Eighty five percent of the cabs in the city are Blue, and the remaining 15% are Green.
> A cab was involved in a hit-and-run accident at night.
> The police investigation discovered that in the neighborhood in which the accident occurred, which is nearer to the Green Cab company headquarters than to those of the Blue Cab company, 80% of all taxis are Green, and 20% are Blue.
> What, do you think, are the chances that the errant cab was Green?

This neighborhood problem (Bar-Hillel 1980, 226) was devised as an example in which it is normatively appropriate to disregard the base rate (i.e., the citywide statistics) in the presence of the additional information (i.e., the local neighborhood statistics). The latter simply replace the former. Rather than providing the likelihood ratio for a Bayesian assessment of the requested probability, the neighborhood statistics provide a direct, and more relevant, assessment of it.

Naive subjects apparently cannot tell the difference between the neighborhood problem and the standard cab problem (Fischhoff and Bar-Hillel 1984). The following problem may foil even more sophisticated readers.

> Kate and Ian FitzGerald were married in a traditional church wedding 17 years ago shortly after graduating from Notre Dame. Three years ago, Ian lost his high-paying job in the aerospace industry and has since taken to heavy drinking. Some time later, Kate, a former prom queen, took their five children and moved out of their home, taking residence close to her parents. She has vowed not to return home before Ian quits drinking and finds new employment.
> Where Ian and Kate live, about one out of every three or four marriages ends in divorce.
> What do you think are the chances that Ian and Kate will divorce?

A nonreflective student of Kahneman and Tversky's Tom W. or engineer/lawyer tasks might use the overall base rate of divorce as the prior probability that Kate and Ian will divorce and then use the individuating information about them to derive a likelihood ratio for their divorce. Multiplying the two according to Bayes's rule would then yield the required posterior.

This individuating information, however, places Kate and Ian in several subpopulations that have their own divorce rates. Most significantly, they appear to be Catholic (but Ian is also unemployed and an alcoholic). An assessment of $P(\text{divorce}/\text{Catholic})$ is actually more natural and probably easier to give than $P(\text{Catholic}/\text{divorce})$. Hence, the individuating information in this scenario, rather than providing a likelihood ratio that can be multiplied with the prior odds to yield the posterior, provides an unmediated estimate of the posterior by replacing one's prior, P(divorce), with a more specific and relevant estimate of the required probability, P(divorce/Catholic). While this estimate may be fine-tuned further to take account of the other facts contained in the individuating information, it is sufficient to render the overall base rate largely irrelevant.

An interesting complication arises if the information with the potential to replace the base rate is known only probabilistically. In the neighborhood problem, for example, this might happen if the neighborhood statistics are themselves a less-than-certain estimate. In the divorce problem, one might have less than full confidence in an inference that Kate and Ian are Catholics—or, more pertinently, practicing Catholics—solely on the basis of the individuating information at hand. Clearly, uncertainty with regard to the accuracy of the additional information reinstates the relevancy of the overall base rates. But the quantitative details of how the different items of information should be integrated in such a case is a normative question that still requires attention (see, however, Peterson 1973).

Assessing the Effect of Changing Base Rates

Suppose that, instead of the one-in-three divorce rate stated in the problem, a one-in-ten divorce rate were given. How should that affect the estimated chances that Ian and Kate will divorce? Well, if the previous base rate could have been ignored, then, by the same token, the new one can also be ignored, which suggests that the change in base rate should not affect the estimated chances that Ian and Kate will divorce at all. On the other hand, it seems that a change in divorce rate might signal changing social trends or tendencies that ought to be taken into account. To decide on the proper response to a change in base rate, a deeper analysis is needed, as follows.

The overall divorce rate in some country or population is a kind of weighted average of the divorce rates among its various subpopulations (whether partitioned into urban vs. rural, socioeconomic classes, ethnic backgrounds, educational levels, age, etc.). Hence, it can be affected by changes either in the population composition (e.g., the absorption of certain ethnic groups into mainstream America, a growth in the relative size of the middle class, an aging of the population, etc.) or in the divorce propensities within subgroups (e.g., removal of social stigma, introduction of no-fault divorce laws, etc.). These effects can counterbalance each other. In fact, it is even possible for the divorce rate in each and every subpopulation to increase at the same time as the overall divorce rate decreases—provided that subpopulations with decreasing divorce rates grow more rapidly than subpopulations with increasing divorce rates. This state of affairs (or its inverse) is known as Simpson's paradox (see, e.g., Blyth 1972).

With respect to our problem, the relevant question prior to deciding how a change in base rates ought to affect one's posterior is to find the right cause, or attribution, for the change in base rates. Thus, for example, if all it tells us is that the FitzGeralds live in an area with a smaller Catholic population than previously assumed, then the change in the stated base rate for divorce should have less effect on their estimated probability of divorcing than if that base rate is taken to reflect the fact that, say, they are members of a far more orthodox or conservative community than was implied by the lower base rate.

The following may be a clearer example of the possible influence of comparing base rates. Suppose you are about to undergo a dangerous type of major surgery and are in the process of selecting a surgeon. You find out that the mortality rates for Dr. A are twice as high as those for Dr. B.[1] Which would you prefer to perform the operation?

Offhand, most people not only opt for Dr. B but do not even see any dilemma. However, a surgeon's mortality rates are a weighted average, reflecting a combination of the surgeon's skill and the nature of his or her cases. Holding skill constant, a higher mortality rate reflects a higher preponderance of tougher cases. Holding case composition constant, a higher mortality rate reflects less skill. In the absence of additional knowledge, little can be inferred from a higher mortality rate. We do know, however, that in real life surgeons differ on both dimensions. There is variability in skill, and cases are not distributed at random—the harder cases tend to gravitate toward the more skilled surgeons. You are interested in finding the more skilled surgeon. That surgeon might well—though not necessarily—be the one with the higher mortality rate.

Simpson's Paradox and Counterfactuals

The fact that the relation between mortality rates and skill is more intuitively available than that between mortality rates and caseload composition is not unlike the fact that the relation between conditional probabilities and their causal implications is more intuitively available than that between conditional probabilities and their diagnostic implication (Tversky and Kahneman 1980). Suppose that Dr. A indeed outperforms Dr. B on every possible type of operation (or patient) but has a practice heavily weighted by severe cases whereas Dr. B's practice is largely composed of light cases. Table 9.2 provides a simplified numerical example for this state of affairs. There are two types of conditions, X and Y. Condition Y is far more severe or dangerous than condition X (the mortality rates, shown in the table, are six to seven times higher for condition Y than for condition X). Dr. A's practice is composed of 10 percent type-X patients and 90 percent type-Y patients, whereas Dr. B's practice is 90 percent type-X patients and 10 percent type-Y patients. For each of the two types, Dr. B's mortality rates are twice as high as Dr. A's, yet, overall, Dr. A's mortality rates are twice as high as Dr. B's.

Suppose you are scheduled to be operated on by Dr. B. You are more likely

---

1. I thank Kahneman and Tversky for this example.

TABLE 9.2
Hypothetical Mortality Rates by Surgeons and Types of Patients

	Type of Patient		
	X (%)	Y (%)	Overall Rate (%)
Dr. A	.6	4	3.7
Dr. B	1.2	8	1.9

to rejoice—erroneously—at the causal implications ("My chances on Dr. B's table are better") than—justifiedly—at the diagnostic implications ("I guess my condition isn't as bad as I thought").

This points out one reason why the probability of counterfactuals is so notoriously controversial and difficult to assess. For suppose, on discovering that you have been assigned for surgery with Dr. B, you now wish to assess your subjective probability of survival had you been assigned to Dr. A. If your condition is fixed, then your estimated (counterfactual) chances with Dr. A would have been higher, as the component rates indicate—not lower, as the overall rates indicate. If you do not know the severity of your condition, however, then your estimated (counterfactual) chances with Dr. A would indeed have been lower—not as a causal result of Dr. A's higher mortality rates (Dr. A is, after all, a more skilled surgeon) but because being (counterfactually) a patient of Dr. A's rather than Dr. B's carries the diagnostic implication that surgery is riskier for you than it is for the majority of Dr. B's patients.

Simpson's Paradox and the Base-Rate Fallacy

Weighted averages can lead to Simpson's paradox. As the example given above showed, surgeons' mortality rates might increase as their skill increases. Similarly, the average wage in academia might decrease while the average wages of professors broken down into the different ranks rise. The average cost of housing might increase while the cost of each of the different categories of housing decreases. The rate of teenage pregnancies can go up unaccompanied by any change in biological fertility and even as contraceptives improve in efficacy.

These are not merely hypothetical examples. Here are some real-life examples. In 1973, the Berkeley campus of the University of California accepted, without exercising sexism, a higher proportion of its male applicants than of its female applicants, even though the latter were more qualified overall (Freedman, Pisani, and Purves 1978). In Israel, the overall mortality rate for Jews is higher than that for Arabs, although in each and every cohort the reverse is true. Also, there are more orthodox Jews among younger adults in Israel than among older ones, though for each of the two major ethnic groups—Ashkenasy and Sephardic—the reverse is true (S. Shay, personal communication, 1987, based on a survey conducted by the Israeli Social Research Institute).

People who find these facts baffling can appreciate why Simpson's paradox is called that. In all these examples, a base-rate consideration can account for the facts. But the base-rate consideration somehow eludes many people.[2] Thus, the paradox in Simpson's paradox is connected to the base rate fallacy.

Consider the following problem (Falk and Bar-Hillel 1980, 106):

> A certain Art School has only two departments—Painting and Music. The school has been collecting statistics since it was founded, and these show that the Painting department admits about 80% of its female applicants versus about 40% of its male applicants, whereas the Music department, which has stricter requirements, admits about 12% of its female applicants versus about 6% of its male applicants. The statistics show, furthermore, that women are more interested in Music, i.e., 90% of the female applicants to the school enroll for Music and 10% enroll for Painting, while amongst the men the opposite is true: 90% of the male applicants enroll for Painting and only 10% enroll for Music.
>
> On the basis of these statistics, who, would you say, has had a better chance of being admitted to this school over the years, men or women?

Table 9.3 summarizes these rates.[3] Although men are actually twice as likely to be accepted into this school as women (37 vs. 19 percent), a majority (56 percent) of our 66 respondents answered that women were more likely to be accepted to this school than men. Apparently, they were more impressed by the fact that in each of the departments the acceptance rate for women is twice as high as that for men than by the fact that women favor the more selective department and men the less selective one.

This bias can be readily explained by the representativeness hypothesis. Global admission probabilities are of a kind with departmental admission probabilities (i.e., both pertain to admission rates) and hence more representative of them than they are of patterns of enrollment preferences, which speak to something quite different. More generally, an average can be the average of many kinds of numerical variables—IQ, income, school grades, life expectancy, fertility rate, and so on. But, if it is weighted, the weights are almost invariably base rates since the averaged components are typically weighted by their relative frequency. For this reason, a weighted average is more compatible with, hence more representative of, its components than their weights. It is thus more natural for people to conclude that a surgeon characterized by higher mortality rates is an inferior surgeon than to consider the alternative possibility that his or her patient load is heavily weighted by hard cases; more

---

2. Women tended to prefer the more selective departments, the Jewish population is older than the Arab population, and the Ashkenasy population is older than the Sephardic population.
3. Table 9.3 was obtained from table 9.2 by multiplying the cell entries by 10 and an appropriate relabeling of the rows and columns.

TABLE 9.3
ADMITTANCE RATES FOR ART SCHOOL DEPARTMENTS

	Music (%)	Painting (%)	Overall Rate (%)
Men	6	40	37
Women	12	80	19

natural to conclude that a student with a higher GPA is a better student than to suspect that she might have avoided demanding courses; more natural, even, to arrive at the counterintuitive conclusion that, if more pedestrians are killed crossing with the light than against it (as seems to have been the case in 1957 in Rhode Island, according to Huff, 1959), then it is dangerous to obey street lights than to recall that considerably more people cross with the light than against it.

Two final observations give anecdotal testimony to the prevalence of this particular form of base-rate neglect. One is the explicit and formal methodological barriers that have been erected to guard against it, most notably the concept of control groups in experimental designs. The other is the relative elusiveness in public-policy debates of distributional consequences of policy changes (in matters such as taxation, wages, contraception, inoculation, and insurance) as compared to appreciation of their direct effects.

Simpson's paradox appears paradoxical because of the base-rate fallacy—the tendency to neglect category size.

WHAT KIND OF BASE RATES WILL OR WILL NOT BE IGNORED?

To enhance our understanding of the base-rate fallacy, and perhaps to design debiasing devices to counter it, we need to explore further when population differences are more likely to be attributed to differences in their size and when to differences in the properties of their members. The following is a possible approach.

A Graphic Representation of Base Rates

Think of a population as a kind of matrix or grid, with the individual members represented by the cells. When a certain base rate applies to the population, it is represented by coloring the matrix in accordance with this base rate. There are two kinds of pure representations. One colors cells in their entirety, so that, if the base rate is, say, P, then a proportion P of the cells are colored fully and the rest not at all (see fig. 9.1). This base rate is a property of the aggregate and of the aggregate only. It is not exhibited by the individual members or by all samples (e.g., same-colored ones). The other representation colors an identical proportion P of each individual cell (see fig. 9.2). This base rate is a property of the individual members as well as of the ensemble and can

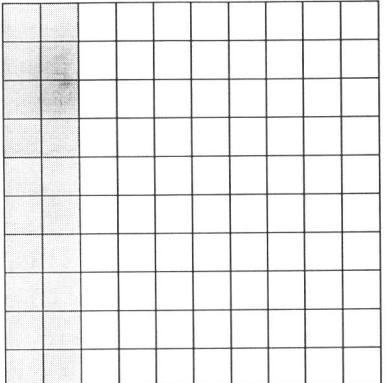

Figure 9.1. Graphic representation of a noncausal base rate that reflects only category sizes.

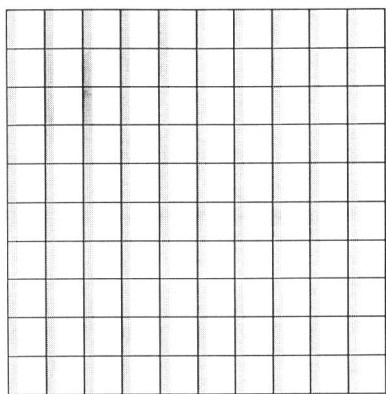

Figure 9.2. Graphic representation of a causal base rate that reflects individual propensities.

Figure 9.3. The relative size of the categories is not preserved in each sample.

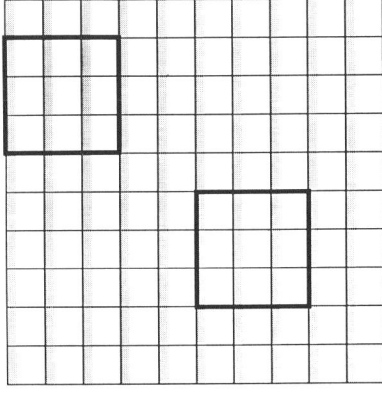

Figure 9.4. The individual propensities are preserved in each sample.

be thought of as a tendency, a propensity, or a disposition. It is manifest also in any sample from the population. In addition to these two pure representations, there can be mixed representations, as when different cells are colored in different proportions.

The hypothesis is that base rates influence probability judgments only insofar as the judge sees both colors and estimates their relative area. Hence, the first type of base rate becomes transparent (which essentially means invisible) when a single cell, or a sample of same-colored cells, is selected as the target event (see fig. 9.3). The second type of base rate never becomes transparent and is constant in any sample of cells (see fig. 9.4). In the mixed representations, things depend on the choice of a sample.

The standard kind of general noncausal base rates are of the first kind, whereas so-called causal base rates are of the second. Thus, the fact that 85 percent of the cabs in some city are Blue cannot be seen in individual cabs—each cab/cell is colored all green or all blue. But, when told that there are equal numbers of Green and Blue cabs yet 85 percent of the cab-related accidents involve Blue cabs, this is represented as accident proneness, a characteristic that is manifested even by individual cabs. Fifty percent of the cabs—those belonging to the Blue cab company—have more of it, which would be represented by coloring 85 percent of each Blue cell/cab, whereas the Green cells/cabs would be colored only 15 percent each. If we are told only that 85 percent of cab-related accidents involve Blue cabs but not what the base rate of Blue cabs is, the appropriate representation is not uniquely determined in the case in which each cell represents a single cab and color represents accident proneness, though it is if each cell represents a single accident and color represents cab color.

Alternative Interpretations, Alternative Representations

It is somewhat awkward to talk about a cab's tendency to be Green, but, with respect to some attributes, it is quite as natural to talk of tendencies to have them as it is to dichotomize them. Examples are *warm, funny, loyal, ambitious,* and so on. When one says, say, that Southern Italians are a warmer folk than Northern Italians, one can mean either that each Southern Italian tends to be warmer than a Northern Italian, ascribing warmth to individuals, or that more Southern Italians are warm than Northern Italians, ascribing warmth to the ensemble (in the second case, but not the first, it makes a difference if by *more* one means in the absolute or proportionately more). According to the proposed hypothesis, people who adopt the former interpretation (warmth as a characteristic of individuals) will be more sensitive to the base rate of warmth than people who adopt the latter interpretation (warmth as a characteristic of the subpopulations). This representation can be exploited to derive further testable hypotheses.

Deep Structure versus Surface Structure

The type of representation can be regarded as the base rate's deep structure, whereas the proportion of the grid that is colored is the surface structure. Different deep structures can underlie the same surface structure, but not vice versa. In linguistics, one way to distinguish between two sentences that have the same surface structure but different deep structures (e.g., "They are drinking glasses" and "They are drinking martinis") is to try to subject them to equivalent rephrasings, under which the nonidenticality of their deep structure is exposed. Likewise, two probability problems may be formally isomorphic in a given formulation but under an identical manipulation may lose this isomorphism. Thus, the standard cab problem and its causal version are formally isomorphic. Both can be solved by Bayes's theorem, and in both the prior odds and the likelihood ratio—therefore also the posterior odds—are the same. But subjecting them both to, say, a neighborhood manipulation (i.e., stating that the accident occurred in a neighborhood where most cabs are Green rather than Blue) has a different normative effect on the two. When 85 percent of the cabs in the city are Blue, the neighborhood base rate simply replaces the city base rate. But, when 85 percent of the accidents in the city involve Blue cabs even though only 50 percent of the cabs are Blue, then the neighborhood base rate must be combined with the different accident proneness to arrive at the normatively appropriate probability that is to be combined with the witness's testimony.

CONCLUSION

The fragments of results and speculations offered in this chapter show that the current version of the base-rate story is overly simplistic. Subjects are wrong to ignore base rates in the standard cab problem and right in considering them in the causal base-rate problem—though the formal, Bayesian analysis of both problems is the same. But subjects are right in their gut feeling that causal base rates differ from noncausal base rates and that ensemble base rates differ from propensities. In some circumstances, whether the base rates are properties of populations or of their members makes a real difference for the normative analysis. The full base-rate story is not yet told. This chapter does no more than suggest where it might go from here.

REFERENCES

Ajzen, I. 1977. Intuitive theories of events and the effects of base rate information on prediction. *Journal of Personality and Social Psychology* 35:303–14.
Bar-Hillel, M. 1980. The base rate fallacy in probability judgments. *Acta Psychologica* 44:211–33.
———. 1983. The base rate fallacy controversy. In *Individual decision making under uncertainty,* ed. R. W. Scholz, 39–61. Dordrecht: Reidel.
———. 1984. Representativeness and fallacies of probability judgments. *Acta Psychologica* 55:91–107.
Bar-Hillel, M., and B. Fischhoff. 1980. When do base rates affect predictions? *Journal of Personality and Social Psychology* 35: 303–14.
Blyth, C. R. 1972. On Simpson's paradox and the sure-thing principle. *Journal of the American Statistical Association* 67:364–66.
Falk, R., and M. Bar-Hillel. 1980. Magic possibilities of the weighted average. *Mathematics Magazine* 53, no. 2:106–7.
Fischhoff, B., and M. Bar-Hillel. 1984. Focussing techniques: A shortcut to improving probability judgments? *Organizational Behavior and Human Decision Processes* 34:175–94.
Freedman, D., R. Pisani, and R. Purves. 1978. *Statistics.* New York: Norton.
Gigerenzer, G., W. Hell, and H. Blank. 1988. Presentation and content: The use of base rates as a continuous variable. *Journal of Experimental Psychology: Human Perception and Performance* 14:513–25.
Ginosar, Z., and Y. Trope. 1980. The effects of base rates and individuating information on judgments about another person. *Journal of Experimental Social Psychology* 16:228–42.

Huff, D. 1959. *How to take a chance*. Harmondsworth: Pelican.

Johnson, J. T., and R. A. Finke. 1985. The base rate fallacy in the context of sequential categories. *Memory and Cognition* 13, no. 1:63–73.

Kahneman, D., and A. Tversky. 1972. Subjective probability: A judgment of representativeness. *Cognitive Psychology* 3:430–54.

———. 1973. On the psychology of prediction. *Psychological Review* 80:237–51.

Locksley, A., and C. Stangor. 1984. Why versus how often: Causal reasoning and the incidence of judgmental bias. *Journal of Experimental Social Psychology* 20:470–83.

Peterson, C. R., ed. 1973. Cascaded inference. *Organizational Behavior and Human Performance* 10:315–432.

Tversky, A., and D. Kahneman. 1980. Causal schemas in judgment under uncertainty. In *Progress in social psychology,* ed. M. Fishbein. Hillsdale, N.J.: Erlbaum.

———. 1982. Evidential impact of base rates. In *Judgment under uncertainty: Heuristics and biases,* ed. D. Kahneman, P. Slovic, and A. Tversky. New York: Cambridge University Press.

Discussion

DAVID SCHUM

ROBYN DAWES

I wish to focus on three points Robyn makes in his chapter: his concern about false consensus, his interesting technique for inferring a base rate from a single datum, and the value of a single datum in such an inference. I will discuss these matters within the context of an experience I once had that, I believe, offers some support to Robyn's conclusions about the consensus effect. This experience involves an analysis I made several years ago of the evidence in a murder trial that took place in Scotland. Had I known about it at the time, I might have used Robyn's base-rate inference scheme for inferring the voting behavior of the 15-person jury that actually reached a verdict in this case; the single datum is my own reaction to the evidence in this case.

In the High Court of the Justiciary in Edinburgh in June 1973, a man named John Preece was tried for murder; though not a cause célèbre, this case attracted substantial interest because there was nothing in the crown's charges against Preece that stated where he allegedly committed the murder. There was some awkwardness here; Preece is English, and the victim's body was discovered in England, but the trial took place in Scotland and under Scots law. In 1975, I received a complete transcript of the evidence in this case from a colleague whose firm of solicitors assisted in the defense of Preece. My colleague asked me not to read either the charge to the jury or the final verdict until I had read the entire transcript of this trial (974 pages). In spite of my curiosity, I did not. But all of us have initial expectations, or "priors" if you like; and mine were related to several discussions I had with my colleague shortly before he sent this transcript to me. These discussions involved the very interesting third alternative in Scots law; in addition to reaching a guilty or innocent verdict, a juror is allowed to vote not proven. I had often wondered what effect a not-proven verdict has on a defendant, and this is what my colleague and I were discussing.

So, when I received the transcript of the Preece trial, my initial expectation was that my colleague had sent me an example of a not-proven verdict. I read the evidence in the order that it was presented at trial. A total of 74 witnesses for the prosecution were heard against 14 for the defense; prosecution witnesses were heard in 5½ days of testimony, defense witnesses in 1½ days.

When I had finished reading the evidence presented in this case, I concluded that the prosecution had utterly failed to prove, beyond reasonable doubt, its case against Preece. Had I been a juror in this case, I would not even have considered a vote for a not-proven verdict. In short, I believed Preece to be innocent.

There are some points of interest about the legal system in Scotland that are relevant to my application of Robyn's inference scheme. In felony cases in Scotland, the jury consists of 15 persons. Further, only a majority and not unanimity is needed for conviction; eight guilty votes is all the prosecution requires to win felony cases. With this as background, I now admit to having had a rather severe case of what has been described as false consensus, that egocentric bias that occurs when people estimate consensus for their own behavior. I was completely confident that Preece would be judged not guilty by a vote of 15 to 0. I could not see how any collection of reasonable people could have voted to convict Preece or even to judge that the case against him was not proven.

Had I known about Robyn's scheme, I could have come fairly close to predicting the actual proportion of innocent votes for Preece, given just my own reaction to the evidence in this case and my vote of innocent. Robyn's scheme for inferring a base rate for this particular juror population allows you to make this prediction, at least in the special case in which you are willing to suppose a uniform prior for this base rate. If we take yes to be a guilty verdict and no to be an innocent verdict, Robyn's scheme yields a predicted proportion of innocent votes by the actual jury to be one to three. If you read the verdict in this trial, you will see that the jury actually voted as follows: nine for guilty and six for not guilty. So Robyn's scheme misses by just .067. It might be argued that I ought to have included myself in this deliberative body since, after all, I read all the evidence and I used my vote as a basis for this prediction. If so, then Robyn's scheme misses by just .104, still not a bad result. In this analysis, I have ignored the not-proven category since I did not consider this alternative and neither did any of the actual jurors.

When I first read Robyn's arguments underlying the inference of a base rate from a single datum, I thought the result slightly counterintuitive; we appear to be getting a lot of mileage out of a single datum. But then I reflected on my own work on probabilistic analyses of the manner in which source credibility acts to influence the inferential value of what the source tells us. In such analyses, it turns out that apparently small values of conditional probabilities analogous to false positives and misses can have a very substantial deleterious effect on the inferential value of testimony. Departures of these conditionals away from zero might easily be justified by only a single item of unfavorable credibility-relevant ancillary evidence. On further reflection, I began to recall other instances of how extremely sensitive a Bayesian inferential scheme is to apparently minor changes in the probabilistic ingredients it requires. As Ward

Edwards and I have discussed on many occasions, there appears to be no flat maximum in Bayesian inferential reasoning.

The adequacy of Robyn's scheme in predicting the proportion of innocent votes by this jury is only part of my story; the rest concerns egocentricity and the alleged falsity of the consensus effect. After his trial, John Preece languished in H. M. Prison, Long Lorton (in England, incidentally). His appeal in 1974 on grounds of insufficient evidence was not sustained, so he faced life imprisonment, the sentence delivered by Lord Avonside, the justice in his trial. Preece somehow found out about my interest in his case, and I subsequently carried on a correspondence with Preece and his family. Preece stoutly maintained that he had never in his life seen the victim, a woman named Helen Will. Then, in 1981, I received from my colleague in Edinburgh a copy of the *Scottish Daily Express* (Saturday, 20 June 1981) having the following headline: "I FORGIVE: Freed Lifer's Pity for Doctor after 8 Years' Prayer."

Of the many very weak items of evidence adduced by the prosecution in Preece's case, I thought the very weakest to be the evidence given by a forensic expert named Dr. Alan Clift. At trial, some of the prosecution's major arguments were based on Clift's analyses of certain fiber and semen samples (Helen Will had been raped). I thought these arguments to be threadbare. Clift's credibility as a forensic witness was challenged in six other cases, with the final result that Clift was suspended from his position in a forensic laboratory. Clift, it turns out, could simply not have achieved the results he reported during Preece's trial. John Preece left Long Lorton prison after serving 8 years for a murder he did not commit.

How egocentric was I to suppose that 15 other persons would draw the same conclusion as I did from the evidence in Preece's case? Apart from Dr. Clift's testimony, there were other, to me, very obvious weak points in the crown's case. A witness whose credibility was never challenged asserted that he saw Helen Will at a location where she could not have been if she had been with Preece, as another witness, of doubtful credibility, had testified. Preece was a truck driver and, allegedly, transported Helen Will's body over a distance and in a time not possible unless he removed the governor on his truck's accelerator (there was no evidence that he did) and made every green light going through Edinburgh and over a further distance of about 100 miles.

I believe that, apart from Clift's very damaging testimony, Preece was convicted for two other reasons: his demeanor and bearing throughout this entire episode (he was justifiably, as it turns out, antagonistic thoughout the whole episode) and the sheer number of prosecution witnesses and the amount of time that they spent in testimony (compared with the defense). Bayes's rule has something else to say about consensus. It is easily shown that Bayes's rule argues against the use of numbers of witnesses alone in the resolution of evidential conflicts or contradictions; that is, simply siding with the majority is nor formally justifiable. What matters is the aggregate credibility of the witnesses on either side. Strongly held beliefs that turn out to be against consensus need not have an egocentric basis, and, even if they do, they are sometimes entirely justifiable. If we suppose that others will have beliefs similar to our own, we may, of course, be entirely mistaken. However, it does not follow that egocentricity always underlies such mistakes.

MAYA BAR-HILLEL

Maya argues that we have more to learn about base rates and about the manner in which people appear to incorporate such information, if they do at all, in their probabilistic judgments. I agree, although for somewhat different reasons that the ones Maya discusses. I might extend my concern here by saying that I believe we have much more to learn about a number of inferential ingredients and attributes apart from base rates. I believe this to be particularly necessary if we, as psychologists, continue to be willing to characterize the behavior of others as fallacious, biased, suboptimal, and so on. Such characterization does no damage, I suppose, as long as we discuss matters among ourselves as we did at this conference in honor of Hilly. The trouble, of course, is that others may be (and, indeed, are) all too ready to accept the "blemished portrait" (Kahneman, Slovic, and Tversky 1982) that some of our research seems to paint of human inferential and decisional competence.

I believe there to be some dangers associated with propagating an overly bleak view of human intellectual competence. On the one hand, if we are all inferentially incompetent, why should anyone ever be held accountable for inferential miscarriage? In a malpractice suit, the defense attorney might well use some of our literature as a basis for excusing the poor diagnosis that led to this lawsuit (perhaps this has already been tried). The defense attorney can argue, "Why is my client being made an example here when, as psychologists tell us, everyone else is inferentially incompetent as well." This attorney will not, of course, mention that, taken seriously, the same behavioral research suggests that the jury may well draw an inappropriate conclusion anyway. On the other hand, if we are indeed inferentially incompetent, we have to toss off correct medical diagnoses, timely and valuable intelligence analyses, appropriate jury verdicts, and so on as being the result of happy accident. But the danger goes a bit farther; studies of debiasing may carry the message, "Come to us psychologists, and we will show you how to avoid all the errors and inadequacies that plague your miserable inferential and decisional lives." This sounds as if psychologists view people at large as belonging to a strange religious cult whose members need to be reprogrammed if they are to lead subsequently useful lives. If this blemished portrait is, indeed, the orthodox view in psychology, I believe that it is an orthodoxy that needs to be continually examined with great care.

I say all this because thoughts like these formed part of my prior attitude before I read Maya's chapter on what has been termed the base-rate fallacy. However, by the time I finished reading Maya's chapter, I was quite optimistic for the following reason. She begins this piece by mentioning the base-rate fallacy a number of times. The use of the term *fallacy* declines as she proceeds, and the term does not appear at all in the very perceptive conclusions she has drawn. As she notes there are different interpretations that might be placed on a given number we call a base rate, and different interpretations do or should make a difference in our thinking about the probabilistic inference tasks we assign research subjects. Maya has had the courage to back off a bit and examine at least one element of this apparent orthodoxy.

In the cab problem, for example, the base rate at issue appears as the prior probability term in calculations using Bayes's rule, the standard against which subjects' responses have been routinely compared. Subjects' behavior in response to early versions of this problem suggested that they ignored this prior probability. I have had more than one person ask me if, by the base-rate fallacy, it is meant that people generally ignore prior probabilities. I have always answered no to this question, for the following reasons. The first involves specific research suggesting that subjects do, indeed, attend to prior probabilities and may, on occasion, attend to them more than they ought to, as least as far as Bayes's rule is concerned (e.g., Peterson and Miller 1965). The second involves a mixture of research and common observation relative to primacy-effect matters. On some occasions, it seems that people refuse to revise initial probabilistic beliefs based on evidence that should cause them to do so. I believe my answers to be correct here in part because, if the base-rate study results had been interpreted to mean the general disregarding of prior probabilities, then we might now be discussing a prior-probability fallacy.

So I am asked what the base-rate fallacy then really means. In reply, I usually say that it means that certain numbers indicating probabilistic rates or relative-frequency estimates of them, that appear in contrived, verbally described scenarios, often seem to be disregarded by subjects who are asked to make probabilistic assessments about various events in these scenarios. I then add something similar to what Maya notes, namely, that a base rate refers to the size of some relevant category or class. The difference is that I emphasize that a base *rate*, by its very nature, refers to something that we can enumerate or count in some way. I do this to point out that the probabilities at issue in base-rate studies are not epistemic in nature and that the results of such studies have no obvious generalization to situations involving singular or unique events for which relative frequencies make no sense. In some base-rate studies, experimenters use the same numbers over again but change their meaning from one usage to another, as we witnessed in various versions of the cab problem. Apparently, a verbal statement accompanying a base rate can mean one thing or have some degree of importance to the experimenter and another thing or another degree of importance to the subjects. Maya has traced various efforts to uncover a base-rate interpretation that subjects will attend to, such as, for example, a base rate that has some causal significance.

All this brings me to the subject of basing theories of human inferential adequacy on the, usually brief, presentation of contrived, verbally described scenarios. I have been away from empirical research for 9 years now, an interval not nearly long enough to make me forget how difficult it was to contrive, in an unambiguous way, an inference problem to be used as part of an empirical study in which very specific issues were being examined. However, I face similar difficulties all the time in contriving problems I include in assignments and on examinations in the probability course I teach. What I do know from considerable experience is that just a very minor change in wording can induce a student to calculate, say, $P(A \& B)$ instead of the $P(A|B)$ that I want the student to be calculating. I have come, by degrees, to think of many verbal descriptions of inference problems as Rorschach inkblots into which many things might be read. In our attempts to understand more about human inference, we have staked our hopes on an experimental vehicle that is exquisitely sensitive to alterations that may seem quite minor.

We also stake many hopes on our understanding of the structural attributes of the inference problems we present to our subjects. Thus, Maya is willing to state that, in Bayesian studies of the base-rate fallacy, the base rate provides the prior and the additional information provides *the* likelihood ratio. The probabilistic ingredients of any likelihood ratio depend on the specific argument one constructs from evidence to possible conclusions being entertained. The trouble is that the layout of any argument is quite arbitrary, as jurists and many logicians have recognized for years. Different persons may construct quite different, but equally valid, arguments from the same evidence to the same conclusions. In the cab problem, for example, evidence G^* from a witness who asserts that the cab in the accident was Green is commonly taken to be direct evidence on G, that the cab in the accident was, in fact, Green. We might say, here, that we have a direct testimonial assertion G^* about a fact in issue $\{G, \text{not-}G\}$ from an eyewitness. For such evidence, all that matters, inferentially, is the competency and credibility of the witness.

Assuming the competency of this witness, let us consider his or her credibility. In the cab problem, what is typically given to the subjects is information from a court-sanctioned test of the witness's color-discrimination ability; probabilistic results of this test are taken as likelihoods: $P(G^*|G)$ and $P(G^*|\text{not-}G)$, where not-G = Blue. The major trouble here is that the court's test is ancillary evidence bearing on just one of the attributes of this witness's credibility, namely, his or her observational sensitivity. But there are other attributes of the credibility of human sources, each of which serves to define additional links in a chain of reasoning from G^* to $\{G, \text{not-}G\}$. For any person who recognizes that there are veracity and objectivity attributes of the credibility of this witness, Bayes's rule cannot be meaningfully applied in the absence of ancillary evidence about these other attributes (Schum 1989, in press). The message here is very simple; we cannot talk about *the* likelihoods for a given item of evidence until we know what precise argument has been constructed from the evidence to the hypotheses.

We have also staked many hopes on the conventional system of probability and Bayes's rule as a canon for probabilistic reasoning. I yield to no one in my acknowledgment of the wide array of evidential and inferential subtleties that can be trapped for study and analysis using Bayes's rule. At the same time, human inference is a remarkably rich intellectual activity; I believe that it is far too much to ask any single formal system to trap all aspects of this richness. It might be a good idea for us to summon some of the courage that Maya demonstrates and extend our thinking about human inference to include some of the non-Bayesian systems currently being discussed. In those inferential contexts with which I have regular contact, it seems that the inference tasks required of people are, in fact, mixtures of deductive, inductive, and the several species of abductive inferences that have been identified. The only pure inductive or probabilistic reasoning tasks that I know of are those encountered in the classroom and in the laboratory. So, when a person who exhibits even an advanced case of the base-rate fallacy is confronted with a contrived, verbally described scenario, he or she ought to not to be dismissed. Perhaps this same person, through an exercise of imagination, generates or has generated a novel possibility that leads to significant advancement in some area.

REFERENCES

Kahneman, D., P. Slovic, and A. Tversky, eds. 1982. *Judgment under uncertainty: Heuristics and biases.* Cambridge: Cambridge University Press.

Peterson, C., and A. Miller. 1965. Sensitivity of subjective probability revision. *Journal of Experimental Psychology* 70, no. 1:117–21.

Schum, D. 1989. Knowledge, probability, and credibility. *Journal of Behavioral Decision Making* 2:39–62.

Schum, D. In press. *Jonathan Cohen and Thomas Bayes on the analysis of chains of reasoning.* In *Rationality and reasoning: Essays in honor of L. Jonathan Cohen,* ed. E. Eells and T. Maruzewski. Amsterdam: Rodopi.

Part Five

INTRODUCTORY COMMENTS

At first glance, the chapters in this part might appear quite unrelated. One—Hammond's—is a discussion of two different approaches to studying judgment and decision making and ways by which they might be integrated. The other—Brehmer's—suggests a new paradigm for studying decision making and provides some intriguing experimental results that augur well for the proposed approach. The commonality between the chapters lies in the fact that both authors are the leading exponents of the methods and the philosophy of research in psychology advocated by Egon Brunswik. In particular, both chapters emphasize the importance of understanding the nature of the environment or task with which people are confronted.

Hammond's chapter poses fundamental issues in research on decision making. What are the metatheoretical foundations of different approaches to studying decision making, and what methodological approaches are most likely to succeed in generating knowledge? Believing that conceptual unity is more likely than diversity to advance knowledge, Hammond seeks ways of integrating what he perceives as different paradigms in decision making. To do so, Hammond first identifies two streams of research that he labels *functionalism* and *illusionism*. With functionalism he equates research carried out within the tradition of Egon Brunswik, in which emphasis is placed on trying to understand how people adapt to the demands of the environment. Indeed, in his own work on cognitive continuum theory, Hammond has explicitly attempted to define a theory of how tasks affect judgmental activities. With illusionism Hammond equates research in the Tversky-Kahneman tradition that has explored the heuristic strategies (e.g., representativeness, availability) that people use in making judgments and choices.

Although, at a conceptual level, Hammond shows more commonalities—and thus possibilities for integration—between functionalism and illusionism than might at first be imagined, it is at the level of methodology that he sees the greatest difficulties. Psychological research, according to Hammond, "has been trapped within a methodology accidentally derived from agricultural research." Moreover, it is this methodology that has been adopted by illusionism, and it is one that is unlikely to lead to cumulative and generalizable knowledge. Hammond's prescription lies largely in the principles of representative design first advocated by Egon Brunswik.

In commenting on this chapter, Doherty questions some aspects of the call for coherence put forth by Hammond. Instead, he counters with Marvin Minsky's arguments concerning the modularity of mental life. It is not clear that evolution has endowed our cognitive processes with a conceptually coherent system. On the contrary, evolution seems to have equipped us with a series of different mental modules that we can use as different situations demand.

The chapter by Brehmer breaks away from the kinds of problems typically studied by psychologists working in behavioral decision making. There are no laboratory-type gambles, no optimal models, no judgments of probability, and he does not calculate any lens model statistics. Instead, Brehmer requires his subjects to make decisions in a simulated fire-fighting exercise. Subjects are seated at a computer terminal and asked to imagine that they are directing a number of fire-fighting units protecting an area of forest. The task is dynamic. An action taken at one time affects the environment, which, in turn, affects what actions need to be taken in the future, and so on. Critical variables isolated by Brehmer in this work are the timing of decisions and the effects of lags in feedback. It is a curious fact that, although many laypersons readily acknowledge the importance of timing in decisions, this topic has received little attention to date in experimental work. However, because Brehmer's paradigm is ideally suited to studying issues of timing, it is to be hoped that this will be the focus of much research in the future. As noted above, in general Brehmer's work emphasizes the importance of task variables (e.g., quality of feedback from actions) in understanding how well people adapt to their (decision) environments.

In his discussion, Doherty admires the research program on dynamic decision making advanced by Brehmer. However, he cautions against assuming that all decisions are dynamic and the claim that Brehmer's paradigm could provide a general framework for psychological research on decision making. There are many situations in which decisions are static, one shot, and isolated in time. Finally, Doherty concludes by enumerating many of the positive aspects of the work on decision making carried out by both Hammond and Brehmer within the Brunswikian tradition.

10

Functionalism and Illusionism: Can Integration Be Usefully Achieved?

KENNETH R. HAMMOND

The lens model and the heuristics-and-biases approach are contrasted in terms of their antecedent metatheories with the aim of integrating these currently disparate efforts. Conceptual differences can be resolved, and their resolution will enhance research efforts. But methodological commitments will constitute an impasse unless efforts are made to cross methods and concepts in a systematic way. Although time consuming and difficult, this step will provide an excellent opportunity for useful integration of the current theoretical derivatives of two metatheories in long-standing opposition and thus advance theory and research in judgment and decision making.

M<small>Y PURPOSES IN WRITING THIS CHAPTER</small> are to describe the characteristics of two metatheories that are antecedent to current theory and research in the field of judgment and decision making, to show how conceptual integration between two derivative theories can be achieved, to address the impasse produced by the methodological commitments of each theory, and to show how that impasse might be turned into an opportunity. My general purpose is to change what are now disparate, independent studies into a unified and thus cumulative, stronger effort to understand human judgment and decision making.

TWO METATHEORIES

I shall use the terms *functionalism* and *illusionism* to identify the two metatheories from which the two current theories are derived. The theories I shall

---

This work was supported in part by the Office of Basic Research, Army Research Institute, Contract MDA903-86-C-0142, Work Unit 2Q161102B74F. The views, opinions, and findings contained in this report are those of the author and should not be construed as an official Department of the Army position, policy, or decision, unless so designated by other official documentation. I thank Berndt Brehmer, Michael Doherty, Reid Hastie, Stephen Hoch, Robin Hogarth, C. R. B. Joyce, Cynthia Lusk, Martha Neal, and Mary Luhring for criticisms of an early draft of this chapter.

here call *lens model functionalism* and *heuristics and biases*. Elsewhere (Hammond, McClelland, and Mumpower 1980), these two theories were distinguished from four other approaches and from one another by the labels *social judgment theory* and *psychological decision theory*, respectively. I make this change both because the scope of social judgment theory (see Brehmer and Joyce 1988) and psychological decision theory has expanded since 1980 and because *heuristics and biases* is the more frequently used descriptor for the latter theory (for examples of recent work, see Slovic, Griffin, and Tversky, in this volume).

Readers are likely to be familiar with the term *functionalism*, but *illusionism* will require some defense, not only because it appears here for the first time, but also because I have been advised that it has a pejorative connotation, which I emphatically deny it should. The study of perceptual illusions has shown them to be striking and powerful phenomena. They have been studied since about 1833, according to Boring (1942), subsequently enticing such giants as Helmholtz, Hering, and Wundt (Boring 1942, 239–46) as well as Ebbinghaus (in 1902) to investigate their causes (although the value of such study has been challenged; Gibson 1979; Brunswik 1952, 1956). Daniel Kahneman and Amos Tversky have explicitly extended research on perceptual illusions to conceptual, or intellectual, illusions. Indeed, they generally refer to *cognitive* illusions (e.g., Tversky and Kahneman 1983, 313) to indicate, I believe, that both types of cognitive activity are subject to the same influences. Therefore, I use the term *illusionism* to name a metatheory that has both a long history of research in perception and a recent history of research in regard to intellectual functions.

ANTECEDENTS

Functionalism

The bedrock of the functionalist view is *adaptation*, the principal cognitive concept is *achievement*, and both, of course, are derived from Darwin. Its central focus is on the relation between organismic and ecological conditions that make for success or failure. Brunswik (1952) described early American functionalism in psychology as the product of "Dewey, Mead, Angell, Carr, and others at the University of Chicago" and gave special attention to Dewey: "In criticizing the traditional molecular physiological emphasis on the reflex arc, Dewey saw the key to the unity of psychological activity in its 'function' or 'successful issue,' the 'organization of means with reference to a comprehensive end.' Reference to the region of distal results was thus established along with a utilitarian, adjustment-centered biological conception of psychology which may be traced to Darwin's views on the struggle for existence" (55).

Brunswik's contribution to functionalism first appeared in 1929. The concept of the "duplicity principle," for which Brunswik gave credit to his teacher, Karl Bühler, was expanded and elaborated on in his book *Wahrneh-*

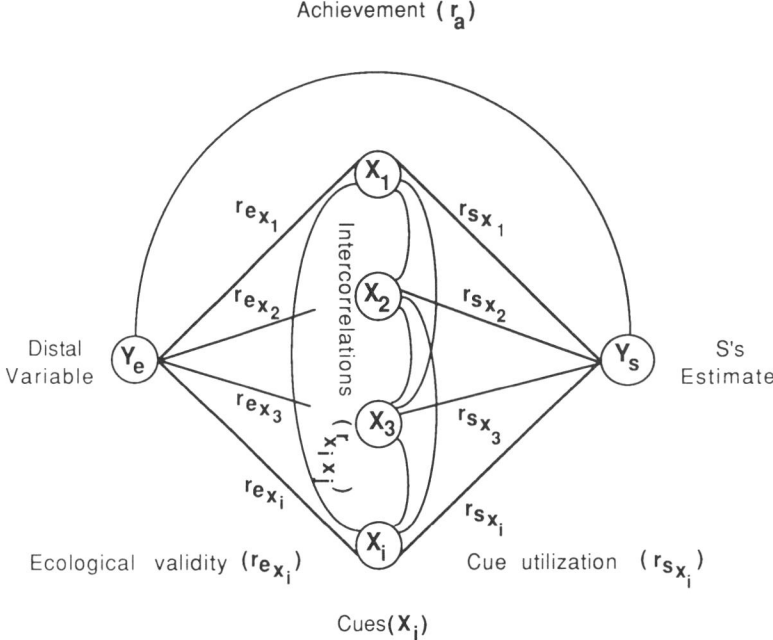

Figure 10.1. This diagram represents Brunswik's lens model as it has been employed in judgment and decision research since 1955 (Hammond 1955), although it represents only part of Brunswik's "composite picture of the functional unit of behavior" presented in 1952 (Brunswik 1952). Here, Y_e = the criterion variable to be judged, Y_s = the subject's judgment of Y_e, r_e = the ecological validity of each of the cues (x_i), $r_{x_{ij}}$ = the intercorrelation among the cues, r_s = the subject's utilization of each cue, and r_a = the subject's achievement, i.e., the correlation between S's judgment and the criterion value. The lens model equation decomposes achievement as follows:

$$r_a = GR_eR_s + C\sqrt{1 - R_e^2}\sqrt{1 - R_s^2}$$

in which R_e = the multiple correlation between X_i and Y_e, R_s = muliple correlation between X_i and Y_s, G = the amount of linear covariations in the two systems, and C = the amount of nonlinear covariation between the two systems. For illustrations of the expansion of the lens model to interpersonal conflict and interpersonal learning, see Hammond and Grassia (1985).

mung und Gegenstandswelt (1934), in which the lens model appears in rudimentary form (see fig. 10.1; for further details, see Hammond 1966; see also Gigerenzer 1987; Leary 1987; Smith 1986).

The essential idea of the duplicity principle is that of "multiple mediation" of information from the distal object to the subject (for a translation of Brunswik's "early conceptualizations" of this topic from his difficult German prose, see Hammond 1966, 514–34). The second point was the "equivocal" nature of the multiple mediators of information, which, as Brunswik increased in scientific sophistication, became the "probabilistic" nature of multiple mediators. The main idea was that of "multiple fallible mediation" (via cues) from the environment, somehow aggregated, integrated, or combined by an organism that could make use of information of this type. This conception of the process gave rise to the lens analogy as he described it then: "Metaphorically speaking, the . . . mediation process then proceeds within the organism through *recollection* [i.e., re-collection, not memory], *binding together and melting together into a single effect,* so to speak, of those *splintered effects* including even those which are separated in time" (Hammond 1966, 518), as in a "condensing lens." A modern translation would refer to the multiple mediation of fallible information to the organism, which aggregates such information into a single judgment regarding distal variables or events.

A third critical feature of Brunswik's lens model functionalism is that it affords a place not only for the multiple mediation of information but for its interrelatedness as well. By 1943, Brunswik was demanding a place for such interrelatedness in the design of experiments in psychology. If interrelated cues did not appear in experiments, he argued, the experiments risked being unrepresentative of the ecology in which the organism functioned because multiple, interrelated cues are ubiquitous in the ecology of most organisms (see esp. Brunswik 1956, 61–62). In addition, "vicarious mediation" of information from an ecology via many interrelated cues would be matched (as the lens model indicates) by the organism's ability to take advantage of such redundancy. As the counterpart to vicarious mediation in the environment, Brunswik introduced the concept of "vicarious functioning" to indicate the capacity of higher organisms to switch reliance to a related cue if a redundant cue were missing (see Brunswik 1956, sec. 6; see also Hammond 1966, 50–71). This was an extraordinary view of behavior to introduce at a time when psychologists were still captivated by a narrow stimulus-response psychology and by research methods inherited from nineteenth-century psychophysics.

Always a thinker on the grand scale, even in 1934 Brunswik saw the application of the lens model to matters beyond perception. For example, under the major heading "Conclusion: Extension of Object-Psychology to the Entire Field of Psychology," he stated, "Our considerations were developed mainly by means of examples drawn from the area of perception. However, we had already stated in the introduction that the facts from other areas of psychology could be dealt with basically in the same manner" (Hammond 1966, 531).

Functionalism appeared in the field of judgment and decision making in the form of the lens model (Brunswik 1934, 1952, 1956), which was modified by Hammond (1955, 1966; Hammond, McClelland, and Mumpower 1980; Hammond et al. 1975; see also, e.g., Brehmer 1970; Stewart 1976; Tucker 1964). The essential elements of the lens model, familiar to most of the readers of this chapter, are described in the legend to figure 10.1 (for further detail, see the references cited immediately above).

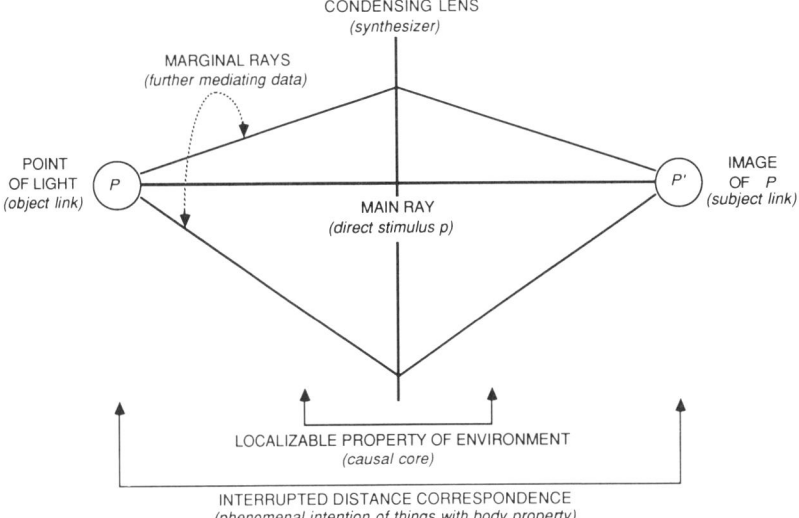

Figure 10.2. The original lens model (reproduced from Brunswik 1934; credit given to Karl Bühler).

In short, functionalism has a long history in psychology. It is best represented in judgment and decision making by the extension and elaboration of Brunswik's lens model, a conceptual and methodological framework that was always intended to have broad application.[1]

Illusionism

Illusionism appeared in the field of judgment and decision making in the work of Kahneman and Tversky (most notably, Tversky and Kahneman 1974; see also Tversky and Kahneman 1982a), who developed the concept in a wide-ranging series of empirical investigations and theoretical articles (see, e.g., Kahneman, Slovic, and Tversky 1982; Tversky and Kahneman 1983, 1986). The broad theme of this work consists of a criticism of the validity of the expected utility model as a descriptor of human judgment and decision making. Kroll, Levy, and Rapoport (1988), for example, describe this general approach as follows: "Employing a variety of decision tasks, mostly choices

---

1. The direct link between lens model functionalism and Darwinian theory (in this instance, sexual selection) can be seen in a remarkable study carried out within the logic of representative design by von Schantz et al. (1989), in which they show that female pheasants choose mates on the basis of the spur length of the male and that such choices in fact result in a greater reproductive success.

between gambles, and investigating different populations of subjects, some of whom were highly sophisticated, these experiments have repeatedly demonstrated the existence of cognitive biases in judgment and choice, and have gradually accumulated ample evidence to convince most students of choice behavior that the celebrated maximization of expected utility model often provides an inadequate description of decision behavior under uncertainty" (407).

This corpus of work is usually viewed as marking a 180-degree shift from the achievement-oriented work emphasized in Peterson and Beach (1967), in which persons are conceived of as "intuitive statisticians" who "gamble well." (The term *intuitive statistician* was first used, I think, by Brunswik [1956, 80] when he referred to "the perceptual system as an intuitive statistician.") Tversky and Kahneman directly challenged the implication that "man, by and large, follows the correct Bayesian rule," asserting that "man is apparently not a conservative Bayesian: he is not Bayesian at all" (Kahneman, Slovic, and Tversky 1982, 46).

The contribution of the traditional theme of perceptual illusionism can be seen in Kahneman and Tversky's presentation of the well-known Müller-Lyer illusion (Tversky and Kahneman 1986, S266–S267). In this instance, the illusion (see fig. 10.3) is used to illustrate the powerful effect on the context or "frame" (i.e., the feathers and arrows) that makes the equal horizontal lines appear to be far different in length. A second illustration (S267) superimposes vertical lines (see fig. 10.4) on the Müller-Lyer illusion to demonstrate how

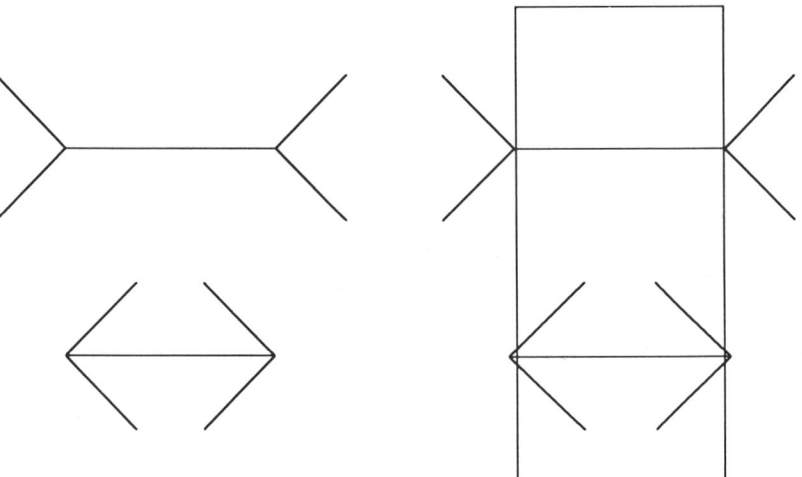

Figure 10.3. The Müller-Lyer illusion (reproduced from Tversky and Kahneman 1986, S266), illustrating the effect of context or frame.

Figure 10.4. The Müller-Lyer illusion (reproduced from Tversky and Kahneman 1986, S267), illustrating how the illusion can be made to disappear.

easily the illusion can be made to disappear by changing the display of information.

Curiously, Brunswik (1956, 16) also used the Müller-Lyer illusion, but for exactly the opposite reason. Brunswik's point was that, as soon as "neighboring variables" (i.e., the feathers and arrows) are added around the horizontal lines, all the generalizations from the rigorous psychophysical studies of isolated stimuli (such as horizontal lines) disappear. Tversky and Kahneman (1986) take a reverse course; they add the vertical lines to the horizontal lines and the neighboring variables in order to make the illusion disappear. But, in both cases, the general point is the same: adding information (or context) changes the results otherwise obtained and thus prevents generalization based on isolated information. This result is obviously relevant to a theory (such as the lens model) that allows for, indeed insists on, the presence of *multiple* fallible indicators in research purporting to increase our understanding of human judgment.

Possible Origins of the Concept of Intellectual Illusions

I examine the several possible origins of the heuristics-and-biases approach below in increasing order of plausibility.

Gestalt Psychology? Kahneman and Tversky's numerous references to cognitive illusions inevitably evoke an association with Gestalt psychology, not only because the Gestaltists used perceptual illusions so frequently to demonstrate what they believed to be the "wholeness" or all-or-none character of perception, but also because the Gestaltists were willing to make extrapolations to intellectual functions as well, as, for example, in the case of "closure." (For recent examples within the heuristics-and-biases approach, see Kahneman, Slovic, and Tversky 1982, 6, 9, 13–14, 215–16, 232–35, 236–38; and Tversky and Kahneman 1983, 313–14; for examples in Gestalt psychology, see Koffka 1935.) The numerous demonstrations by Gestaltists that a perception or judgment can be completely reversed by a small change in the visual field (or by no change at all) would seem to be a natural antecedent for an approach that emphasizes similar phenomena in the judgment of probabilities. In addition, the heuristics-and-biases approach also emphasizes that intellectual illusions are not merely biased away from accuracy or truth but are also biased toward the specific heuristics proposed to account for these illusions. Brunswik (1956, 132) made a similar observation about Gestalt psychologists and "projective testers": "Gestalt psychologists share with projective testers the view that all illusory perception is not only illusion *away from* some ideally accurate or veridical type of response but . . . illusion *toward* something else, that is, assimilation toward some preferred patterns of organization."

But I find no references to any Gestalt psychologist or Gestalt psychology—not even in the context of framing, a key idea in Gestalt psychology—in Kahneman and Tversky's work; there are definitely none in Kahneman, Slovic, and Tversky (1982). So, despite the prominent reference to cognitive illusions in their work, Gestalt psychology does not appear to be the origin of their work.

Functionalism? In the broadest possible interpretation of the heuristics-and-biases approach, it could be argued that this approach is a form of functionalism that studies error or maladaptiveness as the best and surest way to learn about adaptation or achievement or to learn about those cognitive processes that stand in the way of adaptation, success, or survival. It is possible to find traces of functionalism in Tversky and Kahneman (1974), which constitutes the introduction to Kahneman, Slovic, and Tversky (1982):

> The subjective assessment of probability resembles the subjective assessment of physical quantities such as distance or size. These judgments are all based on data of limited validity, which are processed according to heuristic rules. For example, the apparent distance of an object is determined in part by its clarity. The more sharply the object is seen, the closer it appears to be. This rule has some validity, because in any given scene the more distant objects are seen less sharply than nearer objects. However, the reliance on this rule leads to systematic errors in the estimation of distance. Specifically, distances are often overestimated when visibility is poor because the contours of objects are blurred. On the other hand, distances are often underestimated when visibility is good because the objects are seen sharply. Thus, the reliance on clarity as an indication of distance leads to common biases. Such biases are also found in the intuitive judgment of probability. [Tversky and Kahneman 1982a, 3].

This paragraph might well have been written by someone working within the lens-model functionalist tradition and emphasizing achievement rather than error. Indeed, in this passage the word *rule* can easily be replaced by *statistical association* or *relative frequency*. The entire paragraph could have been written to explain the slope of the regression line relating subjective "clarity" to apparent distance in the context of the lens model. Stewart et al. (1984) provide an example of such a study of clarity. Given that the lens model functionalist approach could already explain this phenomenon in the same fashion, one can wonder why different concepts (rule, heuristic) were introduced without explaining how these concepts might differ from those already in use in research on judgment and decision making. The generalization from perception to probability judgments was felicitous, but of course the generalization from perception to judgment had been practiced within the framework of the lens model for at least a quarter century (see, e.g., Hammond

1955). Furthermore, Brunswik had made an explicit argument for probability learning in the rat as far back as 1939 and followed that up in 1943 with a general treatise on probability judgments.

The general spirit of functionalism also appeared in Kahneman and Tversky's explanation of the key concept of *representativeness* (Tversky and Kahneman 1982b). They presented four definitions of "a relation of representativeness" and noted that, "in all four cases, representativeness expresses the degree of correspondence between X [an instance or event] and M [a process or a model], but its determinants are not the same in the four cases. [The reader should note the parallel between cue and distal variable.] In case (1), representativeness is dominated by *perceived relative frequency* or *statistical association*" (Tversky and Kahneman 1982b, 87; italics added).

In case 1, then, should we presume that, the greater the perceived relative frequency of association between X and M, the greater the perceived representativeness of X with relation to M? But why should perceived relative frequency of association of X and M be anything more than a utilization coefficient (or weight) of a cue (X) for M? This concept was already available in the lens model literature in 1943.

But these two examples are only traces of a functionalist approach to subjective probability assessment, and Kahneman and Tversky did not develop them beyond the remarks cited, so far as I know. It would be inappropriate to place the heuristics-and-biases approach within the lens model functionalism approach if for no other reason than that the heuristics-and-biases literature contains no references to the lens model or any associated research on judgment (with one possible exception to be noted later). Rather, the concept of representativeness was explicated in considerable detail in terms of similarity judgments (for the most detailed treatment, see Tversky and Gati 1982). Although similarity judgments would of course evoke great interest from Gestalt psychologists, the methods and procedures used in this research would not; they are more nearly compatible with those found in traditional psychophysics, the third possible origin.

Psychophysics? The psychophysical background for the heuristics-and-biases approach is much more noticeable than that of either Gestalt psychology or functionalism. For, although I can find no references to prior work in the latter two approaches, references to psychophysical journals and articles are numerous (see, e.g., any publication on similarity judgments; see also the prominent analogies to psychophysical functions in prospect theory; Kahneman and Tversky 1979). In addition, such topics as scaling, anchoring (a favorite in psychophysics for a century) and adjustment, bias, the mathematical treatment of responses in relation to carefully isolated stimulus materials, and the comparison of various measurement techniques (matching vs. judgments) occupy a prominent place in all the work on similarity. This work, in turn, is the major basis for the representativeness heuristic. Therefore, the most likely origin for the heuristics-and-biases approach appears to be the psychophysical tradition.

Summary

This brief examination of antecedents of lens model functionalism and the heuristics-and-biases approach should make clear that the current differences between these approaches, delineated in part in Hammond, McClelland, and Mumpower (1980), are neither new nor superficial and that they represent the unfolding of persistent trends in the history of psychology. If it is true that our current activities are often unwittingly guided by implicit, unexamined premises from the past, then making these antecedent premises explicit is useful if only to enlighten us about why we do what we do the way we are doing it. Moreover, examination of the past is constructive if it enables us to cast off old baggage needlessly attached as well as to reaffirm the premises and promises that still guide us—old baggage we cannot do without.

The premises vital to lens model functionalism can be clearly traced. For example, the lens model functionalists of today cannot do without the functionalist premise of adaptation or without Karl Bühler's duplicity principle. That principle, described in Brunswik and Kardos (1929), expanded in Brunswik (1934), brought to maturity in Brunswik (1956), and formally quantified in Hursch, Hammond, and Hursch (1964) and Tucker (1964), formed the basis of the social judgment theory developed in the 1970s by Hammond et al. (1975; see also Hammond, McClelland, and Mumpower 1980; for a current overview, see esp. Brehmer and Joyce 1988) as well as of the cognitive continuum theory of the 1980s (outlined in Hammond et al. 1987; Hammond 1988). Nor can the lens model functionalists do without their methodological commitment to the representative design of experiments (about which more below).

The history of the heuristics-and-biases approach is different, however. The conceptual antecedents of this approach have never been made explicit, possibly because the ideas that gave rise to it were sufficiently innovative that there was no need to build on the past. Be that as it may, there is a definite methodological commitment to the past within this approach, and it is this commitment that places it directly at odds with the methodology to which the lens model functionalists are committed.

NEW CONCEPTS AND RESEARCH TOPICS

The theoretical derivatives of illusionism and functionalism have produced new concepts, and each has addressed new research topics.

Heuristics and Biases

The new concepts introduced by researchers in the heuristics-and-biases approach—representativeness, availability, anchoring and adjustment (Kahneman, Slovic, and Tversky 1982), and the prominence hypothesis (Tversky, Sattath, and Slovic 1988), to mention only a few—are primarily psychological in character. It is this feature that has enhanced the visibility of the field of judgment and decision making. Prior to the appearance of work on heuristics and biases, theory and research in judgment and decision making were almost completely ignored by textbook writers. There is little doubt that the rapid inclusion of this work in textbooks resulted as much from its emphasis on the errors and irrationality of human judgment and from decision processes described in terms of cognitive illusions as from the innovative character, striking directness, and simplicity of the studies. Illustrations of perceptual illusions have always appeared in psychology textbooks and perhaps always will. In fact, a psychological study that found high accuracy in judgments would be like a good-news story in a newspaper. Accuracy and adaptiveness are uninteresting and leave no room for psychology; only error requires explanation. Gibson (1979, 280–83) alluded to this matter in the context of perception, as did Taylor and Thompson (1982) in social psychology and Edwards (in this volume), who has frequently noted that, while two plus two equals four is arithmetic, two plus two equals five is psychology. Christensen-Szalanski and Beach (1984) have gone further, noting that psychologists are biased toward citing research that discovers error or irrationality over research that shows accuracy or rationality.

Professionals in many fields, for example, engineers, clinical psychologists, military specialists, management scientists, and accountants, found much to be learned from the lens model research, Bayesian research, and numerous other types of studies, but mainstream psychology (as defined by textbook content) did not—even though hundreds of articles on judgment and decision making were being published in psychological and other academic journals. Because of the emphasis on error and the strong psychological component in the work on cognitive illusions, Hammond, McClelland, and Mumpower (1980) referred to the heuristics-and-biases approach as psychological decision theory and distinguished it from decision theory, behavioral decision theory, social judgment theory, information integration theory, and attribution theory. Moreover, the expansion of heuristics-and-biases research to many interesting and important topics, including microeconomics, "personality judgment, medical prognosis, decision under risk, suspicion of criminal acts, and political forecasting" (Tversky and Kahneman 1983, 293), doubtless heightened the visibility of judgment and decision making in basic research publications as well as in such popular literature as *Psychology Today* (for a recent example, see Gould 1988).

In short, because the heuristics-and-biases approach emphasized the psychological aspects of judgment and decision making and developed new and interesting psychological concepts, it not only brought this field within the mainstream of psychology but also brought it to bear on new and important topics and thus heightened its visibility and significance.

Lens Model Functionalism

The lens model functionalists also introduced new concepts and topics. The new concepts were not strongly psychological in character, however, but systems oriented in keeping with these researchers' commitment to a Darwinian theme. Indeed, both environment and organism were to be seen as systems. In his last major presentation, Brunswik (1957, 5) stated, "One of the broadest and most universally accepted definitions of psychology conceives of psychology as being concerned with the interrelationships between organism and environment." But this very broad and generally acknowledged definition was followed by a new conception of those interrelationships, namely, "both organism and environment will have to be seen as systems, each with properties of its own." That statement is not merely new; it presents an idea that opens up new research topics. It enables us to ask, What are the relevant properties or functions of an environmental system, and how shall we find and measure them? Prior to Brunswik, psychologists' description of an environmental system had been exhausted by the operational definition of a single stimulus. Brunswik went further, however. "Each system," he asserted, "has surface and depth, or overt and covert regions." Furthermore, "It follows that, much as psychology must be concerned with the texture of the organism . . . it also must be concerned with the texture of the environment as it extends in depth away from the common boundary." No one had thought of this before.

These were new ideas to psychologists. Regrettably, for the most part, they still are. Rarely, if ever, has there been a serious effort to distinguish theoretically or empirically between the surface and the depth or between the overt and the covert regions of an environmental system with which an organism must cope. Rare indeed is the effort to describe—let alone define—the texture of the environment as it extends in depth away from the common boundary. The common boundary might be understood, but what could the texture of the environment possibly consist of? Psychologists have been indifferent to these matters; their preference for developing new organismic concepts far outweighs their interest in and conceptual treatment of the environment. But, as I shall demonstrate, the differentiation of task conditions not only creates the possibility of a systematic attack on task properties and their psychological consequences but opens the door to integration of functionalism and illusionism as well.

The increase in scope provided by the use of systems concepts can be seen in the complexity of topics addressed by the lens model functionalists. These include multiple-cue probability learning, interpersonal learning (Brehmer 1976), interpersonal conflict (Hammond and Grassia 1985), negotiation (see esp. Mumpower 1988), effects of drugs on these capacities (Gillis 1975; Gillis and Blevens 1978; Gillis, Lipkin, and Moran 1981; Gillis and Parkison 1981; Hammond and Joyce 1975), expert judgment (Hammond et al. 1984; Hammond et al. 1987), social policy (Hammond and Adelman 1976; Hammond et al. 1983), judgment in dynamic tasks (Brehmer, in this volume), and more (see Brehmer and Joyce 1988).

The use of systems concepts also increased explanatory power. For example, the lens model equation provided a new method for ascertaining the relative contribution of linear and nonlinear components of a person's judgment policy to accuracy of judgments and thus explained why achievement would be likely to be higher in one judgment task than in another (Hammond et al. 1975; Stewart et al. 1988). The systems-oriented distinction between outcome feedback and cognitive feedback has enabled researchers to explain why it is so difficult for persons to learn to improve their judgments in most judgment tasks that they encounter whereas it is relatively easy for them to do so when cognitive feedback is provided (Balzer, Doherty, and O'Connor 1989; Poses et al. 1986; Wigton, Patil, and Hoellerich 1986).

The increase in theoretical scope and explanatory power provided by the introduction of both psychological and systems concepts enabled both approaches, as well as many others, to address new and more complex topics. Nevertheless, the progress I have described is the result of independent contributions made by investigators within two different approaches who function in isolation from one another and rarely cite one another's work. Does that mean that these conceptual efforts are fundamentally different? Do they contradict each other and thus represent competitive theories? Or can these apparently different approaches somehow be combined so as to further our progress? I shall now try to demonstrate that an integration of these approaches can produce a useful synergism.

TOWARD CONCEPTUAL INTEGRATION

Integration of the theories derived from functionalism and illusionism requires that both theories be placed in a common conceptual framework. To do this, I first place one form of Tversky and Kahneman's concept of representativeness within the lens model framework. I then revise the lens model framework to include a second form of this concept.

Representativeness within the Lens Model Framework

Consider again the lens model in figure 10.1. Now imagine that we are to study an expert who is to make judgments of some distal (or covert or not immediately apparent) state of affairs (Y in fig. 10.1) on the basis of multiple fallible indicators, that is, cues (X_i). The purpose of the study is to understand how the expert makes use of the information provided by the cues. Within this framework, we wish to discover the weights, function forms, organizing principle, and consistency within the expert's judgment policy. In numerous studies, it has been found that these systems concepts are sufficient to account for an expert's judgment policy, to evaluate his or her achievement if criterion data are available, and to discover, if necessary, how the expert's judgments can be improved (for an example in medicine, see Wigton, Patil, and Hoellerich 1986; for an example in hail forecasting, see Stewart et al. 1988; and, for an example in epidemiology, see Hammond et al. 1984).

Now consider the use of the concept of representativeness in terms of Tversky and Kahneman's (1982b) case 1, in which representativeness is described as being "dominated by perceived relative frequency or statistical association" (87). A lens model functionalist's narrow interpretation of this statement would be that, the greater the perceived relative frequency of association between a cue (X) and a distal variable (M), the greater the likelihood that X will be judged to be representative of M. Therefore, the subject can make more or less accurate judgments of M by observing X. This conclusion is supported by the broad definition of a heuristic given above from Tversky and Kahneman (1982a, 3). Thus, the lens model functionalist is apt to conclude that representativeness refers simply to a utilization coefficient for a cue (e.g., size, weight, etc.) for a given subject for inferring M (see fig. 10.1). In this narrow interpretation, nothing is added by the use of the concept representativeness.

Certainly, however, representativeness was intended to be more than a substitute for the term *utilization coefficient*. Further meaning can indeed be found in the statement that, "in all four cases, representativeness expresses the degree of correspondence between X and M" (Tversky and Kahneman 1982b, 87). But the ambiguity of *expresses* is troublesome. When representativeness "expresses the degree of correspondence between X and M," does it suggest a correspondence, does it indicate a correspondence, or does it measure the degree of correspondence? These three interpretations seem to exhaust the reasonable interpretations of *express* as an independently ascertained description of a subject's behavior, but they do not add anything to *utilization coefficient*. Only if *expresses* is intended to mean *explains why* a given degree of correspondence (or utilization coefficient) is found for X in relation to M would representativeness add significance to *utilization coefficient*. For, if representativeness explains why one substantive cue (e.g., height, color, personality characteristic) has a higher utilization coefficient than another, irrespective of the object relation in figure 10.1, then it would indeed be a useful concept. For example, height might well be an objectively measurable cue that is utilized in person perception, but, when it is somehow endowed with representativeness, then height would more often be utilized as a cue or be given greater weight when it is utilized than when not endowed with representativeness.

In such cases, representativeness could be given the status of a secondary cue, in contrast to a primary cue (e.g., height, color, etc.). Such secondary cues are in fact judgments themselves, as Tversky and Kahneman (1982b) have pointed out. The use of such judgments by the subject means that the researchers must construct a hierarchical model of the judgment process. It is

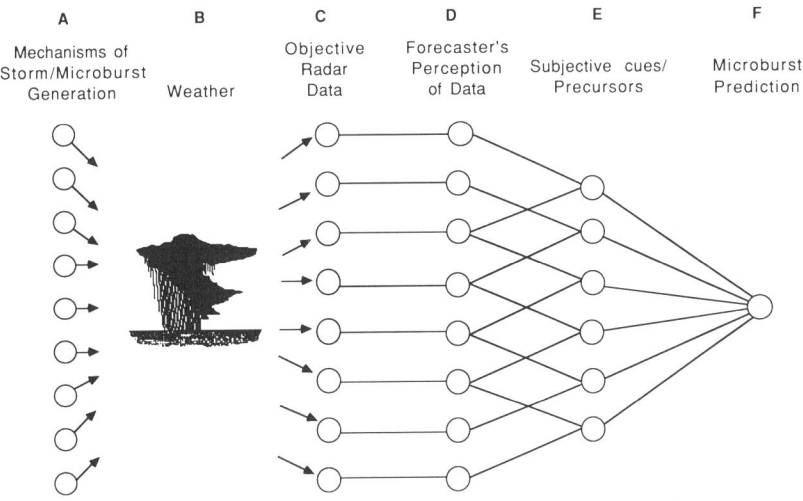

Figure 10.5. Hierarchical model of forecaster's judgments of microbursts.

in this conceptual form that representativeness offers potential for improving the scope and explanatory power of lens model functionalism.

Secondary cues will be found in judgment situations that require hierarchical models. Figure 10.5 shows a hierarchical model of the cognitive activity of meteorologists attempting to "nowcast" the critical weather episode known as the microburst. In this case, the secondary cues serve as inferences about distal physical phenomena mediated by the observation of physical data, mainly color contours on a radar terminal, that serve as primary cues. But it may well be that the meteorologists' judgments are based not on the secondary cues that the meteorologists say they are (e.g., "a descending core," "rotation of winds") but instead on judgments of representativeness, namely, the extent to which the color contours present a configuration that the meteorologists believe a microburst should present. In such cases, the explanatory power of each set of concepts could be pitted against one another. (See also Anderson's [1986] critical treatment of the concept of representativeness in relation to subjective cue values.) In short, the concept of representativeness can enrich understanding of complex judgment processes within the framework of the lens model. I now turn to the case in which the concept of representativeness stands outside the lens model framework and adds explanatory and predictive power independently of it.

Representativeness outside the Lens Model Framework

Representativeness has been defined in terms of similarity as well as of statistical association. Similarity may be explicated either in terms of the similarity between the features of a cognitive template and the features of an array of environmental or task data (for an innovative discussion, see Campbell 1966) or in terms of the similarity between the features of two objects (see esp. Tversky and Gati 1982). The feature-matching equations from the heuristics-and-biases approach and the lens model equation are alike in that both involve linear combinations of data; they are different in that the contrast-model equation, for example, involves a linear combination of features whereas the lens model equation involves a linear combination of functional relations (which may be linear or nonlinear). As a result, it becomes possible to set the predictability of various feature-matching models in competition with the predictability of functional relation models. More important, bringing these two models together allows researchers to ask new questions. Must a person be either a feature matcher or a user of functional relations? Must it be the case that only one form of cognitive activity occurs during the judgment process? Of course not. It is plausible to hypothesize (or believe, as I do) that persons may alternate in their application and use of feature matching or functional relations, using one activity at one moment and the other at another moment, and that these processes must occur in either-or-fashion, that they are not subject to compromise. It may well be found that these processes are used alternatively as task conditions change over time or as success or failure is encountered (for a detailed discussion, see Hammond 1988), but that hypothesis can be tested only if both forms of cognition are in fact used by subjects within the same research project.

Because lens model functionalism has demonstrated that higher organisms can and do make use of functional relations between cue and distal variables, and because the heuristics-and-biases approach has demonstrated that higher organisms can and do make use of similarity relations between objects as well as between cognitive templates and objects, our new research goal should be to determine which conditions induce which type of cognitive activity. For example, Lusk and I are now attempting to ascertain the rate at which these two forms of cognitive activity occur when medical students are being taught by their clinical teachers as well as to determine what circumstances induce the shift between these forms.

Summary

I have attempted to describe how research in judgment and decision making can be advanced by integration of two theories derived from their antecedents, functionalism and illusionism. I hope I have done so in an evenhanded way. I have shown how a central concept explicated in terms of a cue by the heuristics-and-biases approach can be used within the lens model framework and thus enrich it, and I have shown how the same concept, explicated as similarity within the feature-matching model, can be used in combination with the lens model to provide a more complete understanding of the judgment and decision-making process. Nevertheless, we still need to understand which conditions induce various forms of cognitive activity.

INDUCEMENT OF DIFFERENT FORMS OF COGNITION

As long ago as 1977, Slovic, Fischhoff, and Lichtenstein noted that it was not clear when, that is, under which circumstances, heuristics and biases would appear and that it was not possible to predict which, if any, heuristic or bias would appear under particular circumstances. Fischhoff (1983) and others (see, e.g., Fagley and Miller 1987) raised similar points about the framing effect. Tversky and Kahneman (1983) began to address this problem in their article on the conjunction fallacy. Under the heading "Logic versus Intuition," they note that "probability judgments are not always dominated by nonextensional heuristics." In order to specify when they will or will not be, they state, "Judgments of probability vary in the degree to which they follow a decompositional or a holistic approach and in the degree to which the assessment and the aggregation of probabilities are analytic or intuitive (see, e.g., Hammond & Brehmer, 1973)" (310), the citation acknowledging the basic elements of cognitive continuum theory, which I have recently presented in detail (Hammond et al. 1987; see also Hammond 1988).

Most important, they add that "decomposition and calculation provide some protection against conjunction errors and other biases" (Tversky and Kahneman 1983, 310). Exactly. What remains for us to do is to specify the conditions—situational or psychological—that determine when "judgments of probability" will "follow a decompositional or a holistic approach" and when "the assessment and the aggregation of probabilities are analytic or intuitive" and how much "protection" various conditions will afford. Our problem, then, is to describe as definitely as possible those task or environmental conditions that induce, or even permit, specific "nonextensional heuristics" to occur and thus allow us to predict under what task conditions good and poor achievement will occur. Otherwise, research on cognitive illusions offers only a list of heuristics that have been demonstrated to occur under conditions created to demonstrate them, a result that parallels the history of research on perceptual illusions.

However, Tversky and Kahneman (1983) further describe conditions that induce particular cognitive activities, namely, intuition or analysis. They state that "a direct test of the conjunction rule pits an intuitive impression against a basic law of probability" and then argue that the outcome of the conflict is determined by "the nature of the evidence, the formulation of the question, the transparency of the event structure, the appeal of the heuristic and the sophistication of the respondents" (310). Thus, by 1983, Tversky and Kahneman had clearly moved in the direction of lens model functionalism by emphasizing how task conditions determine the form cognition will take. Note also that the first three conditions that they name are environmental systems concepts and that the fourth and fifth are psychological concepts and that, for the first time, lens model researchers are cited. (Payne, Bettman, and Johnson [in this volume] also indicate the need for greater recognition of task conditions.) Earlier, Payne, Bettman, and Johnson (1988) made the important observation that, when these steps are taken, "people appear highly adaptive in responding to changes in structure of available alternatives and to the presence of time pressure. In general, actual behavior corresponded to the general patterns of efficient processing" (534), conclusions that surely support a functionalist point of view.

Nevertheless, more needs to be done. The task conditions that do or do not induce probability judgments to be "dominated by judgmental heuristics" remain largely unspecified.

My own approach to this problem has been to specify those task parameters that I believe induce cognition to occur, not merely at the analytic pole (where logic dominates) or the intuitive pole (where intuition dominates) but at points on a cognitive continuum between these rare polar types, a region in which elements of both may be found—a region that lens model functionalists have labeled *quasi rationality* (Brunswik 1956, 90; Hammond 1980; Hammond et al. 1987). I do this by postulating a task continuum and quantifying it in terms of a task-continuum index. From the task-continuum index, precise predictions can be made about cognitive activity, likewise quantitatively expressed in terms of a cognitive-continuum index (for an empirical test, see Hammond et al. 1987; and, for further elaboration, see Hammond 1988). I believe that the problem of determining which conditions will move cognition away from analytic cognition toward intuitive cognition, and vice versa, can be successfully resolved through the use of cognitive continuum theory. (The question of the accuracy of various forms of cognition needs to be addressed in a different context; see Hammond et al. 1987; Hammond, Hamm, and Grassia 1986.)

Transparency as a Meeting Point

Tversky and Kahneman's (1983, 1986) concept of transparency could provide a conceptual meeting point between the theoretical derivatives of functionalism and illusionism. I select transparency for two reasons. First, Tversky and Kahneman assign a crucial role to this concept for determining whether cognition will be intuitive or analytic—and thus whether the heuristics and biases they discuss will be operative. Second, transparency can be linked to three main concepts in current theory in lens model functionalism, namely, cognitive continuum theory, Brunswik's (1957, p. 5) statement that "each [system] has surface and depth," and cognitive feedback, a linkage I now undertake.

Transparency and Cognitive Continuum Theory. The concept of variability in task conditions is implicit in the statement that "decomposition and calculation provide some protection against conjunctive errors and other biases" (Tversky and Kahneman 1983, 310). For this statement acknowledges that some task conditions will permit "decomposition and calculation" or that, as von Winterfeldt and Edwards (1986) argued, "the use of tools" makes a difference in how we cope with uncertainty. More and more frequently, task conditions make analytic tools (hand-held computational devices for business decisions, etc.) available and thus offer protection against errors of various types. As Kahneman and Tversky note, those task conditions that do permit analytic cognition—whether through the use of tools or otherwise—will be more transparent as a result of calculation and decomposition. Thus, we are protected against whatever errors might accompany intuition. In short, some tasks are transparent (they have properties that make them susceptible to analysis and are thus analysis inducing), and some tasks are opaque (they have properties that prevent analysis and thus induce intuition).

Task conditions, however, vary greatly in their propensity to induce analysis or intuition (Brunswik thought that task conditions varied more than people), and that is why a quantified task continuum (or task-continuum index) is required. It is not enough simply to mention only a few task properties thought to induce one form of cognition or another; we need an abstraction that aggregates information about task properties. Such a concept will provide an index that permits identification, description, and discrimination of tasks. For, once the location of a task can be described quantitatively with the task-continuum index, further predictions about cognitive activity can be made. Tversky and Kahneman's (1983) suggestion that the transparency of the event structure increases the appeal of the heuristic is entirely in accord with my suggestion that different task conditions induce—appeal to—different cognitive processes. In short, there is a direct link between transparency and the development of a task-continuum index and, of course, a cognitive-continuum index as well.

A major premise of cognitive continuum theory is that intuition and analysis are not dichotomous (Hammond et al. 1987). Instead, they are two poles of a cognitive continuum that allows for common sense or quasi rationality between these poles. In addition, the environmental counterpart of cognition is also represented by a continuum, a task continuum that ranges from polar tasks that are highly intuition inducing to those that are highly analysis inducing. "Furthermore, once cognitive processes are defined in terms of their location on a cognitive continuum, they will be found to interact in predictable ways with various task conditions located on a similar continuum" (Hammond et al. 1987, 754). In short, one of the most important advantages of cognitive continuum theory is that it readily allows for movement of cognition on the continuum across time or over changing conditions (Hammond 1988; Hammond et al. 1988).

Transparency, Surface, and Depth. The crucial role of transparency can be seen in Tversky and Kahneman (1986, esp. S266–S267), in which they use the Müller-Lyer illusion to demonstrate the importance of task transparency (see fig. 10.4). The concept of task transparency directly implies a task surface (the display of information) that is to be distinguished from task depth (those properties of the task not displayed or not immediately apparent). Thus, the concept of transparency brings Tversky and Kahneman close to Brunswik's (1957) statement that both environmental systems and organismic systems have surface and depth.

Once the concepts of transparency, surface, and depth are introduced, it is only natural to ask what lies between the surface features and the depth features of any task system. Hammond et al. (1975, 275–76) referred to this region as the "zone of ambiguity" in judgment tasks in order to direct attention to the conditions that reduce or increase ambiguity, or transparency, between surface and depth. Thus, the zone of ambiguity implies a task-system space that requires description. For example, the zone of ambiguity may be shallow or deep, depending on the distance between proximal cues and distal variables and on whether functional relations or feature matching is operative. Thus, the distinction between surface and depth should enhance our understanding of what makes some tasks more difficult than others, why some tasks induce nonextensional heuristics, or, more generally, why some task circumstances induce intuition, quasi rationality, or analysis.

Transparency and Cognitive Feedback. The concept of transparency can also be readily linked to the concept of cognitive feedback (introduced as "lens model feedback" by Todd and Hammond 1965; for an annotated bibliography, see Hammond 1987; and, for a review, see Balzer, Doherty, and O'Connor 1989) and to associated empirical findings from studies of subjects learning to improve judgment under conditions of uncertainty. Cognitive feedback provides the subject with information about the zone of ambiguity between surface features (cue values) and the criterion (depth features). Thus, transparency is enhanced if subjects are provided with such information as cue weights, the form of the functional relations between cues and criterion—the texture of the environment as it extends in depth. As a result, subjects rapidly can learn to improve the accuracy of their judgments.

Logical and statistical considerations make it obvious that outcome feedback (comparisons between the subject's judgment and the correct answer) allows the subject to be right for the wrong reason, and vice versa, and is of little value in tasks involving uncertainty. The empirical results bear out this conclusion (see Poses et al. 1986; Wigton, Patil, and Hoellerich 1986; for practical applications in medicine, see also Faerman, Milter, and Rohrbaugh 1983; Hammond 1971; Hammond et al. 1975). Cognitive feedback, readily provided by computer graphics, increases the transparency between the surface and the depth conditions of the task, and, as Tversky and Kahneman (1983, 1986) would anticipate, learning occurs rapidly. Norman Anderson was correct in observing that "one such picture would easily be worth a thousand of Thorndike's trials and errors" (Anderson 1983, 252).

An Index of Transparency

If the concept of transparency is indeed a step toward the integration of illusionism and functionalism, then some measure of the degree of transparency between surface and depth is required so that various judgment tasks can be compared in this respect. Indeed, such a measure, or index, of transparency will greatly assist us in achieving generalization over tasks.

Summary

Conceptual issues need no longer be a source of division between functionalism and illusionism and their derivative approaches. No longer content with providing a list of explanatory concepts related to cognitive activity independent of task conditions, Tversky and Kahneman (1983, 1986) have begun to specify task conditions from which the appearance or nonappearance of various heuristics and biases can be predicted. This step is welcome because it will add greatly to our understanding of judgment and decision making. In addition, however, their introduction of the concept of transparency also links work on heuristics and biases to current theoretical and empirical work in lens model functionalism. In particular, transparency can be readily linked to cognitive continuum theory, which also emphasizes task conditions and includes a task-continuum index, the concepts of task surface and depth, and cognitive feedback. What is also needed is an index of transparency with which this important task property can be measured. Thus, a common theoretical ground between these approaches can be established; focusing on task conditions is the key to integrating the theoretical derivatives of functionalism and illusionism.

THE COMMITMENT TO DIFFERENT METHODOLOGIES: IMPASSE OR OPPORTUNITY?

Conceptual integration will lead to a more coherent approach to understanding judgment and decision-making processes. But achieving a common theoretical ground will bring us face to face with what may be either a methodological impasse or a methodological opportunity. In this section, my prior commitment to lens model functionalism and its accompanying research design produces a frankly partisan text. I have firmly believed during all my professional life that psychological research has been trapped within a methodology accidentally derived from agricultural research and for generations uncritically driven into the minds of students.

Methodology as Impasse

Tversky and Kahneman (1983) state their methodological commitment in clear and unmistakable terms. They quote Helmholtz under the side heading of "Cognitive Illusions": "Our studies of inductive reasoning have focused on systematic errors because they are diagnostic of the heuristics that *generally* govern judgment and inference. In the words of Helmholtz (1881/1903), 'It is just those cases that are not in accordance with *reality* which are particularly instructive for discovering the laws of the processes by which normal perception orginates'" (italics added). They continue, "The focus on bias and illusion is a research strategy that exploits human error, although it neither assumes nor entails that people are perceptually or cognitively inept" (313). In short, by focusing on error, researchers will learn more and learn better than by any other research strategy.

Tversky and Kahneman do well to cite Helmholtz: he was one of the first to study perceptual illusions, and he used precisely the method he advocated. Thus, although the heuristics-and-biases approach may lack conceptual antecedents, it certainly carries methodological commitments from the past. But my criticisms are as follows. Where is the logical argument for this research strategy? Exactly why should one learn more and better in this way? Apparently because "the same mechanisms produce both valid and invalid judgments" (Tversky and Kahneman 1983, 313). But this statement begs the question. It does not say why that fact—if it is a fact—proves that Helmholtz's methodology is the appropriate one.

The lens model theory, on the other hand, argues that, because multiple fallible indicators (cues, signs) are available to our subjects in many naturalistic circumstances and even in many artificial ones, a design that represents those circumstances is required for our purpose—otherwise, we generalize without justification. For example, a columnist in my morning newspaper tells me that "members of Congress know that making monetary policy is like making legislation; a messy, seat-of-the-pants operation that reflects the pushing, pulling, and contradictory signals of the real world" (Medley 1988, 22). But if research situations must be reduced to those cases that are not in accordance with reality (whatever that might mean), then how can a theory that is prepared to study judgments made under circumstances involving "pushing, pulling, and contradictory signals" (multiple fallible indicators) be tested? How shall we learn what cognitive mechanisms are used when human beings must cope with an array of multiple fallible indicators, a circumstance demonstrably present in so many, if not most, judgment tasks? Is it really advisable to base our conclusions about the ability of human beings to avoid "seductive nonextensional intuitions" (Tversky and Kahneman 1983, 314) on a research strategy that deliberately exploits human error and thus rules out the study of judgments that must be made in circumstances that offer multiple—possibly redundant—cues of varying validity? If we drew conclusions about human perception from studies of perceptual illusions, we would doubt our ability to walk, and driving a car would be unimaginable.

It was precisely because of his commitment to functionalism—in opposition to Gestalt illusionism—that in 1944 Brunswik carried out his study of size constancy with a single subject in her natural environment. Because he found an almost perfect correlation between judged size and actual size (1956, 43–48), he concluded, "The astonishing degree of perfection of the particular stabilization mechanism constituting perceptual size constancy has thus been demonstrated with respect to the universe of situations from which our sample [of objects] was drawn" (47). Since the universe (the Berkeley campus) offered a wide variety of situations and the sample was large, the basis for the conclusion was clear.

Illusionism has clearly demonstrated for over a century that perceptual illusions are powerful and that they are very difficult to overcome, despite our best efforts. But we have also learned that perceptual illusions are fragile and can easily be made to disappear, as Tversky and Kahneman (1986) demonstrated with the Müller-Lyer illusion. Moreover, exactly the correct conditions must be created in order to produce these illusions; that is why they are so rare outside the laboratory. Therein lies the necessity for the representative design of experiments. Its purpose is not to deny that illusions can be created or destroyed. Rather, the reason for using representative designs is to enable us to understand how cognition functions under that variety of conditions representative of those in which a given organism functions.

In summary, although I do not have the slightest doubt about the factual correctness of the empirical results achieved by the heuristics-and-biases researchers in the specific circumstances in which they have been generated, I doubt their generality. If I may set the work on cognitive illusions in parallel with the work on perceptual illusions, then I conclude that the results must be confined to those situations specifically created to demonstrate their occurrence, that is, those situations in which human error has deliberately been exploited. Such demonstrations do not tell me what I should expect when human judgment is applied to circumstances in which human error is not exploited. I believe that the study of what *can* happen when human error is deliberately exploited is of less importance than the study of what *does* happen under various task circumstances representative of an organism's various habitats.

The Representative Design of Experiments

There is a clear conceptual track from the duplicity principle put forward by Brunswik and Kardos in 1929 to the introduction of representative design and the probability point of view presented by Brunswik in 1957. Once the idea has been introduced that much cognitive activity is based on multiple fallible cues to distal objects, the relation between those fallible indicators and distal objects will eventually be treated as a system with properties of its own. When that happens, the formal, not merely substantive properties of task systems must be described and represented in all their variety (see my introduction of this distinction in Hammond 1966, 68–75).

That point of view, once considered bizarre by psychologists, has slowly gained headway. Indeed, Keren and Raaijmakers (1988) recently described representative design as an ideal toward which we should strive, thus: "Ideally, one would like to employ a representative design (Brunswik, 1956) that would most resemble the natural environment" (239).

Much as I welcome recognition of the significance of representative design, I must object to Keren and Raaijmaker's term *real-life circumstances* (1988, 239). The issue is not whether research conditions are removed from "real life," the "real world," "everyday life," "reality," or "natural conditions"; rather, the issue is simply whether the experiment includes those conditions toward which the generalization is intended. For example, if we want to generalize our results to task circumstances that involve, say, nonlinearities or intercorrelated cues of "pushing, pulling, and contradictory signals" (Medley 1988, 22), then such conditions must be included in the circumstances in which the subject is studied. Otherwise, we cannot speak to such conditions in our conclusions. Helmholtz's *reality* and the contemporary term *real world* are unacceptable descriptions of task conditions for precisely the same reason that describing a sample of subjects as *real people* is unacceptable. In short, the justification for accepting generalizations from circumstances in the task studied to task circumstances not yet studied is representativeness (hence the name *representative design*), just as in the case of generalizations from subjects studied in the experiment to the subjects not yet studied. This is exactly the opposite of the justification put foward by Helmholtz and recommended and used by Tversky and Kahneman. Which is correct?

By the logic of induction represented by standard sampling theory, Brunswik is right, and Helmholtz is wrong. But it might be argued that, although the conventional logic of induction is applicable to the subject side of the experiment, somehow it is not applicable to the object (or stimulus) side. Rather than engage in argumentation, let me give a specific example of how a classic result in psychology turns out to be unjustifiable when the conventional logic of induction is applied to the object side of the experiment.

Illusory Correlation: An Illusory Result Created by Systematic Design

Chapman's (1967) finding that persons are subject to illusory correlation has been cited over 1,000 times and has never been doubted, so far as I know. Yet, by applying the argument from representative design, it can be readily demonstrated that not one subject in Chapman's (1967) experiment ever exhibited illusory correlation.

In the first study in which the phenomenon of illusory correlation was reported, Chapman (1967) gave his subjects a paired-associates learning task, six word pairs with high associative value (e.g., *bacon-eggs*) and other neutral word pairs (e.g., *blossoms-notebook*) were presented in such a manner that the word pairs with high associative value appeared one-third of the time. The subjects were then asked to recall the frequency with which all the word pairs occurred in the task. As Chapman indicates, "The correct co-occurrence [of the high associative word pairs] in each case was . . . $33\frac{1}{3}\%$. It was predicted that for the six high associative pairs . . . the reported co-occurrence would be higher than this value. This excess over the correct value is the measure of illusory correlation" (153).

The first question from the standpoint of sampling theory is, Why six word pairs? Why not ten, or five, or four, or one word pair? The answer is, of course, that, if too small a number of word pairs were used, the results would not be convincing. Why not? Because words can vary in several dimensions (meaning, content, etc.) just as persons can vary in several dimensions, and, therefore, characteristics of word pairs other than their associative value might account for the results. Consequently, the experimenter apparently somehow decided that six word pairs would be an adequate number to provide generalizability over a universe of word pairs. But no statistical test was made to determine whether the six word pairs constituted an adequate sample size (irrespective of other sampling considerations) to test the hypothesis, nor is there any discussion of this problem.

But we know that some hypothesis was tested statistically, and that hypothesis was "that for the six high associative pairs . . . the reported co-occurrence would be higher than [33⅓%]" (Chapman 1967, 153). In this test, Chapman compared the mean responses (41.3, 46.7, 43.7, 40.2, 43.3, and 39.1 percent) of the subject sample for the reported co-occurrence of the six critical word pairs with the value 33⅓ percent "by means of a two-tailed, large sample [of subjects] t-test" (153) and found the difference to be "significant for each of the six pairs with high associative connection, $z = 3.45$ or larger, $p < .001$ in *each case*" (153; italics added). Thus, each of the six tests of significance was made over numerous subjects ($N = 55, 49, 59$) but on only one word pair in each test. In accordance with conventional methodology, Chapman concluded that, because the difference was significant in each case, the phenomenon of illusory correlation had been observed with the probability indicated.

Because six word pairs of high associative value were used, however, we can address the question whether any subject responded with a systematic bias in favor of the word pairs with associative value. The weakest test is to ask only that a subject err on the side of overestimation by the minimal amount (34 percent). Even if that is all that is asked, however, a subject would have to overestimate for all six critical word pairs to exceed the customary .05 probability level of significance (by a binomial test). Without access to Chapman's (1967) data, we cannot ascertain whether any subject did overestimate for all six. But this is not a useful test in any event because the small magnitude of the effect (1 percent overestimation) is trivial.

How large an overestimation would not be considered trivial? With a sample size of six word pairs, we can be confident (at the 5 percent level) that, if any subject's mean estimate departed from the 33 percent value by 1.65 standard errors (one-tailed test), the subject was systematically overestimating the appearance of the six critical word pairs. This means that only those subjects whose mean estimate of the frequency of those word pairs exceeded 65 percent could be considered to have become susceptible to illusory correlation. Because the average response of Chapman's subjects in the first series was only 42.3 percent (by the third series, it had dropped to 35.6 percent), it is extremely doubtful that the phenomenon of illusory correlation was demonstrated by any subject. For, if we set the criterion for evidence of systematic departure from 33⅓ percent at 65 percent, the lower (.05) confidence bound for 65 percent for a sample of, say, 50 persons is 54 percent. This bound far exceeds the mean of 42.3 percent obtained by Chapman on the first series, in which the data are most congenial to the illusory correlation hypothesis. The conclusion that a mean estimate of 42.3 percent was a sufficiently large departure from 33⅓ percent to establish the generality of the phenomenon was, therefore, itself an illusion because the statistical test was made in the direction opposite from the direction claimed; it was made in the direction of subjects rather than objects (word pairs).

In short, the logic of sampling theory can be applied to the object side of experiments as well as the subject side, and, when it is, classical results can be shown to be unjustified. Adherence to conventional designs exacts a heavy price.

Chapman should not be singled out for criticism, however; use of this mistaken methodology is common practice. Indeed, the design used by Chapman in 1967 would still be judged appropriate by the great majority of psychology departments (and journal editors) today, despite the growing enlightenment exemplified by Keren and Raaijmakers (1988).

Invariance across Methods

The logic of sampling theory aside, however, representative design also directs us to look at the question of the method dependence of results. Invariance of results across methods is a highly desired research requirement. But Fagley and Miller (1987, 267) have noted that the framing effect—which demonstrates that judgments are not invariant across methods— is itself failing to meet the test of invariance of results across methods and conditions:

> Research on the framing effect presents a varied picture of its impact. Some experiments have not found the mirror image preferences predicted by prospect theory (e.g., Fagley, 1985; Fagley & Kruger, 1986; Miller, 1986). For example, Fagley (1985) reported no significant mirror image preferences, with framing accounting for about 3% of the variance in choice in contrast to the 25% of the variance found by Tversky and Kahneman (1981). McNeil, Pauker, Sox, and Tversky (1982), using a problem with options differing in expected value, also reported that framing accounted for 3% of the variance in choice. Neale and Bazerman (1985), using a negotiation task rather than a decision problem, reported that framing accounted for a "small proportion of variance" (7 and 16% of the variance in concessionary processes and successful outcomes, respectively) in contract negotiation. Thus, evidence for the framing effect is equivocal.
>
> Evidence for the domain effect, on which the framing effect presumably depends, is also variable. Kahneman and Tversky (1979) presented evidence that preferences in the domain of gain were the mirror image of preferences in the domain of loss, as predicted. Hershey and Schoemaker (1980), however, reported significant mirror image prefer-

ences for gains versus losses in only 6 of 28 decision problems. Given the varied evidence for the domain effect, it is not surprising that some research has failed to detect a framing effect.

As a further example of the fragility of illusions, when Hewstone, Benn, and Wilson (1988) compared results obtained by presenting information contrasting base rates and witness's reports by means of a booklet with results obtained by presenting them via a computer terminal, they found "that the base rate fallacy was weaker . . . , with far fewer subjects . . . following the witness" in the latter case. They suggest "that the computer-presentation may have induced a different set in the subjects, whereby they concentrated more on this task and tried to use all the available information" (Hewstone, Benn, and Wilson 1988, 171).

These differences in results all occur in connection with a change in method, procedure, or both and once more raise the specter of method-dependent results, an old story in psychology (see, e.g., Campbell and Fiske 1959). As Meehl (1978) warned, "There is a period of enthusiasm about a new theory, a period of attempted application to new fact domains, a period of disillusion as the negative data came in, a growing bafflement about inconsistent and non-replicable results, multiple resort to ad hoc excuses, and then people just lose interest in the theory and pursue other endeavors" (807). In my view, we must not allow this to happen. The best way to prevent it from happening is not to deny that differences in results occur over different methods or to reject a theory when that occurs but to discover why different methods produce different results. The best way to do that is to develop a theory of task inducement and to apply a research design consistent with it, namely, representative design. Thus, we may change what is now an impasse into an opportunity.

Methodology as Opportunity

As matters stand, functionalism and illusionism produce incommensurable results because results produced by both are method dependent. For example, there can be little doubt that, within what Kahneman and Tversky (1982, 508) have called "the question-answering paradigm," subjects can be shown to ignore base rates and to be likely to make judgments not in accordance with statistical rules. But, for more than 20 years, multiple-cue probability-learning studies have demonstrated exactly the opposite: subjects definitely are sensitive to the standard deviations of the distribution (base rates of occurrence) of cue values when multiple displays are used. Indeed, these studies and policy-capturing studies nearly always provide information about this task parameter as a matter of course (for a recent example, see Klayman 1988; see also Stewart 1988, 41–74). Both conclusions are correct but stand tied to the method used to produce them, and neither conclusion is as general over conditions as we would like it to be.

This situation should surprise no one. Advocates of specific approaches to the study of judgment and decision making (including myself) become wedded to specific ways of doing research and persistently ignore results produced by other methods and procedures, even though they bear on questions central to all investigations (for a description of methods and procedures associated with six approaches to judgment and decision making, see Hammond, McClelland, and Mumpower 1980). Thus, it is not surprising that researchers who think that cognitive illusions are important have never cited the results from lens model studies that used multiple displays and showed sensitivity to base rates. Similarly, functionalists have seldom cited results produced by asking subjects questions. A few investigators, including Einhorn, Hogarth, Doherty, Slovic, and Payne, freed from advocacy of a specific point of view, have undertaken studies in which various methods have been employed. But even these investigators have not systematically crossed methods and concepts, and that is what is needed if we are to achieve generality across methods and conditions.

Incommensurability of method-dependent results is to be expected of an as yet immature discipline in which investigators are still exploring the generality of results within a productive conceptual framework. Anderson (1981, 1983, 1986) is a classic example of a researcher who explores multiple domains by persistent use of a single method. (For an example of method dependence in cognitive psychology, see the analysis of John Anderson and Michael Posner's work in Hammond, Hamm, and Grassia 1986, 264–66).

Method dependence need not be a permanent barrier to the integration of approaches and to what we desire most of all—cumulative results. Indeed, Einhorn, Kleinmuntz, and Kleinmuntz (1979) demonstrated through the use of protocol analysis that judgments made by a clinical psychologist could be described in terms of linear models and "a multiple choice of rules" (471). As Einhorn, Kleinmuntz, and Kleinmuntz noted, Brunswik's concept of "vicarious functioning, by which equivalent judgments can result from different patterns of cues, is central to any theory of judgment" (465). They then demonstrated that the same process (an additive rule) could be captured by different methods (either multiple displays or protocol analysis), thus demonstrating the generality of the additive rule over methods and, in addition, illustrating the role of vicarious functioning in both circumstances. A similar integrative effort can be seen in Einhorn and Hogarth's (1986) landmark essay on judging probable cause.

A more powerful technique is Campbell and Fiske's (1959) multitrait-multimethod methodology that crosses methods and concepts systematically. Because the multitrait-multimethod matrix reflects the logic of "triangulation in empirical space" (Hammond, Hamm, and Grassia 1986, 266), the wide disparity of research methods can be used to great advantage if they are used in a single study across the same subjects (for an example of the use of this method in a study of experts, see Hammond, Hamm, and Grassia 1986). Should similar results indeed be achieved from the use of widely different methods, greater confidence in generality will accrue to concepts as well as results than when methods similar to one another are used. Even if results continue to be method dependent, we still benefit; we no longer overgeneralize, but we learn instead which methods induce which behavior. Specifically, should similar findings be achieved across the question-answering research paradigm and the multiple-display research paradigm, greater credibility would be enjoyed by both approaches precisely because the methods employed are so different. What now appears to be an impasse subject only to endless argumentation could thus become an opportunity.

Correspondence versus Coherence Theories of Truth

I chose to discuss the antecedent metatheories—functionalism and illusionism—of lens model functionalism and the heuristics-and-biases approach for several reasons. First, I believe that the thematic elements of these metatheories still exert considerable control over theory and methodology in judgment and decision research. Thomas Kuhn (1970) rendered us a valuable service when he showed how "normal science" is pursued within theoretical and methodological commitments taken for granted and seldom criticized. Brunswik (1952, 1956) also showed how similar unexamined commitments have guided research in psychology. When implicit commitments to a way of doing things are recognized, however, radical reinterpretations can occur, often with a liberating effect.

Might this occur within the field of judgment and decision research? My answer is yes, which brings me to my second reason for considering antecedents. Without attempting to review the numerous studies that would demonstrate this point, let me simply assert that I believe that a review based on antecedents would find that the vast majority of research carried out by the functionalists, including the lens model functionalists and Bayesians, used tasks with multiple displays of data and thus induced subjects to use the correspondence theory of truth, thereby producing intuitive statisticians. That is, by presenting the subject with multiple displays of data on several dimensions, subjects are induced to base their judgments on relations between the proximal data observed and the distal variables inferred. Thus, the subjects employ the correspondence theory of truth—a theory that argues that truth is based on known or learned functional relations among observations. If success is achieved under these circumstances by the subjects, it will be achieved insofar as they become good intuitive statisticians. Although subjects' achievement will vary with task conditions, the concept of the subject as an intuitive statistician has been highly successful in predicting behavior.

On the other hand, the research that ostensibly refuted the findings summarized in Peterson and Beach (1967) and elsewhere (see Brehmer and Joyce 1988) employed tasks that use the question-answering paradigm instead of multiple displays and thus induced subjects to use the coherence theory of truth (see, e.g., Kahneman, Slovic, and Tversky 1982, 504, 508). That is, by presenting subjects with a set of words that describes individuals (e.g., Tom W., Linda) or events (as in the cab problem), subjects are induced to base their judgments on features rather than variables and thus to seek coherence among the features rather than correspondence between proximal and distal variables. Presented with a highly coherent set of features, as in, for example, Tom W., the subjects are thus (wrongly) induced to base their judgments on the coherence carefully prepared by the experimenters. In sum, the subjects in this research paradigm are induced to base their judgments on the coherence theory of truth, a theory that seeks not validity in terms of multiple observations for each data point or descriptor but coherence among them; the greater the coherence, the greater the truth value of the data (for an attempt to discover differences in the relative weight assigned to each theory of truth by expert engineers, see Hammond, Hamm, and Grassia, 1986; see also Hastie and Rasinski 1987, 204–5). Thus, each methodology—multiple trials and question answering—is tied to either functionalism or illusionism, each of which is tied to its parent theory of truth, correspondence or coherence.

Once induced in the subject, coherence and correspondence theories can, of course, either assist or mislead and thus enhance or impair subjects' performance, depending on which theory is most appropriate for a given set of task conditions. The relative strength of conditions for inducing one or the other theory within subjects should be carefully ascertained and explicitly acknowledged, but it rarely is. The relative advantages of the use of either theory in a task should also be made clear, but seldom is.

In sum, the theories derived from functionalism and illusionism are not competing theories about judgment and decision making; rather, they are complementary theories about cognition that takes place under different conditions, conditions that induce subjects to employ different theories of truth. Because both types of inducement frequently occur in human ecologies, it is costly for *persons* to deny truth to either theory; it is, however, highly beneficial to be able to employ either, particularly when one knows which theory to apply under which conditions. Additionally, it is costly for *researchers* to deny that subjects can employ either or both forms of cognition, but it is beneficial to learn the consequences of their application in various circumstances. It is this argument that leads me to believe that integration could strengthen the research effort to understand human judgment and decision making.

EPILOGUE

This concludes my tribute to my good friend and colleague Hillel Einhorn. I have done my best to unify what I believe to have been historically two very disparate attempts to understand human judgment and decision making that persist to this day. Perhaps because these attempts have been so disparate, there have been no recent attempts to reconcile them. Hilly and I understood unification differently, however. His preference was to enjoy and celebrate diversity within this field of research, whereas my preference has been to attempt to discover the antecedents of diversity, to find their complementarity, and thus to unify them, to find the place of one in relation to the other. Indeed, Hilly and I enthusiastically argued this question on more than one occasion. I only wish that I had been better prepared. But it is the reader who will now have an opportunity to judge which is the better course.

REFERENCES

Anderson, N. H. 1981. *Foundations of information integration theory.* New York: Academic.

———. 1983. Intuitive physics: Understanding and learning of physical relations. In *Perception, cognition, and development: Interactional analyses,* ed. T. J. Tighe and B. E. Shepp, 231–65. Hillsdale, N.J.: Erlbaum.

———. 1986. A cognitive theory of judgment and decision. In *New directions in research on decision making,* ed. B. Brehmer, H. Jungermann, P. Lourens, and G. Sevon, 63–108. Amsterdam: North-Holland.

Balzer, W. K., M. E. Doherty, and R. O'Connor, Jr. 1989. Effects of cognitive feedback on performance. *Psychological Bulletin* 106:410–33.

Boring, E. G. 1942. *Sensation and perception in the history of psychology.* New York: Appleton-Century.

Brehmer, B. 1970. Inference behavior in a situation where the cues are not reliably perceived. *Organizational Behavior and Human Performance* 5:330–37.

———. 1976. Social judgment theory and the analysis of interpersonal conflict. *Psychological Bulletin* 83:985–1003.

Brehmer, B., and C. R. B. Joyce. 1988. *Human judgment: The SJT view.* Amsterdam: North-Holland.

Brunswik, E. 1934. *Wahrnehmung und gegenstandswelt: Grundlegung einer psychologie vom gegenstand her* (Perception and the world of objects: The foundations of a psychology in terms of objects). Leipzig und Vienna: Deuticke.

———. 1939. Probability as a determiner of rat behavior. *Journal of Experimental Psychology* 25:175–97.

———. 1943. Organismic achievement and environmental probability. *Psychological Review* 50: 255–72.

———. 1952. The conceptual framework of psychology. In *International encyclopedia of unified science,* vol. 1, no. 10, pp. 4–102. Chicago: University of Chicago Press.

———. 1956. *Perception and the representative design of psychological experiments.* 2d ed. Berkeley: University of California Press.

———. 1957. Scope and aspects of the cognitive problem. In *Cognition: The Colorado symposium,* ed. H. Gruber, R. Jessor, and K. Hammond, 5–31. Cambridge, Mass.: Harvard University Press.

Brunswik, E., and L. Kardos. 1929. Das duplizitatsprinzip in der theorie der farbenwahrnehmung (The duplicity principle in the theory of color perception). *Zeitschrift für Psychologie* 111:307–20.

Campbell, D. T. 1966. Pattern matching as an essential in distal knowing. In *The psychology of Egon Brunswik,* ed. K. R. Hammond, 81–106. New York: Holt, Rinehart & Winston.

Campbell, D. T., and D. W. Fiske. 1959. Convergent and discriminant validation by the multitrait-multimethod matrix. *Psychological Bulletin* 56:81–105.

Chapman, L. J. 1967. Illusory correlation in observational report. *Journal of Verbal Learning and Verbal Behavior* 6:151–55.

Christensen-Szalanski, J., and L. Beach. 1984. The citation bias: Fad and fashion in the judgment and decision literature. *American Psychologist* 39:75–78.

Einhorn, H. J., and R. M. Hogarth. 1986. Judging probable cause. *Psychological Bulletin* 99:3–19.

Einhorn, H. J., B. Kleinmuntz, and D. N. Kleinmuntz. 1979. Linear regression *and* process-tracing models of judgment. *Psychological Review* 86:465–85.

Faerman, S. R., R. G. Milter, and R. Rohrbaugh. 1983. Modeling the intake process for protective services for children: Texas Department of Human Resources Protective Services for Children Branch. State University of New York at Albany, Nelson A. Rockefeller College of Public Affairs and Policy, Institute for Government and Policy Studies, Decision Techtronics Group. Typescript.

Fagley, N. S. 1985. Factors affecting choice of risky options. Paper presented at the annual meeting of the American Psychological Association, Los Angeles.

Fagley, N. S., and L. Kruger. 1986. Framing effects on the program choices of school psychologists. Typescript.

Fagley, N. S., and P. M. Miller. 1987. The effects of decision framing on choice of risky vs. certain options. *Organizational Behavior and Human Decision Processes* 39:264–77.

Fischhoff, B. 1983. Predicting frames. *Journal of Experimental Psychology: Learning, Memory, and Cognition* 9:103–16.

Gibson, J. 1979. *The ecological approach to visual perception.* Boston: Houghton Mifflin.

Gigerenzer, G. 1987. Survival of the fittest probabilist: Brunswik, Thurstone, and the two disciplines of psychology. In *The probabilistic revolution,* vol. 2, *Ideas in the sciences,* ed. L. Kruger, G. Gigerenzer, and M. S. Morgan, 49–72. Cambridge, Mass.: MIT Press.

Gillis, J. S. 1975. The effects of anti-psychotic drugs on complex learning in schizophrenics. II. Cognitive conflict. In *Psychoactive drugs and human judgment,* ed. C. R. B. Joyce and K. R. Hammond, 147–55. New York: Wiley.

Gillis, J. S., and K. Blevens. 1978. Sources of judgmental impairment in paranoid and nonparanoid schizophrenia. *Journal of Abnormal Psychology* 87:587–96.

Gillis, J. S., J. O. Lipkin, and T. Moran. 1981. Drug therapy decisions: A social judgment analysis. *Journal of Nervous and Mental Diseases* 169:439–47.

Gillis, J. S., and S. Parkison. 1981. The effects of fluphenazine injection and chlorpromazine on symptom severity and learning in outpatient schizophrenics. *Current and Therapeutic Research* 29:1–16.

Gould, S. J. 1988. Review of *Streak: Joe DiMaggio and the summer of '41,* by Michael Seidel. *New York Review of Books* 35 (18 August): 8–12.

Hammond, K. R. 1955. Probabilistic functioning and the clinical method. *Psychological Review* 62:255–62.

———, ed. 1966. *The psychology of Egon Brunswik.* New York: Holt, Rinehart & Winston.

———. 1971. Computer graphics as an aid to learning. *Science* 172:903–8.

———. 1980. *The integration of research in judgment and decision theory.* Technical Report no. 226. Boulder: University of Colorado, Center for Research on Judgment and Policy.

———. 1987. *Annotated bibliography on cognitive feedback.* Technical Report no. 269. Boulder: University of Colorado, Center for Research on Judgment and Policy.

———. 1988. Judgment and decision making in dynamic tasks. *Information and Decision Technologies* 14:3–14.

Hammond, K. R., and L. Adelman. 1976. Science, values, and human judgment. *Science* 194:389–96.

Hammond, K. R., B. F. Anderson, J. Sutherland, and B. Marvin. 1984. Improving scientists' judgments of risk. *Risk Analysis* 4:69–78.

Hammond, K. R., and B. Brehmer. 1973. Quasi-rationality and distrust: Implications for international conflict. In *Human judgment and social interaction,* ed. L. Rappoport and D. A. Summers. New York: Holt, Rinehart & Winston.

Hammond, K. R., E. Frederick, N. Robillard, and D. Victor. 1989. Application of cognitive theory to the student-teacher dialog. In *Cognitive science in medicine,* ed. D. Evans and V. L. Patel, 173–210. Cambridge, Mass.: MIT Press.

Hammond, K. R., and J. Grassia. 1985. The cognitive side of conflict: From theory to resolution of policy disputes. In *Applied social psychology annual,* vol. 6, *International conflict and national public policy issues,* ed. S. Oskamp, 233–54. Beverly Hills, Calif.: Sage.

Hammond, K. R., R. M. Hamm, and J. Grassia. 1986. Generalizing over conditions by combining the multitrait-multimethod matrix and the representative design of experiments. *Psychological Bulletin* 100:257–69.

Hammond, K. R., R. M. Hamm, J. Grassia, and T. Pearson. 1987. Direct comparison of the efficacy of intuitive and analytical cognition in expert judgment. *IEEE Transactions on Systems, Man, and Cybernetics* SMC-17:753–70.

Hammond, K. R., and C. R. B. Joyce, eds. 1975. *Psychoactive drugs and social judgment: Theory and research.* New York: Wiley.

Hammond, K. R., G. H. McClelland, and J. Mumpower. 1980. *Human judgment and decision making: Theories, methods, and procedures.* New York: Hemisphere/Praeger.

Hammond, K. R., J. Mumpower, R. L. Dennis, S. Fitch, and W. Crumpacker. 1983. Fundamental obstacles to the use of scientific information in public policy making. *Technological Forecasting and Social Change* 24:287–97.

Hammond, K. R., T. R. Stewart, B. Brehmer, and D. O. Steinmann. 1975. Social judgment theory. In *Human judgment and decision processes,* ed. M. F. Kaplan and S. Schwartz, 271–312. New York: Academic.

Hastie, R., and K. A. Rasinski. 1987. The concept of accuracy in social judgment. In *The social psychology of knowledge,* ed. D. Bar-Tal and A. Kruglanski, 193–208. Cambridge: Cambridge University Press.

Helmholtz, H. von. [1881] 1903. *Popular lectures on scientific subjects.* Translated by E. Atkinson. New York: Green.

Hershey, J. C., and P. J. H. Schoemaker. 1980. The reflection hypothesis. *Organizational Behavior and Human Performance* 25:395–418.

Hewstone, M., W. Benn, and A. Wilson. 1988. Bias in the use of base rates: Racial prejudice in decision-making. *European Journal of Social Psychology* 18:161–76.

Hursch, C. J., K. R. Hammond, and J. L. Hursch. 1964. Some methodological considerations in multiple-cue probability studies. *Psychological Review* 71:42–60.

Kahneman, D., P. Slovic, and A. Tversky, eds. 1982. *Judgment under uncertainty: Heuristics and biases.* Cambridge: Cambridge University Press.

Kahneman, D., and A. Tversky. 1979. Prospect theory: An analysis of decisions under risk. *Econometrica* 47:263–91.

———. 1982. On the study of statistical intuitions. In *Judgment under uncertainty: Heuristics and biases,* ed. D. Kahneman, P. Slovic, and A. Tversky, 493–508. Cambridge: Cambridge University Press.

Keren, G. B., and J. G. W. Raaijmakers. 1988. On between-subjects versus within-subjects comparisons in testing utility theory. *Organizational Behavior and Human Decision Processes* 41:233–47.

Klayman, J. 1988. Cue discovery in probabilistic environments. *Journal of Experimental Psychology: Learning, Memory and Cognition* 14:317–30.

Koffka, K. 1935. *Principles of Gestalt psychology.* New York: Harcourt, Brace.

Kroll, Y., H. Levy, and A. Rapoport. 1988. Experimental tests of the mean-variance model for portfolio selection. *Organizational Behavior and Human Decision Processes* 42:388–410.

Kuhn, T. 1970. *The structure of scientific revolutions.* 2d ed. Chicago: University of Chicago Press.

Leary, D. E. 1987. From act psychology to probabilistic functionalism: The place of Egon Brunswik in the history of psychology. In *Psychology in twentieth-century thought and society,* ed. M. G. Ash and W. R. Woodward, 115–42. Cambridge: Cambridge University Press.

McNeil, B. J., S. G. Pauker, H. C. Sox, and A. Tversky. 1982. On the elicitation of preferences for alternative therapies. *New England Journal of Medicine* 306: 1259–62.

Medley, R. 1988. A fed Dukakis could love. *Wall Street Journal,* 11 August, p. 22.

Meehl, P. 1978. Theoretic risks and tabular asterisks: Sir Karl, Sir Ronald, and the slow progress of soft psychology. *Journal of Consulting and Clinical Psychology* 46:806–34.

Miller, P. M. 1986. Effect of requesting a decision rationale on the framing effect. Typescript.

Mumpower, J. L. 1988. The cognitive characteristics of negotiators, the structure of negotiation tasks, and the potential for optimal settlement. University Center for Policy Research, State University of New York at Albany. Typescript.

Neale, M. A., and M. H. Bazerman. 1985. The effects of framing and negotiator overconfidence on bargaining behaviors and outcomes. *Academy of Management Journal* 28:34–49.

Payne, J. W., J. R. Bettman, and E. J. Johnson. 1988. Adaptive strategy selection in decision making. *Journal of Experimental Psychology: Learning, Memory, and Cognition* 14:534–52.

Peterson, C. R., and L. R. Beach. 1967. Man as an intuitive statistician. *Psychological Bulletin* 68:29–46.

Poses, R. M., R. D. Cebul, R. S. Wigton, and M. Collins. 1986. Feedback on simulated cases to improve clinical judgment [meeting abstract]. *Medical Decision Making* 6:274.

Slovic, P., B. Fischhoff, and S. Lichtenstein. 1977. Behavioral decision theory. *Annual Review of Psychology* 28:1–39.

Smith, L. D. 1986. *Behaviorism and logical positivism.* Stanford, Calif.: Stanford University Press.

Stewart, T. R. 1976. Components of correlation and extensions of the lens model equation. *Psychometrika* 41:101–20.

———. 1988. Judgment analysis: Procedures. In *Human judgment: The SJT view,* ed. B. Brehmer and C. R. B. Joyce, 41–74. Amsterdam: North-Holland.

Stewart, T. R., P. Middleton, M. Downton, and D. Ely. 1984. Judgments of photographs vs. field observations in studies of perception and judgment of the visual environment. *Journal of Environmental Psychology* 4:283–302.

Stewart, T. R., W. R. Moninger, J. Grassia, R. H. Brady, and F. H. Merrem. 1989. Analysis of expert judgment and skill in a hail forecasting experiment. *Weather and Forecasting* 4:24–34.

Taylor, S. E., and S. C. Thompson. 1982. Stalking the "vividness" effect. *Psychological Review* 89:155–81.

Todd, F. J., and K. R. Hammond. 1965. Differential feedback in two multiple-cue probability learning tasks. *Behavioral Science* 10:429–35.

Tucker, L. R. 1964. A suggested alternative formulation in the development by Hursch,

Hammond, and Hursch and Hammond, Hursch, and Todd. *Psychological Review* 71:528–30.
Tversky, A., and I. Gati. 1982. Similarity, separability, and the triangle inequality. *Psychological Review* 89:123–54.
Tversky, A., and D. Kahneman. 1974. Judgment under uncertainty: Heuristics and biases. *Science* 185:1124–31.
———. 1981. The framing of decisions and the psychology of choice. *Science* 211:453–58.
———. 1982a. Judgment under uncertainty: Heuristics and biases. In *Judgment under uncertainty: Heuristics and biases,* ed. D. Kahneman, P. Slovic, and A. Tversky, 3–31. Cambridge: Cambridge University Press.
———. 1982b. Judgments of and by representativeness. In *Judgment under uncertainty: Heuristics and biases,* ed. D. Kahneman, P. Slovic, and A. Tversky, 84–98. Cambridge: Cambridge University Press.
———. 1983. Extensional versus intuitive reasoning: The conjunction fallacy in probability judgment. *Psychological Review* 90, no. 4:293–315.
———. 1986. Rational choice and the framing of decisions. *Journal of Business* 59:S251–S278.
Tversky, A., S. Sattath, and P. Slovic. 1988. Contingent weighting in judgment and choice. *Psychological Review* 95:371–84.
von Schantz, T., G. Goransson, G. Andersson, I. Froberg, M. Grahn, A. Helgee, and H. Wittzell. 1989. Female choice selects for a viability-based male trait in pheasants. *Nature* 337:166–68.
von Winterfeldt, D., and W. Edwards. 1986. *Decision analysis and behavioral research.* Cambridge: Cambridge University Press.
Wigton, R. S., K. D. Patil, and V. L. Hoellerich. 1986. The effect of feedback in learning clinical diagnosis. *Journal of Medical Education* 61:816–22.

11

Strategies in Real-Time, Dynamic Decision Making

BERNDT BREHMER

This chapter is concerned with decision making in situations in which a number of decisions are required; the decisions are interdependent; the environment changes, both autonomously and as a consequence of the actions taken by the decision maker; and the decisions are made in real time. To perform well in such decision tasks, the decision maker needs a model of the decision task, but the model he or she needs depends on the strategy used. Specifically, a feedforward strategy, involving decisions based on predictions of the future state of the environment, requires a more elaborate model than a feedback strategy, which is based on current information about the environment. The results of a series of experiments on the effects of feedback delays are reviewed. They suggest that decision makers tend to follow a feedback strategy when the task is opaque (i.e., when the reasons for the delays cannot be seen) but that they may develop feedforward strategies when the task is transparent (i.e., when the reasons for the delays can be seen).

CONSIDER THE DECISION PROBLEMS facing a fire chief charged with the task of fighting forest fires. In his command center, he receives information about forest fires from a spotter plane. On the basis of this information, he sends out his fire-fighting units (FFUs), and they report back to him about their position and about their actions. Using this information and that from the spotter plane, the fire chief then sends his FFUs to new locations. This process continues until the fires have been extinguished.

The kind of problem described here differs from those traditionally studied by psychologists in the form of gambles and the like in at least four ways. First, it requires a series of decisions rather than a single decision. These decisions are of two kinds. The first involves a choice of direction or an operational goal. The second involves corrections of the current course of action if it does not seem to lead to the goal. Thus, the fire chief first has to decide which fire to fight and send out his FFUs. He then has to monitor the fire and

The experiments reviewed in this chapter were supported by a grant from the Swedish Countil for Research in the Humanities and Social Sciences.

the performance of the FFUs, redirecting them if the fire spreads in an unexpected direction. Moreover, as new fires start, the fire chief has to redeploy his forces.

Second, the decisions are interdependent; a decision made at a given point in time, t, constrains the possible decisions at time $t + 1$. For example, if the fire chief has already sent out all his FFUs to a given location, he will not have any resources left to fight new fires that start in a different location.

Third, the environment changes, both autonomously and as a consequence of the fire chief's decisions. Thus, fires start spontaneously, but how they actually spread depends on what the fire chief does as well as on factors that he cannot control, such as the strength and direction of the wind.

These three aspects—that a series of decisions is required, that these decisions are interdependent, and that the environment changes—were given as the defining characteristics of a dynamic decision task by Edwards (1962). However, the fire chief's task differs from the kind of dynamic tasks defined by Edwards in one important way: the fire chief has to make his decisions in real time. Thus, it is not sufficient for him to make the correct decisions and make them in the correct order; he also has to make them at the correct moment in time. This is the fourth difference between the fire chief's task and the traditional forms of decision tasks. It has important consequences for understanding the nature of dynamic tasks.

First, the fact that decisions are made in real time means that the decision maker cannot exercise full control over the rate at which he has to make these decisions or choose the moment in time when he will make his decision. As he becomes skilled at the task, he will, of course, gain some control over these aspects, but the world will never stop and wait for him to make his decisions. Real-time decision making is thus often inherently stressful.

Second, the temporal characteristics of the possible actions become important. The fire chief must know how long he has for various actions and how much time these actions require (for discussions of this in other dynamic tasks, see De Keyser [1988] on process control in a modern plant or von Clausewitz [1976] on the need for the commander to know about the time required for different kinds of military operations). Put differently, dynamic decision making in real time requires the decision maker to cope with processes rather than events. Indeed, the problem facing the decision maker in a dynamic environment may be defined as that of finding a way of using one process to control another (Brehmer and Allard 1988c).

There is a third way in which time is important in dynamic tasks. Each task must be defined in terms of a given time scale or set of time scales. Compare, for instance, the tasks facing the commander of an individual FFU and those of the fire chief in the command center. These tasks differ sharply with respect to time scale. The FFU commander works with the immediate fire situation and has to act quickly. There is little time for deliberation, and he can be concerned only with his own unit and with a limited part of the fire. That is, he has only a limited "window" and cannot see the fire as a whole. As a consequence, many FFUs are needed to extinguish a forest fire.

This creates a problem of coordinating the efforts of the individual FFUs, which is the task of the centrally located fire chief. But moving and coordinating many units requires that the fire chief consider his task in a different time scale than the FFU commander simply because it takes much longer to implement the decisions made by the fire chief than those made by the local unit commander. Moreover, it requires information at a different level of abstraction: the local commander needs to know how the fire develops within his immediate vicinity, but the fire chief has to know how the fire develops as a whole. Thus, the tasks of the decision maker of the local commander and the fire chief represent different levels of control, levels that work from different information and in different time scales in a hierarchically organized system. This is typical of complex real-time, dynamic tasks (for further discussion of the problem of time scales and hierarchical organization in complex, dynamic tasks, see Brehmer 1988).

RESEARCH ON REAL-TIME, DYNAMIC DECISION MAKING

Examples of real-time, dynamic tasks are not hard to find; they abound in modern process plants, in the management of patients in medical care, in military circumstances, and in the management of companies. Nonetheless, they have received little attention from psychologists, except in the form of a few scattered studies of process-control tasks (for a review, see, e.g., Umbers 1979). These studies, however, tend to focus on the specific aspects of the process operator's task, and their relevance for understanding real-time, dynamic decision making in general is not always clear (Brehmer [in preparation] discusses these studies in a wider context).

There are at least two possible reasons for this relative neglect of the problem of real-time dynamic decision making. The first is, perhaps, operational: the study of real-time, dynamic decision making requires new forms of research technology. One cannot study dynamic tasks using the ordinary paper-and-pencil approach of psychological research. Instead, interactive computer simulations of dynamic tasks are required. The technology for this has only recently become available in psychological laboratories. The second reason is conceptual: real-time, dynamic decision making cannot be captured by the kinds of normative models used in behavioral decision research (Slovic, Fischhoff, and Lichtenstein 1977).

Seeking an alternative framework, we follow Broadbent, Fitzgerald, and Broadbent (1986), who note that dynamic decision tasks are similar to the adaptive-control tasks studied by engineers. This suggests that the standard engineering tool of control theory (for a good introduction, see Rouse 1980) might provide a useful framework for the study of real-time, dynamic decision making. Whereas the actual mathematics of control theory is, perhaps, not particularly helpful, or even needed, at this stage (for a discussion of control models as descriptions of human behavior, see Bainbridge 1981), it provides a way of clarifying some of the conceptual issues (cf. Hogarth 1981). We therefore use some of its notions.

DECISION MAKING AS CONTROL

The first consequence of this framework is a new view of decision making. This is now seen as the process of achieving control over a system in order to produce a desired outcome rather than as the resolution of a choice dilemma. According to this conception, problems for research center on how, and under what circumstances, control can be achieved.

An important principle in control theory in this context is the model principle, which has been discussed in many different places. It is well stated in the title of the classic paper by Conant and Ashby (1970): "Every Good Regulator of a System Must Be a Model of That System." In other words, to control a system, a control device, such as a decision maker, must have (or be) a model of the system it seeks to control.

The model principle offers a possible definition of the fundamental problem for research on real-time, dynamic decision making: to study the mental models that people develop as they try to control a dynamic system (Brehmer and Allard 1988c). However, this is deceptive and could lead to a limited view of dynamic decision making, just as the corresponding search for models has led to a limited view of decision making in static tasks (cf. Hogarth 1981). Thus, we must remember that the model is an aspect of the decision maker's control strategy. We need to consider the nature of this overall strategy before we consider how we evaluate the decision maker's models.

FORMS OF CONTROL

There are two basic forms of control strategies: feedforward and feedback. For our purposes, the important difference is that feedforward control involves choosing actions on the basis of predictions of the state of the system, whereas feedback control involves choosing actions on the basis of current information about the system. As a consequence, the two strategies differ both with respect to the kind of model needed and the conditions under which they lead to optimal control.

The important factors here are the extent to which the environment remains stable and the feedback delays in the system to be controlled. Thus, a pure feedforward strategy requires that the system does not change and a pure feedback strategy that the delays are insignificant in relation to the time required to affect the system.

FEEDBACK DELAYS

Feedback delay is a complex factor (for a discussion, see Brehmer and Allard 1988a). For example, in the fire-fighting task described above, delays may occur anywhere in the feedback loop: in the transmission of commands to the FFUs, in their response to these commands, in the execution of commands, in reporting results, and in the transmission of these reports.

Since everything takes time, delay is inevitable. Thus, delays due to the time taken to move a FFU from one location to another or to extinguish fire in a given location are inherent in the physical processes that constitute this task. To cope with these delays, the decision maker should ideally initiate his actions before his feedback information indicates that they are necessary. This requires that the decision maker has some model incorporating the time characteristics of these processes and is able to use it in the form of an open loop or a feedforward strategy.

Delays due to lags in the transmission of reports or commands can also be handled by a feedforward strategy. This requires a more complex model that also incorporates some representation of the delays in transmission. However, there is often a simple alternative to such a complex model. This is to decentralize control to the local unit commanders. When there are delays in the transmission of information, the FFU commanders will always have more recent information about the fire and about their own activities than the centrally located fire chief will. However, it is not possible to do away with the fire chief altogether. The need for coordination of different units remains despite the feedback delays.

A feedback strategy also requires a model. But this model can be much simpler. It needs to represent only the way in which the control actions affect the system. In many cases, this model need not even be precise: it is often sufficient to model the direction of the effect of these control actions. The precise adjustment can be taken care of by relying on further feedback.

Provided that there is no error in the feedback information, a feedback strategy will be sufficient for optimal control if there are no feedback delays or when these delays are insignificant in relation to the time taken for the control inputs to affect the system. Feedback control, therefore, is not a general strategy in dynamic decision making; there are systems that cannot be controlled in this way.

In the fire-fighting task, important delays may occur in at least three locations in the feedback loop, making it impossible to achieve optimal control with a simple feedback strategy. First, it may take time for the commands to reach the FFUs and for these units to respond to the commands. Second, it will take time for the FFUs to reach the fire, and, while these units are en route, the fire will spread further. Therefore, the FFUs should not be sent to the location of the fire when the command is issued, but to the location where the fire will be when the units are in place. This requires a feedforward strategy based on predictive models of the behavior of both the fire and the FFUs. Third, the information about the location of the fire and about the location and activities of the FFUs may be delayed. This requires either a model that makes it possible to predict the actual locations of the fire and the FFUs or some decentralization of control. If the fire chief fails to model these aspects, his control will be less than optimal. This does not necessarily mean that he will fail to extinguish the fire, but it does mean that he will lose more trees than necessary.

WHY DECISION MAKERS ARE LIKELY TO ADOPT FEEDBACK CONTROL RATHER THAN FEEDFORWARD CONTROL

Even though feedback control may not be a completely general strategy, real-time, dynamic decision making has features that makes it likely that this will be the preferred mode of control. First, it minimizes cognitive effort because, as noted above, it requires a much simpler model of the task than feedforward control does. Second, if the feedback strategy accomplishes the task at some reasonable level of success, the decision maker may not even notice the need for an alternative strategy. Lack of optimality is not a primary perceptual datum; it is an inference based on a normative model of the task, and, if the decision maker does not have a well-developed model of the task, the possibility of doing better will not be detected. However, since the lack of a well-developed task model is the reason for the feedback-control strategy in the first place, feedback control is likely to be self-perpetuating.

Consequently, we should not be surprised if decision makers opt for feedback control, especially when this strategy enables them to achieve some of their goals. For example, we would expect a fire chief to choose a feedback-control strategy for fighting forest fires if this strategy leads to the eventual extinction of the fire, first, because it accomplishes his main objective and, second, because he may never appreciate the fact that he might have extinguished the fire much faster had he used a different strategy. Thus, if a decision maker chooses a feedback-control strategy, this is not necessarily the result of flawed information processing. It may just as well be seen as a reasonable way of using one's cognitive resources, given what is known about the decision problem.

CONSEQUENCES FOR RESEARCH

An important conclusion from the preceding discussion is that we cannot always expect the decision maker to have a well-developed model of the task. If decision makers follow a feedback-control strategy, the need for such models will not be obvious to them. Although they will need some model of how different actions affect the system, this is not the same as having a general model of the task. Therefore, if our subjects are unable to answer questions about the nature of the task system, this cannot be interpreted as evidence that they are unaware of their model; it may simply mean that we have probed for the wrong model, that is, that we have asked for information pertaining to feedforward control when the subjects are following a feedback strategy. Nor is there any reason to expect that there will be any close relation between insight into the general nature of the task system and level of control if a feedback strategy is sufficient for control. This may explain why Broadbent and his associates have failed to find evidence of mental models of the task, despite high levels of control, in control tasks (Berry and Broadbent 1984; Broadbent, Fitzgerald, and Broadbent 1986; for a discussion, see Brehmer and Allard 1988b).

Before we start probing for possible mental models in dynamic decision making, therefore, we must determine what strategy the decision makers are using. If we were to define the object of research as that of finding subjects' mental models of the task, we would always be evaluating them in terms of a feedforward strategy that they may not be using. As noted by Hogarth (1981), this is exactly what research on decision making has done when it has focused on the accuracy of subjects' predictive models.

Consequently, the first priority in our research has been to establish what kind of strategy the subjects are following. The task of probing for possible mental models has been left for later studies. Specifically, we have been concerned with the effects of feedback delays in a real-time, dynamic task. That is, we have created a situation that requires the use of a feedforward strategy and assessed whether the subjects adopt such a strategy. The remainder of this chapter will review some of our results and discuss some of the implications.

EXPERIMENTS ON THE EFFECTS OF FEEDBACK DELAY IN REAL-TIME, DYNAMIC DECISION MAKING

Before discussing the specific problems studied in the experiments, it is necessary to review our experimental paradigm in some detail.

DESSY: *An Experimental Paradigm*

We are certainly not the first to investigate dynamic decision making experimentally (for a review of different approaches, see Brehmer 1987). However, these earlier attempts have generally not aimed to study dynamic decision making in real time. The only exceptions are the studies of process control referred to above. The experimental tasks used in those studies have usually been physical realizations of some process (see, e.g., Crossman and Cooke 1974; and Brigham and Laios 1975). Such realizations do not allow the experimenter to vary characteristics of the task at will, and they are thus not suited for a general program of research on the effects of task characteristics on dynamic decision making.

Most later experiments on dynamic decision making have used computer simulations of dynamic tasks, but, in these tasks, time has been cut up in discrete units, and the problems have been presented in terms of a series of trials (for examples, see Berry and Broadbent 1984; Dörner et al. 1983; Kleinmuntz 1985; Kluwe and Reimann 1983; Mackinnon and Wearing 1980; Rapoport 1975; Sterman 1989a, 1989b). Not only does this remove the time pressure from the task, but it also means that the task will not have any real process characteristics. The extent to which results from tasks of this kind will generalize to real-time tasks is not known at present. There seem to be some commonalities in results, but these may be related to the complexity rather than the dynamics of these tasks (for a review, see Brehmer 1987). This problem is an important task for future research on dynamic decision making.

Since there was no suitable experimental paradigm for the study of real-time, dynamic decision making, our first task was to develop one. The result of these efforts was the Dynamic Environmental Simulation System, or DESSY for short (Brehmer and Allard 1988c). DESSY is a computer program that allows the subjects to interact with a dynamic environment in real time. It makes it possible to vary seven important characteristics of a dynamic environment: complexity, feedback quality, feedback delay, the extent to which decentralization of control is possible, the rate of change in the process to be controlled, the causal structure of the task, and the relation between the characteristics of the process to be controlled and the characteristics of the process used for control (for a discussion of these characteristics, see Brehmer and Allard 1988c). These characteristics were selected in part on the basis on systems considerations (i.e., with an eye to what is important for control) and in part on the basis of psychological considerations (i.e., with an eye to what may determine the ability of people to control a dynamic task). Thus, the DESSY paradigm may be said to embody both our theory of the nature of dynamic tasks and a preliminary theory of human performance in such tasks.

The Experimental Task

The DESSY experiments reviewed here have utilized a representation of the fire chief's task as outlined in the introduction. This experimental task requires the subject to extinguish forest fires about which he or she receives information on a visual display unit. The subject does this by dispatching FFUs to the location of the fires. This is done by typing commands on the keyboard. In these experiments, DESSY was implemented on a PDP 11/40 system, with two 1.2 Mb discs and a GT 40 display.

Figure 11.1 shows the experimental task as it appears to the subject on the screen. To the right is a map of the forest. It is represented in the form of a grid composed of 256 (16 × 16) squares, coded in terms of letters and numbers. The middle four squares are outlined with heavy lines and represent the location of the base where the subject (the fire chief) is supposed to be lo-

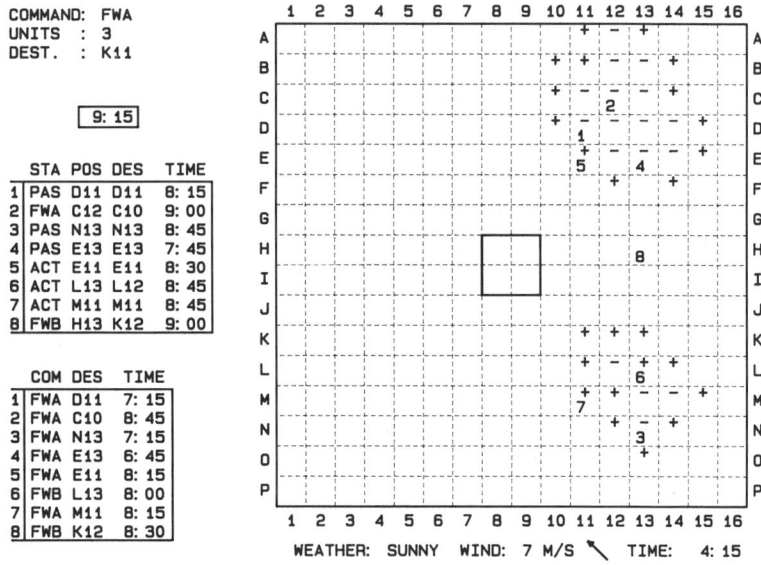

Figure 11.1. The experimental situation as represented on the screen.

cated. Fire, as reported by the spotter plane, is represented on the map in terms of a "+," and fire that has been extinguished is represented by a "−." The reported location of a FFU is represented by its number. This number appears in the square that the FFU reports as its location (possibly after some delay). In these experiments, the subject had eight FFUs at his or her disposal.

Immediately below the display, the current weather report is given. It indicates the general weather conditions, the direction of the prevailing wind, and the time when the report was issued.

To the left on the screen there are four displays. The top display shows the command being typed in. The subject sends out an FFU by typing in its number, the location to which it is supposed to go, and either FWA or FWB. The latter code indicates the extent to which control is decentralized. FWA means that control is centralized: the FFU must go to the location ordered and cannot start fire fighting until it has reached its destination. FWB, on the other hand, indicates a measure of decentralization; the FFU can start fighting any fire it encounters en route to its final destination.

The second display shows the current time. The third display is a list of the reports from the FFUs. Thus, in the figure, unit 1 reports that it is at its final destination D11 and that the report was given at 8:15. The FFU also reports about its activity. ACT means that it is active in fighting fire (this occurs if it is in a location where there is fire and if it has received a FWB command or if it has reached its final destination and found fire there after receiving a FWA command), and PAS that it is passive, that is, that it is not fighting fire (this may mean either that there was no fire in its location or that the fire has been extinguished by the FFU).

The third display is simply a list of the commands that have been given and when these commands were given. Information on the visual display is updated every 20 seconds. A time period of 20 seconds is called 1 "systems time unit."

The subjects had two goals: to extinguish fires as soon as possible and to prevent fires from reaching the base, with the obvious priority ordering. A trial could thus end in two different ways: the base burned down, making further control of the FFUs impossible, or the fires were extinguished before reaching the base.

On every trial, the subjects had to fight two fires. The starting locations of these fires were randomly determined. After 5 time units, the first fire started; then, after 10 additional time units had passed, the second fire started in a different location. As the second fire started, the direction of the wind changed so that the second fire became the most dangerous in that it would reach the base first if nothing were done about it.

The subjects in the experiments were undergraduate students without any previous experience in fighting forest fires. Thus, these experiments study how naive subjects learn to control a dynamic task rather than the performance of actual fire fighters, and we make no claims that the specifics of these results generalize precisely to actual fire fighting. The subjects came to the experiment on three or four different days. On each day, they would go through two trials. This might require anything from 45 minutes to 2 hours.

Feedback Delays in the Experiments

In the experiments to be reviewed here, there were two sources of delay. The first of these was in the time required to carry out commands, that is, for the FFUs to move and put out fire. This was not experimentally manipulated. The second source was in the reporting of results, and this was experimentally manipulated.

In the delay conditions, the FFUs reported their location and activities with some delay. Specifically, half the units reported with a delay of 1 time unit, and the other half reported with a delay of 2 time units (i.e., the average delay was 1.5 time units). Since all reports and commands are timed, it is possible for the subjects to detect this from the information available on the screen. In the no-delay conditions, the units reported immediately.

The spotter plane reported the location of fires without delay in both conditions. Thus, there was an extra source of information about the fact that there was a discrepancy between the information on the screen about the location of fires and the reports from the FFUs about their activity. Note that, although one of the aspects requiring a predictive model (i.e., the delays in reporting) has been removed in the no-delay conditions, the other (i.e., the time required for moving the FFUs and for putting out the fire) remains.

Experimental Results

In this section, we review the results from three studies (Brehmer and Allard 1988a, 1988b, 1988c) concerned with the effects of feedback delays. Each of these studies employed the DESSY paradigm as described above and manipulated feedback delay in the manner described in the preceding section.

Data Analysis. Although the DESSY program stores everything that happens on a given trial, it makes little sense to analyze individual decisions. These individual decisions are interesting only as part of a more general strategy, and it is on this strategy that we focus our analyses. Specifically, we analyze the results on three different levels (Brehmer and Allard 1988c).

First, we analyze the extent to which the subjects are able to meet the two goals: to prevent fires from reaching the base and to extinguish them as quickly as possible. The first aspect is given by the number of trials that end in the based being burned down, the second by the number of squares that are destroyed by fire.

The second level of analysis concerns the subjects' general strategy. In these experiments, we were concerned only with results pertinent to the question of whether subjects respond appropriately to the feedback delays. As noted above, one possibility is to use decentralized control. Consequently, we registered the extent to which the subjects choose FWB commands rather than FWA commands. If subjects show a higher proportion of FWB commands in the delay condition, this would suggest that they are trying to combat the effects of these delays by means of decentralization.

The third level of analysis is concerned with the subjects' tactics. We analyzed two aspects. First is the extent to which the subjects mobilize their resources. This is measured by the proportion of FFUs ordered to go to a given fire 5 time units after this fire has started. Second is the time interval a FFU is left inactive after it has extinguished the fire it had been ordered to extinguish, that is, the number of time units before either an FWA or an FWB command was issued to a unit after it had carried out an earlier command.

The first of these measures shows the extent to which the subjects respond appropriately to the nature of the fire-fighting task. Specifically, it shows the extent to which the subjects learn to respond to the fact that the fire will spread while the FFUs travel to the fire and that the fire will be considerably larger when the FFUs are in place. Because of this, it is necessary to respond massively and rapidly to the fire, that is, to send out as many FFUs as possible as quickly as possible to gain control over the fire. The proportion of FFUs directed to a fire during some suitably short time interval after that fire has started indicates whether the subjects actually respond to this characteristic of the fire-fighting task.

The second measure gives a direct indication of how the subjects respond to the delays. If the subjects manage to develop some model that incorporates the delays, there will, presumably, be no difference in the time a unit is left inactive between a condition in which there are delays and a condition in which there are no delays. If, on the other hand, the subjects completely fail to compensate for the delays, the time a unit is left inactive will be proportional to the delay.

General Results

The results with respect to the effects of feedback delay were similar in all three studies (Brehmer and Allard 1988a, 1988b, 1988c). Thus, the studies agree in showing that, with experience, subjects improve their performance with respect to both criteria.

First, the results show that the number of trials that end in the base being burned down decreases. This indicates that, with practice, most subjects accomplish the primary task of putting out the fire on every trial. This is true in both the delay and the no-delay conditions.

Second, we find that the area lost before fires are extinguished decreases over trials. However, the improvement is much more pronounced when there are no delays. Indeed, we have found no significant improvement with respect to area lost to fire under conditions of feedback delay in any of our experiments so far. The results in figure 11.2, taken from Brehmer and Allard (1988a), are representative.

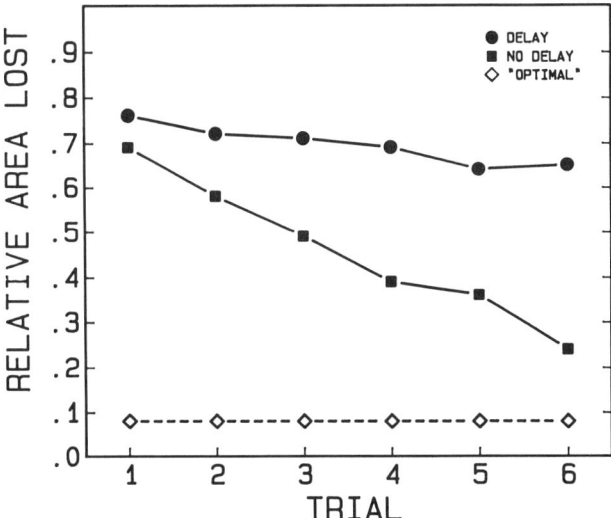

Figure 11.2. Effect of feedback delay on subjects' ability to meet the second criterion, that of putting out the fire quickly, as shown by the relative area of forest lost to fire at the end of a trial (data from Brehmer and Allard 1988a). Since there is no optimal model for this task, the optimal level of performance represents the level of performance of some extremely experienced research assistants.

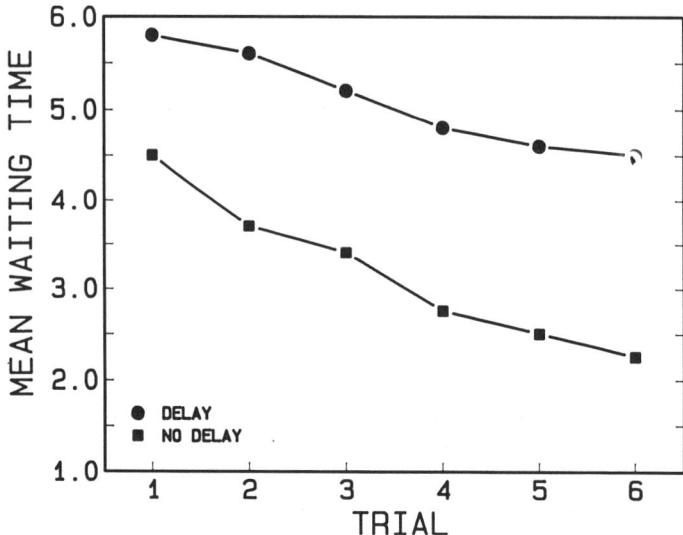

Figure 11.3. The mean number of systems time units an FFU is left inactive after it has carried out its commands as a function of delay and trials. Note that the difference in times between the two conditions is close to the actual delay of 1.5 systems time units, suggesting that the subjects ignore the delays (data from Brehmer and Allard 1988a).

The improvement across time can be explained by a change in tactics. Thus, our results show that subjects quickly learn to respond massively and rapidly, as required by the nature of the fire-fighting task (Brehmer and Allard 1988a, 1988b, 1988c). This means that the subjects adopt a form of open-loop control with respect to at least one aspect of the fire-fighting task. However, the subjects are more successful in doing this in the no-delay than in the delay condition. As a consequence, more trials end in the loss of the base when there are delays than when there are no delays.

Figure 11.3 shows the results (from Brehmer and Allard 1988a) with respect to the time a unit is left inactive. As can be seen from this figure, units are left inactive for a longer time in the delay conditions, and the difference is proportional to the delay (see also fig. 11.5 below).

All our results so far show that subjects generally prefer centralized to decentralized control. This is true both when there are delays in reporting and when there are no delays in reporting. The proportion of FWB commands starts at a low level and generally decreases over trials in all experiments. That is, the subjects do not try to improve their performance in the delay conditions by decentralization of control.

These results suggest that subjects ignore the delays in feedback that are due to late reporting. They do not decentralize control, nor do they develop predictive models incorporating these delays. Instead, they react to the information on their maps as if it related to the current state of affairs rather than to the state of affairs some 1.5 time units ago. One question, then, is whether subjects actually detected that there were delays. Brehmer and Allard (1988a) investigated this problem in a postexperimental interview by asking their subjects in both the delay and the no-delay conditions whether they had detected any delays. One hundred percent (eight out of eight) of the subjects in the delay condition said that they had detected delays, whereas only 25 percent (two out of eight) of the subjects in the no-delay condition said that there were delays. The problem, it seems, is not that subjects fail to detect the delays but that they do not know what to do about them.

These results suggest that subjects use a mixture of feedforward and feedback control. In their rapid and massive deployment of FFUs, they give evidence of open-loop, or feedforward, control, whereas, in their choice of FFUs when giving commands later on in the fire-fighting process, they seem to follow a feedback control or closed-loop strategy.

To investigate these problems further, Brehmer and Allard (1988b) ran a transfer experiment in which delay conditions were changed for two experimental groups. Thus, one experimental group first worked under conditions of no delay in reporting and was then transferred to a condition with delays; a second group first worked under conditions of delay in reporting and was then transferred to a no-delay condition. Subjects in the control groups were run under conditions of delay or no delay throughout the experiment. Figures 11.4 and 11.5 show the results.

Both figures tell the same story. They show that, when delay was introduced for the subjects who learned under conditions of no delay, their performance became virtually identical to that of the subjects who performed under conditions of delay throughout the experiment. This is consistent with the hypothesis that subjects react to the information on the map as if it were information about the current state (which indeed it had been for these subjects during the first stage of the experiment).

The picture for the subjects who learned under conditions of delay appears more complicated. Although their performance changes in the appropriate direction, it does not change to the level of the subjects who performed under conditions of no delay throughout the experiment.

It seems unlikely that this indicates that the subjects do not follow a feedback strategy. The performance of the subjects in the delay condition before the shift is similar to that of the subjects in the earlier Brehmer and Allard (1988a, 1988c) studies, both with respect to the general level of performance (cf. fig. 11.2) and in that FFUs are left inactive for an interval proportional to the delay (cf. fig. 11.3). A more likely explanation, therefore, is that the deviations from expected performance after the shift are due to the shift as such. Perhaps the sudden improvement in performance led to complacency. Whatever the explanation, the deviation from the expected performance is small and does not warrant any change in our general conclusions.

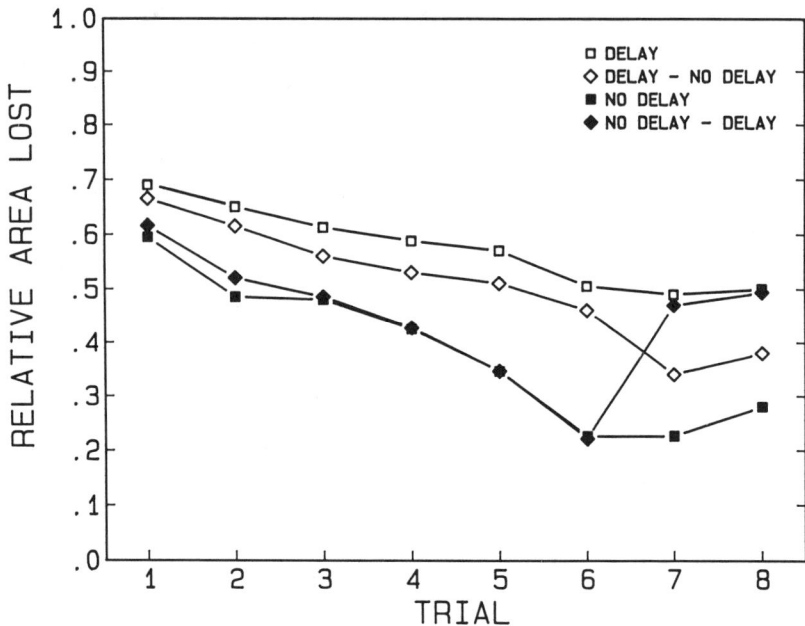

Figure 11.4. Mean area lost to fire as a function of feedback delays before and after a shift in delays. The shift occurs at trial 7 (data from Brehmer and Allard 1988b).

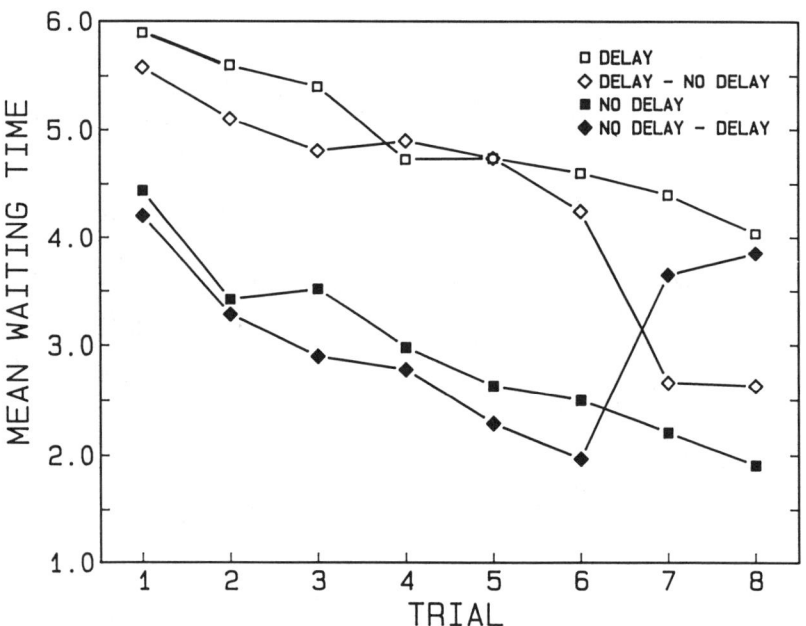

Figure 11.5. Mean number of systems time units an FFU is left inactive as a function of feedback delay before and after a shift in delays. The shifts occurs at trial 7 (data from Brehmer and Allard 1988b).

DISCUSSION

The control-theory framework employed here directs our attention to questions pertaining to the decision maker's model of the task and his or her overall strategy. Strategy in this context is not in the traditional form of maximizing expected utility or minimizing regret but a question of the extent to which the decision maker relies on feedback from the environment, following a general incrementalist framework, or on feedforward, using a model of the world in a more rationalist approach. It leads us to investigate the conditions under which one or the other may be successful. This makes it a psychological parallel to philosophical work on decision making in the critical tradition (Collingridge 1982). As for models of the decision problem, the new framework opens up new possibilities and frees us from the extremely limited conception of traditional decision theory, which asks to see all decision tasks as lists of acts and consequences linked by probabilities.

This framework makes the study of decision making part of the study of action. Decision making, as seen in this framework, becomes a matter of providing direction for the continuous flow of behavior and monitoring one's progress toward some goal rather than discrete episodes involving choice dilemmas (cf. Hogarth 1981). The results from recent studies of executive decision making in organizations (see, e.g., Peters 1979) are consistent with this general view.

As noted in the introduction, there are two possible strategies for achieving control. The results presented here suggest that subjects are capable of both, albeit for different aspects of the task. Thus, they developed a form of open-loop or feedforward control with respect to the delays caused by inherent characteristics of the task, that is, those having to do with the fact that moving FFUs and putting out fires requires time, but not the delays caused by slow reporting. As seen from the results, this led to suboptimal control, with considerable losses of computer-generated forest.

These results agree with earlier findings from process control that subjects are able to learn to adopt a feedforward mode with respect to inherent process characteristics (see Umbers 1979). These studies have not, however, incorporated forms of delay that are comparable to delays due to slow reporting in the present experiments. One important difference between a delay due to inherent characteristics of the physical processes involved, such as time required for extinguishing fires, and a delay due to slow reporting is that the former can be seen as it happens, so to speak, whereas the latter is evident only from the time tags given to reports. Thus, it is possible to see how FFUs move and fires spread, but it is not possible to see the process causing slow reporting; it can only be inferred. Perhaps this makes it easier to form mental models of inherent process characteristics. This observation is supported by results from a study by Brigham and Laios (1975). They found that subjects were unable to learn to control a physical process when given access to measurements from which to infer the nature of the process but not allowed to inspect it. However, they learned to control the process rapidly when allowed actually to see the process while trying to control it. That ability to compensate for delays is not related to whether the delays are due to inherent characteristics as such is also demonstrated by results by Sterman (1989a, 1989b). In these experiments, which studied subjects' behavior in dynamic business games, the actual process producing delays was inherent in the system in the same way as the time required for extinguishing a fire is due to characteristics that are inherent in the system. However, it could not be seen but had to be inferred, just as the delays due to slow reporting had to be inferred in the fire-fighting experiments or the delays caused by the physical process had to be inferred in the Brigham and Laios experiments. Thus, the results suggest that subjects fail to compensate for delays that have to be inferred.

These results, then, suggest that people are capable of both kinds of control strategies but that feedforward control may be possible only under conditions in which the process producing the delays can actually be seen and does not have to be inferred. Such direct information about the nature of a process is, of course, not likely to be a common feature of many complex dynamic tasks, except when the task involves simple and fast physical processes. Consequently, we would expect that feedback control is likely to be a common mode of control in dynamic decision tasks, as the findings by Sterman (1989a, 1989b) suggest for economic decision making. This hypothesis is an important point of departure for our current research program on dynamic decision making.

REFERENCES

Bainbridge, L. 1981. Mathematical equations or processing routines. In *Human detection and diagnosis of system failures,* ed. J. Rasmussen and W. B. Rouse. New York: Plenum.

Berry, D. C., and D. E. Broadbent. 1984. On the relationship between task performance and associated verbalizable knowledge. *Quarterly Journal of Experimental Psychology* 36A: 209–31.

Brehmer, B. 1987. Systems design and the psychology of complex systems. In *Empirical foundations of information and systems science,* ed. J. Rasmussen and P. Zunde. New York: Plenum.

———. 1988. Organization for decision making in complex systems. In *Tasks, mental models and errors,* ed. H. Andersen et al. London: Taylor & Francis.

———. In preparation. The cognitive aspects of process control. Uppsala University, Center for Research on Human-Computer Interaction. Typescript.

Brehmer, B., and R. Allard. 1988a. Feedback delay in real-time dynamic decision making. Uppsala Psychological Reports, no. 407. Uppsala University.

———. 1988b. Learning by doing in real-time dynamic decision making. Uppsala Psychological Reports, no. 408. Uppsala University.

———. 1988c. Real-time dynamic decision making: The effects of complexity and feedback delay. Uppsala Psychological Reports, no. 406. Uppsala University.

Brigham, F. R., and C. Laios. 1975. Operator performance in the control of a laboratory process plant. *Ergonomics* 18: 53–66.

Broadbent, D. E., P. Fitzgerald, and M. P. Broadbent. 1986. Implicit and explicit knowledge in the control of complex systems. *British Journal of Psychology* 77:33–50.
Collingridge, D. 1982. *Critical decision making*. London: Pinter.
Conant, R. C., and W. R. Ashby. 1970. Every good regulator of a system must be a model of that system. *International Journal of System Science* 1:89–97.
Crossman, E. R. F. W., and J. E. Cooke. 1974. Manual control of slow-response systems. In *The human operator in process control*, ed. E. Edwards and F. P. Lees. London: Taylor & Francis.
De Keyser, V. 1988. Temporal decision making in complex environments. Paper presented at the International Workshop on New Technology, Distributed Decision Making and Responsibility, Bad Homburg, 5–7 May.
Dörner, D., H. Kreuzig, R. Reither, and T. H. Stäudel. 1983. *Lohhausen: Von Umgang mit Unbestimmtheit und Komplexität*. Berlin: Huber.
Edwards, W. 1962. Dynamic decision theory and probabilistic information processing. *Human Factors* 4:59–73.
Hogarth, R. M. 1981. Beyond discrete biases: Functional and dysfunctional aspects of judgmental heuristics. *Psychological Bulletin* 90:197–217.
Kleinmuntz, D. N. 1985. Cognitive heuristics and feedback in a dynamic decision environment. *Management Science* 31:680–702.
Kluwe, R. H., H. Reimann. 1983. *Problemlösen bei Vernetzen, komplexen Problemen: Effekte der Verbalisierens auf der Problemlöseleistung*. Technical Report no. 1. Hamburg: University of Defense, Department of Education, Psychology Unit.
Mackinnon, A. J., A. J. Wearing. 1980. Complexity and decision making. *Behavioral Science* 25:285–96.
Peters, T. 1979. Leadership: Sad facts and silver linings. *Harvard Business Review*, November/December, 164–72.
Rapoport, D. 1975. Research paradigms for the study of dynamic decision making. In *Utility, probability and human decision making*, D. Wendt and C. Vlek. Dordrecht: Reidel.
Rouse, W. B. 1980. *Systems engineering models of human-machine interaction*. Amsterdam: North-Holland.
Slovic, P., B. Fischhoff, and S. Lichtenstein. 1977. Behavioral decision theory. *Annual Review of Psychology* 28:1–39.
Sterman, D. 1989a. Misperceptions of feedback in dynamic decision making. *Organizational Behavior and Human Decision Processes* 43:301–35.
———. 1989b. Modeling managerial behavior: Misperceptions of feedback in a dynamic decision making experiment. *Management Science* 35:321–39.
Umbers, I. G. 1979. Models of the process operator. *International Journal of Man-Machine Studies* 11:262–64.
von Clausewitz, C. M. 1976. *On war*. Translated and edited by M. Howard and P. Paret. Princeton, N.J.: Princeton University Press.

Discussion

MICHAEL E. DOHERTY

Before I comment on the chapters by Ken Hammond and Berndt Brehmer, let me just say that I feel honored to have been asked to participate in this conference in Hillel's memory. He was a good man. And that is a profound thing to say of someone. It is also a privilege to be on this program with so many people whose work I have presented in graduate seminars.

There is much dissatisfaction in psychology today. There are major professional rifts. There is malaise not only about the "slow progress of soft psychology," but also about the "lack of cumulativeness" in the discipline, to cite only Meehl (1978) and Hammond (1966; Hammond, Hamm, and Grassia 1986). Maybe such dour judgments are based on too short a time span? Rather than take a serious historical approach and ask whether our insights into human decision making are better in 1988 than in 1888, I will take a more personal, anecdotal approach and ask you to try to recapture for a moment the sense of awe that marks the child's approach to the world.

I suspect that many of you had, as children, the lurking fear that other people could read your mind. I can recall that fear so vividly. Oh those adults! Especially those nuns in grade school. When they were watching you, or even when they were not, you had to make sure that you kept your mind on what you were supposed to. At Sunday mass, when the whole class sat together, you had to make especially sure that you did not have any impure thoughts. I did not even know what impure thoughts were.

I mostly lost that fear, although I occasionally wonder if my wife can tell what I am thinking. But in the everyday world of spelling, arithmetic, and stickball, that sense of wonder about whether others could tell what I was thinking gradually left me. Then, in college in the 1950s, I found out from reading Watson, Hull, and Skinner that none of that "mind stuff" mattered anyway.

Try to recapture for a moment that childish awe. In the everyday world of writing lectures that will not be listened to, papers that will be rejected, and grant proposals that will not be funded, I fear that we too often fail to step back, to take a longer look, and to wonder at the claims that judgment and decision theorists make:

> We claim to be able to tell what people are thinking.
> When a decision theorist elicits a problem scaffolding from clients,

that decision theorist claims to know how those clients are thinking about the world and about themselves.

When we measure utilities, we claim to be able to tell what people think is important.

When we measure probabilities, we claim to be able to tell what people think will happen.

Our descriptive models claim to be a representation of how people understand the world.

Our prescriptive models claim to be a representation of how people ought to behave, given their understanding of the world and given their utilities.

These are no small claims. In many ways, we now claim to be able to do what I feared old Sister Vincent could do as she sat sternly at the end of the pew. It just takes us more work.

Now to a discussion of the chapters by Hammond and Brehmer, who would lead their own Brunswikian cultural revolution.

COHERENCE VERSUS MODULARITY

It may strike you as strange to hear someone question Hammond's call for theoretical coherence, especially given that I believe that coherence is one of Ken's fundamental presuppositions (Holton 1973). It will sound strange, indeed, for we all long for unity and simplicity in our science and in our lives. But that questioning of the call for integration and coherence is one of the main points of my commentary.

In the prologue to his *Society of Mind*, Marvin Minsky writes,

> These ideas have lots of cross-connections. . . . I wish I could have lined them up so that you could climb straight to the top, by mental stair-steps, one by one. Instead they're tied in tangled webs.
>
> Perhaps the fault is actually mine, for failing to find a tidy base of neatly ordered principles. But I'm inclined to lay the blame upon the nature of mind: much of its power seems to stem from the messy ways its agents cross-connect. If so, that complication can't be helped; *it's only what we expect from evolution's countless tricks*. [1986, 17; emphasis added]

This quotation reflects Minsky's version of modularity, a version that differs in detail from Fodor's (1983), especially with respect to whether so-called central systems are what Fodor refers to as epistemically bounded. I find an extension of Minsky's version congenial to my understanding of the cognitive processes that are involved in judgment and decision-making, problem solving, hypothesis testing, and so on. Brunswik's interpretation of reality was, as is Hammond's and Brehmer's, a Darwinian-functionalist one. Ken speaks of the organism's natural habitat and describes it as being marked by multiple fallible indicators. Minsky also uses an evolutionary metaphor and summons up images of millions of years of evolution, during which many special brain systems have evolved in response to evolutionary pressures. Some of those systems are special purpose, evolved and modularized perhaps when our forebears were still arboreal creatures. But such systems endure in our brains yet today, influencing our cognitive processes much as primitive emotions influence the affective dimensions of our lives. Perhaps some are more like Fodor's general purpose central systems. But Minsky envisions a panoply of modules, at different levels of generality, that need not bear any special relation or resemblance to one another.

The picture that I have of the person is of an organism facing an incredible variety of tasks, some static, some dynamic, many laced with uncertainty, an organism coming to terms with a wide variety of environments and doing so by using a wide variety of strategies. Some of these tasks are natural ones, such as coming to know the sizes of things on a campus, and are characterized by multiple fallible indicators. Others are tasks in environments created by people, such as the task of learning arithmetic, inferential statistics, or multiple regression.

I can read Ken's mind. He is saying, "Of course, that's what cognitive continuum theory is all about." Now, I believe that cognitive continuum theory is a truly marvelous accomplishment, deserving far more attention than it has received. It is a highly useful theoretical framework for the investigation of many problems. But I also think that it is, in a deep sense, incomplete. It does not take into account the fact—or at least what I consider a fact—that there are many *kinds* of cognitive tasks and many *kinds* of cognitive strategies. The analytical-intuitive dimension describes but *one* dimension, an important one, on which such tasks and strategies vary. Whether encompassing many dimensions in one is a good strategem from a theoretical standpoint is, of course, arguable. The most important contribution of cognitive continuum theory is that it represents a systematic attempt to delineate the features of cognitive tasks and to show how these task features are determinants of the cognitive activities that are brought to bear on the accomplishment of those tasks. In this regard, the theory is consistent in spirit with Brunswik, with Simon (1969)—and with Aristotle. But tasks differ from one another in a bewildering variety of ways, and so do cognitive strategies. They do not differ only along an analytic-intuitive continuum: they differ in ways that are reminiscent of what Payne, Bettman, and Johnson spoke of and of Edwards's notion of a mental tool kit.

Man-Made Tasks

Sometimes different strategies lead to opposite conclusions on the same problems, especially on those cognitive tasks that are of the man-made sort. Note well that man-made tasks are not to be lightly dismissed as artificial. Borrowing some of that wonderful Hammond rhetoric,

> The time is now past due to consider a shift in point of view; for however valid the Darwinian model, it is a fact that men now control the fate

of the world rather than *vice versa*. . . . It is a *policy-ecology* in which we must learn to survive, for city-ecologies, forest-ecologies, jungle-ecologies and the like are now formed by man's policies. Therefore it is *policy-processes* we psychologists must seek to understand—for it is policies against which men now make sorties, for and against which men are sent to die, and it is man's policies which threaten to eliminate life. [Hammond and Boyle 1971, 103]

If we define man-made policy processes the least bit broadly, then we would certainly include the policy ecology in which we place, for example, our elementary statistics students. It is an ecology not well described as being marked by multiple fallible indicators. Locating the tasks required to survive and prosper in this ecology at the analytic pole of a continuum may give us some insight into the task domain, but it does not help us understand why students have so much difficulty making connections between statistical models or between the statistical models and the empirical procedures they represent. If a number of the cognitive operations (including what are typically called strategies, weighting strategies, heuristics, etc.) that are brought to bear on these tasks are in fact modular, as is suggested by the difficulty of seeing connections among them, what are the consequences for Hammond's exhortations toward theoretical coherence? What are the implications for the generalizability of results from the DESSY environment?

It may just be a reflection of my own limitations, but I have a difficult time seeing the commonalities among some of the cognitive tasks that we ask our subjects to solve. This is one reason that I believe that some of our methods of solution are modular. I suspect that many of you have had students who knew some statistical technique well, who had an experimental test of a scientific hypothesis clearly in mind, but who utterly failed to see that the statistical test was the appropriate model of randomness for the experiment. The students likely expressed astonishment when the mapping was made for them and looked a bit sheepish about their "logic tight compartments," to use Gordon Allport's (1954) term for his early version of encapsulated modularity. Maybe that has even happened to one or two of us?

I'm not sure what would constitute definitive evidence for the hypothesis of modularity in the central region, but the very hypothesis itself is a challenge to the assumption that cognitive theorists should strive for theoretical coherence or for integration of the subfields represented at the conference on which this volume is based. I typically begin my graduate course in judgment and decision making with decision theory, using, for example, Robin Hogarth's (1987) book, then spend a chunk of the course on the lens model. Each has an aesthetic quality, a good Gestalt, if Ken will forgive the term. Then I go on to heuristics and biases, assigning most of Kahneman, Slovic, and Tversky (1982). The contrast is great. The heuristics and biases are a sort of ugly-duckling collection of devices that people often seem to use when they are faced with artificial (remember, that means man-made, not uninteresting or unimportant) tasks. The heuristics lack theoretical coherence. They are modules: they seem to function relatively independently, they are not transparent to introspective analysis, and they are not easily modifiable. The heuristics usually get pretty good answers, just as the same perceptual mechanisms that give us the Müller-Lyer illusion and the Ames distorted-room illusion also give us the perceptual constancies. These perceptual mechanisms are assumed to be modular. Weighting and averaging is a module. In the appropriate circumstances it gives us a pretty good answer. Sometimes it leads us astray.

There is another heuristic not normally identified as such. One of the implications of modularity is that people may often fail to see connections between cognitions, connections that seem all too obvious once they are known. Suppose we apply the idea of modularity to schemata. Often, when people make connections between schemata that had been previously unconnected for them, they do so by the use of analogies. Darden and Maull (1977) refer to the extraordinary power of analogy, or "interfield connections," in the scientific enterprise. Note that, while analogy is not normally included as such among the heuristics talked about in the judgment and decision-making literature, the term appearing in the index of neither Nisbett and Ross (1980) nor Kahneman, Slovic, and Tversky (1982), it is one of the most widely used and powerful heuristics we have.

One goal of judgment and decision-making theorists is exactly the one essayed by Hammond in cognitive continuum theory, that is, the identification of task characteristics that elicit different forms of cognitive activity. But I would frame that goal in terms of identifying the features of cognitive tasks that are associated with the elicitation of different modules, often qualitatively different from one another, rather than focusing only on the analytic-intuitive dimension of those modules.

Who Defines the Task?

There is one great complication facing the theorist who wishes to construct a taxonomy of cognitive tasks and tie it to a taxonomy of cognitive processes. That complication is the active role played by the subject in determining what the task is. In one social judgment study (Roose and Doherty 1976), we had insurance-agency managers rate sales applicants described by 66 items of information taken from their application files. We certainly did not believe that our subjects treated that as a 66-cue task. Nor did we construe it as such. The redefinition of the task by the subject is, I think, one of the problems faced by Ken in the further development of cognitive continuum theory. To turn a phrase, we still need to understand which cognitive activities induce various forms of task characteristics.

One more point, or rather a musing, about the relation between modularity and cognitive continuum theory. Suppose that Ken had, instead of adopting the continuum concept more or less from physical science, taken the evolutionary metaphor to its logical conclusion and used systematics (Hull 1988) as his base analogy. What would a taxonomy of tasks modeled on an evolutionary tree look like? What genera and species of tasks would he have identified, and how would these have related to cognition?

Historical Antecedents

I think that Ken's analogy between the methodological predilections of the Gestalt psychologists and those of the current heuristics-and-biases approach is a good one. I agree with his location of the origins of the approach partly in a reaction against the intuitive statistician and partly in psychophysics. But there is another strong candidate for the intellectual origins of what he formerly called psychological decision theory. That candidate is the research in problem solving in mathematics (Polya 1954) and other domains (Newell and Simon 1972). Certainly therein lie the proximate origins of the general theme of limitations on rationality and of the term *heuristic*.

For a moment, let us adopt the demonstration method of the Gestalt psychologists. Go back and look at the Müller-Lyer illusions that Ken has taken from Tversky and Kahneman (1986). Does the frame make the illusion disappear? It does not for me. It attenuates it and simply allows me to draw the correct inference, much as a straightedge laid on the page would. But the shorter line still *looks* longer. This does not gainsay Ken's point that there is some convergence between approaches in the recognition of the influence of task parameters on strategies. But I fear that I am not so sanguine as Ken about the implications of that and other points of contact for integration. While I have been profoundly influenced by his work and by his exegesis of Brunswik, I must admit that I, too, celebrate the diversity within this field. Perhaps one day some judgment and decision-making theorist will see in an artificial task a key to understanding decision making in the world of multiple, fallible indicators, much as Darwin saw in artificial selection the key to natural selection in evolution (Gruber 1974).

Is There Method Incompatibility?

Even asking the question in this context implies that my answer will be no. I think that heuristics could well be included in a cognitive feedback task. There is no rule that says that we can or should communicate function-form information only via Cartesian coordinates, which some of our subjects probably do not understand anyway. Why not use heuristic devices? A colleague, Bill Balzer, is completing a large cognitive feedback study in which some of the function forms are nonlinear. Recall that the late Clyde Coombs (e.g., 1983) stressed that utility functions are single peaked, and note that people are well aware of some of their utility functions. Why not describe an inverted-U-shaped function to subjects as being "like the amount of sugar you like in your coffee" (an example I borrowed from Ward Edwards many years ago at one of his Michigan conferences, at which I first met Hilly) or "like the amount of salt you like on your French fries"? I do not know the results yet. This may be a trivial example of a confluence of methods, but it is an example nevertheless.

A fundamental Brunswikian principle is that, to know the objects in the world in which we have evolved, we must rely on multiple, fallible indicators. I think that a version of that principle applies to us as scientists as well, except that those people who have worked out much of what I take to be the received view of the way we ought to do science have stressed that the observations we make ought to be as independent of one another as possible—I cite here only Garner, Hake, and Eriksen's (1956) "converging operations," Meehl's (1978) "consistency tests," and Feigl's "triangulation in logical space" (cited in Meehl 1978). If we are to have the cumulative science for which Ken often calls, and if we are going to claim that some process or effect is truly transsituational or, better still, that some parameter value is transsituational, then different methods should be brought to bear on those processes, effects, or measurements. If there is evidence of situation specificity, then perhaps there is modularity involved. But the call for the methods to be as independent as possible suggests that it might well pay, as Ken argued in his chapter, to look long and hard for situations to which lens model methods and some other methods, perhaps those of heuristics and biases, perhaps those of process tracing, might converge. Hillel was one of the very few people actually to do something like that (Einhorn, Kleinmuntz, and Kleinmuntz 1979). What should one infer from the fact that such tasks have not come easily to the field? Or that they do not come easily to mind?

The Focus on Error

I think that we can learn much from errors. Consider Piaget's reliance on errors in the construction of his system. Recall Freud's focus on errors, especially in *The Psychopathology of Everyday Life*. Consider the revolution wrought in the field of sensory psychophysics by the key move of incorporating errors into the analysis rather than using catch trials to discard subjects. Perhaps the value of the relative focus on error versus achievement depends on what sort of module one is investigating. Research on illusory correlation exemplifies the focus on one form of cognitive illusion.

Unlike Ken, I believe that illusory correlation is an extraordinarily interesting phenomenon, one that focuses on error. In fact, I believe that the paradigm, clearly associated with the heuristics-and-biases approach, has much in common with the lens model approach, at least methodologically. In one experiment (Mowrey, Doherty, and Keeley 1979), we showed subjects 48 inkblots, each blot being paired with two signs and two disorders. At the end of the forty-eighth observation, the subjects were asked if they had noticed any relations between signs and disorders. In the eight conditions of the first two experiments, the number of subjects who reported the presence of some relation between signs and symptoms varied between 86 and 93 percent. The vast majority reported the expected associations (e.g., food response–obesity), even though the correlation between food responses and obesity was zero. Let us examine the procedure from the standpoint of a lens modeler. The 48 observations provided the opportunity for the subject to sample a large number of objects, that is, pairings of signs (cues, X_i) and disorders (distal variables, Y_i). After some number of observations, it is likely that the subject made covert judgments, but the paradigm does not call for the assessment of Y_s during learning, and whatever the subjects thought about each observation went unrecorded. The design was orthogonal in that the signs and disorders were unrelated, but the design is in fact quite representative of the natural environment since the signs used are in fact not valid signs. Another dependent varible involved having the subjects make an inference (Y_s) on each of 10 more inkblots, making this phase virtually indistinguishable from a lens model study, except for the number of observations. Still another called for the subject to provide a probabilistic assessment of the degree of relation between selected signs and disorders, that is, a subjectively assessed utilization coefficient.

Are there beliefs out there that are not grounded in valid data? There are clinicians who base their treatment of patients at least in part on the patients' Rorschach responses. There are those who govern their lives, and even their nations, on the advice of astrologers. There are those who believe in the predictive power of dreams, the Bermuda triangle, the master race, and the gambler's fallacy. An exclusive focus on achievement would not readily lead an experimenter to study false beliefs and would leave our science incomplete.

The often-repeated charge that other psychologists are uninterested in research that shows achievement is open to dispute. There are many behavioral scientists who are fascinated by eidetic imagery, mnemonists, or creative geniuses. In the emerging field of the cognitive psychology of science (Tweney, Doherty, and Mynatt 1981), far more attention is devoted to the study of excellence, in the work of giants such as Newton, Faraday, and Einstein, than to the work of progenitors of error, such as Blondlot. Christensen-Szalanski and Beach (1984) took too narrow a view in their identification of error as the source of our interest: it is not error so much as anomaly (Kuhn 1962), that is, systematic deviation from our theoretical expectations, that captures our attention and drives our research.

A Final Note on Integration

Whether Ken's efforts at integration will be successful only time will tell. I do not see clearly at this juncture how one would usefully implement the suggestion that representativeness is a secondary cue, that is, how one might measure representativeness so that ecological validities and utilization coefficients can be calculated. But the celebration of diversity involves not only the appreciation of different theories and different methods but also the appreciation of efforts at simplification. The impulse toward unification is in all of us.

ON DESSY

Perhaps this group has escaped much of the harmful legacy of behaviorism and kept as much of its richer inheritance as any. But legacies there are. One of them is the idea that the experimenter defines the task. Berndt's foray into dynamic decision making is an explicit rejection of this idea. His subjects directly influence the task, irreversibly so. DESSY seems to me to be an excellent starting place for the investigation of real-time dynamic decision making. It is a heroic enterprise, in terms of the sheer complexity of the cognitive task facing Berndt and his collaborators. If higher-order cognition is modular, then generalizations from DESSY will be severely limited. I have some more garden-variety reservations about the generalizability of DESSY data.

We must take care not to think that all decision tasks are dynamic, in the sense described in Berndt's chapter. There are *many* tasks that are static, one-shot tasks that engage deliberative strategies—the decision to get married, get divorced, take a job, leave a job, hire someone. The list is endless. While there are many dynamic tasks, only some are hierarchical, and DESSY results may be limited in important ways to hierarchical tasks. Furthermore, the system constants of DESSY constrain the permissible generalizations tightly. To what degree is the powerful effect of latency of feedback determined by system constants such as the latency levels chosen, the burn rate, and the dynamic equivalent of the lens model component, R_e? To what degree will the generalizations be constrained by the fact that the subjects are spending relatively few hours on the task, looking at a graphic display on a visual display terminal, and using typing as a response mode? These comments are, of course, related to Brunswik's insistence on object sampling. As an aside, it is interesting to note that Gary Klein (Calderwood, Crandall, and Klein 1987) has interviewed a large number of fire commanders and has concluded that the strategy they use involves straight analogical reasoning, that is, "This fire is like Fire X last November, Y worked on that one, so let's try Y."

I introduced this section by referring to legacies of behaviorism. One of the legacies that none of us has fully escaped is not caring sufficiently about what our measures mean. Our colleagues in clinical and industrial-organizational psychology are far more concerned about the construct validity of the measures than are we. Normative measurement is in many ways a different ball game than experimental psychologists usually play, but, with respect to the new program that Berndt is undertaking, I would urge him and his colleagues to be much more psychological in their treatment of their dependent variables. I realize that he, like Ken, is committed to systems concepts, but I disagree strongly with his assertion that it makes little sense to analyze individual decisions. One of the positive legacies of Skinner is the attention to the fine grain of the behavioral stream, to the temporal relations among the stimulus conditions under which responses are made, the responses themselves and the conditions that maintain or fail to maintain those responses. As we move into the reaches of complexity of dynamic decision making modeled by DESSY, can we afford *not* to concern ourselves with the details of the behavior?

A couple of additional notes about Berndt's chapter. The word *feedforward* is being used rather differently than its original use in the static tasks of the multiple-cue probability-learning laboratory. It originally referred to an experimental manipulation; that is, the experimenter provided task information to the subject that the subject could then use on subsequent trials. In the present usage, *feedforward* refers to a strategy that is available to a subject who has a highly detailed understanding of the task environment, a strategy that allows actions to be based on predictions of the future state of the system. Finally, the proposition that feedforward control may be possible only under conditions in which the process producing the delays can actually be seen and does not have to be inferred seems premature. The behavioral differences to which Berndt adverts may reflect only a quantitative difference in the degree to which the subject has learned the task or in the detail of the conceptual model of the task. The argument for a qualitative difference would require that subjects be given much more opportunity to make the necessary inferences, as were, I presume, the "extremely experienced research assistants" who defined optimality in figure 11.2. The performance of those experienced subjects appears to disconfirm the proposition in question.

CONCLUDING REMARKS

When Are We Doing Science and When Technology?

Sometimes it is clear. When a decision analyst goes out and consults with organizations, using standard techniques, that is technology. One of the things that nags me is, When are we doing science? If disconfirmability is truly a hallmark of science, is the hypothesis that one can model a set of results with algebra disconfirmable? The same question applies to regression techniques and certainly to the new wave of connectionist research.

To End on Some High Notes

With all the above criticisms, is there anything positive to say? I think that judgment and decision theory is one of the most exciting and fruitful areas in all contemporary psychology. The lens model and the Brunswikian tradition, almost exclusively through the efforts of Hammond and Brehmer, have given us much: the emphasis on object sampling; explicit models; an emphasis on environmental determinants; a nice mix of basic and applied problems and concerns; the differentiation between motivational and cognitive sources of conflict and the elaboration of the dynamics and power of those cognitive sources; the emphasis on environmental uncertainty; the emphasis on the unreliability of the cognitive system; interesting problems—conflict, the bullet study, the Rocky Flats study, and many more; consequences for human action; the elegance of the lens model and the lens model equation; the use of lens model components to assess the cognitive side effects of psychotropic drugs; and others. But I do want to mention just one more, and that is the wide applicability of the weighting-and-averaging *module*.

REFERENCES

Allport, G. W. 1954. *The nature of prejudice.* New York: Addison-Wesley.
Calderwood, R., B. Crandall, and G. A. Klein. 1987. Expert and novice fireground command decisions. No. KATR-858-87-02F. Yellow Springs, Ohio: Klein Associates. (Prepared under contract MDA903-85-C-0327 for the U.S. Army Research Institute, Alexandria, Va.)
Christensen-Szalanski, J. J. J., and L. R. Beach. 1984. The citation bias: Fad and fashion in the judgment and decision literature. *American Psychologist* 39:75–78.
Coombs, C. H. 1983. *Psychology and mathematics.* Ann Arbor: University of Michigan Press.
Darden, L., and N. Maull. 1977. Interfield theories. *Philosophy of Science* 44:43–64.
Einhorn, H. J., D. N. Kleinmuntz, and B. Kleinmuntz. 1979. Linear regression *and* process-tracing models of judgment. *Psychological Review,* 86:465–68.
Fodor, J. A. 1983. *The modularity of mind.* Cambridge, Mass.: MIT Press.
Garner, W. R., H. W. Hake, and C. W. Eriksen. 1956. Operationism and the concept of perception. *Psychological Review* 63:149–59.
Gruber, H. E. 1974. *Darwin on man: A psychological study of scientific creativity.* London: Wildwood.
Hammond, K. R. 1966. Probabilistic functionalism: Egon Brunswik's integration of the history, theory and method of psychology. In *The psychology of Egon Brunswik,* ed. K. R. Hammond. New York: Holt, Rinehart & Winston.
Hammond, K. R., and P. J. R. Boyle. 1971. Quasi-rationality, quarrels, and new conceptions of feedback. *Bulletin of the British Psychological Society* 24:103–13.
Hammond, K. R., R. M. Hamm, and J. Grassia. 1986. Generalizing over conditions by combining the multitrait-multimethod matrix and the representative design of experiments. *Psychological Bulletin* 100:257–69.
Hogarth, R. 1987. *Judgement and choice.* 2d ed. New York: Wiley.
Holton, G. 1973. *Thematic origins of scientific thought: Kepler to Einstein.* Cambridge, Mass.: Harvard University Press.
Hull, D. L. 1988. *Science as a process: An evolutionary account of the social and conceptual development of science.* Chicago: University of Chicago Press.
Kahneman, D., P. Slovic, and A. Tversky. 1982. *Judgment under uncertainty: Heuristics and biases.* Cambridge: Cambridge University Press.
Kuhn, T. S. 1962. *The structure of scientific revolutions.* Chicago: University of Chicago Press.
Meehl, P. E. 1978. Theoretical risks and tabular asterisks: Sir Karl, Sir Ronald and the slow progress of soft psychology. *Journal of Consulting and Clinical Psychology* 46:806–34.
Minsky, M. 1986. *The society of mind.* New York: Simon & Schuster.
Mowrey, J., M. E. Doherty, and S. M. Keeley. 1979. The effect of negation and task complexity on illusory correlation. *Journal of Abnormal Psychology* 88:334–37.
Newell, A., and H. A. Simon. 1972. *Human problem solving.* Englewood Cliffs, N.J.: Prentice-Hall.
Nisbett, R., and L. Ross. 1980. *Human inference: Strategies and shortcomings of social judgment.* Englewood-Cliffs, N.J.: Prentice-Hall.
Polya, G. 1954. *Mathematics and plausible reasoning.* Princeton, N.J.: Princeton University Press.
Roose, J., and M. E. Doherty. 1976. Judgment theory applied to the selection of life insurance salesmen. *Organizational Behavior and Human Performance* 16:231–49.

Simon, H. A. 1969. *The sciences of the artificial*. Cambridge, Mass.: MIT Press.
Tversky, A., and D. Kahneman. 1986. Rational choice and the framing of decisions. *Journal of Business* 59:S251–S278.
Tweney, R. D., M. E. Doherty, and C. R. Mynatt. 1981. *On scientific thinking*. New York: Columbia University Press.

Part Six

INTRODUCTORY COMMENTS

Both chapters in this final part suggest new topics of research for behavioral decision theory. Kahneman and Snell open with the commonsense notion that, in evaluating the consequences of decisions, people often have to make guesses or predictions about how well they will like different consequences. In choosing where to dine, for example, do we know how much we will like meals in different restaurants? Do we know how much we will like a new job? And so on. Such uncertainty about preferences, however, is antithetical to standard normative models of decision making in which it is assumed that people know their own tastes.

The need to predict one's own preferences raises many important issues. From a theoretical viewpoint, how does one take account of uncertainty concerning preferences? From the descriptive, psychological viewpoint considered by Kahneman and Snell, to what extent are people able to predict their own preferences? Are they accurate in doing so? Can they predict how their preferences might change with experience? Are predictions of preferences biased in systematic ways? In their chapter, Kahneman and Snell show how these issues can be addressed in an illuminating manner by means of psychological experiments and identify several areas in which people seem unable to predict preferences for future activities accurately. As yet, Kahneman and Snell have not developed a model of what they term *predicted utility,* but the empirical groundwork outlined in their chapter may well provide a first step toward this goal.

The agenda for future research set by Camerer's chapter is ambitious. Noting that the psychology of individual decision making has enriched the subject matter of statistical decision theory to produce what is now called behavioral decision theory, he asks whether behavioral findings could not equally well be applied to game theory to produce *behavioral* game theory. To show the feasibility of this approach, he first provides examples of different games that have been studied experimentally (mainly by economists) and points out the kinds of anomalies that occur when people do not seem to act in their economically selfish best interests. One intriguing result that appears in these studies is that, at the beginning of many games, subjects are not able to reason prospectively what actions they should take but that, with experience, they are able to discover the economically appropriate behavior. Camerer also identifies issues in behavioral decision theory that could and should be considered in behavioral game theory. These include the importance of context, different levels of explanation, and—most important—identifying the conditions under which people do or do not learn from experience.

In his discussion, Fischhoff transcends the particular issues raised by Kahneman and Snell and by Camerer. His comments raise important issues about the nature of experience in experiments. What do subjects think they are doing in experiments? What do we think they are doing? How experienced should subjects be in the tasks we ask them to perform? Fischhoff is skeptical about our ability to learn from experiments but helpful in that he suggests ways in which we might think about overcoming some of the difficulties he enumerates.

12

Predicting Utility

DANIEL KAHNEMAN AND JACKIE SNELL

The chapter is concerned with predicted utility, defined as a decision maker's anticipation of the hedonic quality of a future experience. A study of the lay theory of how tastes change identified some areas of broad consensus, a number of areas in which respondents did not agree, and several topics on which opinions did not match research evidence. Decisions about temporally extended aversive outcomes can sometimes be shown to be inconsistent with people's predictions of increasing marginal disutility. A series of studies of self-predictions provided further evidence of generally poor performance in the task of predicting utility. Predictions of future liking can be intrusive. Unlike self-prophecies of future behavior, which are self-fulfilling, predictions of liking may induce a contrast effect.

RATIONAL INDIVIDUALS will attempt to predict the quality of their future experiences to answer questions such as, Are the hideous curtains proposed by my spouse worth a quarrel, if I might adapt to them? Is the ocean view worth paying for, if it might become invisible? Can I ever get to like salt-free food? For the psychologist, such questions raise several topics of investigation. How do tastes change? How do individuals predict future hedonic experiences of enjoyment or discomfort? How accurate are these predictions? Do people make effective use of hedonic predictions in making decisions? Uncertainty about tastes is an important, but neglected, topic for behavioral decision research (March 1978). In this chapter, we report some preliminary explorations of this topic.

The term *utility* has been used in two quite distinct senses in the history of analyses of decisions. In the classic treatments of Daniel Bernoulli ([1738] 1968) and Jeremy Bentham ([1823] 1968), utility was a dimension of subjective experience. Speculations and casual observations about hedonic psycho-

---

The research reported in this chapter was supported by a grant from the Sloan Foundation. We thank Richard Thaler and Amos Tversky for helpful comments and Itamar Simonson for permission to cite results from his current research. Carol Varey and Brian Gibbs were equal participants in some of the research reported here.

physics provided the substance of a utility theory for Bernoulli and Bentham as well as for many early economists (Stigler [1950] 1968). The joys of wealth do not increase linearly, and the pleasure of consuming the proverbial sequence of apples or bananas is diminishing; such commonsense facts of hedonic experience were used to explain choices.

In modern usage, utility is derived from revealed preferences in a way that expresses the positivist spirit: its resistance to subjective notions and its affection for operational definitions anchored in observables. Psychologists who are familiar with the conceptual distinctions of the behaviorist period will recognize that decision theory uses utility as an expendable intervening variable, which merely summarizes a set of coherent choices. The explanatory force of the concept and any link to subjective experience are given up in this conceptual reduction. The focus on decisions rather than on experience is closely linked to the standard assumption of rationality: rational agents can be trusted to know what will be good for them and are entitled to their sovereignty. The notion of consumer sovereignty, in turn, has shaped the modern conception of rationality, in which coherence is the central criterion for the rationality of decisions, to the exclusion of substantive criteria such as the promotion of the agent's objective interests.

In the postbehaviorist period, it should now be permissible to note that the *experience utility* that Bentham talked about and the *decision utility* that is inferred from choices are quite distinct notions. Experience utility is the hedonic quality of experience, whereas decision utility is the sign and weight associated with a consequence in a decision context.

The conceptual separation of experience utility and decision utility raises an immediate question. Is experience utility the criterion for decision utility? The general answer, of course, must be no. Many decisions are governed by moral attitudes that cannot be reduced to pain or pleasure (Sen 1987). However, there remains a large class of decisions for which experience utility is the proper criterion. The flavor one should order at the ice cream parlor, whether to accept those hideous curtains, and perhaps also whether one should accept surgery for throat cancer—all are examples of decisions in which the anticipated quality of future experience should be the dominant consideration.

The consequences of a decision are normally experienced some time after the decision is made. A prediction of future experience is therefore necessary for a decision maker who aims to maximize experience utility. To supplement the analysis of experience utility and decision utility, we therefore need a notion of *predicted utility:* the decision maker's anticipation of the experience utility of outcomes.

Predicting the hedonic quality of an experience may not be a difficult problem when the experience is both familiar and immediate. When the experience is unfamiliar, delayed, or protracted, however, predictions could well be wrong. With few exceptions, notably March (1978) and Kreps (1979), the implications of uncertainty about the quality of future experience have not been explored in much detail. This could be a serious matter: if future tastes are uncertain, the common distinction between decisions under uncertainty or risk and decisions under certainty becomes moot. Indeed, when future tastes are unpredictable, the very feasibility of rational choice could be in doubt.

We have defined three concepts of utility, and these can be paired in three ways, which define problems to be studied.

Predicted utility → *Experience utility.*—The issue here is the validity of predicted utility. We shall consider two aspects of this question in the present chapter: the quality of the lay theory of taste change is discussed in the next section; studies of the validity of individual self-predictions are described in the final section.

Predicted utility → *Decision utility.*—The question is whether the decisions that people make incorporate their own predictions of changes in the quality of experience correctly. A preliminary study of this question is described in the second section of the chapter.

Decision utility → *Experience.*—The answers to the first two questions will ultimately constrain the answer to the third, and most important. Are errors in the prediction of future tastes a significant cause of poor decisions? Under what conditions are people likely not to know what will be good for them?

LAY THEORY OF TASTE CHANGE

The first item on our research agenda is a study of people's beliefs about the determinants of enjoyment and discomfort and of how these change over time. Unlike the studies described in the final section of this chapter, in which individuals predict their own future evaluations of a specified stimulus, our concern here is with the lay theory of tastes and taste changes. Carol Varey and Brian Gibbs are associated with this investigation. Our first objective in these preliminary studies was to identify some of the principles of hedonic psychology on which there is lay consensus. Another objective was to find out how much consensus there is.

We assembled a partial inventory of relevant findings and ideas from psychological research and constructed simple vignettes with multiple-choice questions to test lay beliefs about these topics. Sets of questions were presented to samples of Berkeley students (total $N = 337$), recruited on a busy campus plaza by the promise of a small payment. A selection of questions was also answered by volunteers ($N = 112$) among the participants and audience at the conference on which the present volume is based. This professional group consisted of graduate students and research professionals in various fields of behavioral decision research.

The following question illustrates one of the response modes used in the surveys:

D. and J. both work for a company that is introducing a new abstract logo for its letterhead. D. is just back from vacation and is seeing the logo for the first time; J. has been using the logo letterhead for 2 weeks.

Who likes the logo more today?
Circle your answer   D   J

Lay wisdom and psychological research have identified a long list of factors that can affect the course of taste changes: maturation and aging, satiation, boredom, ennui, adaptation, deprivation, substitution effects (increased or reduced consumption of a substitute may change tastes), mere exposure, dissonance, conditioning, addiction, and opponent process. Our questions in these exploratory studies dealt with only a subset of these topics, with a particular emphasis on issues of adaptation or sensitization to unpleasant stimuli. The number of questions was small for most of these topics, and our conclusions are accordingly tentative.

Some of the questions yielded substantial consensus and agreement with conventional psychological wisdom. The following are examples.

Weber's law.—Eighty-six percent of our sample expected that a person earning $20,000 per year would be happier at winning $100 than a person earning $40,000 would.

Conditioning.—Seventy-five percent of the students thought that a person who hears the company jingle each evening while departing work will like it more than a worker who hears the jingle in the morning while arriving.

Time discounting.—Ninety percent believed that a person who has just won a videocassette recorder that will be delivered today is happier than a winner whose videocassette recorder will be delivered in a month.

Craving and loss of enjoyment in addiction.—We thought it too obvious to ask whether an addict feels more craving or discomfort than a nonaddict when deprived of the stimulus. However, 80 percent of our respondents stated that a light smoker having the second cigarette of the day enjoys it more than a heavy smoker enjoys the fifteenth cigarette of the day.

The students' intuitions did not match several results of recent psychological research about processes of taste change. This is not particularly surprising, of course, since the nonintuitive nature of the results was the main impetus for that research. Some of the respondents' beliefs are listed below.

Little faith in the benefits of insufficient reward (Brehm 1969).—Only forty-three percent believed that a person who is paid $50 to continue for a second day of fasting will be more hungry than an unpaid faster.

Belief in positive reward effect, not in the noxious effects of overjustification (Deci and Ryan 1980).—Seventy-nine percent believed that, of two children making sandcastles, the one who was recently rewarded for this activity is having more fun.

No clear intuitions about the positive effects of mere exposure (Zajonc 1968).—In the sample question shown above, only forty-four percent be-

TABLE 12.1
BELIEFS ABOUT ADAPTATION AND SENSITIZATION

Belief in Adaptation	Belief in Sensitization
Highway noise (91%)	Carrying a heavy suitcase (91%)
Painful injections (daily) (76%)	Push-ups (83%)
Painful injections (hourly) (66%)	Neighbor's stereo (76%)
Foot in ice water (58%)	Headaches over several days (73%)
	Electric shock (69%)
	High-pitched tone (66%)
	Noise of drill (60%)

lieved that a person exposed to a new company logo for 2 weeks will like it more than a person who is seeing it for the first time.

No clear intuition about opponent processes with initially aversive stimuli (Solomon 1980).—For example, the sample was evenly divided on the question of whether novice or expert sky divers have a more prolonged sense of well-being after a jump.

This survey of opinions did not reveal general agreement with Coombs and Avrunin's (1977) dictum that "bads escalate." Respondents expressed highly differentiated beliefs about the long-term response to repeated or maintained aversive stimuli. A detailed assessment of the validity of these differentiated expectations will require much further work. Only a sample is discussed here (for a more complete listing, see table 12.1).

Pain and illness.—Some questions indicated a belief that people do not adapt to pain and illness. For example, 73 percent stated that the subjective experience of a headache that lasts for a few days tends to get worse over time. On the other hand, 66 percent of the students believed in adaptation to the experience of having an hourly injection, and 58 percent believed that the pain of holding one's hand in ice water for a few minutes tends to diminish over that period. (In fact, cold pressor pain increases rapidly, at least over the first minute; see Hilgard et al. 1974).

Noise.—A large majority of respondents (91 percent) believed that the annoyance of an individual who lives near a newly opened highway would diminish over a year. (This could be wrong. Weinstein [1982] found that people affected by a new highway expected to adapt to its noise but that their self-reported annoyance did not actually diminish over a year—although their tendency to talk about it did.) Except for that question, the respondents expected that exposure to intrusive noise would yield sensitization rather than adaptation: 76 percent stated that irritation with a neighbor's loud stereo increases, 66 percent said the experience of a high-pitched tone near one's office gets worse over time, and 60 percent had the same opinion about the noise of a pneumatic drill continuing for 1 week.

Perhaps the most important lesson to be learned from this preliminary study is that the task of predicting future tastes is difficult. The absence of a clear consensus on most questions is the central result of the study: only 27 of 73 questions that required a prediction of experience or a comparison of the experiences of two individuals showed 70 percent or greater agreement. There is lay consensus on a few principles, including satiation and adaptation of hedonic responses. Beyond these common and largely correct intuitions, there is little agreement in lay opinions, even for fairly simple situations.

The professional group ($N = 112$) showed only slightly higher consensus than the student group. The mean percentage endorsing the majority response, over the 17 dichotomous questions in the questionnaire, was 66 percent. The corresponding value for the student groups, on the same questions, was 60 percent. In general, the similarities in the responses of the two groups were more impressive than the differences.

Several of the differences between the two groups reflected fairly directly the professionals' familiarity with specific results or ideas mentioned in the literature. For example, 73 percent of the professionals, in contrast to 44 percent of students, expressed a belief in a mere exposure effect. A large majority of professionals (85 percent) believed that buying furniture at the same time as a new house makes the cost of the furniture less painful than separating the two purchases, but only 51% of the students shared this opinion.

It could be argued, of course, that the lack of agreement reflects the ambiguity of our sketchy vignettes rather than the existence of conflicting views about the effects of the variables featured in these vignettes. On this hypothesis, agreement might improve if more details were provided. For example, if people believe that mere exposure increases liking only for some specified classes of stimuli or under some restricted circumstances, they would need to know more about a company logo and about the measure of the attitude to it to predict the effects of mere exposure. In particular, research suggests that the mere exposure effect is enhanced if the test of the attitude to the stimulus is delayed (for a review, see Harrison 1977). Would there be more agreement on a mere exposure effect if this factor were added to the question? More generally, is there a more detailed version of each of our stories on which agreement would be much higher? Perhaps, but we doubt it. We expect to find out in further work.

Another interpretation of the lack of agreement is that it reflects individual differences in taste dynamics: if individuals differ greatly, they may know more about their own hedonic responses than about those of people in general. This proposition suggests that individuals might do better in predicting changes in their own tastes than in predicting general trends. The results to be presented in the final section of the chapter do not support this claim.

THE UTILITY OF TEMPORALLY EXTENDED OUTCOMES

Many actions have consequences that endure or are strung out over time, but there has been little or no study of decisions about such temporally extended outcomes. In this section, we examine the relation of decision utility to predicted utility for a particular class of extended outcomes: "bads" that are expected to escalate.

To set the stage, consider an individual who faces a choice between several medical treatments. One of the treatments consists of a series of injections, which are expected to become progressively more painful, though not intolerable. What are the implications of the predicted sensitization for decision utility? How will the decision utility of the treatment vary with the number of injections?

For a normative analysis of these questions, we first consider how the utilities of the separate episodes are to be integrated. The simplest rule of integration is a form of within-person utilitarianism, which assigns equal weights to the separate occurrences or to the successive selves that have these experiences (Parducci 1984).[1] Any rule of integration that departs from equal weighting requires special justification. In particular, there is no obvious reason to reduce or discount the last injections relative to the early ones—given the premise that the experience of the injections is expected to get worse.

According to this reasoning, the characteristics of the predicted utility of the separate experiences should determine the decision utility for the sequence. If successive injections get worse, the willingness to pay to eliminate the last injection in a sequence should increase with the length of the sequence. Equal weighting of the episodes in a sequence of escalating bads should also favor risk aversion in choices about the length of the sequence, in contrast to the risk-seeking pattern that is usually observed in the domain of negative outcomes. In collaboration with Carol Varey, we have begun a study of this class of problems, using the casual survey method described in the preceding section. We select aversive outcomes for which most people expect sensitization rather than adaptation, and we use decision problems designed to reveal the curvature of the decision-utility function.

To identify the predicted trend of the hedonic response, we simply ask survey participants whether the subjective experience associated with a repeated or maintained stimulus is getting better or worse, as in the following example:

> Imagine you have a severe headache that has lasted for a few days. Is the overall experience of having a headache getting better or getting worse?
>
> Please circle your answer.   better   worse

In our sample, 73 percent of respondents thought that the discomfort escalates.

The format of the questions used to assess the curvature of the decision-utility function is illustrated below:

---

1. The weighting of utilities considered here is not quite the same as an attribution of successive experiences to different selves, each endowed with preferences that are to be weighted. The normative and descriptive issues that arise in adjudicating between future selves that are expected to disagree have attracted much interest in recent years (Ainslie 1975; Elster 1979; Schelling 1984). In the approach taken here, the successive selves are represented by their (predicted) experiences of pleasure and pain, not by their preferences for currently available courses of action.

An individual suffers from a disease that may require a series of daily treatments with painful side effects: headaches and nausea lasting for 24 hours, until the next treatment. There is uncertainty about the number of treatments that may be required. Which prospect is better (less bad)?

	X	Y
1/3 chance	no treatments	no treatments
1/3 chance	4 treatments	2 treatments
1/3 chance	8 treatments	10 treatments

The format is designed to draw attention away from the probabilities, which are identical for all outcomes in both options. It is also intended to encourage respondents to attend to utility differences between neighboring entries on the same row.[2] The formulation of the consequences highlights the critical differences between the options: X may add a third and fourth treatment to the first two; Y may add a ninth and tenth treatment to the first eight. If treatments 9 and 10 are more painful than treatments 3 and 4, then option Y does not minimize total expected pain.

Table 12.2 presents results for three closely matched problems for which both predictions and decisions were obtained. In all three cases, the proportion of respondents who expressed a risk-averse preference was significantly lower than the proportion who judged that the experience would get worse over time or repetition. There is more risk seeking (less risk aversion) than hedonic considerations warrant. The preferences obtained from the professional respondents were very similar to those of the students.[3] Though many of the matched questions were asked between rather than within subjects, we may infer that 30–40 percent of respondents who believed that the experience is getting worse will nevertheless make risk-seeking decisions that are consistent with decreasing marginal disutility. Whether the results reflect the existence of two subgroups of subjects with different tendencies or a compromise in individual responses is a topic for further research.

We have inferred from table 12.2 that a significant proportion of respondents make decisions that do not adequately reflect their own beliefs about the quality of outcomes. How does this discrepancy between decision utility and predicted utility come about? Casual introspection suggests that the global evaluation of an extended outcome rarely involves a separate evaluation of each of its parts. Instead, we seem able to operate with representations that collapse the time dimension. An *instantaneous representation* projects an extended period of time onto a single moment, much as a three-dimensional

---

2. Other questions in this format have yielded the expected pattern of risk attitudes in some familiar cases (Tversky and Kahneman 1981): more than 70 percent of respondents exhibited risk aversion for monetary gains, for the number of days on a European vacation, and for public health problems described in terms of lives saved. More than 70 percent of respondents were risk seeking for a problem described in terms of lives lost.
3. We did not obtain measures of predicted utility from professionals for heavy suitcases and push-ups, assuming answers to be obvious.

TABLE 12.2
Comparison of Risk Attitude and Predicted Utility

	Students (%)	Professionals (%)
Push-ups:		
Gets worse	83	NA
Risk averse	56	55
Headache days:		
Gets worse	73	65
Risk averse	47	38
Carry heavy suitcase:		
Gets worse	91	NA
Risk averse	45	51

Note. N varied from 57 to 77 in the student surveys. $N = 112$ in the professional survey. Risk aversion refers to choosing the gamble that has the less extreme worst-case outcome.

scene is projected into a flat picture. We propose the hypothesis that people may evaluate a decision utility for an extended outcome by consulting an instantaneous representation of that outcome rather than by integrating the utilities of separate segments.

For an important example of instantaneous representation, consider moments that change one's view of the future. The critical conversation at which the physician breaks the news is, probably for most people, an important part of the scenario of a prolonged illness. Similarly, the event of getting the good news is likely to loom large in fantasies of sudden wealth. As these examples illustrate, the moment of receiving news can be associated with an intense hedonic experience. However, the emotional response to news may have psychophysics of its own, which need not correspond precisely to the intensity of subsequent experiences. In particular, it is a plausible hypothesis that the psychophysical response to symbolic representations of quantity is generally compressive (see also Dawes 1988; and, for a discussion of the psychophysics of number, Rule 1972; Rule and Curtis 1980). In the metric of news, the difference between suffering two or four injections may be noticeable, whereas the news that one may have to suffer eight or 10 injections may be indistinguishable.

It appears easier to imagine and evaluate one's emotional response to receiving news than to imagine responses to a prolonged sequence of events. The assessed response to news can therefore be used as a heuristic for the task of evaluating complex outcomes. The results of table 12.2 could be explained by the hypothesis that our respondents assessed the decision utility of extended outcomes by their news utility rather than by a detailed prediction of the sequence of experiences.[4]

---

4. The notion of "news utility" emerged in conversations with Amos Tversky over the years. He has pursued it in different ways.

We return briefly to the normative question of whether anchoring decision utilities on the utilities of news or of other instantaneous representations can be justified. The quandary can be illustrated by the example of the emotional response to news of a disaster in which lives were lost: the difference between 100 and 200 victims is obviously more impressive than the difference between 1,100 and 1,200. Should this fact of the psychophysics of news affect the valuation of human lives in a decision context? Probably not. Similarly, the acceptability of news utility as a proxy for experience utility in evaluating complex outcomes cannot be taken for granted.

A possible argument that favors reliance on news utility is that the retrospective assessment of the outcome, in memory, may share many of the same characteristics. Amos Tversky has been studying the role of memories in the evaluation of outcomes and the possibility that the ordering of outcomes may change when their memory value is considered. If the memory of a sequence of 10 injections will be essentially indistinguishable from the memory of eight injections, and if the anticipated hedonic quality of memories is important, a risk-seeking choice may be appropriate even if the experience of the treatments worsens steadily.

Finally, we note that results that are compatible with the notion of instantaneous representation have been obtained by Itamar Simonson (1989) in an entirely independent line of research. Simonson visits ongoing classes once each week for 3 weeks. He asks some subjects to choose one of a set of snacks, three sweet and three salty, for immediate consumption. Many subjects will choose the same snack when the experimenter comes to class at weekly intervals for several weeks. Those who do not choose the same snack from week to week will still choose from within the same category, either sweet or salty. However, subjects who are asked to commit themselves in advance to choices of snacks for several weeks usually pick a varied diet that includes both salty and sweet snacks—as they would (and do) if asked to pick several snacks at once for immediate consumption. It is fair to describe subjects' choices for future weeks as a mistake, which they could perhaps avoid by a serious attempt to predict their tastes on each of these weeks separately. The separateness of the episodes may be partially lost in the instantaneous representation, thus biasing the subjects toward the mixed choice that would be appropriate for a single consumption episode. There are other ways of interpreting Simonson's results, but one point is clear: the contrast between the two kinds of choices illustrates the difficulties of decisions that have delayed consequences.

INDIVIDUAL PREDICTIONS OF FUTURE TASTES AND CHOICES

A previous section was concerned with the lay theory of taste and taste change, as expressed in commonly held beliefs about the experiences and preferences of unspecified strangers. The question we address now is whether people have any special insight into their personal hedonic characteristics that might enable them to predict changes in their own tastes more accurately than they can predict changes in the tastes of others. The question will be recognized as a variant of the "privileged access" issue raised in the famous article by Nisbett and Wilson (1977). We ask whether people have privileged access to the dynamics of their own tastes.

The hypothesis to be studied is *not* that people do not know what they like. On the contrary, it appears that people can make accurate choices by consulting a large store of taste facts about the hedonic values of experiences. "We know what we like" in food, music, clothes, and myriad other topics. Because the personal store of taste facts controls approach and avoidance tendencies there are good adaptive reasons to keep tastes for significant consumption items up to date (Rozin 1982; Rozin and Vollmecke 1986). The well-known results on one-trial learning of food avoidance may indicate the operation of a basic taste-updating mechanism (Garcia and Koelling 1966; Pelchat and Rozin 1982). An up-to-date inventory of taste facts permits people to make short-term predictions of experience utility with considerable accuracy. However, tastes do change (Rozin, Ebert, and Schull 1982; Rozin and Schiller 1980)—although some famous economists have argued otherwise (Stigler and Becker 1977)—and decisions that have enduring or delayed outcomes therefore require the individual to predict future hedonic experiences.

In the studies reported in this section, we attempted to induce accelerated change of taste by repeating experiences at an unusually high rate and examined individuals' predictions of the effects of this manipulation. We focused on two questions. How accurate are the predictions of future enjoyment or of future choices? Does the prediction task affect enjoyment or choice?

Table 12.3 gives a brief overview of the studies. In three of the studies (excluding taste/serving), the participants predicted what their future attitude to a particular experience would be after a series of repetitions. The scale of

TABLE 12.3
DESIGN OF SELF-PREDICTION STUDIES

Study	Task	N
Ice cream	Predict rating of liking for ice cream and recorded music after eight daily repetitions	16
Yogurt	Predict rating of liking for plain low-fat yogurt and recorded music after eight daily repetitions	37
Choice	Predict proportion of choices of a default tune (A) in successive trial blocks	22
Taste/serving	Predict rating of liking for a full serving of yogurt after a single taste	31

Note. N is given for the prediction group; all studies had a control group of roughly the same size as the prediction group, except for ice cream and yogurt, which did not have control groups. The choice study also had a third group, which precommitted to choices.

TABLE 12.4
RESULTS OF SELF-PREDICTION STUDIES

Study	Prediction Task	Predicted Change	Predict Group, Actual Change	Control Group, Actual Change
Ice cream	Final rating	Decrease	Decrease	NA
Yogurt	Final rating	Decrease	Increase	NA
Choice	% A choices	No change	Small increase	Large increase
Taste/serving	Rate serving	No change	Decrease	No change

repetition varied greatly, from multiple presentations of a small set of short tunes over a 30-minute period to helpings of a particular flavor of ice cream on 8 consecutive working days. In the taste/serving study, people had small tastes of mildly unusual flavors (plain yogurt and exotic soft drinks) and predicted their liking for a whole serving of the same foods, to be consumed later in the hour. The results of these studies are briefly summarized in table 12.4.

The accuracy with which people can predict changes in their tastes was examined in the ice cream and yogurt studies. The participants in these studies undertook daily repetitions of the same experience: eating a serving of a particular food while listening to a particular piece of music. After an initial exposure (to the entire experience in the case of ice cream or to a single teaspoonful of plain yogurt), the subjects rated their liking for the food and the music and predicted the ratings that they would make on the next day and on the final day of the experiment, about 1 week later. The design allowed us to correlate the difference between the ratings predicted for the first and for the last test days with the difference between the ratings actually made on the two days. The daily repetitions produced fairly substantial changes in the ratings of the food and the music. For instance, average liking for the ice cream decreased 1.81 points on a scale from 6 to -6. Furthermore, these changes varied substantially among individuals (for ice cream, the range was from 2 to -8), allowing fair scope for different predictions. Nevertheless, the correlations between predicted and actual changes of liking were close to zero in both studies.

As we noted earlier, the low validities of predicted changes of taste do not show that people are ignorant of their tastes—they indicate only that people do not know much about their tastes in the future if those are likely to differ from the present. The predictions of future ratings were sometimes correlated with the criterion ratings, but no more so than were the initial ratings.

Participants in the choice study were exposed to two moderately obnoxious computer tunes and told that they would choose which tune to hear for a total of 60 plays. That is, before each trial of the experiment, the subject could choose to hear a default tune, to hear a longer alternate tune, or to have a 15-

second rest followed by the default tune. A control group performed just the choice task. Subjects in the prediction condition were asked to predict the frequencies with which they would choose each of the options in three successive blocks of 20 trials. The correlations between predicted and actual frequencies ranged from .14 to .36. Subjects in the commitment condition were asked to make an advance choice of frequencies for each option in successive blocks of 20 trials but were then allowed to choose on each trial as the other groups did. The correlations between the advance choices and the real-time choices ranged from −.06 to .07.

The preliminary indication from this work is that the prediction of future preferences is indeed a difficult task when tastes are likely to change. It is fair to conclude that these studies provided no evidence that people are skilled in personal taste prediction. Nevertheless, the low validities of taste predictions observed in these studies must be treated with caution: the null hypothesis is not easily proven and is all too easily supported by the noisy data of confused subjects.

The results shown in table 12.4 provide a comparison of average predictions to average outcomes. The mixed picture conforms to what we have learned to expect. Subjects were sometimes correct on the average, for example, in predicting that frequent repetition would dull their enjoyment of ice cream, although individual differences in this effect were not accurately predicted. In the case of yogurt, however, the average change was not in the predicted direction.

Predictions: Self-Fulfilling or Self-Contrasting

Because the ice cream and the yogurt studies were focused on the accuracy of self-predictions, the subjects in these studies all made predictions. This design did not allow a test of possible intrusive effects of the prediction task. Some evidence for such intrusive effects has been reported by Sherman (1980) and by Greenwald et al. (1987). Sherman studied the effect of asking people whether they would engage in a socially desirable act, such as donating time to a charity drive, if asked to do so. He described the predictions as subject to a self-canceling error. The proportion of people who predicted that they would respond positively to a request was very much higher than the proportion that actually agreed to the same request in a control group. However, this error was self-canceling because the individuals who predicted their behavior were much more likely than the control subjects to act charitably. Greenwald et al. obtained similar results with voting as the criterion behavior: individuals who were asked to predict whether they would vote in a forthcoming election were more likely to vote than individuals who were not required to make that prediction.

We obtained results similar to those of Sherman and Greenwald et al. in the only study in which our subjects predicted future choices rather than future ratings. In the experiment described above, in which participants were asked to choose among computer tunes, the control group showed a strong trend toward increasing use of the shortest tune. They chose the default A tune 10 out of 20 times in the first segment and 14.86 out of 20 times in the third segment. Subjects in the prediction group anticipated that their choice of the short tune would average 5.6 on the first block and 5.1 on the last block, indicating a much lower preference for that option. Their actual choices of the short tune changed from 6.8 to 8.4—far less than the control group. Like Sherman and Greenwald et al., we found that predictions of future behavior tend to be self-fulfilling—or that the errors in such predictions tend to be self-canceling. It is worth noting that this pattern does not seem to be restricted to socially desirable behaviors, as Sherman and Greenwald et al. had speculated.

The results of two other experiments suggest an intriguing difference between predictions of future behavior and predictions of future liking: whereas the former appear to be self-fulfilling, the latter appear to be self-negating. In one experiment, we gave students a teaspoonful of yogurt at the beginning of an hour. One group was asked to rate the taste and to predict how much they would like a serving at the end of the hour. A control group tasted and rated but did not make a prediction. At the end of the hour, which was filled by a visual perception experiment, each student was asked to eat a full serving of yogurt (about 5 ounces) and to rate it. Subjects in the prediction group predicted that they would rate the serving as they had rated the taste, but in fact they rated the serving significantly lower. However, subjects in the control group assigned very similar ratings to the taste and to the serving. Thus, the prediction task produced a contrast effect that did not occur under control conditions, $t = 3.08$, 63 df, $p < .01$, for the difference between groups. These preliminary data have intrigued us; extensions and replications of this experiment are in progress.

Why might predictions of future liking induce a self-negating contrast in the criterion ratings? One possibility is that the prediction task produces an artifactual change of attitude. However, we favor the hypothesis that the prediction induces the subjects to articulate a real change, which is masked by an artifact of relative judgment in the responses of the control group. Consider the experience of tasting a spoonful of herb tea or of plain yogurt. Now imagine consuming a whole serving of either substance, trying to assess whether the experience is improving or deteriorating. We speculate that a focus on change may help most people notice a slight but consistent deterioration of the experience. Without this focus on the changing experience, the final evaluation of a serving could be quite similar to the evaluation of the first taste. The serving is compared to a standard serving, and the taste is compared to a standard taste. Thus, we speculate that the prediction task sensitizes subjects to subtle changes in their experience but does not cause these changes. This hypothesis has testable consequences as well as some interesting implications.

SUMMARY

We have introduced the concept of predicted utility and sketched a broad research agenda exploring the characteristics of predicted utility and its relation to decision utility and to experience utility. An initial study of the lay theory of taste and taste changes identified some areas of broad consensus, a striking number of areas in which our respondents did not agree among themselves, and several topics on which their opinions did not match research evidence. Thus, the lay theory of taste changes is inadequate to support generally accurate predictions of such changes. Our study of predicted utility and decision utility for temporally extended aversive outcomes identified a substantial discrepancy: people sometimes apply a decision utility function that is consistent with decreasing marginal disutility for bads that they expect to escalate, such as the discomfort of carrying a heavy suitcase over several blocks on a hot day. We speculated about the mental representations that people employ in evaluating such outcomes. A series of studies of self-predictions provided further evidence of generally poor performance in the task of predicting utility. We also found that the task of predicting future liking is intrusive and that it may induce a contrast effect, perhaps by sensitizing respondents to subtle changes in the quality of their experience.

REFERENCES

Ainslie, G. 1975. Specious reward: A behavioral theory of impulsiveness and impulse control. *Psychological Bulletin* 82:463–96.

Bentham, J. [1823] 1968. An introduction to the principles of morals and legislation. In *Utility theory: A book of readings*, ed. A. L. Page. New York: Wiley.

Bernoulli, D. [1738] 1968. Exposition of a new theory on the measurement of risk. In *Utility theory: A book of readings*, ed. A. L. Page. New York: Wiley.

Brehm, J. W. 1969. Hunger. In *The cognitive control of motivation*, ed. P. Zimbardo. Glenview, Ill.: Scott, Foresman.

Coombs, C. H., and G. S. Avrunin. 1977. Single-peaked functions and the theory of preference. *Psychological Review* 84:216–30.

Dawes, R. M. 1988. *Rational choice in an uncertain world*. San Diego, Calif.: Harcourt Brace Jovanovich.

Deci, E. L., and R. M. Ryan. 1980. The empirical exploration of intrinsic motivational processes. *Advances in Experimental Social Psychology* 13:39–80.

Elster, J. 1979. *Ulysses and the Sirens: Studies in rationality and irrationality*. Cambridge: Cambridge University Press.

Garcia, J., and R. A. Koelling. 1966. Relation of cue to consequence in avoidance learning. *Psychonomic Science* 4:123–24.

Greenwald, A. G., C. G. Carnot, R. Beach, and B. Young. 1987. Increasing voting behavior by asking people if they expect to vote. *Journal of Applied Psychology* 72:315–18.

Harrison, A. A. 1977. Mere exposure. In *Advances in experimental social psychology*, vol. 10, ed. L. Berkowitz. New York: Academic.

Hilgard, E. R., J. C. Ruch, A. F. Lange, J. R. Lenox, A. H. Morgan, and L. B.

Sachs. 1974. The psychophysics of cold pressor pain and its modification through hypnotic suggestion. *American Journal of Psychology* 87:17–31.

Kreps, D. M. 1979. A representation theorem for "preference flexibility." *Econometrica* 47:565–77.

March, J. 1978. Bounded rationality, ambiguity, and the engineering of choice. *Bell Journal of Economics* 9:587–608.

Nisbett, R. E., and T. D. Wilson 1977. Telling more than we can know: Verbal reports on mental processes. *Journal of Experimental Psychology: General* 84:231–59.

Parducci, A. 1984. Value judgments: Toward a relational theory of happiness. In *Attitudinal judgment*, ed. J. R. Eiser. New York: Springer.

Pelchat, M. L., and P. Rozin. 1982. The special role of nausea in the acquisition of food dislikes by humans. *Appetite* 3:341–51.

Rozin, P. 1982. Human food selection: The interaction of biology, culture and individual experience. In *The psychobiology of human food selection*, ed. L. M. Barker. Westport, Conn.: AVI.

Rozin, P., L. Ebert, and J. Schull. 1982. Some like it hot: A temporal analysis of hedonic responses to chili pepper. *Appetite* 3:13–22.

Rozin, P., and D. Schiller. 1980. The nature and acquisition of a preference for chili pepper by humans. *Motivation and Emotion* 4:77–101.

Rozin, P., and T. A. Vollmecke. 1986. Food likes and dislikes. *Annual Review of Nutrition* 6:433–56.

Rule, S. J. 1972. Comparisons of intervals between subjective numbers. *Perception and Psychophysics* 11:97–98.

Rule, S. J., and D. W. Curtis. 1980. Ordinal properties of subjective ratios and differences. *Journal of Experimental Psychology: General* 109:296–300.

Schelling, T. C. 1984. Self-command in practice, in policy, and in a theory of rational choice. *American Economic Review* 74:1–11.

Sen, A. 1987. *On ethics and economics*. Oxford: Blackwell.

Sherman, S. J. 1980. On the self-erasing nature of errors of prediction. *Journal of Personality and Social Psychology* 39:211–21.

Simonson, I. 1989. Consumer choice strategies when making multiple purchases for future consumption. Working paper. Haas School of Business, University of California, Berkeley.

Solomon, R. L. 1980. The opponent-process theory of acquired motivation: The costs of pleasure and the benefits of pain. *American Psychologist* 35:691–712.

Stigler, G. J. [1950] 1968. The development of utility theory. In *Utility theory: A book of readings*, ed. A. L. Page. New York: Wiley.

Stigler, G. J., and G. S. Becker. 1977. De gustibus non est disputandum. *American Economic Review* 67:76–90.

Tversky, A., and D. Kahneman. 1981. The framing of decisions and the psychology of choice. *Science* 211:263–91.

Weinstein, N. D. 1982. Community noise problems: Evidence against adaptation. *Journal of Environmental Psychology* 2:87–97.

Zajonc, R. B. 1968. Attitudinal effects of mere exposure. *Journal of Personality and Social Psychology: Monograph supplement* 9, no. 2, pt. 2:1–27.

13

Behavioral Game Theory

COLIN F. CAMERER

People deviate from the predictions of game theory in two systematic ways. They are not purely self-interested (they care about fairness and try to cooperate with others), and they do not always consider what other players will do before making choices. However, with experience, these deviations sometimes disappear. People learn when they can afford to be unfair and what others will do; their behavior often converges to a game-theoretic equilibrium. A behavioral game theory that explains the initial deviations (and their disappearance) could be useful, especially if the learning process is modeled carefully and better data are gathered.

BEHAVIORAL DECISION THEORY is a catalog of ways in which judgments and choices deviate from normative decision theory and of psychological explanation of these deviations. Despite the formal kinship between decisions and games, there is no behavioral *game* theory. In this chapter, I describe some data that suggest a basis for behavioral game theory.

My approach expands the simple way in which special features of games (as compared to decisions or competitive markets) are treated in normative game theory. Games have two special features: players might care about the payoffs others get, and players must make judgments about the choices others make (and about their own future choices, in dynamic games). In game theory, it is generally assumed that people are self-interested—they do not care about the payoffs of others—and use introspection to make accurate judgments about the choices of others (who are making simultaneous judgments by introspection, ad infinitum).

These assumptions are useful for deriving sharp equilibrium predictions. Without them, game theory is still quite useful as a system for classifying social situations (Aumann 1985). The important question is whether the as-

---

Thanks to Robyn Dawes, Howard Kunreuther, Keith Weigelt, and especially George Loewenstein and Robin Hogarth, for help. This research was supported by National Science Foundation grant SES87-08566.

sumptions are violated systematically enough for an alternative theory to be useful.

A wide array of evidence suggests that they are. Preferences are more complicated than simple self-interest, but they are highly context dependent. Judgments about choices of others are less complicated than introspective equilibrium calculations, but they converge to those calculations as people learn from feedback over time.

There are other useful ways to do behavioral game theory. One way is to ask how the lessons of behavioral decision theory apply in games. For instance, one can ask how outcomes of bargaining situations depend on the way negotiators frame outcomes. This approach has been taken successfully by others in bargaining (e.g., Bazerman and Carroll 1987; Mumpower 1988; I will not retrace their steps. Behavioral decision theory also points out psychological features, like the importance of context and conditions for learning, that are useful in understanding the empirical convergence of behavior to game-theoretic predictions. Another useful direction is to reexamine the normative status of game theory. In this reexaminations, behavioral considerations arise naturally from wondering how people think about games rather than from empirical evidence. Binmore (1987), Rubinstein (1988), and Fudenberg and Kreps (1988) are provocative this way.

NOTATION AND BASIC DEFINITIONS

A *game* consists of *players* ($i = 1, \ldots, n$); *strategies* that players choose (s_i for player i); *outcomes* that result from strategy choices, a function of the vector ($s_1, \ldots, s_n$); *preferences* that players have for outcomes, including lotteries over possible outcomes ($u_i [s_1, \ldots, s_n]$); and rules about the order of moves, the information players have at each point, and so on. I will discuss only games played *noncooperatively,* in which players cannot make binding agreements about what to choose. Whereas noncooperative game theory is concerned with the strategies that players choose, *cooperative* game theory is mostly concerned with the division of gains from the strategies that are chosen by binding agreement. A noncooperative game can be shown in a tree ("extensive form") or in a matrix ("strategic" or "normal form").

The obvious question in a noncooperative game is what strategies players will choose. Nash (1951) suggested that players might choose strategies that are best responses to each other. Such strategies form a *Nash equilibrium*. Formally, ($s^*, \ldots, s_n^*$) is a Nash equilibrium if and only if

$$u_i(s_1^*, \ldots, s_i^*, \ldots, s_n^*) \geq (s_1^*, \ldots, s_i, \ldots, s_n^*) \qquad (1)$$

for all s_i, i. Nash equilibrium is a simple solution concept with attractive properties: an equilibrium always exists for games with finitely many strategies and players, and it is easy to calculate and explain. Many other equilibrium concepts extend Nash's idea (e.g., Aumann 1987) or refine it (see below).

The plan of the chapter is as follows. First, experimental evidence about preferences—tastes for fairness and cooperation—is reviewed. Next, data about judgments of future choices and the choices of others are discussed. (These discussions are extremely selective, intended to illustrate arguments rather than provide comprehensive review. For more thorough reviews, see Roth [1987], Kahan and Rapoport [1984], and McKelvey and Ordeshook [1987] on cooperative games, Colman [1983] on experiments, and Aumann [1985] for wisdom.) Then, some parallels to behavioral decision theory are discussed. A final section offers conclusions and ideas for further research.

PREFERENCES

Fairness

People prefer payoffs that are fair. This is not inconsistent with game theory because players are assumed to have utility for an outcome, which produces a vector of payoffs (one for each player). A player's utility can certainly depend on the payoffs that others get. Assuming that there is no dependence—pure self-interest—is simply a convenient benchmark, like the assumption of risk aversion in risky choice. If we reject the self-interest assumption, we do not reject game theory.

In fact, we can reject the self-interest assumption. Furthermore, we cannot account for fairness preferences by simply assuming that people care about the payoffs of others because their caring depends idiosyncratically on context. Let us see some examples.

The Coase Theorem. The Coase theorem is the conjecture that socially efficient outcomes will result, regardless of who has the right to make decisions about imposition of economic "externalities," as long as people can bargain cheaply.[1]

Many experiments have tested this conjecture in very simple settings (see Hoffman and Spitzer 1982, 1985, 1986). In a typical experiment, a "controller" subject A chooses one of several possible divisions of money between A and B, for example, (4, 10), (6, 6), or (11, 0). (These divisions represent costs and benefits to two parties because of different economic externalities.) The controller and B bargain with each other in an unstructured way, but the controller has the right to choose any division she wishes if they disagree. Since the experimenter has made it easy for the players to bargain, the Coase

---

1. An externality is any effect one party has on another, good or bad, that lies outside their economic relationship. Examples include watching an attractive man or woman, hearing a baby scream on an airplane, or being trapped on a boat listening to a band you dislike. Coase (1960) argued that, if bargaining between parties is easy, the socially efficient outcome would result regardless of who has the "property right" to impose or prevent the externality.

theorem predicts that controllers will choose the division with the largest total payoff (the socially efficient outcome), then demand a payment from B. In the example, the self-interested controller should choose (4, 10), then demand a side payment of at least 7 to bring her total to 11 (because she could pick [11, 0] if she wanted to).

In the experiments, subjects almost always chose the efficient outcome, but controllers got adequate side payments in only a third of the cases; they often split the efficient outcome evenly (7, 7). Similar results are found with larger groups (Hoffman and Spitzer 1986), in a two-firm market setting (Prudencio 1982), and when the subjects bargain over payments for drinking a distasteful substance (Coursey, Hoffman, and Spitzer 1987). Even splits are common in many other bargaining situations too (Roth 1987).

Hoffman and Spitzer (1985) explored two ways to make subjects tolerate uneven splits: in a "moral authority" treatment, subjects were told that they "earned the right" to be controller; in a "game trigger" treatment, subjects became controller if they won a simple game of skill (Nim). Both changes in context led controller subjects toward more uneven allocations. (The moral authority treatment was stronger, which goes curiously unmentioned in many discussions of the results.) Harrison and McKee (1985) found that having several practice periods with no controller, which generally led to disagreement and inefficient outcomes, led to uneven splits in later periods. These data suggest that an unequal division can be acceptable to people if they think that the right to the larger share has been earned.

Ultimatum Games. More evidence of preferences for fair allocations comes from "ultimatum games." In an ultimatum game, the divider divides a $10 "pie" by keeping D and giving $10 - D$ to an accepter (written $[D, 10 - D]$). She accepts the division, and they get paid; or she rejects it, and they get nothing. (Ultimatum games are not common in life, but they are a lens through which attitudes toward others' payoffs can be seen. They also underlie more elaborate theories of bargaining, discussed below, that do apply to common situations.)

There are many Nash equilibria of the ultimatum game, but, in the most reasonable ("subgame perfect")[2] equilibria, the divider should leave a penny (or nothing) to the accepter. A purely self-interested accepter will pick up the penny, unenthusiastically.

People do not actually play ultimatum games so ruthlessly; they leave

2. Any division $(D, 10 - D)$ is a Nash equilibrium if the divider believes that the accepter would reject all other divisions. But such a belief seems paranoid and inconsistent: it assumes actions in parts of the game (subgames) that people would not actually take if those parts were reached. Such an equilibrium is not subgame perfect. The division (5, 5) is a Nash equilibrium, but it is not subgame perfect because it assumes that the accepter will reject (9, 1) (or any other division less favorable than [5, 5]) if the (9, 1) subgame is reached. If the (9, 1) subgame is reached, a self-interested accepter will accept rather than reject.

around 40 percent of the pie for the accepter. Splits leaving less than 20 percent to the accepter are often rejected, contrary to pure self-interest.[3] Auctioning off the right to divide does not change the results much (Güth and Tietz 1986).

Buying from a monopoly is like playing an ultimatum game (see also Thaler 1988, 202–3). For example, in a "posted offer" experiment, a single seller posts a price at which she will sell a good. Buyers should buy if their reservation price is above the offered price and reject the offer otherwise. (Since the price is posted and fixed, there is no room for haggling.) In experiments, buyers sometimes refused to buy, even when the good was worth more to them than it cost (Smith 1981; Coursey, Isaac, and Smith 1984). These buyers were either trying to force prices down or were punishing the monopolist for posting unfair prices. Their efforts resemble boycotts, like the one endorsed by New York City mayor Ed Koch to punish movie theaters for raising ticket prices to $7 in the 1980s. Boycotts inspired by fairness are probably not effective in the long run—Koch's was not—but they may prevent prices from adjusting rapidly to changes.

There is corroborating evidence of tastes for fairness or altruism from many sources. Selten (1987) reports evidence from cooperative game experiments. Loewenstein, Thompson, and Bazerman (1989) found that people disliked differences between their payoffs and others' payoffs (especially differences favoring others) and that their dislike was marginally decreasing. Many earlier studies found similar results.

While people are not purely self-interested, we cannot just assume that they have a utility for payoffs of others; whether they do depends on context (as the Coase theorem data show). Our attention must shift to precisely how context matters.

Surveys of hypothetical situations are one useful way to study the implicit rules that people have for relating fairness to context. The rules uncovered this way do not correspond closely to formal rules in game theory (Yaari and Bar-Hillel 1984) or economics (Kahneman, Knetsch, and Thaler 1986a, 1986b), except perhaps for M.B.A. students (Kunreuther 1986). For example, biological need is considered a fairer basis for a disproportionate claim than simple desire (Bar-Hillel and Yaari 1987). Rationing scarce objects by raising prices is considered less fair than making people wait in lines or win lotteries

---

3. Guth, Schmittberger, and Schwarze (1982) found that dividers left an average of 35 percent of the pie (with experience, 31 percent). In Kahneman, Knetsch, and Thaler (1986a), dividers left 45 percent of the pie; most of the divisions were equal splits. In classroom replications, my students left 39 percent of a $10 pie and 38 percent of a $100 pie. (One pie of each size was actually divided.)

Guth, Schmittberger, and Schwarze's inexperienced subjects rejected two of 21 divisions, which left an average of 10 percent to the accepter. Experienced subjects rejected six of 21, leaving an average of 22 percent. Kahneman, Knetsch, and Thaler's subjects rejected unless they got 23 percent. My students rejected unless they got 21 percent of $10 or 15 percent of $100.

for them. People do not object to wage freezes during times of inflation—which reduce real, inflation-adjusted wages—but they think that absolute wage decreases are unfair. These studies suggest that the context of economic transactions flavors their fairness in subtle, idiosyncratic ways.

Cooperation

The instinct to cooperate is another kind of preference that departs from strict self-interest. Cooperation is indicative of concern for others because it may result from an aversion to the unfairness that results from uncooperative choices. Some examples will illustrate the point.

Social Dilemmas and Public Goods. In a social dilemma, a person's contribution benefits the group more than it benefits her. (In a typical experiment, I can keep $5 or give it back to the experimenter, who distributes $1 each to 10 people.) She prefers to withhold the contribution ("free ride"), but, if everyone withholds, each individual is worse off. Many social situations, for example, bystander helping, resemble social dilemmas (Stroebe and Frey 1982). In economics, social dilemmas arise in the funding of "public goods," goods that can be supplied to additional people at low marginal cost and that people cannot be excluded from consuming (such as national defense or public art).

There have been many experimental studies of social dilemmas (mainly by sociologists and psychologists) and public goods (mainly by economists and political scientists). I will describe them very briefly. For more complete reviews, see Dawes (1980), Dawes and Orbell (1981), Messick and Brewer (1983), and Dawes and Thaler (1988).

The most basic finding is that subjects contribute more to public goods than they should according to pure self-interest. Initial contributions average around half the optimal level, then dwindle to 10–20 percent (Marwell and Ames 1979, 1980, 1981; Brubaker 1982; Isaac, McCue, and Plott 1985; Kim and Walker 1984; Harrison and Hirshleifer, in press). People who value the public good more highly or have more resources contribute more (e.g., Rapoport 1988).

Subjects who contribute initially may do so because they have not learned to free ride or because they are building reputations for cooperativeness, which induces cooperation in others (see the discussion of reputation games below). Andreoni (1988) noticed reputation building among players paired with the same group in a series of 10-period games. In the first 10-period game, contributions began at a high level in the first period and gradually dwindled. In the first period of a second 10-period game, contributions jumped up from the low level to which they had dwindled to a high level, as if some subjects were trying to rekindle cooperation.

Many experiments have studied step-level public goods, which yield increasing benefits to participants in discrete increments (e.g., a bridge or a fleet of ships). An elegant experimental paradigm for such goods was proposed by van de Kragt, Orbell, and Dawes (1983). Each of N players is given E dollars, which they can keep or contribute. If M players contribute (the "minimal contributing set"), the public good is supplied, and all players get R (with $R > E$). In step-level public goods, free riding is not a dominant strategy. If a player expects $M - 1$ others to contribute, then it pays for her to contribute, earning R instead of E.

Roughly half the players contribute to step-level public goods (e.g., van de Kragt et al. 1986; Rapoport 1988) if there is no discussion. (Discussion almost always enables groups to ensure that M players contribute; see van de Kragt, Orbell, and Dawes 1983). In the "no greed" game (Simmons, Dawes, and Orbell 1983), contributions are required from everyone if M people contribute. Contributions are much more frequent (about 90 percent) in this game; it seems that people do not contribute in regular games because they can both keep their endowment and share the public good.

The evidence against strong free riding is so overwhelming that thoughtful researchers have begun to study conditions under which more and less cooperation occurs. In social dilemmas, discussion about contributions works wonders, roughly doubling contributions from one- to two-thirds (Dawes, McTavish, and Shaklee 1977). A "sermon" by the experimenter increases contributions too (cf. the success of telethons). Group discussion about something other than the game and time to think about the dilemma do not help.

Orbell, van de Kragt, and Dawes (in press) found that subjects in a discussion group would contribute twice as often if they thought during the discussion that their contributions benefited members of their own group rather than members of a separate group (created minutes earlier by randomly dividing one large group into two). It seems that discussion creates group identity and loyalty quickly and persistently (Dawes, van de Kragt, and Orbell 1988); moreover, much weaker conditions do too (such as giving subjects a common random payoff; Kramer and Brewer 1986).

Cooperation in Bargaining. In cooperative games with incomplete information, players are assumed to have private information about their own values. The important question is how they will divide the gains from cooperating. Much of the theoretical research in this area centers around a formal equivalence—the "revelation principle"—between freewheeling bargaining among players and structured bargaining guided by an outside arbitrator (e.g., Myerson 1986). The theories usually predict that inefficiencies are necessary to keep players from lying about their information to the (mythical) arbitrator.

For instance, in Forsythe, Kennan, and Sopher's (1987) bargaining games with two players, one "informed" player knew the size of the pie to be split (e.g., either $6 or $1, equally likely). The two players had 10 minutes to decide how to split the pie; if they could not agree, they got nothing. To keep the informed player honest, there must be some penalty for claiming that the pie is small when it is actually large ("we do not have enough profit to pay for a wage increase"). The theoretical penalty is a chance of disagreement when the pie is small (akin to labor strikes); such disagreements are very costly when the pie is actually large. For example, suppose that the pie is $6 but that the informed player says that the pie is $1, offers a $.50–$.50 split, and provokes a disagreement. Then the opportunity to split $6 has been lost. If such disagreements are sufficiently likely, the informed player should not lie.

Another maintained assumption in the theory is that informed players should make the same offers whether the pie is $6 or $1. They did not. About a third of the time, when the informed player knew the pie was $6, she offered more than $1 to the other player (e.g., a $3–$3 split), immediately revealing that the pie was not $1. (Experience did not diminish the number of revealing offers.) Revealing offers were costly because informed players who made them ended up earning $1 less than informed players who were more inscrutable. However, by revealing the size of the pie, informed players provoked fewer disagreements than the theory predicted, which increased the total earnings of all subjects.

Radner and Schotter (1987) experimented with games in which a buyer and seller know their value and cost, respectively, and both players know the distributions of possible values and costs. Each player writes down a bid or ask price. If the bid and ask overlap, a trade takes place at a price midway between them; otherwise, there is no trade. (If the buyer bids $4 and the seller asks $2, a trade takes place at the price of $3.)

It is optimal for players to bid somewhat less than their values (e.g., bid $2 if the valuation is $3) and ask more than their cost. Behaving this way maximizes the expected gain from trading, but it causes inefficiencies because some trades that should take place do not. Subjects in experiments bid much closer to their true values than they should. This "irrationality" caused much less inefficiency than the theory predicted, as if subjects were cooperating to maximize their collective gains from trade (taking the most money from the experimenter). Face-to-face bargaining was the most efficient of all.

The pie-splitting and bid-ask data suggest that subjects are unwilling to conceal their private information completely (or are unable to do so because the "availability" of information in memory makes them think that others know it too; see Camerer, Loewenstein, and Weber 1989). Their behavior is cooperative because it requires personal sacrifice—revealing information hurts informed players—that benefits players collectively, just as contributing in the social dilemma does.

JUDGMENTS ABOUT FUTURE CHOICES IN DYNAMIC GAMES

In decisions, people make judgments about random events; in games, people must make judgments about the choices of others. In dynamic games, people must make judgments in early stages about what they will do later.

These judgments are initially myopic; people do not anticipate what will happen in future plays and use those anticipations to make good choices in early plays. However, in most experiments, people learn not to be myopic.

Sequential Bargaining

Rubinstein (1982) pioneered the study of alternating-offer sequential bargaining games in which player 1 makes an offer, player 2 accepts it or rejects it and makes a counteroffer (which player 1 accepts or rejects), and so on.

One can study the effect of bargaining costs by making the size of the pie shrink each period by a fixed percentage (representing impatience or a discount rate) or by a fixed amount (representing bargaining costs). For a review of theory in this area, see Sutton (1986).

The tendency toward fairness in ultimatum games led many experimenters to study these more complicated sequential bargaining games, which end in ultimatums. For example, Neelin, Sonnenschein, and Spiegel (1988) used 2-, 3-, and 5-period games (cf. Binmore, Shaked, and Sutton 1985, 1988). In the 3-period game, the pie sizes were $5, $2.50, and $1.25. The perfect equilibrium prediction is that the player moving first should keep $3.75 and offer $1.25 to the second player (who should accept the offer).

(In the third period, an ultimatum game, the first player could demand $1.25 in theory. Anticipating this, the second player could demand only $1.25 of the $2.50 pie in the second period; if she took more, the first player would refuse and move on to the third period to get $1.25. Anticipating both stages, the first player can demand $3.75 initially, leaving the second player $1.25, the amount she could get by refusing and moving to the second stage.)

Subjects played very close to the perfect equilibrium prediction in the 2-period game, but they acted as if the 3- and 5-period games would only last 2 periods. For instance, in the 3-period game, subjects typically offered $2.50 (50 percent of the pie) initially, as if the second period were an ultimatum game and the second player could certainly earn $2.50 (though it was not). Perfect equilibrium also predicts badly in the comprehensive study by Ochs and Roth (1989) and in 2-period games in which the pie shrinks by 10 or 90 percent (Güth and Tietz, 1988).

In these experiments, subjects did not usually play the entire multiperiod game because first-period offers were accepted 80–90 percent of the time. In similar experiments on multiperiod assets, subjects underestimate the importance of future periods for current-period asset prices until they have actually lived through the future periods (e.g., Forsythe, Palfrey, Plott 1982). Knowing this, Harrison and McCabe (1988) replicated the 3-period game results of Neelin, Sonnenschein, and Spiegel with a clever twist.

Their subjects played an entire 3-period game, then played a separate 2-period game in which the pies were $2.50 and $1.25. This 2-period game is a subgame of the 3-period game with pies of $5, $2.50, and $1.25: if the initial offer had been rejected in the 3-period game, the players would have found themselves playing two more periods equivalent to the separate 2-period game that they did play. After the separate 2-period game, they played another 3-period game, followed by another 2-period game, and so on.

Subjects initially split the $5 equally in the 3-period game, just like the subjects in Neelin, Sonnenschein, and Spiegel's study. Then they played a 2-period game and saw that the first player ended up with $1.25. Players moving first gradually realized that player 2 would get only $1.25 in the 3-period game if she rejected the initial offer, so they gradually raised their initial demands to $3.75, the perfect equilibrium prediction.

Perfect equilibrium in the 3-period game resulted from seeing the results of future periods (subgames) played out—from experiential backward induction—rather than from hypothetical backward induction.

In this particular game, experiential backward induction also taught them that they did not have to be fair (player 1 gets $3.75 of the $5 pie), though an equal split was a natural division to start with. A reasonable conjecture is that players in unfamiliar bargaining environments begin by behaving fairly. If the environment favors one person over another, they gradually learn of the advantage and exploit it (see Binmore, Shaked, and Sutton 1985).

Strategic and Sincere Voting

Experiential backward induction also teaches people to vote strategically in the presence of a voting agenda. The experiment of Eckel and Holt (1989), shown in figure 13.1, is a good example. Nine subjects vote on three alternatives, A, B, and C. Three subjects, called A voters, prefer A to C to B (written $A > C > B$) because the experimenter pays them $3 if A is elected, $2 if B is elected, and $1 if C is elected. Three B voters have preferences $B > A > C$, and three C voters have $C > B > A$.

Subjects were given a fixed agenda. On the first vote, they chose either {A, B} or {B, C} (i.e., they would decide which one of A and C would later run against B). If {A, B} was voted in, on the second vote they chose A or B; if {B, C} was voted in, they chose B or C.

Players are said to vote "sincerely" if they vote for the set that contains their most preferred alternative. Under sincere voting, A voters would vote for {A, B} over {B, C}. B voters would too, so {A, B} would win. In the {A, B} runoff, A would get only three votes (from the A voters) and lose to B. It is myopic for A voters to choose {A, B} in the first stage because they will end up with B, which they like least of all. It is smarter for A voters to vote "strategically" by choosing {B, C} in the first stage (voting against their true preference), thereby setting up a runoff between B and C that C would win. (A voters would rather end up with C than B. Note that it does not pay for B or C voters to vote strategically.)

The entire 2-period game was repeated about 10 times in the experiment. No A voters voted strategically (for {B, C}) at first, but half their votes were strategic by the fifth repetition. Whether the preference orders of all subjects

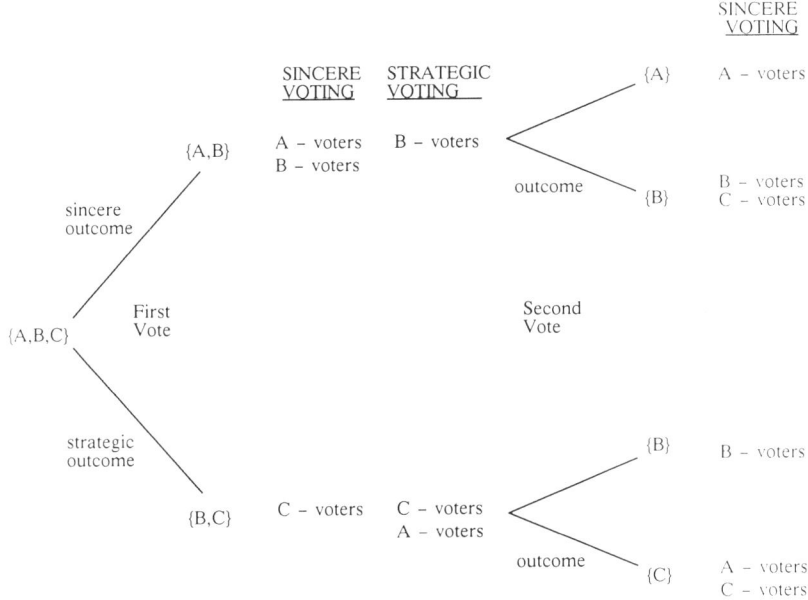

Figure 13.1. A voting game (Eckel and Holt 1989). Preferences: A voters, A > C > B; B voters, B > A > C; and C voters, C > B > A.

were made public before the voting did not matter much: as in the sequential bargaining experiments, subjects seemed to learn by living through future periods (experiential backward induction) rather than by thinking about them (hypothetical backward induction).

JUDGMENTS OF CHOICES BY OTHERS

Players in games must make judgments about choices of other players. (This is what distinguishes games from decisions most sharply.) The decision-theoretic approach treats choices by others as random events, like weather or disease (Kadane and Larkey 1982). The game-theoretic approach treats choices by others as special because their choices can be predicted (nature cannot) if we know what they earn, think they are rational, and believe they have the same presumption of us.

The crucial question is how much faith one has in human rationality. Harsanyi (1982, 121), a game theorist, objects to the decision-theoretic approach because it "would amount to *throwing away essential information*, viz., the assumption . . . that the players will act rationally and will also *expect* each other to act rationally." To call the mutual rationality assumption "information" seems curious (unless a mathematician is talking); an assumption is a hypothesis, subject to test. Game theory just provides a benchmark from which systematic deviations of the mutual rationality assumption are defined.

Reputation Games

Harsanyi (1967–68) suggested that games in which players have private information could be modeled by assuming that nature generates a player's "type," which affects payoffs and which is known only to that player (though others know the probabilities of various types). When played repeatedly, such games provide a natural model of the formation of reputations. Games like this are fashionable in economics and political science as models of labor and product markets, strikes, campaigns, and so on (Wilson 1985).

Camerer and Weigelt (1988) experimented with a reputation game consisting of eight plays of the 1-period ("stage") game shown in figure 13.2. The game is a simple model of building trust. First, nature determines the entrepreneur's (E) type, either honest ($p = .1$) or dishonest ($p = .9$). The banker (B) does not observe E's type. Her ignorance is shown in figure 13.2 by lumping the honest and dishonest nodes of the tree together in an information set enclosed by a dotted ellipse. B knows that she is at one of the two nodes in the information set, but she does not know which one.

B either offers a loan or does not. If the loan is offered, E chooses whether to pay back or renege. Notice that E knows her own type; she knows whether she is on the left (honest) part of the tree or the right (dishonest). If she is dishonest, she prefers reneging (earning 150) to paying back (earning 60). If she is honest, she prefers paying back, earning 60 instead of 0. A single E plays the game eight times against different Bs. Each B can observe what happened before. E knows her own type before the 8-period game, but B knows only the probability of each type.

The sequential equilibrium[4] is complicated. An honest-type E should always pay back. A dishonest-type E should never renege in the first few plays, then should begin using a "mixed strategy"—a probabilistic combination of "pure" strategies—with an increasing probability of reneging each period. (In the eighth period, a dishonest E should certainly renege.) Once the dishonest E begins mixing, B should begin mixing too, lending with a probability of .64. The dishonest E plays a mixed strategy because E wants to maintain a reputation for possibly being honest by paying back loans for as many periods as possible. (Once she reneges, her reputation is shot, and she gets no more loans.) She does not want to renege in the same period every time, or the B's will catch on and withhold loans in that period.

In the first 20 or so 8-period games, subjects deviated from the game-theoretic equilibrium in decision-theoretic ways. For instance, when E reneges in an early period, Bs should learn that she is dishonest and refuse to make loans. Instead, many Bs would lend in later periods, and E would renege again. Thinking decision theoretically, they regarded these bad loans

---

4. Actually, there are many sequential equilibria. The one we pick out is the only one that passes the "intuitive criterion," discussed below.

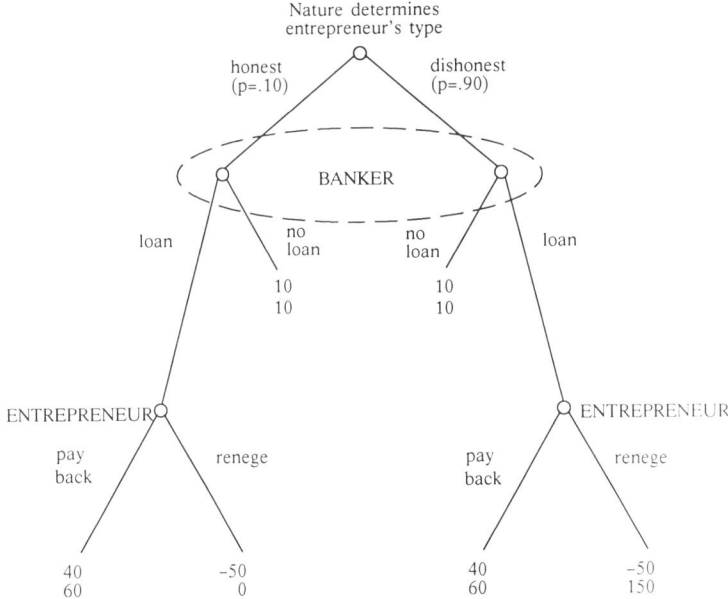

Figure 13.2. The banker-entrepreneur reputation game (Camerer and Weigelt 1988). Note that the upper (lower) payoff is the banker's (entrepreneur's).

as gambles that might be paid back because E's choice is unpredictable. Thinking game theoretically—knowing E's payoffs and assuming her rationality—makes the choice predictable: later loans will not be paid back. (They were not.)

In newer experiments, we measured subjects' estimates of the probability of having a loan paid back in each period of each game. Probabilities were biased in familiar ways (e.g., extreme probabilities are used too often; see Lichtenstein, Fischhoff, and Phillips 1982). The most striking finding is that other E players were better than B players at estimating whether a particular E would pay a loan back, though the Bs and Es had exactly the same objective data available to them when they made estimates. It appears that being in the same game-theoretic role as another player improves insight, helping subjects learn mutual rationality, just as playing future periods helps subjects backward induct.

After many 8-period games, play did converge remarkably closely to the equilibrium predictions. There was one persistent systematic deviation: dishonest E subjects did not renege as early in the game as predicted. This deviation makes sense if players believe that a fraction of dishonest Es (around 16 percent) will always behave honestly. This is further evidence of cooperation, as discussed above, because any E can do better by not behaving honestly but extra honest players increase profits for everyone.

Refinements of Nash Equilibrium

In games with many equilibria, the need to judge others' choices correctly is especially acute. Theorists have developed rules for evaluating the logic of different equilibria, called "refinements."

Many refinements have been described for incomplete-information games like the banker-entrepreneur game. Another example is the education game between students and employers, shown in figure 13.3 (adapted from Cho and Kreps 1987). It is a signaling game in which an informed party chooses a signal that another party sees and responds to.

In the education game, students are of two types, bright and dim. (Assume $p[\text{bright}] = .6$ and $p[\text{dim}] = .4$.) A student observes her type, then decides whether to attend college or not (the signal). Employers see whether a student went to college or not and decide whether to hire her, but employers do not know whether the student is bright or dim. Students get a payoff of 2 units of utility for getting a job, plus 1 for going to college if they are bright or 1 for

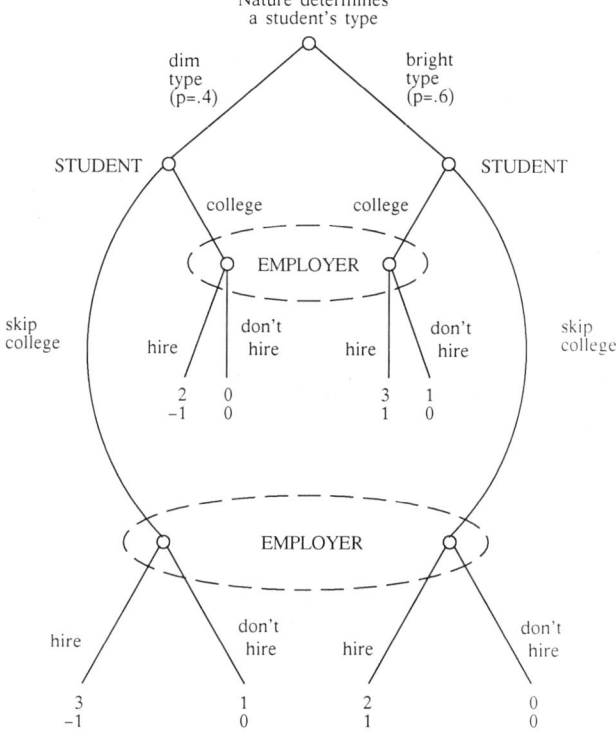

Figure 13.3. The education game (adapted from Cho and Kreps 1987). Note that the upper (lower) payoff is the student's (employer's).

avoiding college if they are dim. Employers get 1 for hiring a bright student and lose 1 for hiring a dim one.

There are two pure-strategy sequential equilibria in the education game. In one equilibrium, both bright and dim students skip college. (This is called a "pooling" equilibrium because both types choose the same strategy and enter a common pool.) Since both types skip college, employers using Bayes's rule realize that p(bright | no college) = p(bright) = .6. They then hire, earning an expected utility of $.6(1) + .4(-1) = .2$ (instead of not hiring and earning 0).

For this to be a Nash equilibrium, employers must not hire a student who went to college. (Otherwise, skipping college would not be a best response for a bright student.) For the equilibrium to be sequential (a refinement of Nash), employers must have beliefs that make not hiring a college skipper rational. To make not hiring rational, employers must believe that p (bright|college) < .5 (then the expected utility of hiring is less than zero, the certain value of hiring).

Since p (bright) = .6, the employer is acting as if going to college lowers the perceived probability that the student is bright. This inference seems backward. Dim students cannot possibly do any better by leaving the "equilibrium path" (where they earn 3) and going to college. Bright students might do better (they earn 2 in the equilibrium and might earn 3 by switching). A logical refinement called the "intuitive criterion" (Cho and Kreps 1987) states that p (bright|college) should be one if bright students might benefit from college and dim students certainly will not. But then it is optimal for employers to hire if they observe college (earning them 1 for sure), which makes going to college a best response for bright types, shattering the equilibrium. The resulting equilibrium does pass the intuitive criterion: all students go to college and get hired; students who skip college are thought probably to be dim and do not get hired.

In experimental tests of such games, the judgments of others' choices are often decision theoretic rather than game theoretic. For instance, undergraduates in a game-theory course made the choices shown in table 13.1. Subjects were asked what they would do at every possible point in the game. If dim, only six of 43 subjects would go to college; if bright, all go to college. As employers, 41 of 43 would hire college goers, but only seven of 43 would hire college skippers. Their logic is not game theoretic because, when dim students decide to skip college, they are apparently not thinking through what rational employers would do—not hire—if faced with a college skipper. (In this experiment, their choices as dim students are inconsistent with their own choices as employers.)

In more thorough experiments (Brandts and Holt 1987), dim types skip college 70 percent of the time. A natural explanation is that subjects are making "maximin" choices, maximizing their worst possible outcome. (In the education game, dim types can get at least 1 by skipping college.) Maximin

TABLE 13.1
EDUCATION GAME RESULTS

	Choice	
	College	Skip
Type:		
Dim	6	37
Bright	43	0
Employer choice:		
Hire	41	7
Not hire	2	36

Note. $N = 43$.

choices are defensible in many contexts (when the sum of all payoffs is constant, a Nash equilibrium necessarily consists of maximin choices), but not here; players choosing according to maximin are regarding choices by others as less predictable (or more malicious) than they truly are. Banks, Camerer, and Porter (1988) reported related results but found that choices were not always consistent with the maximin rule.

SOME PARALLELS WITH BEHAVIORAL DECISION THEORY

My general approach builds behavioral game theory up around the special features of games, deliberately distinguishing it from behavioral decision theory. The two have much in common as well.

Context

Seemingly innocuous changes in context affect the outcomes of games. For instance, experiments and surveys described above suggest that perceived fairness of decisions is sensitive to the method by which decision-making power was granted.

Schelling (1960) noted that many games with several equilibria have "focal points"—"psychologically prominent" equilibria—that are suggested by context and circumscribed by culture. An example appeared in *Games* magazine in November 1988. Readers were shown cartoons of nine celebrities and instructed to "vote" for one celebrity. If you voted for the celebrity receiving the most votes, you became eligible for prizes. The reader's job was to guess what people would do, knowing that those people would be guessing what others would do, ad infinitum.

The *Games* game has nine equilibria in pure strategies, one for each celebrity: those who think that the largest number of people will vote for Pee Wee Herman will vote for him too; those who think that Shirley MacLaine will receive the largest number of votes will vote for her; and so on. Voters man-

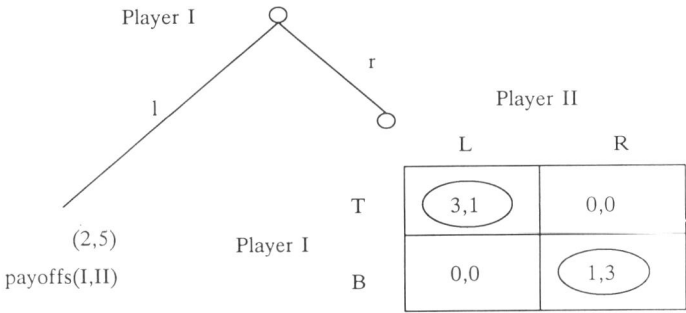

Figure 13.4. A game in which context matters (van Damme 1987).

aged to achieve a remarkable consensus: Bill Cosby won the actual contest (1,489 votes), edging out Lee Iacocca (1,155 voters) and distancing the seven lesser-known celebrities (2,639 votes combined). The same game in another context—with strategies labeled 1–9 or A–I—would not have produced such consensus.

The celebrity game is a "coordination game"; people are better off if they can coordinate their choices, doing what others do. In coordination games, context sets historical precedent, which has great influence (see, e.g., van Huyck, Battalio, and Beil 1988). For instance, driving on the right side of the road is a coordination equilibrium in America (now enforced by law) because of a convention established centuries ago. In England, a different history created a different convention, driving on the left.[5]

A final example of context is shown in figure 13.4 (see van Damme 1987). Player I moves first, choosing 1 or r. If r is chosen, players I and II play a simultaneous move game (shown in matrix form). The matrix game has two Nash equilibria in pure strategies (circled): (T, L), yielding (3, 1), and (B, R), yielding (1, 3).

If the matrix game were played separately, there is no reason to think that either equilibrium is more likely (unless labeling of strategies induces a focal point). But playing the matrix game after player I moved r is different. The matrix game is now circumscribed by context: by giving up her payoff of 2 (from [2, 5]) and taking her chances on the matrix game, player I is hinting to player II that they should play the equilibrium that gives her a payoff of 3 (i.e., [T, L]). Why else would she give up a certain payoff of 2? (This reasoning is

---

5. The American convention was established by farmers driving large teams of horses to market. They sat on the left rear horse so that they could lash the team with a whip, right handed. Since they were sitting on the left, accidents were best avoided if other teams passed on the left; they drove on the right. English drivers sat up on smaller carriages with a load behind them. A whip lashed right handed would get caught in the load if drivers sat on the left, so they sat on the right. Drivers passed on the right. Historical context matters: on an otherwise identical planet with more left-handed drivers, Americans would drive on the left, the English on the right.

called "forward induction": moves are assumed to tell players something about intentions in future subgames.) In this game, foregone choices provide a context; the context might matter because foregoing a choice means something.

Feedback and Learning

The process of learning is crucial and almost completely neglected in game theory. An exceptional model is Harsanyi's "tracing procedure" (1975; cf. Fudenberg and Kreps 1988). Players begin by guessing the probabilities with which other players choose strategies. Then they choose strategies that maximize their own expected utility given their guesses. This procedure yields an optimal strategy for each player; guesses are revised by shifting probability onto each player's optimal strategy, and the procedure is repeated until an equilibrium emerges. The tracing procedure was proposed as a description of the way players think before they play the game, but it seems even more useful as a model of learning across plays.

Behavioral decision theory suggests a simple model of learning: people respond to feedback by changing strategies until they reach a point from which they can do no better—the hallowed grounds of equilibrium. Convergence thus requires three ingredients: feedback must be clear, immediate, and repeated; subjects must interpret feedback correctly, realizing that they can do better; and subjects must change in the correct direction.[6] The most dramatic learning occurs in experiments that satisfy all three conditions. Recall the strategic voting experiment of Eckel and Holt (1989; fig. 13.1 above). In the second stage, A voters get clear feedback about the implications of their first-stage vote. Since their worst outcome is elected, subjects realize that a change can only help. Since there is only one way for them to change (by voting for {B, C} instead of {A, B}), they cannot help but change in the right direction.

In most of the sequential bargaining (pie-splitting) experiments, learning conditions were poor, and convergence was too. Subjects got no feedback about how much better they would do if they made more aggressive offers because initial offers were rarely rejected. When feedback was provided by playing subgames separately (in Harrison and McCabe's experiment), subjects converged remarkably close to perfect equilibrium.

Lack of feedback has an interesting effect in a game studied by Schotter, Weigelt, and Wilson (1988). Their game is depicted in extensive form in figure 13.5 and in normal form in table 13.2.

Player 1 moves first. There are two Nash equilibria, (L, 1) and (R, r). (Only the [R, r] equilibrium survives logical refinements.) If player 1 regards player 2's choice as a random variable rather than an optimal action deducible by introspection, she may choose L because it guarantees a payoff of 4 (it is the maximin strategy). But r dominates 1 for player 2. Player 1 should realize

---

6. Hilly Einhorn's influence here (e.g., Einhorn 1980) should be obvious.

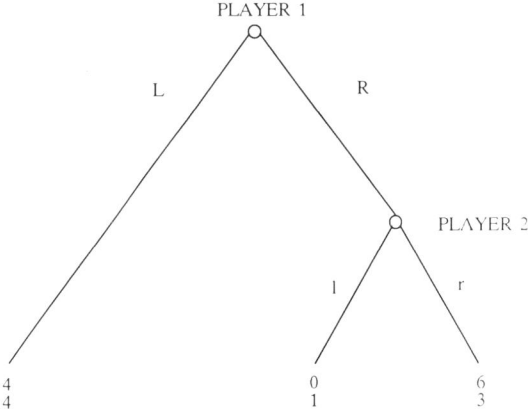

Figure 13.5. A transparency game (Schotter, Weigelt, and Wilson 1988). Note that the upper (lower) payoff is player 1's (player 2's).

TABLE 13.2
A Transparency Game

	Player 2	
	l	r
Player 1:		
L	4, 4	4, 4
R	0, 1	6, 3

Source. Schotter, Weigelt, and Wilson (1988).

this and choose R, earning 6 instead of 4. When the game was shown in tree form (fig. 13.5), player 1 subjects chose R 98 percent of the time. Shown the game in matrix form (table 13.2), player 1 subjects chose R only 44 percent of the time. Presenting the game in tree form seems to make it transparent that r is a dominant strategy for player 2 (cf. Keller 1985).

In this experiment, subjects were told only their own payoffs at the end of each period. When player 1 subjects chose L, they learned that they got 4, but they did not know whether player 2 chose l or r. I suspect that feedback is crucial for generating convergence in this matrix game: without knowing more than just their payoff, player 1 subjects could not be sure that R was a better choice than L. (Feedback on player 2's choices did cause player 1 to switch from L to R in classroom experiments.)

Levels of Explanation

An important finding in behavioral decision theory is that simple linear models may explain complicated judgments "paramorphically," without de-

TABLE 13.3
A Game with a Mixed-Strategy Equilibrium

	Column Player				Frequency	
	1	2	3	J	Predicted	Actual
Row player:						
1	−5, 5	5, −5	5, −5	−5, 5	.20	.221
2	5, −5	−5, 5	5, −5	−5, 5	.20	.215
3	5, −5	5, −5	−5, 5	−5, 5	.20	.203
J	−5, 5	−5, 5	−5, 5	5, −5	.40	.362
Frequency:						
Predicted	.20	.20	.20	.40		
Actual	.226	.179	.169	.426		

Source. O'Neill (1987).

scribing the detailed process of judgment very well (Einhorn, Kleinmuntz, and Kleinmuntz 1979). Models that work well at one level (overall judgment) work poorly at a less-aggregated level (judgment process). A similar phenomenon occurs with predictions of mixed-strategy play. A mixed strategy is a random choice (or "probabilistic mixture") of pure strategies.

Consider the game in table 13.3 (used by O'Neill 1987). There is no pair of strategies that are mutual best responses. However, if the column player chooses the strategies (1, 2, 3, J) with probabilities (.2, .2, .2, .4), then the row player's expected utility is the same for all strategies (-1). A mixed strategy with the same probabilities is therefore a weak best response to the column player (no other strategy is better; no other strategy is worse either).

O'Neill (1987) found that subjects played each strategy with an overall frequency remarkably close to that predicted (the data are shown in table 13.3), but the predictions are much less impressive at the individual level. (Brown and Rosenthal [1987] reject the predictions for a third of the subjects at $p < .05$.) Like paramorphic models, the mixed-strategy prediction works well at one level but fails at another.

In banker-entrepreneur reputation games (Camerer and Weigelt 1988), relative frequencies of choices were remarkably similar to the predicted probabilities overall, but individuals chose different patterns, which were often deterministic rather than mixed (e.g., pay back until period 5, then renege). Since different people chose different deterministic patterns, a player facing a randomly chosen opponent confronted an unpredictable strategy choice, which was effectively mixed.

Bull, Schotter, and Weigelt (1987) observed the opposite phenomenon in their experimental "tournaments." A tournament is a labor contract in which players choose effort levels (higher effort is more costly) and output is the sum of effort and a random variable. The player with the largest output wins a fixed prize (e.g., tenure or the company presidency). In their experiments, there is a unique pure-strategy equilibrium—subjects should choose the same effort level each time. Average effort was remarkably close to the level predicted, but individual effort varied dramatically over time and across people (perhaps because subjects tried to outguess the random variable, as in probability matching). The Nash equilibrium prediction was quite accurate in the aggregate but cannot explain individual variation. People cannot generate random sequences easily (e.g., Baddelcy 1966), though they can learn to do so with extensive feedback (Neuringer 1986). Thus, it is not surprising that people do not mix strategies randomly (for almost half O'Neill's subjects, choices depended on their own previous choices). Nonrandom mixing is troublesome for game theory because it changes equilibrium strategies if subjects can detect it. It would be useful to know if they can detect it.

CONCLUSION

My argument is that game theory relies on descriptively inadequate assumptions of the two features that distinguish games from decisions. The first feature is that games yield a payoff to each player. If players care about others' payoffs, predictions based purely on self-interest will be wrong. A wide variety of data suggest that people typically do prefer fair payoffs (often equal ones) but that their concern for fairness is context dependent. People also try to cooperate by making personal sacrifices to maximize joint gains.

The second feature is that, in games, players must judge the choices that others will make (including themselves in the future). The special assumption of equilibrium analysis in game theory is that such judgments are made by considering how others will behave if they are rational. Data suggest that people do not consider others. They are also myopic in anticipating their own future choices.

Of course, we should not abandon game theory simply because people violate it. Equilibrium predictions provide a handy, precise target that people move toward. Subjects usually begin experiments playing fairly, myopically, and decision theoretically. Gradually, they learn to accept unfair outcomes, plan ahead, and expect rational choices by others (if the equilibrium dictates that they should). A central question for *behavioral* game theory is learning conditions for convergence.

The natural hypothesis is that clear, informative feedback and the ability to adapt are necessary for convergence. Most of the experiments surveyed are especially conducive to learning, and convergence usually occurs (but never immediately). More experiments that are less conducive to learning (like the sequential bargaining experiments in which unreached subgames are not played) would be useful to see if convergence fails.

Then we must ask when people converge to equilibria in the natural world. Is the world more like the first period of an experiment or the last? The answer is surely mixed. Novice negotiators, first-time home buyers, and newlyweds are probably initially myopic in sequential bargaining, like inexperienced subjects. Veterans of painful strikes or divorces have lived through subgames (as experienced subjects have); they are probably not so myopic in new games. Practice may help too: novice salesmen rehearse the closing of a sale (imagining the end of their sequential bargaining with customers before it begins); hopeful lovers might do the same before a date.

If subjects can learn, an important question is how well learning in one setting transfers to another setting. Is behavior in the first period of an experiment like that in the last period of a similar experiment? There are good reasons to be pessimistic about transfer (on the "winner's curse," see, e.g., Kagel and Levin 1986, 909–10), but there are too few data to say anything more.

Broader data would be especially useful in developing behavioral game theory. In virtually all the experiments described in this chapter, researchers collected only the data needed to test the normative theory that they considered (choices, typically). It is easy to collect lots of other data, like judgments of what others will do (e.g., Selten and Stoecker 1986), process measures, or protocols. From those data, we can make game theory more behavioral, and better.

REFERENCES

Andreoni, J. 1988. Why free ride? Strategies and learning in public goods experiments. Working paper. University of Wisconsin, Department of Economics.

Aumann, R. J. 1985. What is game theory trying to accomplish? In *Frontiers of economics*, ed. Kenneth J. Arrow and Seppo Honkapohja. Oxford: Blackwell.

———. 1987. Correlated equilibrium as an expression of Bayesian rationality. *Econometrica* 55:1–18.

Baddeley, A. D. 1966. The capacity for generating information by randomization. *Quarterly Journal of Experimental Psychology* 18:119–28.

Banks, J., C. F. Camerer, and D. Porter. 1988. Experimental tests of Nash refinements in signaling games. Working paper. University of Pennsylvania, Department of Decision Sciences.

Bar-Hillel, M., and M. Yaari. 1987. Judgments of justice. Working paper. Hebrew University, Department of Economics.

Bazerman, M. H., and J. S. Carroll. 1987. Negotiator cognition. In *Research in organizational behavior*, ed. B. M. Staw and L. L. Cummings. Greenwich, Conn.: JAI.

Binmore, K. 1987. Modeling rational players. *Economics and Philosophy* 3:179–214.

Binmore, K., A. Shaked, and J. Sutton. 1985. Testing noncooperative bargaining theory: A preliminary study. *American Economic Review* 75:1178–80.

———. 1988. A further test of noncooperative bargaining theory: Reply. *American Economic Review* 78:837–39.

Brandts, J., and C. A. Holt. 1987. An experimental test of equilibrium dominance in signaling games. Working paper. University of Virginia, Department of Economics.

Brown, J. N., and R. W. Rosenthal. 1987. Testing the minimax hypothesis: A reexamination of O'Neill's game experiment. Working paper. State University of New York, Stonybrook, Department of Economics.

Brubaker, E. R. 1982. Sixty-eight percent free revelation and thirty-two percent free ride: Demand disclosures under varying conditions of exclusion. In *Research in experimental economics,* vol. 2, ed. V. L. Smith. Greenwich, Conn.: JAI.

Bull, C., A. Schotter, and K. Weigelt. 1987. Tournaments and piece rates: An experimental study. *Journal of Political Economy* 95:1–33.

Camerer, C., G. Loewenstein, and M. Weber. 1989. The curse of knowledge in economic settings: An experimental analysis. *Journal of Political Economy* 97:1232–54.

Camerer, C., and K. Weigelt. 1988. Experimental tests of a sequential equilibrium reputation model. *Econometrica* 56:1–36.

Cho, I.-K., and D. M. Kreps. 1987. Signaling games and stable equilibria. *Quarterly Journal of Economics* 102:179–221.

Coase, R. 1960. The problem of social cost. *Journal of Law and Economics* 3:1–44.

Colman, A. 1983. *Game theory and experimental work.* London: Pergamon.

Coursey, D. L., E. Hoffman, and M. L. Spitzer. 1987. Fear and loathing in the Coase theorem: Experiments involving physical discomfort. *Journal of Legal Studies* 16:217–48.

Coursey, D. L., R. M. Isaac, and V. L. Smith, 1984. Natural monopoly and contested markets: Some experimental results. *Journal of Law and Economics* 27:91–113.

Dawes, R. M. 1980. Social dilemmas. *Annual Review of Psychology* 31:169–93.

Dawes, R. M., J. McTavish, and H. Shaklee. 1977. Behavior, communication, and assumptions about other people's behavior in a common dilemma situation. *Journal of Personality and Social Psychology* 35:1–11.

Dawes, R. M., and J. Orbell. Social dilemmas. In *Progress in applied social psychology,* vol. 1, ed. G. Stephenson and J. Davis. Chichester: Wiley.

Dawes, R. M., and R. H. Thaler. 1988. Anomalies: Cooperation. *Journal of Economic Perspectives* 2:187–97.

Dawes, R. M., A. J. C. van de Kragt, and J. M. Orbell. 1988. Not me or thee but we: The importance of group identity in eliciting cooperation in dilemma situations: Experimental manipulations. *Acta Psychologica* 68:83–97.

Eckel, C. and C. A. Holt. 1989. Strategic voting in agenda-controlled committees. *American Economic Review* 79:763–73.

Einhorn, H. J. 1980. Learning from experience and suboptimal rules in decision making. In *Cognitive processes in choice and decision behavior,* ed. T. S. Wallsten. Hillsdale, N.J.: Erlbaum.

Einhorn, H. J., D. N. Kleinmuntz, and B. Kleinmuntz. 1979. Linear regression and process tracing models of judgment. *Psychological Review* 86:465–85.

Forsythe, R., J. Kennan, and B. Sopher. 1987. An experimental analysis of bargaining and strikes with one sided private information. Working paper no. 87–4. University of Iowa, Department of Economics.

Forsythe, R., T. Palfrey, and C. Plott. 1982. Asset valuation in an experimental market. *Econometrica* 50:537–67.

Fudenberg, D., and D. Kreps. 1988. A theory of learning, experimentation, and equilibrium in games. Working paper. Stanford University, Graduate School of Business, July.

Güth, W., R. Schmittberger, and B. Schwarze. 1982. An experimental analysis of ultimatum bargaining. *Journal of Economic Behavior and Organization* 3:367–88.

Güth, W., and R. Tietz. 1986. Auctioning ultimatum bargaining positions—how to act if rational decisions are unacceptable? In *Current issues in West German decision research,* ed. R. W. Scholz. Frankfurt: Lang.

———. 1988. Ultimatum bargaining for a shrinking cake—an experimental analysis. In *Bounded rational behavior in experimental games and markets,* Lecture Notes in Economics and Mathematical Systems, vol. 314, ed. R. Tietz, W. Albers, and R. Selten. Berlin: Springer.

Harrison, G., and J. Hirshleifer. In press. An experimental evaluation of weakest-link/best-shot models of public goods. *Journal of Political Economy*.

Harrison, G., and K. McCabe. 1988. Testing bargaining theory in experiments. Working paper. University of Western Ontario, Department of Economics.

Harrison, Glenn, and M. McKee. 1985. Experimental evaluation of the Coase theorem. *Journal of Law and Economics* 28:653–70.

Harsanyi, J. C. 1967–68. Games with incomplete information played by "Bayesian" players. I–III. *Management Science* 14:159–82, 320–34, 486–502.

———. 1975. The tracing procedure: A Bayesian approach to defining a solution for n-person noncooperative games. *International Journal of Game Theory* 4:61–94.

———. 1982. Subjective probability and the theory of games: Comments on Kadane and Larkey's paper, and rejoinder to reply. *Management Science* 28:120–24, 125.

Hoffman, E., and M. Spitzer. 1982. The Coase theorem: Some experimental tests. *Journal of Law and Economics* 25:73–98.

———. 1985. Entitlements, rights, and fairness: An experimental examination of subjects' concepts of distributive justice. *Journal of Legal Studies* 14:259–97.

———. 1986. Experimental tests of the Coase theorem with large bargaining groups. *Journal of Legal Studies* 15:149–71.

Isaac, R. M., K. F. McCue, and C. R. Plott. 1985. Public goods provision in an experimental environment. *Journal of Public Economics* 26:51–74.

Kadane, J. B., and P. D. Larkey. 1982. Subjective probability and the theory of games, and reply. *Management Science* 28:113–20, 124.

Kagel, J. H., and D. Levin. 1986. The winner's curse and public information in common value auctions. *American Economic Review* 76:894–920.

Kahan, J. P., and A. Rapoport. 1984. *Theories of coalition formation*. Hillsdale, N.J.: Erlbaum.

Kahneman, D., J. L. Knetsch, and R. H. Thaler, 1986a. Fairness and the assumptions of economics. *Journal of Business* 59:S285–S300.

———. 1986b. Fairness as a constraint on profit seeking: Entitlements in the market. *American Economic Review* 76:728–41.

Keller, L. R. 1985. The effects of problem representation on the sure-thing and substitution principles. *Management Science* 31:738–51.

Kim, O., and M. Walker. 1984. The free rider problem: Experimental evidence. *Public Choice* 43:3–24.

Kramer, R. M., and M. B. Brewer. 1986. Social group identity and the emergence of cooperation in resource conservation dilemmas. In *Experimental social dilemmas*, ed. H. Wilke, D. Messick, and C. Rutte, 205–34. Frankfurt am Main: Lang.

Kunreuther, H. 1986. Comments on Plott and on Kahneman, Knetsch, and Thaler. *Journal of Business* 59:S329–S335.

Lichtenstein, S., B. Fischhoff, and L. D. Phillips. 1982. Calibration of probabilities: The state of the art to 1980. In *Judgment under uncertainty: Heuristics and biases*, ed. D. Kahneman, P. Slovic, and A. Tversky. Cambridge: Cambridge University Press.

Loewenstein, G., L. Thompson, and M. Bazerman. 1989. Social utility and decision making in interpersonal contexts. *Journal of Personality and Social Psychology* 57:426–41.

Marwell, G., and R. E. Ames. 1979. Experiments on the provision of public goods. I. Resources, interest, group size, and the free-rider problem. *American Journal of Sociology* 84:1335–60.

———. 1980. Experiments on the provision of public goods. II. Provision points, stakes, experience, and the free-rider problem. *American Journal of Sociology* 85:926–37.

———. 1981. Economists free ride, does anyone else? Experiments on the provision of public goods. IV. *Journal of Public Economics* 15:295–10.
McKelvey, R. D., and P. C. Ordeshook. 1987. A decade of experimental research on spatial models of elections and committees. Social Science working paper no. 657. California Institute of Technology.
Messick, D. M., and M. B. Brewer. 1983. Solving social dilemmas: A review. In *Review of personality and social psychology*, ed. L. Wheeler and P. Shaver, vol. 4, 11–44. Beverly Hills: Sage.
Mumpower, J. L. 1988. Heuristics, biases, and optimality in negotiations. Working paper. State University of New York, Administration and Policy.
Myerson, R. B. 1986. Negotiation in games: A theoretical overview. In *Uncertainty, information, and communication: Essays in honor of Kenneth J. Arrow*, vol. 3, ed. W. Heller, R. Starr, and D. Starrett, 3–24. New York: Cambridge University Press.
Nash, J. 1951. Non-cooperative games. *Annals of Mathematics* 54:286–95.
Neelin, J., H. Sonnenschein, and M. Spiegel. 1988. A further test of noncooperative bargaining theory: Comment. *American Economic Review* 78:824–36.
Neuringer, A. 1986. Can people behave "randomly"? The role of feedback. *Journal of Experimental Psychology: General* 115:62–75.
Ochs, J., and A. E. Roth. 1989. An experimental study of sequential bargaining. *American Economic Review* 79:355–84.
O'Neill, B. 1987. Nonmetric test of the minimax theory of two-person zero-sum games. *Proceedings of the National Academy of Sciences, U.S.A.* 84:2106–9.
Orbell, J. M., A. J. C. van de Kragt, and R. M. Dawes. In press. Explaining discussion-induced cooperation in social dilemmas. *Journal of Personality and Social Psychology*.
Prudencio, Y. C. 1982. The voluntary approach to externality problems: An experimental test. *Journal of Environmental Economics and Management* 9:213–28.
Radner, R., and A. Schotter. 1987. The sealed-bid mechanism: An experimental study. Working paper no. 87-41. New York University, C. V. Starr Center for Applied Economics.
Rapoport, A. 1988. Provision of step-level public goods: Effects of inequality in resources. *Journal of Personality and Social Psychology* 54:432–40.
Roth, A. E. 1987. Bargaining phenomena and bargaining theory. In *Laboratory experimentation in economics: Six points of view*, ed. A. E. Roth. Cambridge: Cambridge University Press.
Rubinstein, A. 1982. Perfect equilibrium in a bargaining model. *Econometrica* 50:97–109.
———. 1988. Comments on the interpretation of game theory. Discussion paper no. TE/88/181. London School of Economics.
Schelling, T. 1960. *The strategy of conflict*. Cambridge, Mass.: Harvard University Press.
Schotter, A., K. Weigelt, and C. Wilson. 1988. Strategic choice and presentation effects: Some experimental evidence. Working paper. New York University. C. V. Starr Center for Applied Economics.
Selten, R. 1987. Equity and coalition bargaining in experimental games. In *Laboratory experimentation in economics: Six points of view*, ed. A. E. Roth. Cambridge: Cambridge University Press.
Selten, R., and R. Stoecker. 1986. End behavior in sequences of finite prisoner's dilemma supergames. *Journal of Economic Behavior and Organization* 7:47–70.
Simmons, R. T., R. M. Dawes, and J. M. Orbell. 1983. An experimental comparison of the two motives for not contributing to a public good: Desire to free ride and fear

of being gypped. Working paper. University of Oregon, Department of Psychology.

Smith, V. L. 1981. An empirical study of decentralized institutions of monopoly restraint. In *Essays in contemporary fields of economics,* ed. G. Horwich and J. Quirk. West Lafayette, Ind.: Purdue University Press.

Stroebe, W., and B. S. Frey. 1982. Self-interest and collective action: The economics and psychology of public goods. *British Journal of Social Psychology* 21:121–37.

Sutton, J. 1986. Non-cooperative bargaining theory: An introduction. *Review of Economic Studies* 53:709–24.

Thaler, R. 1988. Anomalies: The ultimatum game. *Journal of Economic Perspectives* 2:195–206.

van Damme, Eric. 1987. Stable equilibria and forward induction. Working paper. University of Bonn.

van de Kragt, A. J. C., J. M. Orbell, and R. M. Dawes. 1983. The minimal contributing set as a solution to public goods problems. *American Political Science Review* 77:112–22.

van de Kragt, A. J. C., J. M. Orbell, and R. M. Dawes with S. R. Braver and L. A. Wilson II. 1986. Doing well and doing good as ways of resolving social dilemmas. In *Experimental social dilemmas,* ed. H. Wilke, D. Messick, and C. Rutte. Frankfurt am Main: Lang.

van Huyck, J. B., R. C. Battalio, and R. O. Beil. 1988. Strategic uncertainty, equilibrium selection principles, and coordination failure in average opinion games. Working paper no. 88-20. Texas A&M, Department of Economics.

Wilson, R. 1985. Reputations in games and markets. In *Game-theoretic models of bargaining,* ed. A. E. Roth. Cambridge: Cambridge University Press.

Yaari, M., and M. Bar-Hillel. 1984. On dividing justly. *Social Choice and Welfare* 1:1–24.

Discussion

BARUCH FISCHHOFF

Hilly would have enjoyed these two fine chapters. Each deals with an issue critical to the development of our field. Each attempts to structure a dauntingly messy area with as formal a perspective as its substance and empirical results will allow. Each draws on a diverse set of methods and literatures. Each makes bridges between psychology and other disciplines and between our kind of psychology and everyone else's. Each tries to create, rather than just elaborate, a research paradigm. Each is concerned with some nonintuitive aspects of everyday experience, of the sort that set psychology's version of common sense apart from that of mere mortals.

I would have loved to have heard what Hilly would have had to say about them. What follows is my part in soldiering on without him. I envy the opportunity that his colleagues at Chicago had to see Hilly on a regular basis compared to my too-brief intense interactions at a conference or so a year. However, there is an advantage that I might have had. Hilly and I overlapped for a year at Wayne State, he as a graduate student, I as an undergraduate. In the course of studying his research in graduate school, I gradually convinced myself that he had been the T.A. in one of the courses I had taken at Wayne. I am an accomplished name-face amnesiac, so not having a clear memory of him posed little barrier to this illusion. Every time I saw Hilly, I meant to, but never got around to, asking him. I guess that I was, and continue to be, comfortable with the (slightly untested) feeling that I had the opportunity to begin learning from Hilly a few years before the rest of us did.

One way to read these two papers goes something like this. According to Danny and Jackie, unless you have experienced something, there is some substantial chance that you will not know what it is like. If you do not know what it is like, then you cannot be sure how much you will like it. Realizing that complicates decision making for you by adding a source of uncertainty to it. Not knowing whether you realize it, and, if you do, how you go about managing the uncertainties surrounding your future tastes, complicates life for those of us who are in the business of predicting your choices.

According to Colin, even if you know what you want, there is some substantial chance that you will not know how to get it—under the conditions of the "games" that life (including experiments) offers you. Realizing this complicates decision making for you insofar as you are uncertain which strategy gives you the best chance of getting what you want (or think you want). Not knowing whether you realize it, and, if you do, how you go about managing the uncertainty regarding strategy selection, complicates life for those of us who are in the business of explaining choices. It is hard to explain your behavior when we have to make inferences simultaneously regarding what you want and what strategy you use in trying to get it. So you're damned to suboptimize if you do not understand your own preferences, and you may be damned to suboptimize even if you do. And so are we.

Furthermore, as the phenomena are described in these chapters, at least some of these uncertainties seem almost inevitable in most of life's tasks. In an important sense, there is some element of novelty (and hence uncertainty) in all experiences—insofar as the history of our experiences shapes the enjoyment (or disenjoyment) of subsequent ones. For example, with things that we have enjoyed, there is always some chance that we will discover that we have had, say, one too many drinks (or donuts or European capitals). Health spas sign up more people than they could possibly accommodate as yearly members by counting on new members to discover within the first few months that the three thousandth sit-up or bench press is a lot less enjoyable than they thought it would be. (These spas can always count on the bankruptcy laws if they cannot count on people's inability to predict their preferences.)

Tasks involving other people have analogous uncertainties arising from their own histories. Even when we think that we have understood the rules, we cannot be certain that the other players have, too—so our wisdom may be wasted or even counterproductive. Worse yet, we do not know how the other players have been affected by the stumbling about in our own learning process (and that of the other learners that they have had to play with). By the time you finally discover how to get along with a significant other, the scars may be so deep that neither of you has the energy to apply that understanding in the current relationship. Perhaps it does not apply to a relationship having that kind of history. Perhaps it applies only to relationships with other players who have been similarly scarred, but at the hands of other learners. Such worries make life very difficult for protective parents (who do not even know what to wish their kids).

Anecdotally, it seems as though we abandon many of life's games before we have really got the hang of them. Maybe they do not seem worth playing, given the hand that we have been dealt. Maybe we cannot get a grip on the basic rules constraining what we, and others, can get away with. Maybe we understand those rules but cannot fathom their interactions. Maybe we are just too aroused to keep our wits about us and think our ways through to gaming the system. So we either act out or get out. Examples might be the take-this-job-and-shove-it school of career planning or the it's-my-party-and-I'll-cry-if-I-want-to approach to analyzing zero-sum games with scarce human resources as stakes.

The hope of avoiding some of these complications underlies the construction of most single- and multiple-player experiments. We try to keep things cool so that subjects think their way through to decisions rather than emote their way through. We try to use unfamiliar stimulus combinations so as to eliminate carryover effects of prior commitments while still exploiting familiar stimulus components (e.g., receiving dollars, eating single helpings of ice cream, hearing single plays of a record, listening to single drops of water). We have unfamiliar subjects play one another so as to avoid carryover effects of prior social relations. We lay out (what we perceive to be) the unique rules of our game clearly so that there need be no guessing about what gives. We use common response modes (bids, choices, matches) so as to reduce what gets lost in the translation as subjects try to tell us what they think or want in terms that we will find acceptable.

How well do we get away with it? Perhaps a fairer question is, How well could we get away with it? Colin mentions a couple of curses that provide conceptual anchors in this (accursed?) field. I thought that I would toss out a couple more, what I will call the curse of context and the curse of cleverness. (Neither term has quite the zip I would like, but at least they have alliteration going for them.)

People can respond to our tasks at all only because they have performed a lot of related tasks in the course of their lives. To do our job, we need, somehow or other, to evoke only those aspects of that experience that are relevant to our experiment. We need to create an evocative context but also to decontextualize it. We need people who have gambled enough to have general attitudes toward gambling but not people who will bear the scars or glories of any recent experiences. In a sense, we want subjects to be both mammals and reptiles: the products of a long nurturing process yet freshly hatched at t_1. We need people whose learning has come from the rich settings that life provides but who will then put up with reduced circumstances focused on those few elements that interest us. We want subjects to be creatures of context but to resist the temptations to recontextualize. We want to study the social norms (like altruism) that are evoked by social settings unlike any that our subjects have seen. We want subjects to act as though this is like life but often without a clear theory of what kind of life it is like or could be like should subjects choose to add lifelikeness to it.

The curse of cleverness holds that science progresses through our ability to think up just the right set of tasks to tease out the principles underlying people's behavior (e.g., Are they risk averse? How much do they like gazpacho? Do they believe in fairness? Do they reason like Yogi Berra?) under some assumptions regarding the savviness of their behavior (in the sense of their being able to identify courses of action in their own best interest). However, in doing so, we create tasks that threaten that very savviness. Faced with a new task, subjects who care about optimizing must first understand the set of relevant rules (both those contained in the task description and those drawn from their own repertoire) and then figure out their mutual implications (perhaps under some assumptions regarding how the parallel processes have been undertaken by other players). One possible correlate of the probability that subjects will solve the problem that we set for them is the amount of time that it took us to solve it. Even if subjects understand and confidently believe that they understand the rules of our games, there may still be special behavioral rules that apply to initial plays of novel games (e.g., misplaying to check one's comprehension, cautious playing just to be sure one has it down, exploitative playing to capitalize on a perceived imbalance in sophistication).

As Colin notes, one way that some behavioral (and not so behavioral) game theorists have attempted to address some of these problems is by providing repeated rounds of a task. However, such experience might do a variety of things in parallel: it could provide a positive or negative reinforcer for particular behaviors; it could provide revealing (or apparently revealing) information about other players (including the experimenter); it could provide apparent clues to how the game works; it could change the conditions of the game (e.g., reducing the stakes to simulate bargaining costs); it could change the other players; it could give one a chance to sample the stakes; it could give one time to think about the nature of those stakes and one's tastes for them; or it could generate interpersonal rivalries or affinities among the players, creating stakes beyond those provided by the experimenters. With all this potentially going on, it may be hard to take away any clear, simple lesson—or for us to make inferences regarding either stability or change in behavior.

These are, of course, irresponsible comments. They are just variants on the general theme of radical skepticism about the possibility of interpretable experimental research. It is piling on the problems in a spirit of "anything goes." Fortunately, these two chapters offer two generic approaches to developing (rather than bludgeoning) research programs out of concern over these potential artifacts.

Danny and Jackie's chapter might be considered a special case of the general strategy that William McGuire (I think) called turning an artifact into a main effect. Rather than worrying about the possibility that (unrecognized) instability of tastes will mess up the interpretation of single-person choice tasks, they make stability and the recognition of tastes into matters of study in their own right. Worked imaginatively, these prove to be worthy, fascinating topics that allow us to exploit work done elsewhere in psychology. It is the sort of detailed work needed to counter the feeling that we cannot test everything (regarding our auxiliary assumptions) and that therefore we cannot do better than just relying on our intuitions regarding what is going on. The chapter shows that there may be some systematic accounting for tastes and accounting for people's accounts of tastes.

The details of Colin's chapter offer a variety of methodological thoughts and reservations of the sort that I have mentioned. However, its overall structure represents another generic strategy: identifying some sort-of-true "stylized facts" that seem to emerge from a hard-nosed multimethod review. None of these "facts" are completely tied down, but they give one some handy, at least partially valid principles for analyzing complex, real-world events. In some cases, these are principles that we never would have thought of without the conduct of carefully controlled experimental studies testing precise theories that allowed them to emerge as clear surprises. In other cases, these are commonsense principles that these studies have enabled us to rescue from some ravenous theoretical ashcan (usually that of economics). So it now appears that (yes, Virginia) people do value fairness (sometimes) and do have an altruistic bone in their bodies.

If there had been a few more chapters in this session, what other strategies might they have undertaken? One additional strategy is to take the rule-learning process even more seriously. Much of our formal and informal education involves mastering some set of rules sufficiently well that we can apply it to some set of cases. The learning of math and physics, in particular, has drawn considerable research attention (e.g., Chi, Glaser, and Farr 1988). As I understand that literature, the learning of formal rules is an excruciatingly slow process, with students being unsure of the meaning of individual rules and the complications of their combination. Even the best high school physics students get by mainly because they get only textbook problems (containing the relevant facts and nothing but the relevant facts) within a few pages of the relevant formulae. Any intuitive understanding of how physical systems work seems to come much later, percolating up from having solved many concrete problems rather than trickling down from understanding a set of general principles. As experimentalists, we might wonder how rapidly subjects' mastery develops for the tasks that we concoct for them. We might try to learn from the science education literature how to accelerate the learning process. We might even consider the possibility of there being experiment anxiety akin to math anxiety, where fear that they cannot figure a task out arouses subjects and encourages them to grab onto some simple strategy just to get out of the experiment. A lot of life may be like that. However, it seems like a design decision whether we want our tasks to be.

A further research strategy would be to find out what subjects believe our games to be all about. If we opened this can of subjects, then we might focus on two aspects of subjects' intuitive theories of our experiments, each aimed at one curse. Regarding the curse of cleverness, we might ask how subjects think these games work. How do they interpret the rules, what do they see as their corollaries, what do they believe to be the best ways to express various tastes and obtain various goals, what do they believe to be permissible ways to act, and how stationary do they assume the rules and their implications to be? Regarding the curse of context, we might study subjects' default assumptions. That is, what do they read between the lines of our tasks? If they want to act in a lifelike way, what kind of life do they think that the experiment is like? What flesh do they add to the bare bones of our tasks in order to feel at home with them? In social science, we often seem to have a preference for sins of omission over sins of commission. That is, we go to greater lengths to avoid saying things that would explicitly misrepresent our tasks than to ascertain that subjects have not added misrepresentative details on their own (Fischhoff and Furby 1988).

An analogous challenge might be found with rational expectations theory in economics. If I understand correctly, proponents of this approach attempt to predict economic behavior by assuming that people are rational not only in the small sense of optimizing local hedonic decisions but also in the larger sense of anticipating economic trends and policies. You could undertake that enterprise either by assuming that lay people have absorbed the latest wrinkle in macroeconomic theory or by asking them flat out how they think the economy works. Jim Voss has some results showing no differences in the solving of economics problems (e.g., "How does the balance of trade affect interest rates?") among people with and without degrees in economics (although having some college degree did make a difference; Voss et al. 1986). Understanding how people interpret our games and their world would put us in a better position to answer Hilly and Robin's challenge to make more responsible assessments of others' rationality (see Einhorn and Hogarth 1981). It would also provide us with an intuitive theory of games and economic behavior.

REFERENCES

Chi, M., R. Glaser, and M. Farr eds. 1988. *The nature of expertise.* Hillsdale, N.J.: Erlbaum.

Einhorn, H. J., and R. M. Hogarth. 1981. Behavioral decision theory: Processes of judgment and choice. *Annual Review of Psychology* 32:53–88.

Fischhoff, B., and L. Furby. 1988. Measuring values: A framework for interpreting transactions. *Journal of Risk and Uncertainty* 1:147–84.

Voss, J., J. Blais, M. L. Means, T. R. Greene, and E. Ahwesh. 1986. Informal reasoning and subject matter knowledge in the solving of economics problems by naive and novice individuals. *Cognition and Instruction* 3, no. 4:269–302.

THE SCIENTIFIC PUBLICATIONS OF
Hillel J. Einhorn

1970

Einhorn, H. J. Comment on Hebb's criticism of Jensen. *American Psychologist* 25:1173–74.

———. The use of nonlinear, noncompensatory models in decision making. *Psychological Bulletin* 73:221–30.

1971

Einhorn, H. J. Use of nonlinear, noncompensatory models as a function of task and amount of information. *Organizational Behavior and Human Performance* 6:1–27.

Einhorn, H. J., and A. R. Bass. Methodological considerations relevant to discrimination in employment testing. *Psychological Bulletin* 75:261–69.

Einhorn, H. J., and N. J. Gonedes. An exponential discrepancy model for attitude evaluation. *Behavioral Science* 16:152–57.

1972

Einhorn, H. J. Alchemy in the behavioral sciences. *Public Opinion Quarterly* 8:367–78.

———. Expert measurement and mechanical combination. *Organizational Behavior and Human Performance* 7:86–106.

Einhorn, H. J., S. S. Komorita, and B. Rosen. Multidimensional models for the evaluation of political candidates. *Journal of Experimental Social Psychology* 8:58–73.

Rosen, B., and H. J. Einhorn. Attractiveness of the "middle of the road" political candidate. *Journal of Applied Social Psychology* 2:157–65.

1973

Einhorn, H. J. Reply to Morgan and Andrews. *Public Opinion Quarterly* 36:129–31.

1974

Einhorn, H. J. Cue definition and residual judgment. *Organizational Behavior and Human Performance*, 12:30–49.

———. Expert judgment: Some necessary conditions and an example. *Journal of Ap-*

plied Psychology 59:562–71. (A shortened version appears in *Judgment and decision making: An interdisciplinary reader*, ed. H. R. Arkes and K. R. Hammond. Cambridge: Cambridge Univesity Press, 1986.)

1975

Einhorn, H. J., and R. M. Hogarth. Unit weighting schemes for decision making. *Organizational Behavior and Human Performance* 13:171–92.

1976

Einhorn, H. J. A synthesis: Accounting and behavioral science. *Journal of Accounting Research* 14:196–206.

Gallagher, W. E., and H. J. Einhorn. Motivation theory and job design. *Journal of Business* 49:358–73.

Hogarth, R. M., and H. J. Einhorn. Optimal strategies for personnel selection when candidates can reject offers. *Journal of Business* 49:478–95.

1977

Einhorn, H. J., R. M. Hogarth, and E. Klempner. Quality of group judgment. *Psychological Bulletin* 84:158–72.

Einhorn, H. J., and W. P. McCoach. A simple multiattribute utility procedure for evaluation. *Behavioral Science* 22:270–82. (Also appears in *Multiple criteria problem solving*, ed. S. Zionts. Berlin: Springer, 1978.)

Einhorn, H. J., and S. Schacht. Decisions based on fallible clinical judgment. In *Judgment and decision processes in applied settings*, ed. M. Kaplan and S. Schwartz. New York: Academic.

1978

Einhorn, H. J. Decision errors and fallible judgment: Implications for social policy. In *Judgment and decision in public policy formation*, ed. K. R. Hammond. Denver, Colo.: Westview/American Association for the Advancement of Science.

Einhorn, H. J., and R. M. Hogarth. Confidence in judgment: Persistence of the illusion of validity. *Psychological Review* 85:395–416.

1979

Einhorn, H. J., D. N. Kleinmuntz, and B. Kleinmuntz. Linear regression *and* process-tracing models of judgment. *Psychological Review* 86:465–85.

1980

Einhorn, H. J. Learning from experience and suboptimal rules in decision making. In *Cognitive processes in choice and decision behavior*, ed. T. S. Wallsten. Hillsdale, N.J.: Erlbaum. (A shortened version appears in *Judgment under uncertainty:*

Heuristics and biases, ed. D. Kahneman, P. Slovic, and A. Tversky. Cambridge: Cambridge University Press, 1982.)
———. Overconfidence in judgment. In *New directions for methodology of social and behavioral science,* vol. 4, ed. R. A. Shweder and D. W. Fiske. San Francisco: Jossey-Bass.

1981

Einhorn, H. J., and R. M. Hogarth. Behavioral decision theory: Processes of judgment and choice. *Annual Review of Psychology* 32:53–88. (Also appears in *Journal of Accounting Research* 19 (1981): 1–31; and *Decision making: An interdisciplinary inquiry,* ed. G. R. Ungson and D. N. Braunstein. Boston: Kent, 1982.)
———. Rationality and the sanctity of competence [Commentary]. *Behavioral and Brain Sciences* 4:334–35.

1982

Einhorn, H. J., and R. M. Hogarth. Prediction, diagnosis, and causal thinking in forecasting. *Journal of Forecasting* 1:23–36. (Also appears in *Behavioral decision making,* ed. G. Wright. New York: Plenum, 1985.)
———. Reply to commentaries on, "Behavioral decision theory: Processes of judgment and choice." In *Decision making: An interdisciplinary inquiry,* ed. G. R. Ungson and D. N. Braunstein. Boston: Kent.
Einhorn, H. J., and C. T. Koelb. A psychometric study of literary-critical judgment. *Modern Language Studies* 12:59–82.

1984

Einhorn, H. J. Random strategies and "ran-dumb" behavior [Commentary]. *Behavioral and Brain Sciences* 7:104.

1985

Einhorn, H. J. A model of the conjunction fallacy. Working paper. Center for Decision Research, University of Chicago, June.
Einhorn, H. J., and R. M. Hogarth. Ambiguity and uncertainty in probabilistic inference. *Psychological Review* 92:433–61.
———. A contrast/surprise model for updating beliefs. Working paper. Center for Decision Research, University of Chicago, April.

1986

Einhorn, H. J. Accepting error to make less error. *Journal of Personality Assessment* 50, no. 3:387–95.
Einhorn, H. J., and R. M. Hogarth. Decision making under ambiguity. *Journal of Business* 59, no. 4, pt. 2:S225–S250. (Also appears in *Rational choice: The contrast between economics and psychology,* ed. R. M. Hogarth and M. W. Reder. Chicago: University of Chicago Press, 1987.)
———. Judging probable cause. *Psychological Bulletin* 99:3–19.

1987

Einhorn, H. J., and R. M. Hogarth. Decision making: Going forward in reverse. *Harvard Business Review* 87, no. 1:66–70.

Goldstein, W. M., and H. J. Einhorn. Expression theory and the preference reversal phenomena. *Psychological Review* 94, no. 2:236–54.

1988

Einhorn, H. J. Diagnosis and causality in clinical and statistical prediction. In *Reasoning, inference, and judgment in clinical psychology,* ed. D. C. Turk and P. Salovey. New York: Free Press.

Einhorn, H. J., and R. M. Hogarth. Decision making under ambiguity: A note. In *Risk, decision, and rationality,* ed. B. Munier. Dordrecht: Reidel.

1989

Goldstein, W. M., and H. J. Einhorn. Expression theory and the measurement of apparently labile values. *Annals of Operations Research* 19:51–78.

Hogarth, R. M., and H. J. Einhorn. Order effects in belief updating: The belief-adjustment model. Working paper. Center for Decision Research, University of Chicago, May.

———. Venture theory: A model of decision weights. *Management Science,* in press.

Author Index

Abbott, V., 103
Abelson, R. P., 131, 151
Aboul-Ezz, M. E., 149
Abrams, R. A., 97
Adelman, L., 118, 122, 239
Ainslie, G., 301
Ajzen, I., 201, 203
Allais, M., 56, 77
Allard, R., 263, 265, 266, 268, 269, 272, 273, 274, 275
Allport, G. W., 283
Alpert, M., 60
Ames, R. E., 316
Anderson, N. H., 241, 246, 254
Andreoni, J., 316
Anzai, Y., 145
Arkes, H. R., 149
Armstrong, J. S., 117
Aschenbrenner, K. M., 120
Ashby, W. R., 265
Aumann, R. J., 311, 313
Avrunin, G. S., 121, 158, 299

Baddeley, A. D., 331
Bainbridge, L., 265
Balzer, W. K., 239, 246, 285
Banks, J., 326
Bar-Hillel, M., 195, 201, 202, 203, 204, 207, 211, 315
Barron, F. H., 113, 120
Battalio, R. C., 327
Bazerman, M. H., 312, 315
Beach, L. R., 130, 135, 149, 156, 232, 237, 255, 287
Becker, G. S., 305
Becker, S. W., 31, 37
Bedard, J., 50
Behn, R. D., 33, 36, 121
Beil, R. O., 327

Bell, D., 68, 107, 111
Benn, W., 253
Bentham, J., 295–96
Ben Zur, H., 155
Bernoulli, D., 295–96
Berry, D. C., 268, 269
Bettman, J. R., 131, 132, 138, 140, 143, 146, 147, 148, 149, 150, 155, 244
Biller, W. F., 34
Binmore, K., 312, 319, 320
Black, M., 29
Blank, H., 203
Blevens, K., 238
Blyth, C. R., 208
Boring, E. G., 228
Bowman, E. H., 114
Boyle, P. J. R., 282–83
Brainard, R. W., 6
Brandts, J., 325
Brehm, J. W., 298
Brehmer, B., 147, 228, 230, 236, 238, 239, 243, 255, 263, 264, 265, 266, 268, 269, 272, 273, 274, 275
Brewer, M. B., 316, 317
Breznitz, S. J., 155
Brier, G. W., 190
Brigham, F. R., 268, 277
Broadbent, D. E., 264, 268, 269
Broadbent, M. P., 264, 268
Brown, A. L., 129
Brown, J. N., 330
Brown, R. V., 110
Brownson, F. O., 31, 37
Brubaker, E. R., 316
Brunswik, E., 46, 228–30, 232, 233, 236, 237, 244, 246, 248, 249, 255
Budescu, D. V., 30, 31, 32, 35, 36, 38, 39, 40, 67, 108, 110, 118
Bull, C., 330

347

AUTHOR INDEX

Calderwood, R., 288
Camerer, C., 114, 318, 322, 326, 330
Campbell, D. T., 242, 253, 254
Canela, J. A., 193
Card, S. K., 133
Carroll, J. S., 312
Casey, J., 52
Chapman, L. J., 250–52
Chase, W. G., 142
Chassin, L., 182, 183
Chew, S. H., 78
Chi, M., 341
Cho, I. K., 324, 325
Christensen, C., 149
Christensen-Szalanski, J. J. J., 155, 237, 287
Clemen, R. T., 119
Coase, R. H., 313
Cohen, B. L., 36, 38, 39
Collingridge, D., 277
Colman, A., 313
Conant, R. C., 265
Cooke, J. E., 268
Coombs, C. H., 121, 158, 285, 299
Corrigan, B., 114, 123
Coursey, D. L., 314, 315
Cox, J. A., 38
Crandall, B., 288
Creyer, E. H., 146, 149
Cronbach, L. J., 191
Crossman, E. R. F. W., 268
Curley, S. P., 97
Curtis, D. W., 303

Dansereau, D. F., 142
Darden, L., 284
Dawes, R. M., 114, 123, 149, 184, 193, 303, 316, 317
Deci, E. L., 298
de Finetti, B., 32
De Keyser, V., 263
Delquié, P., 24–25
de Neufville, R., 24–25
Denniston, W. B., 117
Desvousges, W., 70
Doherty, M. E., 239, 246, 284, 286, 287
Dorner, D., 269
Dosher, B. A., 130, 131
Dummett, M., 29, 30
Dyer, J. S., 115, 123

Easterling, D. V., 30, 37
Ebert, L., 305

Eckel, C., 320
Edwards, W., 33, 36, 46, 47, 48, 51, 52, 54, 57, 60, 61, 75, 94, 107, 108, 113, 114, 118, 122, 193, 244, 253
Einhorn, H. J., 22, 24, 37, 38, 40, 72, 81, 82n, 92, 97, 107, 110, 111, 114, 118, 122, 129, 130, 131, 132, 143, 147, 149, 151, 155, 156, 159, 160, 169, 170, 173, 192, 254, 286, 328, 330, 342
Eliashberg, J., 110
Ellsberg, D., 30–31, 35, 37, 77, 96
Elster, J., 196, 301
Eppel, T., 49
Erev, I., 36, 39, 40
Eriksen, C. W., 286

Faber, M. D., 148
Faerman, S. R., 246
Fagley, N. S., 243, 252
Falk, R., 211
Farquhar, P. H., 107, 108, 111
Farr, M., 341
Feagans, T. B., 34
Fillenbaum, S., 38
Fineberg, H. V., 120–21
Finke, R. A., 205–6
Fischer, G. W., 25, 108, 110, 113, 117, 119, 120
Fischhoff, B., 5, 53, 60, 71, 92, 93, 97, 101, 104, 107, 108, 110, 120, 122, 202, 203, 243, 264, 323, 342
Fishburn, P. C., 51, 107, 111
Fisher, S., 53
Fiske, D. W., 253, 254
Fitts, P. M., 6
Fitzgerald, P., 264, 268
Fodor, J. A., 281
Ford, C., 49
Forsythe, R., 317, 319
Freedman, D., 210
Frey, B. S., 316
Fryback, D. G., 46
Fudenberg, D., 312, 328
Furby, L., 342

Gage, N. L., 191
Garcia, J., 305
Gärdenfors, P., 32
Gardiner, P. C., 122
Garner, W. R., 286
Gati, I., 235, 242
Gettys, C., 52, 53

Gibbs, Brian, 297
Gibson, J., 228, 237
Gigerenzer, G., 203, 229
Gillis, J. S., 238
Ginosar, Z., 203
Glaser, R., 341
Gold, E., 193
Goldberg, L. R., 114
Goldberger, L., 155
Goldstein, W. M., 22, 24, 82, 110, 147, 173
Goodman, B. C., 46
Gordon, M. M., 117
Gough, H. G., 183
Gould, S. J., 237
Graham, J. D., 35
Grassia, J., 238, 244, 254, 256, 280
Greene, D., 180
Greenwald, A. G., 307–8
Grether, D. M., 14
Griffin, D., 69–70, 71
Groen, G. J., 142
Gruber, H. E., 285
Güth, W., 315, 319

Hagen, J., 56
Hake, H. W., 286
Hamm, R. M., 244, 254, 256, 280
Hammerton, M., 103
Hammond, K. R., 114, 117, 118, 122, 130, 188, 228, 229, 230, 234–35, 236, 237, 238, 239, 240, 242, 243, 244, 245, 246, 249, 254, 256, 280, 282–83
Hanson, R. D., 155
Harrison, A. A., 300
Harrison, G., 314, 316, 319
Harsanyi, J. C., 321, 322, 328
Hastie, R., 256
Hauser, J. R., 110
Hawkins, S. A., 25
Hayes-Roth, B., 147
Hayes-Roth, F., 147
Heerboth, J., 52
Hell, W., 203
Helmholz, H. von, 247
Henrion, M., 97
Hershey, J., 24, 85, 98, 103, 110
Hewstone, M., 253
Hilgard, E. R., 299
Hirshleifer, J., 316
Hoch, S. J., 181, 188–90
Hoellerich, V. L., 239, 240, 246
Hoffman, E., 313, 314

Hogarth, R., 37, 38, 40, 41, 54, 67, 81, 92, 97, 103, 107, 108, 109, 110, 111, 118, 119, 122, 130, 132, 149, 151, 155, 156, 159, 169, 170, 173, 254, 265, 268, 277, 283, 342
Holt, C. A., 320, 325
Holt, V. E., 62
Holton, G., 281
House, P., 180
Howard, R., 31, 67, 108, 122
Huber, J., 149
Huff, D., 212
Hull, D. L., 284
Hursch, C. J., 114, 188, 236
Hursch, J. L., 188, 236

Isaac, R. M., 315, 316

Jagacinski, C. M., 148
Janis, I. L., 155, 160, 170
John, R., 49
Johnson, E. J., 23, 24, 119, 132, 134, 138, 140, 142, 143, 146, 147, 150, 155, 244
Johnson, J. T., 205–6
Jones-Lee, M. W., 103
Joyce, C. R. B., 228, 236, 238, 239, 255

Kadane, J. B., 61, 321
Kagel, J. H., 332
Kahan, J. P., 313
Kahneman, D., 13, 15, 16, 18, 19, 24, 26, 33, 46, 54, 56, 57, 75, 78, 83, 92, 96, 98, 101, 103, 107, 109, 113, 119, 147, 148, 149, 159, 169–70, 174, 187, 191, 200, 201, 202, 203, 204, 209, 220, 228, 231, 232, 233, 234, 235, 236–37, 240, 243, 244, 245, 246, 247, 248, 249, 253, 255, 283, 284, 285, 302, 315
Kardos, L., 236
Keating, J. D., 155
Keeley, S. M., 286
Keeney, R., 49, 52, 98, 102, 122
Keinan, G., 160
Keller, L. R., 99, 329
Kennan, J., 317
Keren, G. B., 103, 249, 252
Keynes, J. M., 31, 32
Kim, O., 316
Klayman, J., 253
Klein, G. A., 288
Klein, N. M., 146
Kleindorfer, P. R., 100

Kleinmuntz, B., 114, 160, 173, 254, 286, 330
Kleinmuntz, D. N., 114, 115, 120, 122, 160, 173, 254, 269, 286, 330
Kluwe, R. H., 269
Knetsch, J. L., 315
Knight, F. H., 31
Koelling, R. A., 305
Koffka, K., 233
Kramer, R. M., 317
Kreps, D. M., 296, 312, 324, 325, 328
Kroll, Y., 231
Kuhn, T. S., 255, 287
Kulik, R. M., 157
Kunreuther, H., 38, 41, 67, 70, 97, 100, 108, 110, 315

Laios, C., 268, 277
Langer, E., 193
Langley, P., 147
Larkey, P. D., 321
Larsen, J. B., 123
Larsson, S., 77
Laskey, K. B., 110, 117, 119, 120
Lave, L. B., 34, 35
Leal, A., 52
Leary, D. E., 229
Levi, A., 131, 151
Levi, I., 32
Levin, D., 332
Levy, H., 231
Lichtenstein, S., 5, 13, 14, 22, 23, 24, 25, 46, 47, 53, 60, 71, 77, 92, 93, 96, 103, 104, 107, 108, 110, 114, 117, 120, 150, 243, 264, 323
Lindley, D. V., 110, 120
Lipkin, J. O., 238
Locke, E. A., 156, 160, 165, 170
Locksley, A., 203–4
Loewenstein, G., 315, 318
Loomes, G., 68, 97
Lopes, L. L., 174
Luce, R. D., 40

McCabe, K., 319
McClelland, G. H., 135, 228, 230, 236, 237, 254
McCoach, W., 118, 122
MacCrimmon, K. R., 37, 67, 77, 78, 82, 83, 84, 85
McCue, K. F., 316
MacGregor, D., 95, 117
Machina, M. J., 33, 78, 96, 107, 111

McKee, M., 314
McKelvey, R. D., 313
Mackinnon, A. J., 269
McNeil, B. J., 103
MacPhillamy, D., 23
McTavish, J., 317
Mann, L., 155, 160, 170
Manning, C., 52
Mano, H., 155, 165
March, J. G., 67, 193, 295, 296
Marks, G., 180–81
Marschak, J., 130
Marwell, G., 316
Maull, N., 284
Medley, R., 248, 250
Meehl, P. E., 114, 195, 253, 280, 286
Mefferd, R. B., 160
Mehle, T., 53
Melton, G. B., 195
Messe, L. A., 196
Messick, D. M., 316
Miller, A., 221
Miller, N., 180–81
Miller, P. M., 243, 252
Milter, R. G., 246
Minsky, M., 281
Mitchell, T. R., 130, 149, 156
Moran, L. J., 160
Moran, T. P., 133, 238
Morgan, M. G., 101
Morgenstern, O., 32, 74
Mowrey, J., 286
Mullen, B., 180, 192
Mumpower, J., 228, 230, 236, 237, 238, 254, 312
Murphy, A., 60
Myerson, R. B., 317
Mynatt, C. R., 287

Nash, J., 312
National Research Council, 33
Neelin, J., 319–20
Neuringer, A., 331
Newell, A., 131, 132, 133, 174, 285
Nisbett, R., 185, 284, 305

Ochs, J., 319
O'Connor, R., Jr., 239, 246
Okrent, D., 102
O'Neill, B., 330
Orbell, J., 316, 317
Ordeshook, P. C., 313

AUTHOR INDEX

Palfrey, T., 319
Parducci, A., 301
Parkison, S., 238
Parkman, J. M., 142
Patil, K. D., 239, 240, 246
Payne, J. W., 121, 132, 134, 135, 138, 139, 140, 143, 146, 147, 149, 150, 151, 155, 156, 244
Pearl, J., 52
Peele, E., 70
Pelchat, M. L., 305
Peters, T., 277
Peterson, C. R., 208, 221, 232, 255
Phillips, L. D., 60, 108, 323
Pisani, R., 210
Pitz, G., 52
Plott, C. R., 14, 316, 319
Politser, P. E., 120–21
Polya, G., 285
Porter, D., 312, 326
Poses, R. M., 239, 246
Presson, C. C., 182
Prudencio, Y. C., 314
Purves, R., 210
Puto, C., 149

Raaijmakers, J. G. W., 249, 252
Radner, R., 318
Raiffa, H., 60, 122
Ramsey, F. P., 74
Rapoport, A., 36, 38, 107, 231, 313, 316, 317
Rapoport, D., 269
Rasinski, K. A., 256
Rasmuson, D. M., 30
Ravinder, H. V., 115
Reder, L. M., 146
Reder, M. W., 107
Reimann, H., 269
Rohrbaugh, R., 246
Roose, J., 284
Rosen, A., 195
Rosenthal, R. W., 62, 330
Ross, L., 180, 181, 185, 284
Roth, A. E., 313, 314, 319
Roth, J., 193
Rouse, W. B., 264
Rozin, P., 305
Rubinstein, A., 312, 319
Ruckleshaus, W., 34
Rule, S. J., 303
Russo, J. E., 130, 131, 142, 150
Ryan, R. M., 298

Sachs, N., 52
Sagaria, S. D., 101
Sahlin, N.-E., 32
Salch, J., 52
Samuelson, P., 96
Sanders, G. S., 192
Sarin, R. K., 99
Sattath, S., 5, 22, 23, 25, 26, 49, 83, 109, 237
Savage, L. J., 32, 55, 74, 79, 96
Sawyer, J., 114
Schelling, T., 180, 181, 301, 326
Schiller, D., 305
Schkade, D. A., 23, 24, 119, 122
Schmittberger, R., 315
Schoemaker, P., 24, 85, 98, 103, 108, 110
Schotter, A., 318, 328, 330
Schull, J., 305
Schum, D., 222
Schwarze, B., 315
Seaver, D., 60
Seeger, C. M., 6
Selten, R., 315, 332
Selvidge, J., 60
Sen, A., 296
Shaked, A., 319, 320
Shaklee, H., 317
Shanteau, J., 46, 50
Shapira, Z., 67, 193
Shay, S., 210–11
Sherman, S. J., 182, 183, 307–8
Sicoly, F., 181
Simmons, R. T., 317
Simon, H. A., 107, 130, 131, 132, 135, 145, 149, 174, 282, 285
Simonson, I., 149, 304
Sivacek, J. M., 196
Slovic, Paul, 5, 13, 14, 15, 16, 18, 19, 22, 23, 24, 25, 26, 35, 46, 47, 49, 53, 68, 69–70, 70, 71, 77, 83, 92, 93, 95, 96, 101, 104, 107, 108, 109, 110, 113, 114, 117, 120, 148, 150, 220, 231, 232, 233, 234, 236–37, 243, 255, 264, 283, 284
Smith, L. D., 229
Smith, M. R., 82, 83, 84, 85
Smith, V. L., 315
Solomon, R. L., 299
Sonnenschein, H., 319–20
Sopher, B., 317
Spiegel, M., 319–20
Spitzer, M., 313, 314
Staelin, R., 150

Stangor, C., 203–4
Sterman, J. D., 269, 278
Stewart, T. R., 230, 234, 239, 240, 253
Stigler, G. J., 32, 296, 303
Stoeker, R., 332
Stroebe, W., 316
Sugden, R., 68, 97
Summers, D. A., 114
Sutton, J., 319, 320

Taylor, S. E., 237
Terry, C., 155
Tetlock, P. E., 149
Thaler, R. H., 57, 315, 316
Thompson, L., 315
Thompson, S. C., 237
Thorngate, W., 130, 134, 135
Tietz, R., 315, 319
Toda, M., 84
Todd, F. J., 114, 246
Tolcott, M. A., 62
Trope, Y., 203
Tucker, L. R., 188, 230, 236
Tversky, A., 5, 6, 13, 15, 16, 18, 19, 22, 23, 24, 25, 26, 33, 46, 49, 54, 56, 58, 69–70, 71, 75, 78, 83, 92, 96, 98, 101, 103, 107, 109, 110, 113, 119, 130, 132, 147, 148, 149, 151, 159, 169–70, 174, 187, 191, 193, 200, 201, 202, 203, 204, 209, 220, 231, 232, 233, 234, 235, 236–37, 240, 242, 243, 244, 245, 246, 247, 248, 249, 253, 255, 283, 284, 285, 302, 303n, 304
Tweney, R. D., 287

Umbers, I. G., 264, 277

van Damme, E., 327
van de Kragt, A. J. C., 317
van Huyck, J. B., 327
Varey, Carol, 297, 301
Vaupel, J. W., 33, 36, 121
Vesely, W. E., 30
Vollmecke, T. A., 305

von Clausewitz, C. M., 263
von Neumann, J., 32, 74
von Schantz, T., 231
von Winterfeldt, D., 33, 36, 48, 49, 51, 52, 54, 57, 60, 61, 94, 108, 113, 114, 118, 244
Voss, J., 342

Wagenaar, W. A., 101, 103
Walker, M., 316
Wallsten, T. S., 29, 30, 31, 32, 34, 35, 36, 38, 39, 40, 67, 75, 107, 108, 110, 118
Wearing, A. J., 269
Weber, M., 318
Wehrung, D. A., 67
Weigelt, K., 322, 328, 330
Weinberg, A., 68
Weinberg, S., 36, 38
Weinhouse, S., 33
Weinstein, N. D., 299
Weitz, B., 155
Wessel, D., 71
Whitfield, R. G., 30
Wickens, C. D., 6
Wigton, R. S., 239, 240, 246
Wilson, A., 253, 305
Wilson, C., 328
Wilson, R., 322
Winkler, R., 60, 61, 108, 119
Wohl, J. G., 53
Wooler, D., 134, 155
Wright, P., 155
Wright, W. F., 149

Yaari, M., 315
Yates, J. F., 37, 97, 148, 157

Zajone, R. B., 298
Zakay, D., 134, 155
Zimmer, A. C., 36
Zukowski, L. G., 37
Zwick, R., 29

Subject Index

Accounting, 54–55, 58
Achievement in functionalism, 228
Adaptation in functionalism, 228, 236
Allais paradox, 56–57, 68, 77–78, 84–85, 96
Altruism, 315
Ambiguity, 29, 67; avoidance of, 37, 79, 96–97
Analogy as heuristic, 284
Anchoring and adjustment, 24–25, 173–74; in compatibility effects, 13–14, Einhorn-Hogarth model, 159, 170; in goal setting, 159, 164, 168–69; in heuristics-and-biases approach, 236
Artificial intelligence, 62
Availability, 236

Base-rate fallacy, 200–202, 206, 220–23; and Simpson's paradox, 208–12
Base rates: causal and noncausal, 212–15; conditions for use, 201–3; deep and surface structures in, 214–15; effect of changing, 208–9; with indicant information, 203–5; prediction of, 183–96; use and understanding of, 220–23
Behavioral decision theory. *See* Decision theory, behavioral
Behavioral game theory. *See* Game theory, behavioral
Belief, 5, 297, 298, 299
Benefit/risk equity, 99–100
Benefits, 34–39, 121–23
Bootstrapping, 114, 117

California Psychological Inventory (CPI), 183, 184, 191
Choice: editing process in, 147–48; imagination in, 169; judgments about in dynamic games, 318–26; matching and, 20–23; measuring accuracy of, 134–35; Monte Carlo simulations of, 132–40; by others, 321–26; pricing and, 6, 14–19, 20–21, 24; process for in decision analysis, 69–72; role of compatibility in, 5–6. *See also* Editing processes in choice and cognition; Prominence effect
Coase theorem, 313–14
Cognitive continuum theory, 243, 244–45, 282; and modularity hypothesis, 284; and transparency concept, 247
Cognitive effort: in choice, 140–42; in decision-making strategy, 130, 148; effect of deadline penalty on, 165–66; effect of stress on performance in, 170; influences on, 130; regulation of, 129; for strategy selection, 130, 132–34
Cognitive feedback, 244, 246
Coherence, 134, 296
Coherence theory of truth, 255–56
Compatibility: in decision making and preference reversal, 14–23, 82–83; effect on prediction and preference, 25; between input and output, 6; in judgment and choice, 6–14; and prices and payoffs, 17
Compatibility hypothesis, 5–6, 11–14; anchoring and adjustment in, 13–14; in matching, 20–23; to predict market value, 7–10; rationale for, 5–6; statement of, 7; weighting of for analysis, 7, 9, 11–12. *See also* Choice; Judgment; Matching; Preference reversal; Prominence effect
Conceptual integration, 247
Conflict, interpersonal, 238
Consensus, 297–300
Consistency, 109–17, 122–23
Contingent strategy selection, 129, 147
Contingent-weighting model, 15–17, 26
Control theory: feedforward and feedback, 265–78, 288–89; model principle in, 265. *See also* Dynamic Environmental Simulation System

Convergent validity, 113–14
Cooperation, 316–18
Correspondence theory of truth, 255–56
Costs, 34–39, 121–23
CPI. *See* California Psychological Inventory
Cues, 240–42, 248, 249, 254

Deadline with penalty: analysis of effect of, 160–68; and decision making, 154–55, 159; effect of on cognitive effort, 165–66
Decision analysis: choice process in, 69–72; consistency in, 109–17; costs and benefits of, 121–23; errors in, 78; hypothesis invention in, 53; input issues for, 59–62; interaction of with artificial intelligence, 62–63; level of detail for, 120–21; normative and descriptive theory in, 107–8, 111; option invention in, 51–53; resets management in, 54–59
Decision making: under deadlines, 154–55; ethical basis for, 104; purposive and flexible behavior in, 155; real-time, 262–65; use of feedback and feedforward, 265–67. *See also* Control theory
Decision rules, 130
Decision strategies: analysis of cognitive effort in choice, 140–42; changing of, 145–47; different, 131–32, 135, 138–40
Decision theory, behavioral, 96–97, 311, 311–12, 312; compared with behavioral game theory, 326–31; feedback and learning in, 328–29; levels of explanation in, 329–31
Decision utility, 296–97
Decomposition process: in decision analysis, 108, 117, 122; dependent errors in, 119–20; and expected utility, 112–13; level of detail in, 120–21; and multiattribute evaluation, 112; and probability assessment, 111–12. *See also* Bootstrapping; Error
DESSY. *See* Dynamic Environmental Simulation System
Dual pair paradigm, 75–85
Duplicity principle, 236, 249
Dynamic Environmental Simulation System (DESSY), 268–75, 287–89
Dynamic games, choice in, 318–26. *See also* Sequential bargaining games; Voting, strategic and sincere

EBA. *See* Elimination by aspects
Ecological validity, 46–48
Editing processes in choice and cognition, 147–48
Effort-accuracy approach, 145–50; in decision-making strategy, 148–49; information displays in, 149–50
Einhorn-Hogarth anchoring-and-adjustment model, 159, 170. *See also* Choice; Judgment
Elementary information processes (EIPs), 132–34, 140–42, 174–75
Elicitation methods, 23, 45, 51; construction in, 5; and convergence, 48–49; and compatibility effect, 14–26; values in, 61. *See also* Framing
Elimination by aspects (EBA), 131, 132, 134, 139, 140
Ellsberg paradox, 30–31, 67, 77–81, 84–85
Epistemic reliability, 32
Equal weighting rule (EQW), 131, 132, 135, 136, 140
Equilibrium analysis in game theory, 331–32
EQW. *See* Equal weighting rule
Error: attention to 286–87; dependent, 119–20; in judgment, 109–11; random, 114–17; reduction of, 117–19; systematic, 113–14. *See also* Bootstrapping
Error theory, 108–9
EV. *See* Maximization of expected value
Expected-utility maximization, 56–57, 130
Expected-utility theory, 32–33, 85–86, 134; in behavioral decision theory, 93, 96–97; paradoxes of, 74–75, 77–84
Experience utility, 296–97
Expertise, 50

Fairness: preference for, 313–16; in ultimatum games, 314–16, 319
False consensus effect, 180–81
Feedback: cognitive, 246; in strategy selection, 145–47; use of in decision making, 146–47
Feedback and feedforward control, 265–78, 288–89
Framing, 103, 252
Free riding, 316–17
Functionalism, 234–35; and illusionism, 239–42, 246, 247–49, 255–56; as metatheory in judgment and decision making, 227–33, 255. *See also* Lens model functionalism

Game theory: cooperative and non-cooperative, 312–13; distinguished from

SUBJECT INDEX

decision theory, 331–32. *See also* Nash equilibrium
Game theory, behavioral, 311–12; compared with behavioral decision theory, 326–31; effect of changes in context in, 326–28; learning and feedback in, 328–29
Goal setting: anchoring-and-adjustment process in, 159, 168–69; input-output cost/benefit model for, 156–60; process model for analysis of, 159–66

Heuristics: in decision strategy, 131–32, 135, 138–39, 283–84; representativeness in, 201. *See also* Elimination by aspects; Equal weighting rule; Lexicographic choice rule; Self-inquiry
Heuristics-and-biases approach, 228, 233, 235, 248, 249; functionalism in, 234–35; Gestalt psychology in, 233–34; new concepts in, 236–39; psychological aspects of, 236–37; psychophysics in, 235–36
Hypothesis invention, 53, 69

Illusionism: and functionalism, 239–42, 246, 247–49, 255–56; as metatheory in judgment and decision making, 227, 255
Illusions, 233–34
Illusory correlation, 250–52
Imagination in judgment and choice, 169–70
Incentive effects, 148–49
Information: costs of communicating, 34–39; display of, 6, 149–50, 245–46; incomplete, 317–18; indicant, 203–5; multiple mediation of, 229–30; in predicting base rates, 187; vague and precise, 34–39. *See also* Misinformation; Understanding
Information processing, 25, 131, 149–50, 155; behavior for, 142–45; vague, 34–39
Invariance, 24–26, 83–84, 109

Judgment: averaging to reduce errors in, 118; about choice in dynamic games, 318–26; errors in, 108–9; expert, 238; imagination in, 169; role of compatibility in, 5–6; systematic and random components of, 114; under uncertainty, 159, 170. *See also* Choice
Judgment strategy: analysis using RKD model for, 115–17; in goal setting, 159–66; random error in, 114–17; systematic error in, 111–14. *See also* Bootstrapping; Consistency; Convergent validity; Decomposition process; Error

Learning: in decision making, 147; interpersonal, 238; multiple-cue probability, 238
Lens model functionalism, 228, 229–31, 234–35, 236, 248; and representativeness, 240–42; systems concepts in, 238–39. *See also* Cognitive continuum theory; Cognitive feedback; Surface and depth
Lexicographic choice rule (LEX), 130, 131, 132, 135, 136, 139, 140
Lexicographic semiorder (LEXSEMI), 132
Likelihood function, 53
Locke's goal-setting theory, 160, 165
Logical consistency, 109–17, 122–23

Magical thinking, 196
Majority of confirming dimensions (MCD), 132, 140
Market value prediction, 7–10
Matching, 20–23; payoff, 20–21, 83, 85; probability, 20–21, 85
Maximization of expected value (EV), 134, 135, 175
MCD. *See* Majority of confirming dimensions
Metacognition, 129
Metatheories in judgment and decision making. *See* Functionalism; Illusionism
Misinformation, 100–102
Misunderstanding. *See* Understanding
Modularity hypothesis, 283–84
Monte Carlo simulations, 132–40
MOUSELAB system, 140–44
Müller-Lyer illusion, 232–33, 245, 249, 285. *See also* Transparency
Multiattribute-evaluation models, 112, 120
Multiple preference orders, 26

Nash equilibrium, 312–13, 314; game theoretic choice of, 324–26; in tournaments, 330–31; in ultimatum games, 314–15
Negotiation, 238
Numeraire hypothesis. *See* Compatibility effect

Option invention, 51–53, 69

Payoff matching, 20–21, 83, 85
Performance, effect of stress on, 170
PR. *See* Preference reversal
Precision, defined, 29–30
Predicted utility, 296–97, 309
Prediction: and base rates, 202–3; compatibility effects in, 7–14

SUBJECT INDEX

Preference, 97, 102–4; construction of, 5; and preference reversal, 74–75; revealed, 296. *See also* Coase theorem; Cooperation; Fairness; Prominence effect; Ultimatum games

Preference reversal (PR), 84–85; compatibility effect for, 82–84; compatibility hypothesis in, 14–23; and risk, 17–19; in strategy selection, 150; types of, 20–23. *See also* Allais paradox; Ellsberg paradox; Slovic-Lichtenstein paradox

Probability: in choice and pricing, 14–19; multiple-cue, 238; and risk, 95–104; selection of in uncertainty, 39–41

Probability matching, 20–21, 85

Probability theory, and uncertainty, 29–34, 66

Procedure invariance, 24–26, 83–84, 109

Process consistency, 109–17, 122–23

Prominence effect, 22–23, 237

Psychology, 236–38

Psychophysics, 235–36

Public goods, 316–17

Rational choice, 14, 25–26, 296

Ravinder-Kleinmuntz-Dyer model (RKD model), 115–17, 119, 120

Representativeness, 211, 235; in heuristics-and-biases approach, 236; and lens model framework, 240–42

Reputation games, 322–23, 330

Resets, 54–57, 78; and multiple transaction streams, 57–59; requirements for, 76

Risk: assessment of, 69–72; perception of, 68–69, 97–100; and uncertainty, 32, 34–36, 68

Risk equity and neutrality, 98–100

RKD model. *See* Ravinder-Kleinmuntz-Dyer model

Satisficing (SAT), 131, 132, 140

Scenarios, 53

SDM. *See* Societal decision maker

Self-inquiry, 180–81

Sequential bargaining games, 319–20

SHOR paradigm, 53

Simpson's paradox, 208–12

Slovic-Lichtenstein paradox, 77, 81–85, 150

Social dilemmas, 316

Social policy, 239

Societal decision maker (SDM), 91–104

Strategy effort. *See* Cognitive effort

Strategy selection: adaptive, 142–45; contingent, 129, 149; editing processes in, 147–48; incentives in, 148–49; measuring accuracy in, 134–35; measuring cognitive effort in, 132–34. *See also* Information processing

Stress, 160, 170

Sure-thing principle, 79, 96

Surface and depth, 214–15, 238, 245–46

Task conditions, 245–46, 247

Task-continuum index, 244, 245

Tastes; changes in, 297–300; predicting, 304–8

Time pressure: and decision making, 154–55; and strategy selection, 143–45. *See also* Deadline with penalty

Tournaments, 330–31

Transaction streams, multiple, 57–59

Transparency, 244–45; and cognitive feedback, 246; and integration of functionalism and illusionism, 246–47

Truth theories, 255–56

Ultimatum games, 314–16

Uncertainty: analysis of judgments under, 159, 170; errors in assessment of, 108; representation of for analysis and communication, 28–30; and risk, 32, 34–36, 68; use of probability theory in, 29–33. *See also* Ambiguity; Precision; Vagueness

Understanding and vague uncertainty, 36–39

Utility: and extended outcomes, 300–304; predicting, 307–8; theory of, 96, 111, 295–96; zero utility, 54. *See also* Decision analysis; Decision utility; Experience utility; Predicted utility

Utilization coefficient, 240

Vagueness, 29–41, 67, 96–97. *See also* Ambiguity; Uncertainty

Validation of output, 50–51

von Neumann–Morgenstern utility theory, 111

Voting, strategic and sincere, 320–21

WADD. *See* Weighted additive rule

Weighted additive rule (WADD), 132, 133, 134, 139, 140–41, 175

Weighting, in compatibility analysis, 7, 9; and decomposition effort, 118–19

Wohl's paradigm: 53

Zero utility, 54